Understanding the
Book of Mormon

Understanding the Book of Mormon

A Reader's Guide

GRANT HARDY

OXFORD
UNIVERSITY PRESS

2010

OXFORD
UNIVERSITY PRESS

Oxford University Press, Inc., publishes works that further
Oxford University's objective of excellence
in research, scholarship, and education.

Oxford New York
Auckland Cape Town Dar es Salaam Hong Kong Karachi
Kuala Lumpur Madrid Melbourne Mexico City Nairobi
New Delhi Shanghai Taipei Toronto

With offices in
Argentina Austria Brazil Chile Czech Republic France Greece
Guatemala Hungary Italy Japan Poland Portugal Singapore
South Korea Switzerland Thailand Turkey Ukraine Vietnam

Published by Oxford University Press, Inc.
198 Madison Avenue, New York, NY 10016

www.oup.com

Oxford is a registered trademark of Oxford University Press

Library of Congress Cataloging-in-Publication Data
Hardy, Grant, 1961–
Understanding the Book of Mormon : a reader's guide / Grant Hardy.
p. cm.
Includes bibliographical references and index.
ISBN 978-0-19-973170-1
1. Book of Mormon—Criticism, interpretation, etc. I. Title.
BX8627.H33 2010
289.3′32—dc22
2009026675

9 8 7 6 5 2 3 2

Printed in the United States of America
on acid-free paper

For Heather

Strange, the extravagance of it—who needs
those eighteen-armed black Kalis, those musty saints
whose bones and bleeding wounds offend good taste,
those joss sticks, houris, gilded Buddhas, books
Moroni etched in tedious detail?
We do; we need more worlds. This one will fail.

—John Updike, "Religious Consolation"

Contents

Acknowledgments

I offer my sincere thanks to Phil Barlow, Kent Brown, Richard Bushman, Terryl Givens, Royal Skousen, and Jack Welch for going over the manuscript and offering valuable comments and suggestions. Others who read the manuscript in whole or in part include Laurie Maffly-Kipp, Michael and Douglas VanDerwerken, Melissa Mann, Mary Wilson, Lisa Holmstead, Christie Nielsen, Sheryl Sawin, and Nirmal Dass. Mark Thomas and other members of his annual Book of Mormon Roundtable provided stimulating conversation and a first reading of several sections of this book. Extraordinary generosity came from Cynthia Read and Joellyn Ausanka, both of Oxford University Press. But it is my wife, Heather, to whom I owe the greatest debt. I gave her a readable Book of Mormon, and in return she taught me how to read it. The words that follow are mine, but many of the ideas (including most of the best ones) originated with Heather, and all of them have been worked out in conversation with her. It is sometimes said that no one should study Talmud alone. The Book of Mormon has nowhere near the depth and complexity of the Talmud, but I have nevertheless benefited enormously from having Heather as a study partner. Indeed, my task in writing has often been to try to capture just a few items from the seemingly endless stream of insights and observations that she makes, and then to rewrite them until they are an accurate reflection of what she had in mind. She has been more a coauthor than a muse, but when I offered her joint authorship status, she just laughed. The love of such a woman is a gift beyond comparison.

Our urge to read the Book of Mormon closely and creatively was nurtured in Sunday school discussions in the first two years of the New Haven Second Branch (the first Mormon congregation at Yale University). More than twenty years later, we are still profoundly grateful to members of that small community, including Dorothy and Curtis Alva, Doug Dickson, Effa and Ron Farnsworth, CarrieLyn Guymon, Lisa and Jeff Holmstead, Katherine Lahti, Kathy Vinson-Mack and Gary Mack, Cinco Paul, Heather Heuston Rosett, Judith and Scott Smith, Mary Jane and Michael Smith, and Tina and Michael VanDerwerken.

And finally, I want to thank my parents, Herb and Karleen Hardy, for a Mormon upbringing that included regular readings of LDS scripture, as well as my children, Liza and Elliot, for their patience and long-suffering. Their childhood years were spent listening to their parents talk nonstop about the Book of Mormon (among other things).

Introduction

> The reader must begin this book with an act of faith and end it
> with an act of charity. We ask him to believe in the sincerity and
> authenticity of this preface, affirming in return his prerogative to
> be skeptical of all that follows it.
>
> —John Barth

It perhaps comes as no surprise when Richard Bushman, the distinguished
Latter-day Saint historian and biographer of Joseph Smith, complains that
"the Book of Mormon, in my opinion, has never been examined in its full
complexity by outside scholars."[1] True believers of all sorts feel a twinge of
shock and dismay when others fail to take seriously what they hold dear.
Yet one may be more inclined to concede the point when Bushman is
joined by Nathan Hatch, an eminent non-Mormon scholar of early American religion—"For all the recent attention given to the study of Mormonism, surprisingly little has been devoted to the Book of Mormon itself"—
especially in light of the pronouncement by Gordon Wood that "the Book
of Mormon is an extraordinary work of popular imagination and one of
the greatest documents in American cultural history."[2] More recently,
Daniel Walker Howe, in his Pulitzer Prize–winning *What Hath God
Wrought*, has observed that "the Book of Mormon should rank among the
great achievements of American literature, but it has never been accorded
the status it deserves."[3]

Monographs on Joseph Smith or Mormonism usually offer a quick
synopsis of the Book of Mormon and perhaps a general interpretation,

but the book itself remains something of a mystery. It has been described as "whole-heartedly and completely Arminian" in its theology, with an emphasis on egalitarianism and democracy;[4] a text that "plays and replays established biblical ideas of obedience and disobedience to God" with a minimum of theological novelty;[5] an optimistic expression of America's sense of national destiny and individual potential;[6] and a manifestation of "premillennialist disillusionment with contemporary society"[7]—a characterization close to Hatch's own opinion that the book is best read as a "document of profound social protest" that fulminates against the rich, the proud, and the learned.[8] Book-length studies of the Mormon scripture have been similarly diverse, seeing it as an attempt to "defend God against deism, rationalism, and sectarianism";[9] a participant in a long-running cultural conversation on the origins of the Indians,[10] an "American apocrypha,"[11] a work of crypto-Masonry that challenges mainstream Evangelical culture,[12] and a "disguised version of Smith's life" whose characters are in fact his "fantasy alter-egos."[13] The Book of Mormon is an extraordinarily rich text, and its complicated narrative—which includes a great many theological discourses—allows for any number of interpretations by scholars interested in one aspect or another of Mormonism.

The book's obvious significance in American history is matched by the importance it holds in the lives of the more than thirteen million Latter-day Saints around the world who believe it to be God's word, "another testament of Jesus Christ" that stands alongside the Bible.[14] If, as Jan Shipps has argued, Mormonism is an emerging world religion, the Book of Mormon may someday take a place not only with the Bible but also with the Daodejing, the Dead Sea Scrolls, the Lotus Sutra, the Bhagavad Gita, the Nag Hammadi library, the Qur'an, and the Zohar as one of the world's foremost religious texts.[15] In addition to what it might tell us about American religion of the nineteenth century or the rise of Mormonism, a close analysis of Mormon scripture may also offer broad insights into the nature of scriptural production and human religious yearnings.

Yet the very reasons that draw readers to the Book of Mormon can also tempt them to read it poorly. Most studies tend to mine the text for evidence in larger arguments about the nature of Mormonism as a religious movement or the credibility of its first prophet. In doing so, they can misrepresent or distort what the book actually says. For instance, Dan Vogel's biography of Joseph Smith offers a thorough reading of the Book of Mormon, yet he is much less interested in Mormon scripture than in demonstrating that every detail can be attributed in some way or another to Smith's personal experiences or cultural environment. As a result, he misses a great deal of what makes the book unique and engaging.[16] Richard Rust, on the other hand, is much more attuned to the book's structure, voices, and rhetoric—the means by which it communicates whatever ideas it has—but he is so eager to portray it as an inspired literary masterwork that he ignores the awkwardness that is all too evident to outsiders.[17]

While historians have searched the Book of Mormon for clues about nine-teenth-century America or Joseph Smith, Mormon writers have generally focused either on evidence for the book's historical claims or correlations with current LDS theology.[18] And for many Latter-day Saints, careful scrutiny of the volume's contents is secondary to the direct relationship with God that the book makes possible. Those investigating the faith are encouraged to pray about the Book of Mormon, in accordance with the promise that God "will manifest the truth of it . . . by the power of the Holy Ghost" to those who "ask with a sincere heart, with real intent" (Moro. 10:4). Individuals who feel they have received such a spiritual witness are often content to redirect their energies from textual analysis toward living the wholesome sort of lifestyle that Mormonism advocates.

What all these approaches have in common is the urge to start with something outside the Book of Mormon—Joseph Smith, Jacksonian America, Mesoamerican archaeology, ancient Near Eastern culture, Mormon theology, or a personal spiritual quest—and then selectively identify and interpret pertinent passages.[19] The book, after all, is long and complicated, and the double-columned verses of the official edition offer little guidance to those trying to make sense of the narrative. In addition, the copious references at the bottom of pages steer readers toward doctrinal or topical approaches. Literary theorist Dominick LaCapra has offered a general warning that "the rhetoric of contextualization has often encouraged narrowly documentary readings in which the text becomes little more than a sign of the times or a straightforward expression of one larger phenomenon or another. At the limit, this indiscriminate approach to reading and interpretation becomes a detour around texts and an excuse for not really reading them at all."[20] Or as the Catholic sociologist Thomas O'Dea famously pointed out, "The Book of Mormon has not been universally considered by its critics as one of those books that must be read in order to have an opinion of it."[21]

The situation is similar to how David Bell has characterized reading books on a computer screen:

> If physical discomfort discourages the reading of texts sequentially, from
> start to finish, computers make it spectacularly easy to move through
> texts in other ways—in particular, by searching for particular pieces of
> information. Reading in this strategic, targeted manner can feel empow-
> ering. Instead of surrendering to the organizing logic of the book you
> are reading, you can approach it with your own questions and glean
> precisely what you want from it. You are the master, not some dead
> author. And this is precisely where the greatest dangers lie, because when
> reading, you should not be the master. Information is not knowledge;
> searching is not reading; and surrendering to the organizing logic of a
> book is, after all, the way one learns.[22]

Few readers, even if we count Latter-day Saints, have surrendered to the organizing logic of the Book of Mormon as a whole. This is perhaps because it appears at first glance to be a confused jumble of strange names and odd stories, told in a quirky style, and all of very suspicious origins. An 1841 critic described it as "mostly a blind mass of words, interwoven with scriptural language and quotations, without much of a leading plan or design. It is in fact such a production as might be expected from a person of Smith's abilities and turn of mind."[23] The world's general impression has not changed much in the last 180 years. What is one to do with such a text other than scan it for phrases and incidents that might have some bearing on a particular thesis?

There has never been a detailed guide to the contents of the Book of Mormon that meets the needs of both Latter-day Saints and outsiders, undoubtedly because they come to the text with such different perspectives and expectations. In this study, I suggest that the Book of Mormon can be read as literature—a genre that encompasses history, fiction, and scripture—by anyone trying to understand this odd but fascinating book. If we keep our focus squarely on the narrative, it turns out that there *is* an organizing principle at work, but it is fairly subtle. Mormons, who are familiar enough with their scripture to have discerned large-scale patterns, have been so overwhelmed by the needs of practical theology and the desire to defend the book's historicity (both of which tend to shift the focus to individual verses or short passages) that they have largely missed the implications of this principle. By contrast, non-Mormons, naturally expecting much less in the way of consistency or coherence, have generally not even tried to take the book's arrangement into consideration when formulating their interpretations.[24] Nevertheless, reading the Book of Mormon well—that is, comprehensively, following the contours and structure of the text, perceiving how the parts fit into the whole, and evaluating fairly the emphases and tensions within the book—requires a recognition of the central role played by its three major narrators: Nephi, Mormon, and Moroni.[25]

This realization came only gradually to me as I edited *The Book of Mormon: A Reader's Edition* (published by the University of Illinois Press in 2003). Without changing any of the words, I added paragraphing, quotation marks, headings, section breaks, some poetic forms, and a few footnotes so that readers might more easily view incidents in context, see sermons as extended arguments, and grasp the form and structure of the book as a whole.[26] What surprised me was the degree to which this relatively minor revision in formatting minimized the awkwardness and repetition of the book while at the same time highlighting the contributions of the narrators. Even a device as simple as marking the four major segments of the text—the Small Plates of Nephi, Mormon's explanatory comments, Mormon's abridgment of the Large Plates, and Moroni's additions—served to give prominence to these figures. Time and again, in trying to discern patterns and organization, I came up against the narrators, who are quite unlike the anonymous storytellers of the Hebrew Bible. In the Book of Mormon, Nephi, Mormon, and Moroni are major characters themselves, and each has a distinctive life story, perspective, set of concerns, style, and sensibility. Furthermore, they have a sense of who their audience will be and they deliberately shape their messages accordingly. In short, they exhibit clear communicative strategies, and there is a certain sort of aesthetic pleasure in watching them work. Contrary to what many readers have expected, the Book of Mormon is not simply a wisdom text of homespun aphorisms, a series of theologically tinged Indian adventure tales, or a confused congeries of biblical quotations and the popular beliefs of Joseph Smith's day. Rather, it appears to be a carefully constructed artifact.

It may be easy to lose sight of this when looking at verses out of context, but the starting point for all serious readers of the Book of Mormon has to be the recognition that it is first and foremost a narrative, offered to us by specific, named narrators. Every detail and incident in the book has to be weighed against their intentions and rhetorical strategies. We might imagine a history of the Nephites written by an impersonal, omniscient narrator whose point of view was similar to Joseph Smith's, but that is not what we have. The heterogeneous materials in the Book of Mormon— including historical accounts, prophecies, sermons, letters, poems, allegories, and apocalypses supposedly written by different authors in different periods—are all presented as the work of the three primary editor/historians.

The pervasive presence of narrators can make the Book of Mormon more engaging and literary than is often assumed. The situation is a little like the *Odyssey*: everyone knows the stories of the Cyclops, Circe, and the Sirens, but Homer does not tell these tales directly; instead he has Odysseus recount them for the Phaeacians in an extended speech/flashback in books 9–12. There is considerable scope for imaginative interpretation here since we can guess at our hero's motivations for telling these particular stories to this particular (and decidedly unheroic) audience.[27] Similarly, the multilayered texture of the Book of Mormon has been noted by Richard Bushman:

> In his narrative, derived from the available source materials, [Mormon] quotes other prophets and sometimes quotes them quoting still others. Moroni injects a letter from his father, and Nephi inserts lengthy passages from previous scriptures. Mormon moves in and out of the narrative, pointing up a crucial conclusion or addressing readers with a sermon of his own. Almost always two minds are present, and sometimes three, all kept account of in the flow of words.[28]

If the Book of Mormon is a work of fiction, it is more intricate and clever than has heretofore been acknowledged. And although there is some truth to the charge of didacticism often leveled against it, the fact that everything is deeply embedded in narrative makes it rather more interesting—narratives are always susceptible to multiple interpretations.

At this point, a few readers may want to jump right to Joseph Smith, asking whether the Book of Mormon demonstrates that he was a prophet, a religious genius, or a fraud. This is a significant religious and historical question, but it is not the focus of this present study. Mormons and non-Mormons will never agree on the basic nature of the text—to come to agreement would be to move from one camp to the other—and there is a world of difference between a religious novel by an early nineteenth-century American farmer (even if inspired by God) and a divine translation of an ancient document written by pre-Columbian prophets. Consequently, when believers and outsiders talk about the Book of Mormon, it often seems as if they have been reading entirely different books. Yet if we shift our attention away from Joseph Smith and back to the Book of Mormon itself, a common discourse becomes possible.

Someone, somewhere, made choices about how the narrative of the Book of Mormon was to be constructed. We can look closely at the text—how it is arranged, how it uses language, how it portrays itself, how it conveys its main points—without worrying too much about whether the mind ultimately responsible for such decisions was that of Mormon or Joseph Smith. So I propose bracketing, at least temporarily, questions of historicity in favor of a detailed examination of what the Book of Mormon is and how it operates. In the chapters that follow I will outline the major features of the book and illustrate some of the literary strategies employed by the narrators. It does not matter much to my approach whether these narrators were actual historical figures or whether they were fictional characters created by Joseph Smith; their role in the narrative is the same in either case. After all, narrative is a mode of communication employed by both historians and novelists.[29]

In his groundbreaking book, *The Eclipse of Biblical Narrative*, Hans Frei noted that "the historical critic does something other than narrative interpretation with a narrative because he looks for what the narrative refers to or what reconstructed historical context outside itself explains it. He is not wrong when he does this, but unfortunately he is also not apt to see the logical difference between what he does and what a narrative interpretation might be and what it might yield."[30] So it is with the Book of Mormon. Historical studies on the relationship of the Book of Mormon to its environment (whether this is assumed to be ancient or modern), to Joseph Smith, or to the church that claims it as scripture are important and engaging, but they frequently miss much of what makes the book both coherent and unique. The present study is an experiment in what a narrative interpretation of the Book of Mormon might look like.[31] For the most part, the focus of my attention remains on the text itself and the world that it creates. Because I adopt the internal perspective of the book, I will often write about the narrators as if they were actual people with complex motivations and developing understandings, yet I am fully aware that speaking of Nephites as if they were real does not make them so; at the same time, imagining them as having life experiences and independent minds does not necessarily mean that one accepts their historicity (non-Mormons are welcome to place virtual quotation marks around the names Nephi and Mormon whenever they appear in the chapters that follow).

The type of narrative analysis that I practice is not quite historical and not quite literary, because neither exactly fits the Book of Mormon. While it is clearly a "history-like" text—to borrow a term from Frei—it is impossible to read the book as an ordinary history since it is alleged to be a translation from an otherwise unknown language, and because it takes place in an unknown location somewhere in the New World. We might look for anachronisms or parallels with ancient North American or Mesoamerican cultures in order to evaluate the historical claims of the book in general, but there are no independent records or authenticated artifacts from Nephite civilization that would help us get at an objective reality behind the narrative. The task of historians is to reconstruct the past by triangulating from multiple primary sources, and these do not exist for the Book of Mormon. (It can certainly be read as a product of the nineteenth century, but this requires treating it as an indirect or coded source; one must start with the assumption that it is something very different from what it professes to be.)

Yet there are also problems with reading the Book of Mormon as a novel. Under close scrutiny, it appears to be a carefully crafted, integrated work, with multiple narrative levels, an intricate organization, and extensive intratextual phrasal allusions and borrowings. None of this is foreign to fiction, but the circumstances of the book's production are awkward: the more complicated and interconnected the text, the less likely it is that Joseph Smith made it up spontaneously as he dictated the words to his scribes, one time through. A standard refrain in LDS commentary is "Joseph Smith could not have written this book." This apologetic point, however, is not the subtext of the present study. I will argue that parallels and allusions in the Book of Mormon are deliberate and meaningful rather than coincidental, but literary analysis does not compel belief. (Weighing the relative probability of human creativity against divine intervention is always a subjective judgment, and Latter-day Saints exhibit remarkably low levels of skepticism toward angels and miracles.) My basic thesis is that the Book of Mormon is a much more interesting text—rewarding sustained critical attention—than has generally been acknowledged by either Mormons or non-Mormons. Rather than making a case for Smith's prophetic claims, I want to demonstrate a mode of literary analysis by which all readers, regardless of their prior religious commitments or lack thereof, can discuss the book in useful and accurate ways. Anyone can perceive and appreciate the nuances of Book of Mormon narrative in much the same manner that he or she might be persuaded by Michael Sells' work that the Qur'an was written in refined, eloquent Arabic poetry.[32] Was such a style beyond the capabilities of Muhammad, as many believers allege? Perhaps, but entering into that debate is not mandatory for those who simply wish to know something more about Muslims, their scripture, and its appeal.

Adopting the path of narrative interpretation is not to deny the problematic archaeology or anachronisms that can make the Book of Mormon difficult to take seriously, but non-Mormons who are willing to suspend disbelief long enough to read through the text attentively, on its own terms, may discover something of the literary power and religious vision that make it so convincing to Latter-day Saints, even if they themselves have little inclination to join in.[33] When the Book of Mormon is approached from the perspective of the narrators, there are aesthetic principles seen to be at work, though they may be distinct from those of mainstream literature. It is possible that such a book might have something to say about life and the human condition, and when undertaken in the right spirit, reading the Book of Mormon might even be pleasurable. I will leave it to others to prove or disprove the historical and religious claims of the book; my goal is to help anyone interested in the Book of Mormon, for whatever reason, become a better, more perceptive reader.

For those who see it as the work of Joseph Smith, it is crucial to recognize that its complex form makes it difficult to draw a firm connection between the author and any particular passage in the text; if Joseph (adopting the LDS convention of referring to Smith by his first name) is commenting on contemporary politics or theological disputes or ethnographic speculations, he does so only indirectly, and there is never a single viewpoint with which he can be completely identified. As the literary critic Bernard Duyfhuizen has written, "Any complete reading of a narrative depends, in part, on an understanding of the distinctions that mark the narration's relationship to the narrated events," and he warns that "all readers of narrative risk eliding narrating levels, and only careful reading can avoid misconstruing one level for another or excluding a level altogether."[34] It is a commonplace of literary theory to distinguish between narrators, implied authors, and authors. The Book of Mormon, if regarded as fiction, needs to be read more thoroughly, employing these distinctions along with other tools of literary criticism.

For Latter-day Saints, on the other hand, who see Nephi, Mormon, and Moroni as actual historical figures and the Book of Mormon as a translation, there is even less overlap with the mind of Joseph Smith (except insofar as authentic prophets share a basic understanding of spiritual truths). Yet Mormons also have not carried their convictions as far as they might. They are often content with paraphrases or didactic interpretations, whereas reading the Book of Mormon in a more history-like fashion, as the product of particular authors and editors in times past, requires an imaginative reconstruction of the circumstances of the act of literary production. (This can be done even while staying within the bounds of the text.) Why did Book of Mormon prophets write the way they did? What kinds of experiences, motivations, and personalities might have resulted in the narrative as it is presented? How did they perceive their lives and work? What did they choose to omit from their record? These are all issues that Nephi, Mormon, and Moroni address explicitly in the writings ascribed to them, and readers trying to make sense of these figures need to be asking the same sorts of questions. In addition, because they rarely read the text with the narrators in mind, Mormons have largely missed the literary coherence and aesthetic qualities of the book.

From either perspective, the narratives of the Book of Mormon do not provide direct access to either God or Joseph Smith; everything is mediated by the narrators. And *this* is the underlying logic of the text from which all interpretation has to proceed. The present study, arising out of my own decade-long experience in editing the *Reader's Edition*, is an attempt to develop a poetics of the Book of Mormon—that is, to identify some of the characteristic structures, conventions, subjects, levels of diction, and literary techniques through which its narrators speak to us. In each chapter that follows, I focus on a different aspect of Book of Mormon poetics, providing a tutorial of sorts in reading the text carefully. While I cannot comment on every major event or discourse, I have adopted the organizing principle of the Book of Mormon as the framework for my own book. Arranging my comments according to the basic sequence of narrators will allow for a relatively comprehensive treatment of the Book of Mormon, one that will provide a basic introduction for those who are new to the text. Latter-day Saints will benefit from a broad overview as well. Perhaps because they most often encounter the Book of Mormon in a verse-by-verse format, they rarely read in terms of large-scale narrative contexts or weigh the parts against the whole. (It is an unusual Latter-day Saint, for example, who can differentiate between the three major conflicts in the book of Alma, much less recognize that the last phase of the Amalickiahite Wars was fought on two fronts simultaneously.)

For Mormons who view the book as a gift from God, every word should be savored and pondered as potentially revelatory. Indeed, recent LDS prophets have urged the faithful to make the study of the Book of Mormon a lifetime pursuit, and the urge to see and understand more should lead to very close readings.[35] For non-Mormons, expectations are different, yet a book that has changed millions of lives as well as the course of American history is certainly worth a thoughtful look. Despite the Book of Mormon's somewhat archaic and unpolished style, close scrutiny will reveal more intellectual interest and literary value than many readers have previously supposed. Too often we have read Mormon scripture as if it were "The Book of Joseph Smith." There is nothing wrong with that, but we will see more if we take it seriously as "The Book of Mormon (and Nephi and Moroni)."

Abbreviations

References to biblical books follow standard abbreviations. (In keeping with Book of Mormon usage, citations of the Bible are given in the King James Version.) For books within the Book of Mormon, the following abbreviations are used:

1 Ne.	1 Nephi
2 Ne.	2 Nephi
Jacob	Jacob
Enos	Enos
Jarom	Jarom
Omni	Omni
W. of M.	Words of Mormon
Mosiah	Mosiah
Alma	Alma
Hel.	Helaman
3 Ne.	3 Nephi
4 Ne.	4 Nephi
Morm.	Mormon
Ether	Ether
Moro.	Moroni

Understanding the
Book of Mormon

1

A Brief Overview

Narrator-based Reading

For some books, the fact that they exist at all is reason enough to take a look. One thinks, for example, of Jean-Dominique Bauby's *The Diving Bell and the Butterfly* (1997), spelled out letter by letter by a quadriplegic stroke victim whose only means of communication was blinking his left eye; or the *Popol Vuh*, an anonymous sixteenth-century manuscript that managed to save a few Mayan traditions from oblivion and survived only because it was copied by a parish priest shortly before 1700; or Margery Kempe's (ca. 1373–1438) autobiography, dictated to a scribe and then lost until it was rediscovered in the 1930s; or *The Declarations of the Perfected*, a collection of Daoist sacred texts dictated by "perfected beings" to Yang Xi (fl. 364–370), a servant in the Xu family, and then collected a century later by a scholar who used Yang's extraordinary calligraphy to determine which manuscripts had been authentic revelations.[1]

The Book of Mormon is another such book, produced in a sudden rush of revelation as a young, poorly educated New York farmer dictated the text, one time through, to a series of scribes from April through June 1829. Joseph Smith claimed that his words were a translation of a record of the ancient Americas written on thin gold plates that had been delivered to him by an angel, and that he had made his translation with the help of a seer stone. Joseph himself lacked the means to publish the book, but a family friend stepped in to pay for the printing, and five thousand copies of the Book of Mormon were offered for sale to the public on March 26, 1830.[2] Curiosity about what sort of book an angel might bring could be enough to attract some readers, but the Book of Mormon's postpublication history is equally astonishing. Smith went on to found a new form of Christianity—based on the Book of Mormon—that became the most successful native-born religious movement in American history, and today there are millions of Latter-day Saints around the world. It is no coincidence that these believers are generally known as "Mormons," named after their signature scripture.

Thanks to the missionary zeal of Latter-day Saints, the Book of Mormon is widely available, with over 140 million copies published since 1830 in more than a hundred different languages. Yet while the close association of the book with Smith's prophetic claims and the LDS Church may provide additional reasons to examine it—from the perspectives of American history, religious studies, individual curiosity, or even spiritual yearning—the external connections and claims made for and against the Book of Mormon can make it more difficult to read. It is easy to lose sight of the text in the welter of arguments about what Joseph Smith could or could not have known in 1829 about the ancient Americas or pre-exilic Israel, or which elements seem to reflect nineteenth-century American society, or how we should judge the reliability of various witnesses, or the ways in which later church leaders have interpreted the book. Indeed, most studies of the Book of Mormon move fairly quickly from the text to secondary concerns (though perhaps this should not come as a surprise—we know much more about the world of Joseph Smith, or even the ancient world, than we do about the scripture that he produced).

For those who have devoted their lives to Mormonism as well as those who see such devotion as spiritually perilous, issues of historicity and veracity are not peripheral; indeed, one's eternal salvation may hang on the question of whether the book is a genuine revelation from God. Yet not every reader approaches the Book of Mormon in the midst of an existential, religious crisis, and there can be value in deferring questions of ultimate significance until we better understand the text and how it operates. Even those who come to the book seeking insights into American history or world religions are better served by beginning with a close examination of what the text says about itself and how it says it.

A Few Generalizations

We can start with ten quick, relatively uncontroversial observations about the text. Believers and skeptics may account for these features differently, and they may assign to them different levels of significance, but together they provide a basic description of the book before us. Many of these characteristics are unexpected, and each probably constitutes a challenge to examining the Book of Mormon carefully, at least for some readers.

1. *It is a long book.* The Book of Mormon began as 588 densely printed pages in 1830, and the current official edition (reformatted with substantial grammatical editing) still runs to 531 pages. In some ways this is surprising. If the primary purpose of the Book of Mormon were to function as a sign—as tangible evidence that Joseph Smith was a true prophet of God—that mission could have been accomplished much more concisely.[3] A fifty-page book delivered by an angel is no less miraculous than a thick volume; it's the heavenly messenger part that makes it hard to believe. In fact, Thomas B. Marsh (an early LDS apostle) and his wife were converted to Mormonism after reading only the first sixteen pages of the Book of Mormon—that is, the first signature sheet, which Martin Harris had given him right off the press as the book was being printed.[4] A longer tome might be more impressive to some, but it would put off other readers, in addition to offering a broader target for critics. In any case, the book represents a significant amount of work on the part of Joseph Smith and his scribes, and just getting through it can be a daunting task, especially in light of the next point.

2. *It is written in a somewhat awkward, repetitious form of English.* Nearly every page contains examples of archaic English constructions, phrases that reappear several times in quick succession, and locutions such as "and it came to pass" and "for behold" that are annoyingly pervasive. (Indeed, the constant refrain of "and it came to pass" was so offensive to Gallic sensibilities that the French translation for many decades replaced the phrase with an asterisk wherever it appeared.) Similarly, much of the grammar was awkward in the original edition, and despite several thousand minor revisions—for example, *is* to *are*, *them which* to *those who*, and *had fell* to *had fallen*—there are still sentence fragments, misplaced prepositional phrases, pronouns with unclear antecedents, and verses in which the subject changes midsentence. Nonbelievers naturally attribute all this to Smith's limited education and abilities, whereas Latter-day Saints have argued that the awkwardness may actually be the result of a too-literal translation process, and they have delighted in identifying ancient literary devices that make use of various types of repetition as evidence of the book's miraculous origins.[5] Mormons tend to ignore much of the linguistic gracelessness, and as readers get used to the rhythms of the text there are passages where the repetitions attain a particular sort of literary power. If the Book of Mormon is not high art, it is certainly folk art; it appears that there are patterns in its awkwardness, which may represent a kind of nonmainstream literary aesthetic.[6]

3. *It imitates the style of the King James Bible.* Even a cursory glance reveals that the Book of Mormon wants to be seen as a companion to the Bible. It is divided into books named after prophets; biblical phrases and even chapter-length quotations are scattered throughout; and it is written in the diction of the Authorized Version, including the general use of archaic words such as *thou, doth, hath,* and all

manner of verbs ending in -*eth*. This style of English marked the Book of Mormon immediately as "scripture," but the KJV set a very high literary standard, and the Jacobean forms are not always employed consistently, even after the many additional changes that sought to regularize these forms. The Bible-like impression of the text was enhanced in the first edition of 1830, published in binding modeled on mass-distribution Bibles of the time.[7] Since 1830, the LDS Church has further emphasized the biblical nature of the Book of Mormon by dividing it into numbered verses with cross-references (1879) and double columns (1920) and adding brief summaries at the beginning of chapters (1920; revised in 1981), extensive cross-references (1981), and a new subtitle: *Another Testament of Jesus Christ* (1982).

4. *It claims to be history.* The first edition listed Joseph Smith as "author and proprietor," but that technical legal phrase clearly was used to assert copyright ownership.[8] Joseph and his associates insisted from the beginning that the Book of Mormon was a translation from an authentic ancient document written in "Reformed Egyptian" on metal plates and buried by the last ancient author about AD 421. The book tells the story of three groups of people (Jaredites, Lehites, and Mulekites) who sailed at different times from the Near East to the Americas and established large civilizations. The primary narrative traces the history of the family of Lehi and their descendants from about 600 BC until the destruction of the righteous portion of the people in AD 384. Even though these claims generally have not been corroborated by archaeologists, Mormons have not been willing to read the book as inspired fiction.[9] There is no indication in the text itself of literary license on the part of Joseph Smith, and indeed, other than a page-and-a-half preface in the 1830 edition, his voice is never heard.[10] The book is narrated, from first to last, by ancient prophets, who admit the possibility of human error in their writing, but never the possibility that they are not fully historical. In fact, the last author—Moroni—was apparently so ontologically substantive that he became the resurrected being who delivered the plates to Joseph Smith. The strong historical assertions of the book seem to allow for only three possible origins: as a miraculously translated historical document, as a fraud (perhaps a pious one) written by Joseph Smith, or as a delusion (perhaps sincerely believed) that originated in Smith's subconscious.[11]

5. *It presents a complicated narrative.* Not only are there more than a thousand years of history involving some two hundred named individuals and nearly a hundred distinct places, but the narrative itself is presented as the work of three primary editor/historians—Nephi, Mormon, and Moroni. These figures, in turn, claim to have based their accounts on dozens of preexisting records. The result is a complex mix that incorporates multiple genres ranging from straightforward narration to inserted sermons and letters to scriptural commentary and poetry. It requires considerable patience to work out all the details of chronology, geography,

genealogy, and source records, but the Book of Mormon is remarkably consistent on all this. The chronology is handled virtually without glitches, despite several flashbacks and temporally overlapping narratives; there are only two potential geographical discrepancies (at Alma 51:26 and 53:6);[12] and the narrators keep straight both the order and family connections among the twenty-six Nephite record keepers and forty-one Jaredite kings (including rival lines). The complexity is such that one would assume the author worked from charts and maps, though Joseph Smith's wife—the person who had the longest and closest view of the production of the text—explicitly denied that he had written something out beforehand that he either had memorized or consulted as he translated, and indeed she claimed that Joseph began sessions of dictation without looking at the manuscript or having the last passage read back to him.[13]

6. *It is a religious text.* The Book of Mormon portrays a world where prayers are regularly answered with revelations, prophets predict the future with astonishing accuracy, and God punishes the wicked and rescues the righteous by miraculously intervening in human history. Societies prosper to the degree that they keep God's commandments, with pride, greed, and unbelief being the most dangerous of sins.[14] Though wealth has a corrosive effect, faith is rewarded materially in this life, but resurrection and final judgment await everyone. Morality is a matter of both individual and collective responsibility, and religious communities—led by prophets and bound together by covenants—are held accountable by God for the way they treat the poor and vulnerable. And all of this is overtly and emphatically Christian. The New Testament gospel—including the Sermon on the Mount—is preached by the resurrected Christ himself in the New World. Perhaps even more startlingly, the Book of Mormon asserts that long before the birth of Jesus there were Christians, who were taught by prophets to believe in a redeemer who would one day come into the world. This universalization of the Christian message, making it accessible to sincere seekers before the Christian era, is further expanded with the notion that God has scattered multiple, discrete offshoots of the House of Israel throughout history and around the globe. As a religious text, the Book of Mormon insists that the world it describes is in fact the world in which readers actually live, and its historical narratives, explicit sermonizing, and invitations to repent and ask God directly are all intended to convince readers of that fact. Readers may or may not find this a compelling worldview, but the Book of Mormon does offer a consistent moral and religious vision.

7. *It is basically a tragedy.* If there is any validity to the Talmud's observation that the phrase "it came to pass" signals impending trouble, we know that things will not turn out well in the Book of Mormon.[15] It relates how God led three groups to the New World, and each migration ended disastrously. The primary narrative describes Lehi and his family, whose attempt at civilization lasted a thousand years

before they destroyed themselves. The brief account of the Jaredites (in Ether—the next-to-last book, but set before the arrival of the Lehites) began with a group of friends rather than a family, yet it also concluded with mass self-destruction. The Mulekites, a colony from Jerusalem with strong political leadership including a Davidic king, did not last for more than a few generations before internal warfare and cultural drift led them to join with the Lehites and cease their existence as a separate people (their very sparse account is found in the book of Omni). For the most part, the contents of the Book of Mormon are grim. While there is hope for individuals and groups who choose rightly, general social catastrophe seems inevitable. This insistent focus on tragedy appears intentional; the single two-hundred-year period of general peace and prosperity is related in just half a chapter (4 Ne. 1:1–23). Narrators, having given up on their contemporaries, write a cautionary tale for future generations with sorrow and disappointment as prominent modes. In the words of the final writer, Moroni: "Give thanks unto God that he hath made manifest unto you our imperfections, that ye may learn to be more wise than we have been" (Morm. 9:31). It is somewhat surprising that Mormonism—generally regarded as an optimistic, forward-looking faith—has as its foundational scripture such an unrelenting record of human folly and ruin.

In even more general terms, the unifying theme of the book, from the first chapter to the last, is that God's mercies are ever extended to those who exercise faith. Nephi introduces his account with the words "Behold, I, Nephi, will show unto you that the tender mercies of the Lord are over all those whom he hath chosen, because of their faith, to make them mighty even unto the power of deliverance" (1 Ne. 1:20), a sentiment echoed in Moroni's concluding exhortation to his readers: "Behold, I would exhort you that when ye shall read these things . . . that ye would remember how merciful the Lord hath been unto the children of men, from the creation of Adam even down until the time that ye shall receive these things" (Moro. 10:3).[16] The tragedy, of course, is that so few people take advantage of God's compassionate offer.

8. *It is very didactic.* Although it takes time and patience to work out the details of various prophets, narrators, events, and records, the general message of the Book of Mormon is obvious on nearly every page. Narrators do not let readers puzzle over how to interpret various incidents, nor do they encourage speculation on who was right or wrong in a given situation. Their message is clear—repent and turn to God or suffer the consequences—and the stories they tell, the sermons they reproduce, and the comments they offer in passing are all directed toward "the convincing of the Jew and Gentile that Jesus is the Christ, the Eternal God, manifesting himself unto all nations" (Book of Mormon title page). Meir Sternberg has described the Bible as a book that is "difficult to read, easy to underread and overread and even misread, but virtually impossible to, so to speak, counterread."[17] The

Bible achieves this through very different means—biblical narration is anything but didactic—but the same can be said of the Book of Mormon. Even casual readers come away with a fairly accurate impression of the point of the book; it is hard to miss its insistence that readers change their lives and accept its values and assertions as an authoritative revelation from God.

Strikingly, the Book of Mormon's claims encompass the future as well as the past, and its narrators promise that they will someday meet each reader in the flesh at the judgment day:

> And if [these] are not the words of Christ, judge ye—for Christ will show unto you, with power and great glory, that they are his words, at the last day; and you and I [Nephi] shall stand face to face before his bar; and ye shall know that I have been commanded of him to write these things, notwithstanding my weakness. (2 Ne. 33:11)[18]

This nicely illustrates one of the surprising features of the text. In the gospels, when Jesus says "Verily, I say unto you . . .," he is speaking to his Jewish contemporaries, and modern readers are free to apply his words to themselves or not, as they wish. By contrast, when Mormon and Moroni use the second-person pronoun, they actually mean "you, the reader." Unlike religious writings that offer generic aphorisms or vague mystical pronouncements, the Nephite narrators make specific demands on their readers, whom they want to push to a religious crisis. In fairness to the text, I will convey their intentions, but it is certainly possible to read from a more disinterested, academic point of view. One does not have to take these challenges personally, even though they were obviously meant as such. This is a book designed to polarize readers, and subtlety about its central message is not among its virtues.

9. *It is a human artifact.* Strangely enough, both believers and nonbelievers agree on this point. Outsiders generally view the Book of Mormon as a product of Joseph Smith's imagination, while Mormons hold that it is the work of inspired, but quite human, ancient American prophets. In either scenario, choices were made by someone as to what to include and what to omit, and how to represent characters and situations.[19] The Book of Mormon draws on the same set of narrative tools used by both novelists and historians, including direct and indirect speech, digressions, framing narratives, quoted documents, metaphors, allusions, juxtapositions, explicit commentary, variations in duration, chronological disruptions, repetitions, contrasts, motifs, and themes. Causation can be specified or implied, details can be revealed or withheld at critical junctures, and some time periods receive much more attention than others. Although at times Latter-day Saints want to speak of God as "the primary author of the Book of Mormon,"[20] clearly the Book of Mormon is not like the Qur'an, with God speaking in the first person (or even like Joseph's own revelations in the Doctrine and Covenants, for

that matter). Rather, the word of God is articulated by very human narrators who continually draw attention to the editorial choices they have made. The combination of human effort and inspiration is captured in the title page, which states: "And now, if there are faults they are the mistakes of men; wherefore, condemn not the things of God."

10. *Its basic structure is derived from the three narrators.* The Book of Mormon explains its origins as an abridgment of the Large Plates of Nephi—the official history of the Nephites—made by the prophet/general Mormon around AD 350. He reports that when he was about to hand this record on to his son Moroni, he was inspired to add the Small Plates of Nephi—a shorter, alternative account of the first generations of Nephites, written primarily by Nephi. Moroni in turn added an abridgment of Jaredite records, some letters and sermons of his father, and a few comments of his own before burying the plates; fourteen hundred years later, as an angel, he delivered them to Joseph Smith. After Joseph and his scribe Martin Harris had translated 116 pages of Mormon's abridgment of the Large Plates, Martin asked for and received permission to take the manuscript home to show his skeptical wife. The manuscript was stolen and Joseph was commanded not to retranslate the lost pages, but rather to translate the Small Plates of Nephi in its stead. Latter-day Saints, following hints in the Book of Mormon itself (1 Ne. 9:5, 19:3; W. of M. 1:6–7), interpret this as an example of God's foreknowledge. Critics since Fawn Brodie have seen this incident much less providentially, as a personal crisis that became a pivotal moment in Joseph Smith's progression from village seer to prophet.[21] In either case, the basic structure of the Book of Mormon is as follows:

> Small Plates of Nephi—1 Nephi through Omni (150 pages)
> Mormon's explanatory comments—Words of Mormon (2 pages)
> Mormon's abridgment of the Large Plates of Nephi—Mosiah through
>   ch. 7 of Mormon (380 pages)
> Moroni's additions to his father's records—ch. 8 of Mormon through
>   Moroni (50 pages)[22]

It appears that after the loss of the first part of the manuscript, Joseph continued his dictation with the book of Mosiah, worked his way to the end of Moroni, and then produced 1 and 2 Nephi, the books that now stand at the beginning of the text. This means that the Book of Mormon narrative was produced out of chronological order, with Words of Mormon being the last section dictated.[23]

These ten observations give a basic overview of the Book of Mormon, but they do not make a strong case for reading it carefully. Indeed, several of them seem to suggest just the opposite. Certainly the book matters to Latter-day Saints, but are the details engaging enough to sustain the interest of readers who are not already committed to the faith? After all, life is short and libraries are full of literary curiosities. The answer can be found in the extraordinary creativity exhibited in the text. In reading the Book of Mormon as a work of literature, it is difficult to improve on Daniel Walker Howe's synopsis (already cited in the introduction):

> True or not, the Book of Mormon is a powerful epic written on a grand scale with a host of characters, a narrative of human struggle and conflict, of divine intervention, heroic good and atrocious evil, of prophecy, morality and law. Its narrative structure is complex. The idiom is that of the King James Version, which most Americans assumed to be appropriate for divine revelation. Although it contains elements that suggest the environment of New York in the 1820s (for example, episodes paralleling the Masonic/Antimasonic controversy), the dominant themes are biblical, prophetic, and patriarchal, not democratic or optimistic. It tells a tragic story, of a people who, though possessed of the true faith, fail in the end. Yet it does not convey a message of despair; God's will cannot ultimately be frustrated. The Book of Mormon should rank among the great achievements of American literature, but it has never been accorded the status it deserves, since Mormons deny Joseph Smith's authorship, and non-Mormons, dismissing the book as a fraud, have been more likely to ridicule than to read it.[24]

Even apart from its significance in the rise of Mormonism and the history of nineteenth-century America, the story itself is of considerable interest.

Another set of reasons for undertaking a detailed reading comes from the field of religious studies. The Book of Mormon is one of the most successful new scriptures of the last few centuries (arguably second in importance only to the Adi Granth of the Sikhs), yet most recent sacred texts consist of doctrinal expositions, ritual instructions, moral codes, scriptural commentary, or devotional poetry. The Book of Mormon, by contrast, is narrative—a much rarer genre of religious writing—and for examples of canonized sacred history one would have to look to previous millennia and writings such as the Christian gospels, the historical portions of the Hebrew Bible, Buddhist Jataka stories, or Hindu Puranas and epics such as the Mahabharata and the Ramayana. Even so, the fact that the Book of Mormon consists of an extended, integrated, nonmythological, history-like narrative makes it quite distinctive. The narrators are a natural focus for making sense of the book as a whole, and their dual function as both characters in the story and tellers of that story make them potentially intriguing from a literary perspective. We can begin by considering the position of Nephi, the first voice that we hear in the Book of Mormon.

Nephi as Narrator

When the Book of Mormon begins with "I, Nephi, having been born of goodly parents . . .," it is not immediately obvious that these words are set within a framing story, which can only be perceived a bit later.[25] We learn in the first chapter that Nephi is writing a memoir that is based, at least in part, on a record made by his father, Lehi: "after I have abridged the record of my father then will I make an account of mine own life" (v. 17). Then in chapter 9 he mentions that he has already written a longer, more detailed history of his family, and that the text we are currently reading is a second version, commanded by God "for a wise purpose in him, which purpose I know not" (1 Ne. 9:5). It is left to readers to make the connection that this purpose was to provide a substitute narrative for the 116 pages of translation that would be lost by Martin Harris in 1828.[26]

In chapter 19, Nephi returns again to this theme, noting that after the family's arrival in the Promised Land, "the Lord commanded me, wherefore I did make plates of ore that I might engraven upon them the record of my people . . . and I knew not at the time when I made them that I should be commanded of the Lord to make these plates . . . and an account of my making of these plates shall be given hereafter" (1 Ne. 19:1–5). And then, nearly seventy pages after we first meet Nephi, we finally get an account of the creation of the record we are now reading:

> And thirty years had passed away from the time we left Jerusalem. And I, Nephi, had kept the records upon my plates, which I had made of my people thus far. And it came to pass that the Lord God said unto me, "Make other plates . . ." Wherefore, I, Nephi, to be obedient to the commandments of the Lord, went and made these plates upon which I have engraven these things . . . And it sufficeth me to say that forty years had passed away, and we had already had wars and contentions with our brethren. (2 Ne. 5:28–34)

At this moment, the narration shifts from the recounting of events in the narrator's past to the telling of events in his present. In Seymour Chatman's vocabulary, "story-time" has caught up with "discourse-time."[27] Yet by this point, Nephi has also given us all the historical details that he will divulge—the family is already in the Promised Land, Lehi's descendants have split into the two opposing groups of Nephites and Lamanites, and Lehi himself has died. In the remainder of his writings, Nephi offers no further dates or political events, only chapters consisting entirely of sermons and prophecies.

When they arrive at 2 Nephi 5, readers would do well to return to the first chapter of First Nephi, because the situation of the narrator has finally become clear.

Nephi is not recording events as they happen. Instead, he is a middle-aged man recounting incidents from his teens and early twenties, with the full knowledge that life in the Promised Land has soured, that there has been an irreparable breach with his brothers, and that his closest relatives have spent years trying to kill each other. We are reading a second version of his memoirs, based in part on writings of his father and focusing particularly on spiritual matters (as God had commanded in 1 Ne. 9:3–4).[28] This information is crucial in trying to sort out the narrator's attitudes and perspective, but because it is mentioned only in passing much later in the text, few readers of First Nephi realize that their conception of Nephi is still incomplete.

To use the technical language of narratology, the book of First Nephi constitutes an autodiegetic, temporally distant, embedded narrative.[29] That is to say, Nephi relates incidents from his own life, long after the fact, and the main narrative is framed by a more comprehensive story—the story of God commanding Nephi to write a second record, which was an abridgment of his first draft. The tale of Joseph Smith, angels, and gold plates is paratext (material that is separate from the narrative but which nevertheless shapes the way that readers read), and most publications on the Book of Mormon have focused on the issue of the implied author or, as H. Porter Abbott prefers, the inferred author.[30] All readers can agree that Nephi is the narrator, but they differ in the mental image they construct of the author: they either imagine Joseph Smith inventing a narrator who in turn constructs an edited narrative, or they think of Nephi himself picking and choosing what to include in order to create a persona—the narrator—who will instruct and inspire future generations (with Joseph Smith as the translator).

In this book I propose that the best approach to reading the Book of Mormon is one that focuses on the narrators. At this level, readings are more likely to be comprehensive (since this is the way the book is actually structured) and they can deal with larger literary units such as complete discourses, multichapter prophecies, and extended stories rather than isolated verses. Whether Nephi operates as a fictional character or an ancient prophet, he presents a life story with a particular point of view, a theological vision, an agenda, and a characteristic style of writing, all of which can be found within the confines of the text itself. Nephi, along with Mormon and Moroni, tells us a great deal about himself—not only through what he says directly but also through the way he creates narratives and edits sources.

The other reason to favor a narrator-centered approach is that it opens up the Book of Mormon to literary appreciation. Since the nineteenth century, critics have complained that the book is simply a pastiche of biblical passages "chiefly garbled from the Old and New Testaments," "a miserable attempt to imitate the style of King James the first," an awkward synthesis of ideas cobbled together from the popular culture of Joseph Smith's time, or even "spontaneous free association."[31] For reasons enumerated in the previous section, the Book of Mormon, unlike the

Bible, will probably never be praised for literary excellence by anyone who does not already love the book for its religious message. While Latter-day Saints have always felt a certain power in its language, it is only in recent years that they have begun to employ techniques of literary criticism to identify the book's characteristic features. Several authors have proclaimed the Book of Mormon a literary masterpiece, supporting this assertion by exhaustively cataloging the rhetorical devices they have found in the text, from anaphora and chiasmus to epanalepsis, parallelism, and word pairs.[32]

The presence of literary forms, however, does not guarantee that a book is a work of literature, nor does the identification of these features constitute a full reading. As Meir Sternberg has written of the Bible: "The listing of so-called forms and devices and configurations—a fashionable practice, this, among the aspirants to 'literary criticism'—is no substitute for the business of reading. Since a sense of coherence entails a sense of purpose, it is not enough to trace a pattern; it must also be validated and justified in terms of communicative design."[33] Literary devices of various kinds may indeed be present in the text—some more engaging than others—but what gives them meaning is how they fit into the particular designs of the three editor/historians. If we read the Book of Mormon in large sections rather than fragmented verses, we can learn to discern the individual personalities, methods, and intentions of these figures. The ongoing and explicit interaction between narrators, narratives, and audience—the Book of Mormon's "communicative design"—is the aspect of the text that seems most likely to interest students of literature.

Nephi is somewhat like Pip in *Great Expectations*: he is narrating events from his own past, with a full understanding of how the story will turn out. This allows for a certain sort of irony—the narrator knows things of which his younger self is unaware. In the case of Nephi, we can see him shape the narrative for certain ends, and we can form a picture of his character and personality, his biases and blind spots. If he employs literary devices, he does so for his own purposes. There may be an aesthetic at work in the Book of Mormon, but it is not that of nineteenth-century novels, nor even of the Bible; repetitions, direct speech, and poetry have to be evaluated in terms of the conventions of the text itself. And because of the way the book is structured, close readings of narrative techniques often become character studies.

Latter-day Saints are attuned to how the Book of Mormon resembles the Bible, but just as important are the ways in which the two books are dissimilar. Indeed, a narrator-centered approach immediately highlights one crucial difference. It may appear that both works are library-like collections of distinct books written over time by various authors, but where scholarly scrutiny suggests that many of the biblical books as we have them today were produced by multiple, self-effacing redactors, the Book of Mormon presents itself as the work of known abridgers with precise dates, life stories, and motivations. From its first verses, the extended first-person narrative of Nephi offers a mode of writing almost entirely absent from the Hebrew Bible (the only exceptions are a few chapters of Ezra-Nehemiah). This means that the primary narrators of the Book of Mormon—Nephi, Mormon, and Moroni—are accessible to readers in a way that the dominant narrative voice of the Bible is not.

The narrators in the Hebrew Bible are anonymous, omniscient, reticent, and unobtrusive. They speak from no particular time or place, reporting words, actions, and secret thoughts (even, at times, what God is thinking). They rarely comment on the story, offer judgments, mention themselves, refer to their own editing, or address their audience directly.[34] We are seldom told how we should react to specific incidents, and as a result, biblical narratives are generally open to multiple readings and interpretations. This is part of their literary appeal. As Robert Alter has observed: "Many of these habits of reticence may be plausibly attributed to an underlying aesthetic predisposition. The masters of ancient Hebrew narrative were clearly writers who delighted in an art of indirection, in the possibilities of intimating depths through the mere hint of a surface feature, or through a few words of dialogue fraught with implication."[35]

Without exception, Book of Mormon narrators operate very differently. They reveal their identities from the beginning and exercise strict control over their material. They write from limited, human perspectives—that is, they give us their personal view of what happened and why it is important (though for those within the faith, the prophetic authority of these men makes them uniquely qualified to render such judgments). They do not hesitate to address readers directly to explain their intentions, their writing processes, their editorial decisions, and their emotional responses to the events they recount. They demarcate textual units for our consideration.[36] They interrupt the narrative to offer explicit judgments. They even admit the possibility of human error and ask indulgence for their "weakness in writing" (Eth. 12:23, 40; cf. 2 Ne. 33:1, 4).

The narrative itself is constructed with a minimum of moral ambiguity, and there are regular passages that begin with some variation of "Thus we see that . . .," wherein the narrators tell readers exactly how they should interpret particular events. This is not to say that the meaning is entirely determined—the humanity of the narrators and the ample narrative details they provide leave some space for independent readerly analysis—but the first round of interpretation has been done for us, and we owe this additional clarity (perhaps at the cost of aesthetic pleasure) to the narrators. All this gives the Book of Mormon a very different feel from the narrative portions of the Bible, let alone the prophetic books or the wisdom texts. In summary, we might say that while the Bible appears to be divine in its authorship and human in its textual transmission, the Book of Mormon seems to be just the opposite—it claims to have been written by specific, historic individuals but was transmitted to modern readers through divine intervention.

A volume of the size and complexity of the Book of Mormon required deliberate choices about how to tell the story, and those decisions can be analyzed through conventional literary means. When is direct speech employed? Which incidents are given more space? How is characterization indicated? When are there disruptions in the chronology? Is there repetition of key phrases? Are events arranged into patterns? When does the narrator interrupt the story? When are earlier documents quoted? Where are poetic forms found? Are there significant juxtapositions? Does the text set up expectations that can be thwarted at pivotal points? When is crucial information revealed or withheld? These sorts of questions were originally formulated in the study of fiction, but they also apply to history. Historians obviously are not free to simply make things up, but when they tell stories they draw on many of the same narrative techniques used by novelists. In the Book of Mormon these choices are presented as the work of the editor/historians.

Nephi Returns with the Plates

As an example of what might be gained from an attentive, narrator-based reading of a text that might otherwise seem literarily dismissible, we can look at a story—quite familiar to Latter-day Saints—from 1 Nephi chapters 3–5. The background, as reported in the first chapter of the Book of Mormon, is that Lehi received a vision in 597 BC warning him that Jerusalem was about to be destroyed. Lehi prophesied this message of impending doom to his neighbors and was rejected by them. Indeed, they were so angered they wanted to kill him, though Lehi does not realize this until the second chapter, when God revealed the murder plot to him in a dream and commanded him to gather his family and leave as quickly as possible. This is the moment at which our story begins.

After traveling some distance into the wilderness, Lehi had yet another dream in which God directed him to send his sons back to Jerusalem to get the Brass Plates—an early version of the Hebrew Bible written in some form of Egyptian or Egyptian script (Mosiah 1:3–4) that was in the possession of a distant kinsman, Laban. When his brothers hesitated, Nephi announced that he would go because he knew that "the Lord giveth no commandments unto the children of men, save he shall prepare a way for them that they may accomplish the thing which he commandeth them" (1 Ne. 3:7). His brothers joined him and, after what would have been about a two-week journey (according to maps available to Joseph Smith), they arrived at Jerusalem and drew lots as to who should make the first attempt.[37] The lot fell to the oldest brother, Laman, who went to Laban's house and asked for the record, only to retreat in haste when Laban threatened to kill him. Next, Nephi had the idea that they should gather the valuables they had abandoned at their old home and try to buy the plates. When they approached Laban, he had his servants chase them away and then claimed as his own the gold and silver they left behind.

At this point the two oldest brothers wanted to give up and return to their father empty-handed. Indeed, they tried to persuade Sam and Nephi by beating them, but an angel appeared, chastised them, and promised success for the next attempt. Only Nephi rose to the challenge. He went into the city alone at night, where he came across a very drunk Laban lying on the street, passed out. The Spirit of the Lord urged him to slay Laban, which Nephi did with Laban's own sword, justifying his actions by observing that Laban had stolen their property and tried to kill them first. In addition, Nephi realized that the Brass Plates would be necessary if his descendants were to have any chance at keeping the laws of Moses in the Promised Land. Nephi then put on the dead man's clothes and, pretending to be Laban, ordered a servant to fetch the plates and follow him outside the city, where he met his brothers. When Zoram, the servant, realized the ruse, the brothers convinced him to join their family in the wilderness, promising him his freedom. Then the five of them headed back into the wilderness for the two-week journey back to Lehi's tent. It is here, at the moment the family is reunited, that Nephi's narration becomes particularly interesting.

So far, this somewhat grim tale has emphasized Nephi's role in his family and especially his superiority to his two older brothers: they were unbelieving, he was faithful; they were terrified, he had courage; they received an angelic rebuke, he enjoyed divine favor; they failed, he succeeded. This much is clear from Nephi's own version of these events, but given the unexpected complications that arose in acquiring the plates, it would have been helpful to have followed up the story with some external, explicit commendation of Nephi's actions. The one person who could have bestowed such validation—Lehi—is silenced in Nephi's retelling (making this incident something other than simplistic didactic fiction; Lehi does not speak the words that Nephi the storyteller was hoping to hear). We can imagine that a father might have had a lot to say upon the return of his sons, particularly when Nephi brought with him not only the Brass Plates but also a bloody sword, a tale of a roadside killing, and a kidnapped, recently freed slave.[38] We are informed that Lehi was happy to see them (this seems to have come before the brothers had a chance to tell their story), but we are given not a single word from Lehi to his sons. Instead, Nephi offers a prior conversation between his parents, Lehi and Sariah. Nephi often claims that he cannot include everything in his record (1 Ne. 1:16, 6:1–3, 8:29, 9:1–4, 10:15, etc.), but it is difficult to avoid the suspicion that something is being suppressed here.

Watch how skillfully the narrator handles this:

> And it came to pass that we took the Plates of Brass and the servant of
> Laban, and departed into the wilderness, and journeyed unto the tent of
> our father. [*No mention here of Laban's sword, which we know from later
> verses (2 Ne. 5:14, Jacob 1:10) was in Nephi's possession.*]
>
>   And it came to pass that after we had come down into the wilderness
> unto our father, behold, he was filled with joy [*this is where we might
> expect Lehi to say something, but our attention is immediately shifted to
> Sariah*], and also my mother, Sariah, was exceedingly glad, for she truly
> had mourned because of us. For she had supposed that we had perished
> in the wilderness [*the desert, rather than Laban, was her greatest concern*];
> and she also had complained against my father, telling him that he was a
> visionary man; saying, "Behold, thou hast led us forth from the land of
> our inheritance, and my sons are no more, and we perish in the wilder-
> ness." And after this manner of language had my mother complained
> against my father. (1 Ne. 4:38–5:3)

The narrator makes three remarkable moves here. First, he disrupts the chronology of the story by telling us about previous events—something always worth
noting. Second, he puts his mother in a negative light by reporting her grumbling
(though it is only because of her love for her sons), and because we are never told in
the text exactly how long the brothers were gone, it is hard to assess how justified her
complaints might have been. Third, he provides his mother's exact words. This last
move is particularly significant since it goes against the conventions of the text; outside of this verse and verse 8 below, Nephi *never* quotes women. If his intention is to
distract readers from the situation at hand, he has chosen something particularly
effective—a woman's voice in the Book of Mormon is very rare and very engaging.

> And it had come to pass that my father spake unto her, saying, "I know
> that I am a visionary man; for if I had not seen the things of God in a
> vision I should not have known the goodness of God, but had tarried at
> Jerusalem, and had perished with my brethren. [*Is there a hint here that
> Laban would have perished later anyway?*] But behold, I have obtained a
> land of promise, in the which things I do rejoice [*this is the first time in
> the Book of Mormon that Lehi mentions the Promised Land; the only earlier
> references were in a revelation to Nephi and in Nephi's justification for
> slaying Laban (1 Ne. 2:20, 4:14)*]; yea, and I know that the Lord will
> deliver my sons out of the hands of Laban [*worries about Laban appear
> here for the first time—a concern that Sariah will pick up in her response*],

and bring them down again unto us in the wilderness." And after this manner of language did my father, Lehi, comfort my mother, Sariah, concerning us, while we journeyed in the wilderness up to the land of Jerusalem, to obtain the record of the Jews. [*Apparently the conversation dates back to just after their sons' departure, a month or so earlier. When did Lehi or Sariah inform Nephi of this discussion that he was not around to overhear?*] (1 Ne. 5:4–6)

It is striking how Lehi's profession of faith makes us think of Nephi and his brothers as vulnerable, potential victims rather than as the perpetrators of a deed that, without a considerable amount of explanation, would look a lot like murder and robbery. Perhaps not coincidentally—given the fact that Nephi has chosen to include this information as a direct quotation—Lehi's words reflect (or prefigure) the key ideas in Nephi's wrestling within himself about whether or not to slay Laban, with similar appeals to revelation, the perishing of entire peoples, the family's destiny in the land of promise, and the Lord's deliverance (compare 1 Ne. 4:10–18).

And when we had returned to the tent of my father, behold their joy was full, and my mother was comforted. [*Here the flashback catches up with the main narrative and there is another opportunity for Lehi to speak; instead, Sariah continues the conversation that had started long ago. It is not clear to whom she is speaking, but she responds to Lehi point by point.*] And she spake, saying, "Now I know of a surety that the Lord hath commanded my husband to flee into the wilderness; yea, and I also know of a surety that the Lord hath protected my sons, and delivered them out of the hands of Laban [*this sounds more like a response to Lehi's prediction rather than to the brothers telling their story*], and given them power whereby they could accomplish the thing which the Lord hath commanded them." [*An echo of Nephi's assertion at 1 Ne. 3:7 that God will always provide a way*].[39] And after this manner of language did she speak. And it came to pass that they did rejoice exceedingly, and did offer sacrifice and burnt offerings unto the Lord; and they gave thanks unto the God of Israel. (1 Ne. 5:7–9)

Thus doubts are resolved and commandments are fulfilled, all in the same terms by which Nephi narrated the story of the slaying of Laban, with full credit given to God. Nephi continues with a lengthy description of his father's eager perusal of the Brass Plates (it is essential to the narrative to establish that the plates were worth the cost Nephi paid), and then concludes the chapter—the first in the 1830 edition—by sounding the now familiar themes one last time:

And it came to pass that thus far I and my father had kept the commandments wherewith the Lord had commanded us. [*Note that there is no
space between the two men here; in the following, "we" always refers to
Nephi and Lehi.*] And we had obtained the records which the Lord had
commanded us, and searched them and found that they were desirable;
yea, even of great worth unto us, insomuch that we could preserve the
commandments of the Lord unto our children. Wherefore, it was
wisdom in the Lord that we should carry them with us, as we journeyed
in the wilderness towards the land of promise. (1 Ne. 5:20–22)

From the perspective of the family, however, regardless of the spiritual value of
the plates, the slaying of Laban marked a decisive moment in their history. Before
that fateful night some family members could have held out the hope that their
flight was a temporary matter, just until the immediate threats against Lehi had
dissipated. After Laban's death, however, the brothers are fugitives; there is no
going back to their old life—not with the family property gone, Laban dead, the
Brass Plates missing, and the brothers' recent intense interest in the plates common
knowledge, at least among Laban's servants.

In dealing with reticent biblical texts, Meir Sternberg has introduced the useful
distinction of "gaps" (conspicuous absences from a narrative that demand some sort
of closure) and "blanks" (things that might be interesting to know but which are hardly
crucial to the story, such as someone's physical appearance).[40] Lehi's response to the
killing of Laban is a gap. This is why, in the *Book of Mormon Movie* (2003)—a not
entirely successful attempt to bring the Book of Mormon to the big screen—there is a
scene in which Lehi greets the returning brothers and is introduced to Zoram: "Welcome to the family," he says. The scriptwriters understood that some sort of comment or reaction was needed to round out the story, though they chose not to think
too hard about how much explaining Nephi would have had to do to his father.[41]

Lehi was undoubtedly happy to see his sons again (we are told that three
times), yet he may have had some stern words for Nephi, or at least some pointed
questions. S. Kent Brown has observed that burnt offerings, such as those Lehi
sacrificed at 1 Nephi 5:9, were intended to purge sin, so Lehi must have felt somewhat ill at ease with how his request to procure the plates had been carried out.[42]
Nephi, as a narrator who is anxious for us to perceive him as spiritually superior to
his brothers and in harmony with his father at all times, omits the homecoming
dialogue. (If Lehi had said, "Surely God was directing you," or "You alone among
my sons have been faithful," wouldn't Nephi have mentioned it?) But this is not
just a case of simple elision; at the crucial moment in the narrative, when we are
most likely to feel the gap, Nephi quickly substitutes something else—something
quite distracting—hoping that we won't notice.

This analysis of Nephi's narration does not, however, constitute a complete reading of the passage. It is also important to note how carefully, even artfully, it is structured. The section (1 Ne. 5:1–9) begins and ends with rejoicing. There are three quotations that each conclude with "after this manner of language," and the two occurrences of "complained" in the first half are matched by two appearances of "comfort" in the second.[43] Sariah's three criticisms starting at "behold" (loss of inheritance, loss of sons, loss of lives in the wilderness) are countered by Lehi's three reassurances, also starting at "behold" (a land of promise, the sons delivered, the family reunited in the wilderness). So in schematic form, the passage looks something like this:

5:1   Parents rejoice
    5:2–3 Quotation 1: Sariah "complained . . . saying, Behold [three items] . . .
        and after this manner of language had my mother complained"
    5:4–7 Quotation 2: Lehi's response, "But behold [three matching items] . . .
        after this manner of language did my father, Lehi, comfort my
        mother, Sariah . . . and my mother was comforted"
    5:8   Quotation 3: Sariah's rejoinder, "Now I know . . . [three items] . . .
        and after this manner of language did she speak"
5:9   Parents rejoice[44]

Yet there is more here than mere repetition and balance, because Nephi has portrayed his mother as a dynamic, changing character; with each repetition there is also development. Sariah moves from doubt to acceptance, and specifically she comes to adopt Lehi's perspective on things. Or rather, she comes to see the Lord's hand in their family's history. Compare her initial complaint with her final affirmation: "thou [Lehi] hast led us forth from the land of our inheritance" versus "the Lord hath commanded my husband to flee in the wilderness"; "my sons are no more" versus "the Lord hath protected my sons," and "we perish in the wilderness" (with the implication of it having been pointless) versus having "power whereby they could accomplish the thing which the Lord hath commanded." The first set of statements focuses on what has been lost; the second set focuses on divine protection and assistance. And where Nephi introduced Sariah's complaints by noting how she "supposed" that disaster had overtaken them, now she proclaims (twice), "I know of a surety."

Faith was a crucial issue for Nephi, and it appears throughout his writings. How do people come to accept the words of prophets as the word of the Lord? What is faith founded upon? How is prophetic credibility established? Is there a way to convince his brothers—and modern readers, for that matter—to accept his spiritual authority? Sariah provides one particular answer. Her husband predicts a number of things; when one of those turns out to be true (i.e., her sons return safely), she is inclined to trust Lehi on the rest ("Now I know of a surety," she begins, though she continues by expressing faith in more than just God's deliverance of her children).

The problem of false prophets was a critical concern in late pre-exilic Judah (as it was in Joseph Smith's day, but we will continue to view Nephi as a character rooted in a particular time and place). The issue figured prominently in both Deuteronomy and Jeremiah—two of the writings Nephi specified were included in the Brass Plates (1 Ne. 5:11–13)—and the *New Oxford Annotated Bible* (3rd ed.) describes the situation in this way:

> Having established an Israelite model of prophecy, the law provides two criteria to distinguish true from false prophecy. The first is that the prophet should speak exclusively on behalf of God and report only God's words. The second makes the fulfillment of a prophet's oracle the measure of its truth. . . . If a false prophet is distinguished by the failure of his oracle to come true, then making a decision in the present about which prophet to obey becomes impossible. (Deut. 18:20–23, fn.)

It is crucial that Lehi's commands are not his but God's (1 Ne. 3:5: "behold, I have not required it of them, but it is a commandment of the Lord"), and Nephi wants to portray the brothers' successful return from Jerusalem not just as an example of divine intervention but also as the fulfillment of prophecy. Only in this way can Lehi's status as a true prophet be established. Sariah's grasp of those principles is meant to be a model for readers.

So in just nine verses we have seen (1) a narrative gap, (2) the narrator's attempt to disguise it, (3) a chronological disjunction, (4) a deviation from narrative convention (that of silent women), (5) shifts between paraphrase and direct discourse, (6) significant repetition, (7) the demarcation of a literary unit, (8) the balancing of key phrases, (9) allusions to earlier and later events, (9) strong characterization, and (10) an illustration of a theological issue of urgent importance to the narrator.

Even a relatively short passage can demonstrate many of the points made in my earlier list, including the awkward biblical-style language, the insistence on historicity, the relatively complicated narrative, the pervasive religiosity, the central role of narrators, and the didacticism. It will be readily apparent that the narrators not only show us what they want us to see but also tell us what to think about it. As the Catholic sociologist Thomas O'Dea noted long ago, in the Book of Mormon "good and evil are easily discernible at all times."[45] Yet the constant interplay of original event and later narration opens up some intriguing possibilities for literary analysis. As we learn to read the Book of Mormon in terms of Nephi's editorial, behind-the-scenes decisions, our understanding of the narrator (regardless of whether he was fictional or historical) gradually unfolds in complex ways, and the same will be true of Mormon and Moroni.

We can compare the frustrations and concerns that arise from their personal circumstances with their interest in relating specific incidents. We can identify their distinctive themes and techniques. We can see where they have shaped their accounts to elicit particular reactions. We can read against the text to determine where their qualms and apprehensions have interfered with a straightforward telling of stories. We can weigh the finished work against their stated intentions and then go back to see where there are gaps—either things they deliberately omitted, blind spots that are apparent to later readers, or places where they misjudged their target audience. A truly didactic book only needs to be read once to grasp its full meaning, but the intersecting perspectives of Book of Mormon narration allow for nuanced interpretations and multiple rereadings as we deconstruct the text in order to construct the narrators.

When Nephi tells the story of his family, he touches upon many themes of considerable interest—the nature of revelation and prophecy, the origins of faith and how it can be passed to the next generation, conflict within families, immigration and new beginnings, physical survival and divine deliverance, reliving sacred drama (in this case, the biblical Joseph's conflicts with his brothers and the Israelites' exodus from Egypt), religious violence, the significance of books and records, God's knowledge and power, and the purpose of afflictions—but everything must be interpreted through the perspective of the narrator. Nephi's favorite themes and primary literary techniques are not those of Mormon or Moroni, and Joseph Smith's own opinions on such matters are perhaps still more difficult to ascertain, whether one regards him as a translator or as an author who deserves a degree of separation from the inferred author and narrators of his book. But the narrators are explicit, self-disclosing presences in the text in a way that Joseph Smith never is.

A Note on Methodology

As may be surmised from the example above, this book will offer character studies of figures from the Book of Mormon—particularly the three major narrators—and I will write about them, in many ways, as if they were real people. Hence I have opinions about what Nephi left out of his account, how Lehi probably would have reacted to news of Laban's death, and how Nephi hoped his actions would be perceived by his readers. To Latter-day Saints, who as a matter of faith believe Nephites to have been historical individuals, these are reasonable questions. Non-Mormons, however, may be reminded of L. C. Knights' famous 1933 essay "How Many Children Had Lady Macbeth?" in which he criticized a Romantic mode of literary criticism popular at the time. Knights' whimsical title—as opposed to anything he actually said in his essay—has become a shorthand for the commonsense observation that literary figures are not living beings and have no independent existence apart from the words of their authors.[46] If Nephi was, in fact, a fictional creation of Joseph Smith (and this seems to be the most useful, plausible way for outsiders to approach the text), can we speak of Nephi's mind and ambitions or his life apart from what is explicitly reported in the Book of Mormon? I would argue that we can.

Imagining the feelings and motivations of literary characters as if they were our friends or acquaintances has always played a large part in the enjoyment of fiction. In the last half century, theorists have produced a number of sophisticated studies explaining the process by which readers come to know characters and why this is a valid response to literature. In reply to those who say, "We cannot ask how many children Lady Macbeth had, or what courses Hamlet pursued at Wittenberg," Seymour Chatman writes:

> Because one question is idle, does it mean that all questions concerning characters are idle? How about "Is Lady Macbeth a good mother, and if so, in what sense of 'good'?" . . . Or about Hamlet: "What sort of a student was he? What is the relation between his scholarly interests and his general temperament?" In short, should we restrain what seems a God-given right to infer and even to speculate about characters if we like? Any such restraint strikes me as an impoverishment of aesthetic experience. . . . Of course Hamlet and Macbeth are not "living people" but that does not mean that as constructed imitations they are in any way limited to the words on the printed page.[47]

Philosopher Peter Lamarque observes that "both literary critics and ordinary readers take it for granted that inferences beyond what is explicit are not just permissible but indispensable in understanding fiction," and he explains, "Readers, somewhat like scientists or historians, frame and modify hypotheses about fictional content, assessing the quality and connectedness of the data, attempting to construct (fictional) states of affairs such that they render maximally coherent the evidence available."[48] This is a dynamic and creative process that should take into account not only direct descriptions, reported words and actions, and ascribed beliefs and thoughts, but also what is presumed from the reader's own life experiences and what can be inferred about the normal workings of the fictional world, as well as more literary concerns such as structure, themes, and modes of expression, including irony, hyperbole, satire, figurative usage, allusion, and point of view. Yet in the end, even the most detailed fictions will leave a number of "facts" about characters unspecified (these are the gaps and blanks mentioned in the previous section). Can we speak meaningfully about these? Again Lamarque:

While I would agree that propositions for which we have no evidence at all, either from the text or from the background, might best be considered as lacking a truth-value, I do not think we should automatically dismiss in the same way all propositions about a character's (or narrator's) attitudes and beliefs over which there is some indeterminacy. I am inclined to say, at least of some propositions of this kind, that they are true on some readings of the text and false on others or that they are true *relative to an interpretation.* . . . [Literary interpretation] is not a matter of discovering truths about a world so much as assigning thematic significance to component parts of a work. It is a search for coherence and sense. It involves making connections by subsuming more and more elements in a work under a network of thematic concepts. Part of this literary interpretation will involve making sense of the actions and thoughts of characters. But interpretation goes well beyond that. It is also concerned with general themes or symbolic structures that bind together all the elements in a work, not just psychological factors. Again there is no a priori reason why any one interpretation should capture all the possible or interesting connections.[49] [Emphasis in the original]

This quotation provides a useful context for my project, which tries to make sense of the actions and thoughts of the narrators in order to provide a coherent, comprehensive reading of the Book of Mormon as a whole (all the while acknowledging that other interpretations are possible).

Despite its length, the Book of Mormon is a rather elliptical work that includes a great deal of indeterminacy. I will be reconstructing the attitudes and beliefs of its major narrators based on a close reading of the text. To do so, I will make observations about elements that are present, as well as those that are absent but expected (in accordance with the conventions of the story world or general assumptions of human psychology and behavior). I will also point out features of literary organization, rhetoric, and tone. Inevitably, I end up giving more weight to some details than others as I fit together an interpretation that makes sense of as many of the narrative elements as possible, but because the Book of Mormon represents itself as a history that is told and edited by participants, the entirety of its contents and structure—including omissions, juxtapositions, repetitions, and selectivity—can be read as speech acts that reveal the personalities of its narrators.

At times I imagine what sorts of life experiences might have resulted in the narration as it is presented, but only insofar as there is at least indirect textual support. I do not, for instance, ask questions about Nephi's favorite foods or how old Mormon was when he married. Readers are free, of course, to ask anything they want, but since these speculations are entirely outside the text and its thematic concerns, they are not arguable assertions. On the other hand, in the next chapter I will suggest that Nephi's narration is more coherent if we imagine that he had no sons, and I identify verses that seem to support this hypothesis. I am not, however, making a claim about a historical Nephi; I am trying to make sense of a text. There may be other readings that connect data in different ways to provide a better explanation for why Nephi tells his story the way he does, but because this is something we can argue about, based on textual evidence, there is some truth-value to my proposition regardless of whether Nephi was a historical figure or a fictional construct. Although it may sometimes appear as if my analysis assumes the historicity of the text, the sorts of observations and inferences I put forward could just as readily be made about an intricately constructed, multivocal, narrated novel such as Nabokov's *Pale Fire*.

An approach suitable for fiction is not necessarily inappropriate for history. Both genres are *representations* of reality, and consequently, readers come to know all of the characters they meet in books in much the same way. Baruch Hochman has explored this phenomenon at some length in his *Character in Literature*,[50] but it is once again Seymour Chatman who provides a particularly succinct summary:

> Why should we be any less inclined to search through and beyond the words of Shakespeare for insights into the construct "Hamlet" than through and beyond the words of Boswell for insight into the construct "Samuel Johnson"? Samuel Johnson did indeed live, but any current attempt to "know" him requires reconstruction, inference, and speculation. No matter that the facts and views provided by Boswell are more numerous than those provided by Shakespeare—there is always more to reconstruct, to speculate about.[51]

In the final accounting, there is an absolute, existential difference between fictional characters and historical figures, with Mormons and non-Mormons never coming to agreement about which category the Nephites fit into, but at the level of narrative analysis, the reading and interpretive strategies of both insiders and outsiders converge. This is the domain of the present study. I treat the Book of Mormon as a "history-like" narrative (a term that can encompass both historical fictions and authentic histories),[52] but I stop short of actual historical criticism, which would require one to choose between incommensurate backgrounds in order to assess the accuracy and meaning of the narrative; reading almost any passage in the context of the ancient world will yield very different interpretations than if we start with the assumption that it is a product of Joseph Smith and his upstate New York environment.

In reconstructing the mind of Samuel Johnson, we can consult sources in addition to Boswell's biography for information about both the man and eighteenth-century

England. By contrast, though a few chapters of the Book of Mormon take place in a recognizable historical setting—hence my comments on likely travel times in Arabia and the topography of Jerusalem—after Nephi's family arrives in the New World their exact location is unknown and a rigorous historical-critical approach is impossible, even if one were so inclined. There are no independent, verifiable sources for Nephite history that would shed light on specific details of the narrative. Consequently, I avoid arguments that appeal to the world outside the text (especially after Nephi's genera-tion), with one significant exception: I regularly refer to the Hebrew Bible, which plays an integral role in the Book of Mormon. Because the Bible exists both in the ancient background posited by the narrative and also in Joseph Smith's world, identifying bib-lical connections (such as the problem of false prophets in Deuteronomy) should not automatically divide readers into believers and nonbelievers.

It was Stanley Fish who first introduced the idea of "interpretive communities" into literary studies.[53] The details of his theory are controversial, but there is little doubt that readers are greatly influenced by the interpretive assumptions and hab-its of their peers. And rarely is the divide between communities as great as the one that separates insiders and outsiders when they pick up the Book of Mormon. To non-Mormons, the book is obviously a fiction or a hoax. The idea of reading it as an actual history of a lost Christian civilization in the ancient Americas is so pre-posterous that it is hard to imagine how otherwise educated and rational people can take it seriously in this way (tales of angels, gold plates, and seer stones do not help). For Latter-day Saints, accustomed to a community that unquestionably accepts the text as history, the complexity and beauty of the book—in addition to what they see as profound religious truths—would seem to make it impossible for thoughtful, open-minded people to doubt (especially those willing to listen to the promptings of the Holy Spirit). My goal is not to move readers from one side to the other but rather to provide a way in which they can speak across religious bounda-ries and discuss a remarkable text with some degree of rigor and insight.

There is great value in studies of how the Book of Mormon was received in nineteenth-century America, the role the book has played in the lives of believers, and the identification of its major themes—all of which have been ably handled by Terryl Givens in his *By the Hand of Mormon* and *The Book of Mormon: A Very Short Introduction*—but these approaches cannot replace thorough, detailed readings of the text in its entirety. A comprehensive understanding of the book's contents depends on a careful examination of its structure, which in turn requires tempo-rarily adopting the book's internal perspective, at least until we can grasp the func-tion of the narrators. For nonbelievers reading the Book of Mormon, adopting the proverbial willing suspension of disbelief may seem like a surrender to fanciful naiveté, yet it is just as necessary for religious narratives as it is for novels (the Bud-dhologist Noble Ross Reat has suggested something even stronger—"temporary conversion"—as a practical method in religious studies).[54] In order to conceptual-ize the Book of Mormon as fiction, we must picture Joseph Smith imagining a history of the Nephites and then imagining narrators who interact with that history and with each other.

On the other hand, it may be just as beneficial for Latter-day Saints to allow for a willing suspension of *belief*, that is, to think of the Book of Mormon as a work of literature, with an emphasis on its creativity and artifice. Becoming more aware of how the book appears to outsiders can sharpen Mormon perceptions, but even more importantly, analytical tools that were originally developed for the study of fiction can expose the ways in which the Book of Mormon, even if it is a transla-tion of an ancient record, is not an objective, straightforward history (as if there were such a thing). Close readings suggest that Nephi, Mormon, and Moroni are presenting theological ideas in the guise of history, as they deliberately highlight or elide certain facts in accordance with their individual, prophetic agendas. For both insiders and outsiders, reading the Book of Mormon from the perspective of the narrators will reveal that there is more to this engaging book than first meets the eye.

This present study is intended as a guide to the Book of Mormon that will introduce readers to its most significant characters, events, and themes. Yet it is more than simply a synopsis. I want to demonstrate a method by which the Book of Mormon can be read more insightfully and comprehensively. Each chapter focuses on a representative writing strategy adopted by the narrators. We will see, for example, how Nephi adapts biblical passages to reflect his own circum-stances, how Mormon organizes his material to provide a rational, evidentiary basis for faith, and then how Moroni comes to reject that model of belief. We will investigate characterization, parallel structures, and verbal allusions, all the while looking for both coherence and inconsistencies. I will provide some sense of how Mormons typically approach their scriptures (with more information about LDS scholarship in the notes), but there is also a great deal here that will be new to Latter-day Saints. My rather narrow focus on the text itself is something of a depar-ture from many Mormon commentaries, and several of the specific interpretations that I advance are novel. While recognizing that believers and outsiders bring very different assumptions to their readings of the Book of Mormon, I nevertheless try to present an overview of its characteristic features that is fair to both the book and its message.

PART I

Nephi

2

Sons and Brothers

Characterization

The story of the Book of Mormon is told, to a large extent, as a series of interlocking biographies. First one and then another individual comes to the forefront of the national narrative to carry the plot forward. In his biography of Joseph Smith, Richard Bushman provides a quick, enthusiastic overview of the Book of Mormon, noting:

> Among the leading characters are Nephi, the unbendingly good younger brother; Sariah, the dutiful, outspoken mother; Benjamin, the righteous king who speaks to his people from a tower; Ammon, the warrior missionary who wins hearts by faithfully serving a Lamanite king; Alma, the prodigal son who is converted like Paul and becomes a champion of the gospel; the hot-blooded General Moroni; Samuel, the brave Lamanite prophet who stands on a wall to warn the Nephites until they drive him away. Then there are the heretics, Sherem, Nehor, and Korihor, who challenge the Nephites with wayward dogmas ranging from universalism to atheism. . . . Along with the heretics are the villains Kishkumen, the assassin of judges, and Gadianton, the organizer of secret bands for robbery and murder.[1]

Dan Vogel, in his own biography of Joseph Smith, is decidedly less impressed with the variety and richness of Book of Mormon figures: "Rarely are his characters' inner moral conflicts reflected. Most often we encounter flat, uncomplicated, two-dimensional heroes and villains. Generally the plots are simple and frequently improbable."[2]

How someone responds to the personalities in the Book of Mormon will vary according to his or her tastes and inclinations, but it is also a function of how well he or she reads. The narrators have deliberately shaped their characterizations to provoke certain reactions in readers, and this process is more interesting than a simple up-or-down judgment on whether any particular figure is compelling or inspiring. Nephi, while he may appear at first glance as the "unbendingly good younger brother," is also the narrator who is our sole source for everything we know about his rebellious older brothers. That adds a certain nuance to his account, as well as allowing for more sophisticated interpretations.

Like the biblical story of Joseph, the narrative of Nephi and his brothers is both a family drama and the founding narrative for a nation. The difference is that Nephi tells the story himself, in retrospect and with a clear agenda. His goal is to show that "the tender mercies of the Lord are over all those whom he hath chosen, because of their faith, to make them mighty even unto the power of deliverance" (1 Ne. 1:20). To accomplish this, he needs villains from whom deliverance is necessary, preferably scoundrels who themselves exhibit a decided lack of faith. For the first few chapters, the unbelieving Jews at Jerusalem and then Laban are the primary opposition, but after the family leaves the area of Jerusalem permanently, the role of antagonist is taken up by Nephi's older brothers Laman and Lemuel. When Nephi begins writing this particular account, at least thirty years have elapsed since the family left Jerusalem (2 Ne. 5:28–31), the Nephites and the Lamanites have separated, and it is clear that conflict between the two lineages will be the driving force of Nephite history. As he covers the next decade in a few verses, he notes: "It sufficeth me to say that forty years had passed away, and we had already had wars and contentions with our brethren" (2 Ne. 5:34). Nephi knows the tragic results of the family tensions of his teenage years, and he has little sympathy for his rebellious brothers.

In fact, his ambition is not simply to illustrate theological principles or outline the origins of political divisions; Nephi wants his readers to actually adopt his religious beliefs—"For the fulness of mine intent is that I may persuade men to come unto the God of Abraham, and the God of Isaac, and the God of Jacob, and be saved" (1 Ne. 6:4)—and there was also a political dimension to his account.[3] As Noel Reynolds has observed, "Nephi carefully structured his writings to convince his own and later generations that the Lord had selected him over his elder brothers to be Lehi's political and spiritual successor."[4] Given his admitted penchant for plain speaking ("my soul delighteth in plainness unto my people, that they may learn," 2 Ne. 25:4), we might expect a very didactic history. And that is exactly what we get.

Nephi is faithful and hence chosen by God; Laman and Lemuel are disbelieving and disobedient. Readers are not asked to analyze ambiguous situations or puzzle out moral implications. Although there are occasional tense confrontations, there is never really any question as to how things will turn out: God will ensure that justice is done; that is, the righteous will be rewarded and the wicked punished. Yet watching the narrative unfold along entirely expected lines offers little of the drama we expect from literature. While it may be religiously satisfying to see life presented in terms of absolute good and evil (with the former reliably winning out), this is a reduction of reality rather than a representation of it. In the Book of Mormon, Laman and Lemuel are stock characters, even caricatures. They don't develop much, and it seems that their sole mode of communication is complaining.

This sort of didacticism follows from Nephi's intentions. To make his points, he needs opponents who are strong enough to highlight the miraculous nature of his deliverances, yet are not so interesting that readers might be tempted into taking their point of view seriously (making Satan a more compelling figure than God is a criticism that has often been leveled against Milton's *Paradise Lost*). Yet if Laman and Lemuel are flat, two-dimensional, entirely predictable characters, it is because Nephi has made them so. Careful readings reveal a certain degree of tension between what Nephi knows and what he shows, and this may open space for more literary approaches to the text. The key is to shift our focus to what lies beneath the surface story line, to the editorial activity that Nephi explicitly acknowledges and implicitly practices. By watching him at work—shaping his narrative, highlighting certain features while downplaying others—we gradually come to see him as a much more complex, realistic, and even moving character.

Selective Characterizations

The first thing to notice is that Nephi flattens his older brothers by treating them as a single unit rather than as individuals. The only time that Laman does anything independently is when he goes to Laban's house to ask for the plates (1 Ne. 3:9–14); otherwise, he always speaks and acts in conjunction with Lemuel. Lemuel, in turn, never opposes Laman in any way, and never appears without Laman close by (Nephi writes of them the way that people sometimes talk about twins). A powerful part of the appeal of the Book of Mormon is its insistence on its historicity, but such claims also invite readers to speculate about its characters as full-bodied individuals with lives outside of whatever may be explicitly reported in the text. Nephi lived with these brothers for more than three decades, often in very close quarters, and it is difficult to imagine that in his mind they were virtually indistinguishable or that his relationships with both of them were identical.

Similar questions might arise with regard to Sam—a rather passive ally of Nephi's in family dynamics—who is bland to the point of being nearly a nonentity.

His presence is not registered at moments of intense family conflict (the broken bow incident of 1 Ne. 16, the confrontation over shipbuilding in ch. 17, or the nearly fatal arguments at sea in ch. 18), and Nephi never quotes a single word that Sam spoke. Was he really so self-effacing, or has Nephi downplayed Sam's role in order to sharpen the main conflict between himself and Laman and Lemuel? The pattern of selective representation is even more pronounced in the case of the shadowy sons of Ishmael, who join the family in the desert and generally side with Laman and Lemuel, though they are so unindividualized that we don't even know their names.

Aside from brief appearances by Sariah and one of the daughters of Ishmael (1 Ne. 7:19), Nephi has reduced thirty years of tumultuous family interactions among some two dozen people to a conflict between Laman and Lemuel on one side and himself and Lehi on the other.[5] From the beginning, he structures the narrative in such a way as to prevent readers from sympathizing with his older brothers. We know their names from the headnote at the beginning of First Nephi and from the list of family members in 1 Nephi 2:5, but the first time we actually meet the brothers is a few verses later when the family sets up camp in the wilderness and Lehi names two local landmarks after his oldest sons, hoping that characteristics of the landscape will somehow be transfused into Laman and Lemuel:

> And when my father saw that the waters of the river emptied into the
> fountain of the Red Sea, he spake unto Laman, saying,
> "O that thou mightest be like unto this river,
>   continually running into the fountain of all righteousness!"
> And he also spake unto Lemuel,
> "O that thou mightest be like unto this valley,
>   firm and steadfast and immovable in keeping the commandments of
>   the Lord!"
> (1 Ne. 2:9–10)

Lehi appears to be wishing for something that is not already the case, and indeed Nephi hardly takes a breath before he informs us that there are serious problems with these two brothers, which he goes on to describe in some detail:

> Now this he spake because of the stiffneckedness of Laman and Lemuel;
> for behold, they did murmur in many things against their father,
> because he was a visionary man, and had led them out of the land of
> Jerusalem, to leave the land of their inheritance, and their gold, and
> their silver, and their precious things, to perish in the wilderness.
> And this they said he had done because of the foolish imaginations
> of his heart.

And thus Laman and Lemuel, being the eldest, did murmur against
their father. And they did murmur because they knew not the dealings of
that God who had created them. Neither did they believe that Jerusalem,
that great city, could be destroyed according to the words of the
prophets. And they were like unto the Jews who were at Jerusalem, who
sought to take away the life of my father. (1 Ne. 2:11–13)

Note how Nephi quickly slides from descriptions of stubbornness and selfish
complaints to murderousness. Eventually Laman and Lemuel will try to kill Nephi
(1 Ne. 7:16)—as the middle-aged, retrospective narrator well knew—but the
description at this point in the narrative is unwarranted. (Somewhat ironically, the
first death in the story is when Nephi himself dispatches Laban.) Moreover, Nephi
undermines their reasonable concerns for an abandoned estate by observing that
their complaints were tied to their status as the oldest sons; apparently they had
already begun to think of the family property as "*their* inheritance, and *their* gold,
and *their* silver." Because Nephi has already presented Lehi's visions and prophecies as fact, readers can immediately perceive Laman and Lemuel's skepticism as
wrongheaded, and just as these sons show disrespect for their father, so also they
remain willfully ignorant of "that God who had created them." The allusion to
creation here is curious. Perhaps it highlights Laman and Lemuel's utter dependence on God for everything (including the property of which they are so jealous),
or it may give emphasis to Lehi's prophetic warnings for Jerusalem (surely the God
of creation is also a reliable source for information about impending destruction),
or it may hint at a new beginning in the Promised Land (a fate at this point unknown
to anyone in the family).

In the next verse Lehi, finding that gentle, poetic persuasion is not enough,
compels obedience in Laman and Lemuel with Spirit-infused words so powerful
that "their frames did shake before him" (1 Ne. 2:14). Nephi here heightens the
contrast between his brothers and himself as he describes his own reaction to his
father's words:

having great desires to know of the mysteries of God, wherefore, I did
cry unto the Lord; and behold, he did visit me, and did soften my heart
that I did believe all the words which had been spoken by my father;
wherefore, I did not rebel against him like unto my brothers. (1 Ne. 2:16)[6]

Nephi never openly admits doubting his father—he characterizes his motivation as
a search for greater spiritual understanding—but the result of his prayer suggests
that Lehi's explanation of why the family had to flee Jerusalem so suddenly was
not immediately convincing to everyone; belief comes to Nephi only after
God softens his heart. And Laman and Lemuel's complaints are now seen as open

rebellion against their father. Nephi manages to win over Sam, but he is rejected by Laman and Lemuel. Then, in a moment that the mature Nephi must have savored as poetic justice, God speaks directly to Nephi, blessing him and promising that if his brothers rebel, he will "be made a ruler and a teacher" over them (1 Ne. 2:21–22), a revelation that comes while he is praying on behalf of those same brothers (v. 18). (Note also the echoes of the biblical Joseph, whose older brothers were appalled at his dream of the sheaves in Gen. 37:8, asking, "Shalt thou indeed reign over us? or shalt thou indeed have dominion over us?")

By the beginning of the third chapter, the lines are clearly drawn. Yet Nephi, as narrator, has another tool at his disposal. In this section of the story direct discourse is rare, and allowing individuals to speak in their own voices gives those opinions tremendous weight, particularly when a character speaks for the first time (psychologists speak of the "primacy effect," whereby we privilege first impressions over later data).[7] Of course we have heard Nephi's mature voice from the opening verse, but the first time he quotes his teenage self we read this ringing affirmation of faith:

> And it came to pass that I, Nephi, said unto my father, "I will go and do
> the things which the Lord hath commanded, for I know that the Lord
> giveth no commandments unto the children of men, save he shall
> prepare a way for them that they may accomplish the thing which he
> commandeth them." (1 Ne. 3:7)

Not content to let readers assess his declaration independently, Nephi follows immediately with a commendation from Lehi: "And it came to pass that when my father had heard these words he was exceedingly glad, for he knew that I had been blessed of the Lord" (1 Ne. 3:8).

The first direct words of Laman and Lemuel in the Book of Mormon are, naturally, a joint speech (or perhaps unnaturally; it seems unlikely that they spoke the same words simultaneously, like members of a Greek chorus):

> And after the angel had departed, Laman and Lemuel again began to
> murmur, saying, "How is it possible that the Lord will deliver Laban into
> our hands? Behold, he is a mighty man, and he can command fifty, yea,
> even he can slay fifty; then why not us?" (1 Ne. 3:31)

Although we know of their murmuring from earlier paraphrases, this quotation still comes as something of a shock. Not only are the brothers characteristically complaining and doubting, but they also are shown dismissing the words of an angel, within minutes of his leaving, who had told them explicitly that "the Lord will deliver Laban into your hands." It is one thing to discount the opinions of a younger brother or even a father, but brushing aside the authoritative command of a divine messenger reveals Laman and Lemuel to be hardened skeptics indeed.

Nephi, writing from the spiritual and political needs of thirty years later, takes care to present his brothers in the worst light possible, but readers can also reconstruct the story from a perspective in which Laman and Lemuel's hesitancies are reasonable, their beliefs orthodox, and their actions faithful, at least to some extent. Imagine the scene again. Lehi dreams of a death threat and quickly packs up his family, who assume that they will be away just long enough for things to cool down. God had commanded Lehi to take nothing other than the most basic provisions, and indeed it would not have made sense to leave money behind if they knew they were embarking on a lengthy, one-way trip; after all, provisions are quickly depleted, and as long as there is any chance of contact with other people, gold is worth its weight. After a breathless flight, the family sets up camp and various members start thinking and questioning.

It could all have happened very quickly. We are not told how long Lehi's preaching career lasted. A month? A week? Conceivably the requirements of the text could have been met by the events of one very discouraging afternoon: "[B]ehold he went forth among the people, and began to prophesy . . . and when the Jews heard these things they were angry with him" (1 Ne. 1:18, 20). Then suddenly the brothers find themselves refugees in the wilderness, cut off from all property, resources, friends, and whatever personal or business dealings had been occupying them. But the anger of one's neighbors is not the same thing as an impending murder attempt, and Lehi believed his life was in immediate danger only because of a dream. That was perhaps the first problem.

Although dreams could be a legitimate means of divine communication (Gen. 40–41), they were also subject to considerable skepticism (Deut. 13:1–5; Ps. 73:20), and in Lehi's time they were regarded as the least reliable form of prophecy (Jer. 23:25–32). As biblical scholar John Bright writes, "So far as we know, the classical prophets never received divine revelation through dreams (as contrasted to visionary experiences). Jeremiah clearly regarded dreams as subjective experiences having nothing to do with Yahweh's word."[8] In this case, God used a dream to preemptively warn Lehi of a plot that had not yet reached fruition. The only evidence Laman and Lemuel had of an actual death threat was Lehi's own interpretation of his dream, and they were well aware that people have nightmares all the time, most of which don't mean much. In his telling, Nephi mentions the plot before he describes the dream, so that readers never question Lehi's perspective (1 Ne. 1:20, 2:2), yet the natural suspicion of dreams might explain why even Nephi felt the need for some independent confirmation from God. (It also accounts for the slight uneasiness Nephi exhibits when reporting other dreams: "I [Lehi] have dreamed a dream; or, in other words, I have seen a vision" [1 Ne. 8:2]; "after my father had spoken all the words of his dream or vision" [1 Ne. 8:36]; and at 1 Ne. 1:8 Nephi explicitly labels his father's experience a "vision," even though it came when Lehi was in bed, exhausted.)

Despite their likely hesitancy, Laman and Lemuel joined the family's flight into the wilderness, even though they were both grown men at the time. It is not clear, however, that they had any idea how long they would be gone. The urgent issue, after all, was a conspiracy against Lehi. Gradually, however, Lehi and Nephi began to talk of a promised land, and of escaping not just a personal, particular danger but the final destruction of Jerusalem by the Babylonians (which at the time the family left was still a decade off). In Lehi's words:

> I know that I am a visionary man; for if I had not seen the things of God
> in a vision, I should not have known the goodness of God, but had
> tarried at Jerusalem, and had perished with my brethren. But behold, I
> have obtained a land of promise. (1 Ne. 5:4–5)

Unless he is referring to his fellow prophets as his "brethren," his reasons for leaving have expanded dramatically; he seems to be speaking of the destruction of the Jews in general.

Similar ideas underlie Nephi's arguments as he tries to persuade his brothers to make a second attempt to gain the Brass Plates. He suggests that the Lord had commanded Lehi to leave behind gold and silver just for this moment, so that they could use them to buy the plates:

> And all this he [Lehi] hath done because of the commandments of the
> Lord. For he knew that Jerusalem must be destroyed, because of the
> wickedness of the people. For behold, they have rejected the words of the
> prophets. Wherefore, if my father should dwell in the land after he hath
> been commanded to flee out of the land, behold, he would also perish.
> Wherefore, it must needs be that he flee out of the land. And behold, it is
> wisdom in God that we should obtain these records, that we may
> preserve unto our children the language of our fathers. (1 Ne. 3:16–19)

Again, the key issue is the general destruction of Jerusalem, not a death threat against Lehi, and there is suddenly talk, among four unmarried brothers, of the spiritual needs of their descendants, who apparently will not have access to the prophets and traditions of the holy city. Laman and Lemuel are not so sure. Even after years in the wilderness, after they become fathers themselves, they are still willing to defend their associates back home:

> And we know that the people who were in the land of Jerusalem were a
> righteous people; for they kept the statutes and judgments of the Lord,
> and all his commandments, according to the law of Moses; wherefore,
> we know that they are a righteous people; and our father hath judged
> them, and hath led us away because we would hearken unto his words;
> yea, and our brother is like unto him. (1 Ne. 17:22)

(The note of self-reproach at the end for their own gullibility is a nice touch.)

Was their opinion justified? Not by the hindsight of history, which records the Babylonian destruction of Jerusalem in 586 BC, but Laman and Lemuel were certainly not alone in their assessment of the times. The family left the city in 597 BC. Within the previous year Nebuchadnezzar's forces had captured Jerusalem, deposed the ruler, raided the temple, deported thousands of people to Babylon, and installed Zedekiah as a puppet king. More political turmoil was not unlikely. Yet there were many leading citizens, including prophets and priests, who interpreted promises made to David (2 Sam. 7:13–16; Ps. 46, 48, 132:11–18) as well as the verses of Isaiah 31:4–5 and 37:33–35 to mean that God would never allow Jerusalem to fall. Jeremiah nearly lost his life when he preached against this attitude (sometimes referred to as "Zion Theology") in his Temple Sermon of 609 BC (Jer. 7.1–15, 26.1–24).[9] Laman and Lemuel's particular version of faith in God's protection may have been misguided, but it was based on accepted scriptural interpretations that were defensible, conservative, and held by the majority of the religious establishment of the time.

Whatever else they may have been, Laman and Lemuel appear to have been orthodox, observant Jews. Nephi—who has a vested interest in revealing their moral shortcomings—never accuses them of idolatry, false swearing, Sabbath breaking, drunkenness, adultery, or ritual uncleanness. Indeed, when he is describing their sins during their voyage to the New World that bring upon them the wrath of God, the worst he can come up with is "rudeness," a nonbiblical term that appears to denote inappropriate levity: "my brethren and the sons of Ishmael and also their wives began to make themselves merry, insomuch that they began to dance, and to sing, and to speak with much rudeness" (1 Ne. 18:9).[10]

It is true that Nephi several times describes Laman and Lemuel as would-be murderers, but they seem to be rather halfhearted assassins. Although there are two of them, both living side by side with Nephi for years on end, they never kill him or even wound him, despite numerous opportunities and provocations. Rather than actually stoning or stabbing him, they threaten him (1 Ne. 16:37; 2 Ne. 5:1–4) or they tie him up (1 Ne. 7:16, 18:11)—actions that could be interpreted as attempts to quiet him or teach him a lesson (much like their beating of him at 1 Ne. 3:28, unsavory behavior that nevertheless left Nephi healthy enough to immediately return to Jerusalem and contend decisively with Laban).

Laman and Lemuel's rough treatment of their younger brother is difficult to justify, but it is understandable. Nephi apparently had a speaking style that was less than diplomatic. He regularly characterizes his older brothers as "angry with me" (seven times); only in Lehi's last words do we discover that Nephi could appear just as enraged (2 Ne. 1:26), something that may be reflected obliquely in his psalm of 2 Nephi 4: "Rejoice, O my heart . . . do not anger again because of mine enemies" (vv. 28–29). He seems not to have kept to himself the Lord's promise to make him a "ruler and a teacher over [his] brethren" (1 Ne. 2:22, 3:29), a claim that Laman and Lemuel found particularly grating (1 Ne. 16:37–38, 18:10; 2 Ne. 5:3), and one that Nephi felt had been fulfilled even though he never had formal leadership over the entire family (2 Ne. 5:19).[11] And finally, Laman and Lemuel would have been aware that the scriptural penalty for false prophets was death (Deut. 18:20; cf. 13:1–11). Their first attempt on Nephi's life immediately follows a particularly strong prophecy—which they believed was mistaken—when he warned them that

> the word of the Lord shall be fulfilled concerning the destruction of
> Jerusalem . . . Now behold, I say unto you that if ye will return unto
> Jerusalem ye shall also perish with them. And now, if ye have choice, go
> up to the land, and remember the words which I speak unto you, that if
> ye go ye will also perish; for thus the Spirit of the Lord constraineth me
> that I should speak. (1 Ne. 7:13, 15)

The brothers might well have recalled that the Deuteronomic judgment on false prophets required a summary execution, even for "thy brother, the son of thy mother" (Deut. 13:6).

One of the most remarkable observations concerning Laman and Lemuel is that despite their doubts, complaints, and anger, they nevertheless continue to stay with the family. In fact, they usually end up doing exactly what Lehi and Nephi have requested of them, whether it is fleeing Jerusalem initially, going back to get the Brass Plates (a round trip of some five hundred miles),[12] going back yet again for Ishmael and his family (which included the five daughters that the brothers and Zoram would marry), building a ship, or leaving the land of Bountiful to cross the ocean. For eight years (1 Ne. 17:4) they have the means and the motivation to give up on the enterprise and return home to Jerusalem, and indeed they make moves in that direction twice (1 Ne. 7:6–7, 16:35–36), but each time they stop short.

Similarly, they continue to support Nephi, grudgingly, even when things go badly. For example, they complained when their father had another dream commanding them to go to Jerusalem for the Brass Plates (1 Ne. 3:5), but they went anyway. When the lot fell to Laman to make the first attempt, he went, and nearly lost his life in the process. Laban responded to Laman's straightforward request with the accusation "Behold, thou art a robber, and I will slay thee" (1 Ne. 3:13). Undoubtedly Laman did not just march up to the door and ask for the family treasure as a favor; he would have explained that he was there by divine decree (Nephi implies as much when he notes that Laban "would not hearken unto the commandments of the Lord," 1 Ne. 4:11). Perhaps Laman had hoped for a miraculous softening of Laban's heart, as appears to have happened later with Ishmael (1 Ne. 7:4–5). In any case, when Laman's naive but faithful attempt failed disastrously, he and the other older brothers were inclined to give up and return to

Lehi. Nephi talked them into trying to purchase the plates, even suggesting that God had commanded Lehi to leave his money behind for that very purpose.[13] The result of that idea was even worse—they lost the family's gold and silver (Laman and Lemuel's inheritance) and again almost got themselves killed by Laban's servants. At this point frustrations ran so high that Laman and Lemuel began to beat Nephi, only to be interrupted by an angel. Nephi urged one more attempt, and rather than abandon him to his own foolhardiness, they went along: "Now when I had spoken these words, they were yet wroth, and did still continue to murmur; nevertheless, they did follow me up until we came without the walls of Jerusalem" (1 Ne. 4:4).

There is something to be said for belated obedience and reluctant faith, which, after all, are still obedience and faith (strong enough that Laman and Lemuel agree to sail over the open ocean on a ship they built themselves; 1 Ne. 17:17–18, 18:1–8), but this is not a case that Nephi makes. Instead, he reduces the family's decade in the wilderness to a repetitive sequence of his brothers "murmuring" (some fifteen times), his own "grieving for the hardness of their hearts" (1 Ne. 2:18, 7:8, 15:4, 16:22, 17:19, 46–47), and then their being humbled either by persuasion (7:19, 15:20, 16:4–5, 24, 18:4) or by some divine manifestation (2:14, 16:39, 17:48–55, 18:20). The only development he allows them is negative—whereas in 1 Nephi 7:19–20 they spare Nephi because of the pleas of family members, at 18:11–20 they pointedly disregard the petitions of their parents or any other relatives and refuse to untie Nephi until they are facing imminent death by drowning. Indeed, Nephi plays with the chronology to reinforce this point. He presents the story of their crisis at sea as:

1. The brothers bind Nephi (v. 11).
2. A great storm arises (vv. 13–14).
3. Their sense of self-preservation leads them to untie Nephi (v. 15).
4. Lehi had asked them to relent; Sariah was distraught, as were their two youngest brothers; Nephi's wife and children had also begged—all to no avail (vv. 17–19).
5. Laman and Lemuel panic in the storm and untie Nephi (v. 20).

Clearly, event 4 happened between events 1 and 3, and Nephi was freed once, not twice, but Nephi, as the narrator, wants to disrupt any sense that the appeals of family members were even a partial cause of his brothers' change of heart.

If the pattern of resentment, rebellion, rebuke, and repentance seems familiar, it is intentional. Nephi employs yet another literary device to gain the sympathy of readers and alienate them from his brothers, and that is to make allusions to sacred history. When Nephi shows Laman and Lemuel "murmuring" in the wilderness on their way to the Promised Land, readers are supposed to make a connection between the brothers and the ungrateful, unfaithful children of Israel during the Exodus.

And if they miss that hint, Nephi (the narrator) makes the analogy even clearer when he reports how Nephi (the character) urged his brothers to follow him in re-creating Moses' deliverance:

> Let us be strong like unto Moses, for he truly spake unto the waters of
> the Red Sea and they divided hither and thither, and our fathers came
> through out of captivity, on dry ground; and the armies of Pharaoh did
> follow and were drowned in the waters of the Red Sea . . .
> The Lord is able to deliver us, even as our fathers,
> and to destroy Laban, even as the Egyptians. (1 Ne. 4:2–3)

Later, in his pointed recounting of the Exodus story to his brothers, Nephi explicitly notes that God "did straighten them in the wilderness with his rod; for they hardened their hearts, *even as ye have*" (1 Ne. 17:41; emphasis added).[14] The Exodus precedent is never far from Nephi's mind, and he refers to Moses' example or writings in nine different chapters in First and Second Nephi.[15]

Nephi's story also replicates some of the main features of the tale of Joseph in Genesis. Like his biblical counterpart, Nephi is a teenager with older brothers who resent his apparent self-righteousness and favored status with their father. He receives a revelation promising that someday he will rule over them, and they respond by trying to kill him: at 1 Nephi 7:16 their plan was to tie him up and "leave [him] in the wilderness to be devoured by wild beasts"—the same scenario that Joseph's brothers painted for Jacob (Gen. 37:20, 33). Nephi, like Joseph, is miraculously delivered and eventually saves his entire family from starvation (1 Ne. 16:17–32; cf. 2 Ne. 1:24). And his brothers do indeed bow down before him (1 Ne. 7:20 and then 17:55, where Nephi criticizes their response as inappropriately worshipful; cf. Gen. 37:5–11, 44:14).

It is probably possible to find parallels between the story of Joseph and any narrative of sibling rivalry, but are the echoes in the Book of Mormon intentional? Are such allusions a deliberate element of Nephi's storytelling strategy? A few details suggest that readers are supposed to read Nephi's account with Joseph in mind. Nephi reminds his audience of Joseph's life when he recounts Lehi's first perusal of the Brass Plates: "wherefore he knew that he was a descendant of Joseph; yea, even that Joseph who was the son of Jacob, who was sold into Egypt, and who was preserved by the hand of the Lord, that he might preserve his father, Jacob, and all his household from perishing with famine" (1 Ne. 5:14). As we learn elsewhere, Lehi actually belonged to the tribe of Manasseh, Joseph's son (Alma 10:3; keep in mind that two of the traditional twelve tribes, Ephraim and Manasseh, were named for Joseph's sons rather than his brothers), yet Nephi takes pains to avoid saying this:

> And now I, Nephi, do not give the genealogy of my father in this part of
> my record; neither at any time shall I give it after upon these plates
> which I am writing; for it is given in the record which has been kept by
> my father; wherefore, I do not write it in this work. For it sufficeth me to
> say that we are descendants of Joseph. (1 Ne. 6:1–2)

Tribal affiliation was significant in Lehi's day, and although it would have taken much less space to write "tribe of Manasseh," Nephi wants to highlight the Joseph connection at this point in his narrative.

For the eight-year period that the family traveled in the wilderness between Jerusalem and Bountiful, suffering "many afflictions and much difficulty" (1 Ne. 17:4, 6), Nephi reports only one story in detail—the time when, like Joseph, he saved his family from starvation (in this case, Nephi makes a new bow and uses it to bring back game). This was also the one moment when even Lehi murmured (1 Ne. 16:20). Nephi could have circumspectly omitted this brief and uncharacteristic lapse of his father (as well as his mother's complaining in 1 Ne. 5:2–3), yet his mention of it may bring to mind the way that Joseph outshines his parents at Gen. 37:9–10. And the fact that his bow plays a central role in the incident may also be an allusion to Joseph (see Gen. 49:22–24).[16]

In his last words to his son Joseph, who was born in the wilderness, Lehi quotes extensively from prophecies made by Joseph of Egypt that were contained on the Brass Plates (2 Ne. 3:4–22). It is a lengthy discourse compared to the blessings that Nephi records for his other brothers, and in some ways it is surprising that Joseph (Nephi's brother) receives so much attention here, because he is not a major figure in the narrative. Nephi tells us that when the family divided after Lehi's death, his two younger brothers Jacob and Joseph went with him, and that he later appointed them to be priests and teachers (2 Ne. 5:6, 26). Other than that, Joseph never does anything or says anything for the rest of the story (Jacob, by contrast, will become a primary character). It seems that his sole function in the narrative is to be the recipient of this blessing, which explicitly ties the family's past (and future) to Joseph of Egypt.

And finally, there is a clear verbal echo when Lehi and Sariah lament the abuse that Nephi suffered at the hands of his brothers on the ship: "Yea, their grey hairs were about to be brought down to lie low in the dust / yea, even they were near to be cast with sorrow into a watery grave" (1 Ne. 18:18), reminding alert readers of the thrice-repeated description of Jacob's fear that his son Benjamin would perish like Joseph: "Then shall ye bring down my gray hairs with sorrow to the grave" (Gen. 42:38, 44:29, 31).

Of course there are also differences between the stories of Nephi and Joseph, and two immediately stand out. First, the biblical story ends with reconciliation—a happy outcome that escapes Nephi and his brothers. And second, the Genesis account is a much better story. Despite (or because of) its minimal descriptions and near absence of narrator intrusions, the tale of Joseph features a degree of psychological realism and a range of emotion that Nephi never comes close to. The irony of Joseph in disguise, the telling details of how he loses his composure or warns the brothers not to quarrel on their way back home, the long-buried guilt of the brothers that surfaces regularly, the overwhelming emotion of Jacob when his son seems to return from the dead, the unexpected generosity of both Judah and Joseph, and, most importantly, the sense that the brothers are real people caught in genuine moral dilemmas (will they sacrifice another brother?) all make the last chapters of Genesis a masterpiece of well-crafted storytelling.

Nephi, by contrast, offers a didactic, one-sided narrative that severely truncates events and flattens characters, but it is not entirely devoid of literary interest, for the one character who achieves some degree of depth and hidden complexity is himself. There is obviously another side to the family drama, and in fact later in the Book of Mormon we catch a glimpse of how things might have looked to the older brothers. Their descendants complain that Laman and Lemuel "were driven out of the land of Jerusalem because of the iniquities of their fathers [Lehi and Ishmael?], and they were wronged in the wilderness by their brethren [Nephi and Sam], and they were also wronged while crossing the sea . . . they said that he [Nephi] had taken the ruling of the people out of their hands . . . they said that he robbed them [by taking the Brass Plates when the family divided after Lehi's death]" (Mosiah 10:12, 15–16).[17] Yet Nephi, as an overt narrator, uses all the literary tools at his disposal—including direct quotations, biblical allusions, selective details, and intrusive comments—to shape an account that he believes will persuade his readers. In doing so he inadvertently provides some hints about the personal costs of his monolithic perspective. A careful reading of what he chooses to reveal and to obscure suggests that his faith was also accompanied by sorrow, frustration, and spiritual anguish. Nephi never doubts, but his position in the family and even with God may not have been as clear-cut as would appear from a first reading. There is much more to Nephi.

Telling Omissions

It might be tempting to dismiss Nephi as a biased, self-aggrandizing character, but that would be a mistake. Instead, we ought to ask why he writes the way he does. Fortunately, he is fairly explicit about his methods, which he describes in four separate chapters (1 Ne. 6, 9, 19 and 2 Ne. 5). The story is always the same—shortly after his arrival in the land of promise, Nephi was commanded by God to write a history of the family that included his father's record, the family genealogy, details of their journeys in the wilderness, and both his own and Lehi's prophecies. The record was regularly updated to include events in the New World, including the reigns of kings and the "wars and contentions and destructions of my people" (1 Ne. 19:4). Some thirty years after the family left Jerusalem (and probably twenty years after their arrival in the Promised Land), Nephi was surprised by a new commandment from God to write yet another history of the family, one that would highlight "the ministry and the prophecies, the more plain and precious parts of them" (1 Ne. 19:3), that is, the things that were particularly "pleasing unto God" (1 Ne. 6:5; 2 Ne. 5:32). Nephi believed this record would be valuable for the instruction of his descendants and also perhaps for some other, unknown purpose (which turned out to be replacing the first 116 pages of the Book of Mormon manuscript lost by Martin Harris). Thus, the account from 1 Nephi 1 to 2 Nephi 5 was written between thirty and forty years after the initial flight from Jerusalem (2 Ne. 5:28, 34), long after the family had divided into Nephites and Lamanites.

Nephi's second, revised history (referred to by later writers as the "Small Plates") offered an opportunity to reflect on why things had gone wrong so quickly in the Promised Land. A single family, led by a prophet and by God, had been providentially delivered from destruction and miraculously transported across the ocean to a fertile paradise. Yet within just a few years, they had had "wars and contentions and destructions" (1 Ne. 19:4). Surely this was not at all what Nephi had pictured when God first told him about a promised land (1 Ne. 2:20). An explanation was obviously needed, and God had requested a history that focused on spiritual causation. When a narrator suggests that he has produced the text at hand primarily by deleting things from an earlier, more extensive record, it is natural to ask what was left out and why. The answers to such questions reveal something of the narrator's character and values, even if talking about absences is a delicate matter; readers must take care not to stray too far from omissions and gaps that are clearly hinted at in the narrative itself. For instance, Nephi tells us that he has a wife and children (1 Ne. 16:7, 18:19; 2 Ne. 5:6, 14).[18] Yet despite the fact that we see a great deal of him as a brother and a son, we know virtually nothing of Nephi as husband or father. He reports no names, no conversations, and no stories. It is somewhat surprising that he takes so much interest in his descendants, as we shall later see, and yet pays so little attention to his own children. (The situation is as puzzling as the fact that Henry Adams, in his remarkable autobiography, the *Education of Henry Adams*, never once mentions his thirteen-year marriage.)

Perhaps he left out the details because they were not pertinent to his main themes—God's mercy and deliverance, the nature of faith, and the effects of disbelief and disobedience. Or perhaps the complications of ordinary family life seemed to work against clear-cut moral lessons. There is considerable evidence that Nephi, despite his faith, was not immune from family difficulties. For instance, it appears that many in the party blamed Lehi and Nephi for the death of Ishmael:

> And it came to pass that the daughters of Ishmael did mourn exceedingly because of the loss of their father, and because of their afflictions in the wilderness; and they did murmur against my father, because he had brought them out of the land of Jerusalem, saying, "Our father is dead; yea, and we have wandered much in the wilderness, and we have suffered much affliction, hunger, thirst, and fatigue; and after all these sufferings we must perish in the wilderness with hunger." And thus they did murmur against my father, and also against me; and they were desirous to return again to Jerusalem. (1 Ne. 16:35–36, with echoes again of the Exodus story; cf. Ex. 15:24, 16:2–3, 17:3)

As the father of at least seven adult children (five marriageable daughters and two sons), Ishmael would have been advanced in years, but fatigue, exposure, and hunger were clearly factors in his death. Nephi identifies the bitter family members as "the daughters of Ishmael," a group that would have included his own wife.[19]

Nephi and Lehi never deny that their revelations brought real hardships to their loved ones; indeed, the words *affliction*, *suffering*, and *sorrow* appear often in their speech. Yet to those who had not been blessed with prophetic assurances of deliverance, Lehi and Nephi could have seemed callous. They push the family onward and enforce a strange commandment to avoid fire and eat uncooked food—an unnatural diet perhaps intended to remind the family of the manna of the Exodus (1 Ne. 17:12–13), but a particular hardship for the young wives who were becoming pregnant and bearing children:

> We did travel and wade through much affliction in the wilderness; and our women did bear children in the wilderness. And so great were the blessings of the Lord upon us, that while we did live upon raw meat in the wilderness, our women did give plenty of suck for their children, and were strong, yea, even like unto the men; and they began to bear their journeyings without murmurings. (1 Ne. 17:1–2)[20]

Nephi presents the stoic strength of the women as miraculous. He does not report his wife's perspective.

By contrast, Laman and Lemuel seem much more attuned to the feelings and concerns of female family members.[21] After the daughters of Ishmael decide that they want to return to Jerusalem, the brothers immediately seize the opportunity to second that opinion (1 Ne. 16:36–38). And later they complain again on behalf of their wives:

Thou [Nephi] art like unto our father, led away by the foolish imaginations of his heart; yea, he hath led us out of the land of Jerusalem, and we
have wandered in the wilderness for these many years; and our women
have toiled, being big with child; and they have borne children in the
wilderness and suffered all things, save it were death, and it would have
been better that they had died before they came out of Jerusalem than to
have suffered these afflictions. Behold, these many years we have suffered
in the wilderness, which time we might have enjoyed our possessions
and the land of our inheritance; yea, and we might have been happy.
(1 Ne. 17:20–21)

There is a world of bitterness in the phrase "we might have been happy," but they
seem to have been sincerely solicitous to their wives. Several years later, Nephi's
younger brother Jacob reports that the Lamanites were much better husbands and
fathers than the Nephites. Not only were they more faithful to their marriage vows,
but "their husbands love their wives, and their wives love their husbands; and their
husbands and their wives love their children" (Jacob 3:7).

And what of Nephi's children? When God promised that faith and obedience
would be rewarded, Nephi undoubtedly expected that his blessings would include
sons to inherit that promise. This may not have happened. At the age of about seventy, Nephi entrusted his record not to a son but to his brother Jacob. Indeed, the
prominence of Jacob in 2 Nephi (chs. 6–10 are a transcription of one of Jacob's
sermons) seems like an attempt by Nephi to smooth the way for an unexpected
succession of spiritual leadership. The plates were then inherited by Jacob's son,
grandson, great-grandson, and so on.[22] Yet at one point Nephi expected his direct
descendants to carry on his labors—"Wherefore, I shall give commandment unto
my seed, that they shall not occupy these plates with things which are not of worth
unto the children of men" (1 Ne. 6:6). This sounds as if he had sons in mind rather
than nephews and grandnephews.[23]

Nephi assumed political leadership of his people when they made him a king,
but there appears to be some ambivalence here as well. He describes his coronation
as follows: "And it came to pass that they [Nephi's people] would that I should be
their king. But I, Nephi, was desirous that they should have no king; nevertheless, I
did for them according to that which was in my power" (2 Ne. 5:18). This is somewhat coy; after all, he has already informed readers that the large plates contained
"an account of the reign of the kings" (1 Ne. 9:4), he refers to his "reign and ministry" (1 Ne. 10:1), and Jacob explicitly calls him a king (2 Ne. 6:2).[24] Perhaps Nephi's
reticence was derived from antimonarchical traditions in the history of Israel (e.g.,
1 Sam. 8), but there may also have been concerns about how the institution would
fare after his death. Jacob reports Nephi's last days in this way:

> Now Nephi began to be old, and he saw that he must soon die; where-
> fore, he anointed a man to be a king and a ruler over his people now,
> according to the reigns of the kings. The people having loved Nephi
> exceedingly . . . wherefore, the people were desirous to retain in remem-
> brance his name. And whoso should reign in his stead were called by the
> people "Second Nephi," "Third Nephi," and so forth, according to the
> reigns of the kings; and thus they were called by the people, let them be
> of whatever name they would. And it came to pass that Nephi died.
> (Jacob 1:9–12)

Note that even at the end of his life, Nephi does not yet have a clear successor.
He anoints "a man" who will then take on his name, perhaps as a sort of formal
adoption. Elsewhere in the Book of Mormon father/son successions are clearly
noted both among the Nephites (Omni 1:23; Mosiah 6:4) and the Lamanites (Mosiah
10:6), and this follows the pattern in the books of First and Second Kings in the
Bible. The description of the next king after Nephi is an anomaly.

We know that Nephi had children and descendants (Mormon lays claim to this
distinction as late as the fourth century AD; Morm. 1:5), but perhaps he only had
daughters, in which case the next king may have been a son-in-law or even a grandson.[25] It is curious that at exactly this moment, when Nephi died, the descendants
of Sam disappear entirely from the record. Jacob reports, "Now the people which
were not Lamanites were Nephites; nevertheless, they were called Nephites, Jaco-
bites, Josephites, Zoramites, Lamanites, Lemuelites, and Ishmaelites" (Jacob 1:13).
Every male of that generation is accounted for except one—there are never any
"Samites" in the Book of Mormon. At his deathbed, Lehi had blessed Sam that his
progeny would be combined with Nephi's:

> Blessed art thou [Sam], and thy seed; for thou shalt inherit the land like
> unto thy brother Nephi. And thy seed shall be numbered with his seed;
> and thou shalt be even like unto thy brother, and thy seed like unto his
> seed; and thou shalt be blessed in all thy days. (2 Ne. 4:11)

It may be that Sam's sons married Nephi's daughters (nearly everyone would have
married cousins in that generation) and then adopted the label of "Nephites" as
they dropped their own father's name.

Or if Nephi did have sons, perhaps they died at a relatively young age (not an
unusual occurrence in the premodern world), or even followed their uncles Laman
and Lemuel when the family divided. There is at least a hint of the latter possibility.
If one tries to keep straight the pronouns in Nephi's first revelation, the result is:

> And inasmuch as thou [Nephi] shalt keep my commandments,
>   thou shalt be made a ruler and a teacher over thy brethren.

For behold,
in that day that they [thy brethren] shall rebel against me,
I will curse them even with a sore curse,
and they shall have no power over thy seed
except they [thy seed] shall rebel against me also. (1 Ne. 2:22–23)

In this worst-case scenario, it is not the descendants of Laman and Lemuel who will have power over the descendents of Nephi; rather, it is the brothers themselves who are leading away Nephi's sons.

The details of Nephi's fatherhood may not just have been irrelevant to his main themes; they may have been too painful to relate. Given his cultural background, it would have been impossible for Nephi not to have viewed the absence or loss of sons as a chastisement from God.[26] And the fact that his rebellious brothers clearly had male offspring (they are mentioned explicitly at 2 Ne. 4:3, 8, 9) would have led to soul-searching as well as heartbreak. This is admittedly a speculative reading, but the text does report that Nephi saw in vision that the descendants of his brothers would eventually destroy his own posterity (1 Ne. 12:13–20). Nephi took this information hard, and indeed never really recovered from the shock and disappointment of that vision. It must have been an unpleasant surprise to learn his descendants would be wiped out, especially since this revelation came before he ever set foot in the Promised Land, and even before he married and had children. Years later, when Nephi was prophesying the final end of the Nephites, he exclaimed, "[W]hen these things have passed away, a speedy destruction cometh unto my people; for notwithstanding the pains of my soul, I have seen it . . . and this grieveth my soul" (2 Ne. 26:10–11). There is an undercurrent of grief and weariness that runs throughout his writings. Nephi certainly affirms that he was blessed by the Lord, but it may not always have been in ways he expected or desired.

After his marvelous vision of the future of the Lehites in the Promised Land, which included the traumatic disclosure of the tragedy awaiting his own descendants, Nephi returned to his father's tent only to find his older brothers "disputing one with another concerning the things which my father had spoken unto them" (1 Ne. 15: 2). He continues—and note that this is *not* a conditional prophecy—by saying:

Now I, Nephi, was grieved because of the hardness of their hearts, and
also because of the things which I had seen, and knew they must unavoidably come to pass because of the great wickedness of the children of
men. And it came to pass that I was overcome because of my afflictions,
for I considered that mine afflictions were great above all, because of the
destructions of my people, for I had beheld their fall. (1 Ne. 15: 4–5)

Nephi is frequently misjudged by his brothers (who apparently do not see in him either a new Joseph or a new Moses), but here we perceive something of the emotional cost of his prophetic calling. He regarded his own private sorrows as weightier than anything they could imagine—"great above all." It is not surprising that Nephi has little patience for his brothers' petty doubts and squabbles. They, on the other hand, perceive him as ill-tempered and quick to condemn (charges that Nephi records Lehi as answering directly at 2 Ne. 1:24–27).

There was a profound misunderstanding between Nephi and his older brothers. They could never comprehend his unwavering faith and assumed it was a cloak for ambition, particularly when following Lehi resulted in such obvious hardships and pain. Nephi, in turn, was impatient with their persistent skepticism, the way they repented and then quickly fell back into old habits of grumbling, suspicion, and jealousy. "Ye also know that an angel hath spoken unto you; wherefore can ye doubt?" he says to them—a theme he returns to at least twice more (1 Ne. 4:3, 7:10, 17:45). Laman and Lemuel, responding to claims of angelic visitations, retort, "[W]e know that he lies unto us; and he tells us these things, and he worketh many things by his cunning arts, that he may deceive our eyes, thinking, perhaps, that he may lead us away into some strange wilderness; and after he has led us away, he has thought to make himself a king and a ruler over us, that he may do with us according to his will and pleasure" (1 Ne. 16:38). (Of course, when our narrator reports this challenge to his credibility, he cannot allow such charges to sink into the minds of readers; he follows it immediately with an account of a divine rebuke in which the "voice of the Lord came . . . and did chasten them exceedingly" so that they "did repent of their sins" [1 Ne. 16:39].)

Concerns about his immediate family, as well as ongoing conflict with Laman and Lemuel, would have made Nephi's life difficult, but there are also indications that he did not always see eye to eye with Lehi. We might question why, given the strained family relations in the wilderness, Lehi named a new infant son Joseph. Did it send a message to Nephi that he was not necessarily the only favored child? Hadn't Nephi already staked his claim to the Joseph role in the family drama? Nephi may well have seen his situation differently than his father did. Why, in 2 Nephi 11:2–3, does Nephi list himself, his brother Jacob, and Isaiah as the three witnesses of Christ, ignoring the testimony of his father? In the last chapter we noted that Nephi omitted Lehi's reaction to his returning with the plates of Laban. Even more telling is Nephi's missing blessing. At the end of his life, following the pattern of the biblical patriarch Jacob, Lehi gathered his kin around him to give counsel and blessings. The recipients included Laman, Lemuel, Sam, and the sons of Ishmael (2 Ne. 1:28–29), Zoram (2 Ne. 1:30–32), Jacob (2 Ne. 2:1–13), Joseph (2 Ne. 3:1–25), the children of Laman (2 Ne. 4:3–7), the children of Lemuel (2 Ne. 4:8–9), again the sons of Ishmael (2 Ne. 4:10), and Sam (2 Ne. 4:11). Nephi concludes, "And it came to pass after my father, Lehi, had spoken unto all his household, according to the feelings of his heart and the Spirit of the Lord which was in him, he waxed old. And it came to pass that he died, and was buried" (2 Ne. 4:12). Nephi's blessing is conspicuous for its absence, despite his admission that Lehi "had spoken to all his household" and precedents in the Hebrew Bible (Gen. 27, 49). Why doesn't Nephi report what his father said to him?

Robert Alter, in his commentary on Genesis, observed at one point that "in the laconic narrative art of the Hebrew writer, this is left as a gap for us to fill in by an indeterminate compound of careful deduction and imaginative reconstruction."[27] Reading the Book of Mormon requires a similar combination of deduction and imagination to make sense of Nephi's inexplicable gaps. In that spirit, I suspect that Lehi's deathbed instructions to Nephi may have included a last, desperate plea for him to keep the family together (something that would have been both awkward and painful for Nephi to record). It is clear from Lehi's other speeches that family unity was a high priority, and he would have charged Nephi, as both the next leader and the focal point of conflict, with the responsibility to make sure they remained unified. In 2 Nephi 1, Lehi speaks as "a trembling parent," and despite the fact that his "heart hath been weighed down with sorrow from time to time," fearing that God would punish his sons for the hardness of their hearts, he still holds out hope that "these things might not come upon you, but that ye might be a choice and a favored people of the Lord" (2 Ne. 1:14, 17, 19). He continues, perhaps a bit unrealistically:

> And now, that my soul might have joy in you,
>> and that my heart might leave this world with gladness because of you,
>> that I might not be brought down with grief and sorrow to the grave:
> Arise from the dust, my sons, and be men,
>> and be determined in one mind and in one heart
>> united in all things . . .
> Awake, my sons; put on the armor of righteousness.
>> Shake off the chains with which ye are bound,
>> and come forth out of obscurity,
> and arise from the dust. (2 Ne. 1:21, 23)

Lehi had long ago taught that it was necessary for the family to be led "with one accord" to the Promised Land (1 Ne. 10:13), and at this late date he still hopes for unity among his sons. Putting aside for the moment the question of how he would have had access to Second Isaiah, which was presumably written several decades after his family's departure from Jerusalem, there seem to be clear echoes of Isaiah 52:1–2:

Awake, awake; put on thy strength, O Zion; put on thy beautiful
garments, O Jerusalem, the holy city: for henceforth there shall no more
come into thee the uncircumcised and the unclean. Shake thyself from
the dust; arise, and sit down, O Jerusalem: loose thyself from the bands
of thy neck, O captive daughter of Zion.[28]

Lehi seems to be holding out the possibility that just as Jerusalem can be restored,
so also his family—perhaps in response to his death—could free themselves of old
wounds and habits and awake to a fresh realization of their situation. He never
abandoned the hope that a renewal, a return to more cooperative relationships, was
still an option.

But it wasn't. Within days of Lehi's death conflict between the brothers broke
out again, and shortly thereafter family ties were permanently severed when Nephi
led those who would follow him into the wilderness. It is possible that Nephi omitted his blessing because he did not want it to appear as if he had let his father down.
Actually, Nephi not only leaves out his blessing but also deflects his readers' attention from this omission by immediately following his account of the family gathering with an original psalm—a literary exercise in which he tries to work through
some significant spiritual and psychological anxieties (2 Ne. 4:15–35).

By reading between the lines, I have presented an uncharacteristically generous assessment of Laman and Lemuel, but it is a perspective that Lehi perhaps
would have shared. He is not blind to the problems of his two oldest sons, but he
never gives up on them either. After he sees them reject the fruit of the tree in his
dream in 1 Nephi 8, "he exceedingly feared for Laman and Lemuel; yea, he feared
lest they should be cast off from the presence of the Lord. And he did exhort them
then with all the feeling of a tender parent, that they would hearken to his words,
that perhaps the Lord would be merciful to them, and not cast them off" (1 Ne.
8:36–37). Nor does Lehi ever exhibit a disregard for the significance of birth order:
when the family entered the ship, they did so in order, "every one according to his
age" (1 Ne. 18:6), perhaps signaling to Laman and Lemuel that their precedence in
the family was not irretrievably lost (they had just recently "humble[d] themselves
again before the Lord"; 1 Ne. 18:4).[29] Lehi's final blessings also appear to have been
given in order, from oldest to youngest and then to the next generation (with the
sons of Ishmael and Zoram inserted in Nephi's place, between Sam and Joseph).
And even on his deathbed Lehi continues to tell his older sons, "[I]f ye will hearken
unto the voice of Nephi ye shall not perish," urging them to "choose eternal life,"
as if this were still a real possibility (2 Ne. 1:28, 2:28).

After reading Nephi's account, we tend to see Lehi's hope for a change of heart
in his older sons as wishful thinking, but Nephi writes as a disappointed, reviled-
against younger brother, not as a "tender parent." There was one moment, not long

after they left Jerusalem, when he had believed that Laman and Lemuel might have a chance—"It came to pass that they did humble themselves before the Lord; insomuch that I had joy and great hopes of them, that they would walk in the paths of righteousness" (1 Ne. 16:5)—but years of unpleasant interactions led Nephi to a more judgmental, harsher view. While Lehi held out a hope for repentance, Nephi had a much more realistic assessment of Laman and Lemuel's spiritual state, and when they threaten him again shortly after Lehi's death he takes them at their word and flees with whoever will follow him; in fact, just as with Lehi, God himself warned Nephi to leave (2 Ne. 5:5).

This difference in attitude is most evident in the way that Lehi and Nephi interpret the same vision. Lehi dreams of a great open field with a beautiful tree on one side and a large, tall building on the other. In between are crowds of people trying to get to the tree. Many cannot see the path, and their confusion only increases when a mist of darkness rolls in. The solution is an iron rod that runs along the path, which they can grasp and then follow to the tree. Numerous individuals do just that, though some later leave when they see the jeering of the well-dressed, haughty inhabitants of the building. Other people are more interested in the large building in the first place, but in making their way there they get lost or even drown in a nearby river. When Lehi tells his family of his dream, he notes that Sariah, Nephi, and Sam joined him at the tree, while Laman and Lemuel ignored his shouts and gestures of encouragement.[30]

Nephi prays for an interpretation of the dream and is granted an apocalypse-style vision—complete with a spirit journey, an angelic guide, and a tour of the end times—that cleverly combines elements of his father's dream with a vision of future events, thus transforming a family drama into an allegory of everyman and an outline of the future history of the world. As explained by the angel, the tree represented God's love (particularly as manifest in Jesus), the iron rod was the word of God (exemplified in the still-to-be-written Christian Bible), and the great and spacious building was the pride of the world (later embodied as persecutors of the faithful).[31] Nephi shares these sorts of explanations with his brothers, but the tenor of his account is markedly different from Lehi's:

> I said unto them that the water which my father saw was filthiness; and
> so much was his mind swallowed up in other things that he beheld not
> the filthiness of the water. And I said unto them that it was an awful gulf,
> which separated the wicked from the tree of life, and also from the saints
> of God. And I said unto them that it was a representation of that awful
> hell, which the angel said unto me was prepared for the wicked. And I
> said unto them that our father also saw that the justice of God did also
> divide the wicked from the righteous; and the brightness thereof was like

unto the brightness of a flaming fire, which ascendeth up unto God
forever and ever, and hath no end. (1 Ne. 15:27–30)

Lehi apparently had not told Laman and Lemuel everything that he had seen,
and indeed, according to Nephi, he had even missed a few crucial aspects of the
vision because "his mind [was] swallowed up in other things" (undoubtedly worries about some of his children). Nephi is not exactly improvising here—much of
his description is derived from the narration provided by his angel guide (see 1 Ne.
12:16–18)—yet this is the first time the brothers have heard their father's dream
portrayed with words such as *hell, gulf,* and *justice.*

In Lehi's gentle account, the invitation was open to all to come and partake of
the fruit of the tree, and the only thing hindering anyone was his or her inability to
find the path or a refusal to grasp the iron rod. The water was a hazard, but it
seemed more of a danger for those trying to get to the spacious building (1 Ne.
8:31–33), and in any event, there was a clear and simple technique in place to guide
wanderers safely through the mists. By contrast, when Nephi offers his interpretation of the dream imagery, the river becomes a barrier set up to keep the wicked
away from the tree. It sternly separates the occupants of the spacious building from
the saints of God, and there is a brightness associated with it "like the brightness of
a flaming fire." Lehi was concerned about how the building might entice people
away from the tree; Nephi worries that the tree might attract people from the building who are not worthy to eat of its fruit.

Latter-day Saints usually refer to this vision as "Lehi's dream of the tree of life,"
but it is striking (and significant) that Lehi himself never uses that term from the
Garden of Eden story. Rather, it is Nephi who first introduces the label at 1 Ne.
11:25. Lehi's tree is not in a garden, there is no angel guarding it, and it does not
confer eternal life (according to 1 Ne. 8:25–28, it is possible to eat of its fruit and
then fall away), but Nephi is reminded of the Genesis account of a tree kept off-
limits from the unrighteous by a "flaming sword which turned every way" (Gen.
3:24).[32] When talking to his brothers he emphasizes the connotations of judgment
and justice associated with the "tree of life" and never mentions the "love of God"
that played such a prominent role in the his own perception of the meaning of the
tree (1 Ne. 11:17, 22, 25).

For Lehi, the wicked tragically refuse what is freely offered by God; Nephi
reverses this and has God refuse the wicked. As he says at the end of his explanation
to his brothers of his father's dream: "Wherefore, the wicked are rejected from the
righteous, and also from the tree of life, whose fruit is most precious and most
desirable above all other fruits; yea, and it is the greatest of all the gifts of God"
(1 Ne. 15:36).[33] Of course, God is both merciful and just, and some prophets may
stress one aspect of his character while others emphasize different features. Lehi

speaks as a concerned father, Nephi as a condemning brother (and a younger one at that). No wonder Laman and Lemuel's response is to complain that Nephi has "declared unto us hard things, more than we are able to bear" (1 Ne. 16:1).[34]

A difference of opinion between Nephi and Lehi as to how best to deal with Laman and Lemuel would have strained their relationship, yet the theological issues at stake are appropriate to the time period claimed by that narrative. Are prophecies—such as those concerning the destruction of Jerusalem or the fate of the Lehites in the Promised Land—contingent? After punishment has been decreed, is repentance still an option? When do people reach the point where God's wrath is unavoidable? *The New Oxford Annotated Bible* introduces the book of Jeremiah, who would have been Lehi's contemporary, with these words:

> Much of Jeremiah's prophetic preaching is based on the theme of the covenant relationship between God and the people of Israel and Judah. Drawing on traditions at home in northern Israel, Jeremiah considered the covenant to be a conditional one, which could be broken by the people's persistent apostasy. Influenced by Hosea, Jeremiah used imagery of the people as an unfaithful wife and as rebellious children (chs. 2–3). Such infidelity made judgment virtually inevitable. . . . Interspersed with the words of judgment and anguish, however, are a number of references to repentance and the renewal of the covenant relationship. Because of the complex ways in which the book has been edited, it is difficult to determine whether Jeremiah considered it possible that the people's repentance might forestall judgment or whether he considered repentance and a new beginning possible only after judgment had fallen.[35]

Lehi believes that Jerusalem is doomed but that his two older sons still have a chance. Nephi believes that all three are beyond help.

If Nephi was spared doubt, he nevertheless had to bear other burdens—knowing that he was responsible, to a degree, for hardships and sorrows of loved ones; being frequently misunderstood and scorned; foreseeing the eventual destruction of his descendants (while prophetically witnessing the preservation of his brothers' line); perhaps facing challenges with his own wife and children; dealing with disappointment when life in the Promised Land turned out badly; evidently disagreeing with his father on how best to respond to Laman and Lemuel; and even leading family members into war against their relatives (2 Ne. 5:14, 34). He also bore the responsibility—given by divine injunction—to produce a record of these events that would highlight spiritual truths. His account, not surprisingly, emphasizes his side of the story while minimizing his personal struggles, weaknesses, and mistakes, but they are surely there. We have been reading First Nephi against the grain, so to speak, in an attempt to uncover tensions that Nephi only hints at, but there is an astounding passage in which Nephi does reveal his spiritual insecurities—the psalm mentioned earlier, which he inserts exactly between the arguments among the brothers that broke out within a few days of Lehi's death and the permanent division of the family (2 Ne. 4:15–35).

There we read of Nephi's weaknesses and sorrows (vv. 17, 26), his sins and temptations (vv. 17–19, 27–28), his slackened strength (vv. 26, 29), and his anger and agitation (vv. 27, 29)—and all this from the one person in the family who never complained! We gain in these verses surprising insight into Nephi's inner struggles, yet he has constructed his narrative in such a way that this passage does not tempt us into misreading his record and empathizing too much with the wrong parties. In the first place, his descriptions are rather general—we are not informed of any specific sins, and his lamentations are never connected to particular events in the preceding account. Second, by this point in the narrative our sympathies are firmly established: we know who was right and who was wrong. And third, he keeps all mention of his struggles within these few verses, where he is less concerned with exploring his weaknesses than in working through them to a clear resolution. Although Nephi mentions long-term challenges, his bracketing of them in this manner prevents us from drawing erroneous conclusions at other points in the narrative.

The Psalm of Nephi is an intricate passage exhibiting a great deal of parallelism, as well as chiastic structures and an intriguing interweaving of things said and done by his "heart" and his "soul."[36] The basic train of thought, however, is easy enough to follow. Nephi's pondering of the scriptures brings a realization of his own weaknesses, which leads to a divided mind, but he quickly identifies his one source of security:

> And when I desire to rejoice,
>> my heart groaneth because of my sins;
> nevertheless, I know in whom I have trusted.

He goes on to recount the miracles that he has experienced in his life, and then he berates himself for wavering, both emotionally and physically:

> O then, if I have seen so great things,
>> if the Lord in his condescension unto the children of men
>> hath visited men in so much mercy,[37]
> why should my heart weep and my soul linger in the valley of sorrow,
>> and my flesh waste away,
>> and my strength slacken,
> because of mine afflictions?

He continues in the same mode, asking, "[W]hy should I yield to sin . . . why am I angry because of mine enemy?"

In a somewhat surprising move, Nephi then steps outside his unhappy, vacillating self and orders his heart to rejoice, even providing it with the appropriate words:

> Awake, my soul! No longer droop in sin. . . .
> Rejoice, O my heart,
>> and cry unto the Lord, and say:
>> "O Lord, I will praise thee forever."

His psyche is still divided, but here the faithful half is forcefully taking control of the situation. Yet in the act of asserting control, Nephi also acknowledges his utter dependence. He turns to God and asks for future deliverance in a series of questions that begins somewhat plaintively—"O Lord, wilt thou redeem my soul?"—and then shifts to more insistent, more urgent, more confident requests: "May the gates of hell be shut continually before me . . . O Lord, wilt thou encircle me around in the robe of thy righteousness!" (providing a striking contrast to the temptations that "encompassed" him earlier in the poem). Nephi ends with a strong affirmation of faith, addressed directly to deity: "Behold, my voice shall forever ascend up unto thee / my rock and mine everlasting God."

Given his faith-promoting agenda, Nephi may have included this psalm more as a model for dealing with doubts and weakness than as a window into his soul, but it does offer an unexpected moment of introspection and vulnerable self-disclosure. We have seen how reading for gaps, omissions, inconsistencies, and unexpected details can fill out our understanding of a person. These are the means by which Nephi provides literary characterization, both of himself and also of his brothers, but a full assessment of his character would have to take into account the more explicitly religious portions of his record, that is, the two-thirds of First and Second Nephi that we have so far largely ignored. We cannot understand Nephi apart from the non-narrative elements of his record, namely, his visions and prophecies.

3

Prophets of Old

Scriptural Interpretation

When Latter-day Saints think of Nephi, they generally have in mind the young man featured so prominently in the opening chapters of the Book of Mormon. This is the Nephi portrayed in pageants, paintings, films, songs, skits, and even toy action figures. The real Nephi, however (at least as we encounter him directly through the text), is a much older, middle-aged character, someone who has spent several decades reflecting on how his life fits into the broader scheme of God's relationship with humankind. Nephi repeats stories from his early years to explore themes of deliverance, faith, revelation, records, obedience, and prophecy, but those narratives make up only one-third of his literary production. The tale of Lehi's family and their journey to the New World ends abruptly at 1 Nephi 18; of the remaining thirty-seven chapters of First and Second Nephi, only one consists primarily of narrative (2 Ne. 5). The rest are made up of quotations from discourses of Lehi and Jacob (Nephi's younger brother), whole chapters borrowed from Isaiah, Nephi's own reflections and interpretations of scripture, and original prophecies.

Aside from the single chapter of 2 Nephi 5, Nephi tells us nothing of life in the Americas. Even though we know that he was made king over his people (2 Ne. 5:18), he provides no information about his reign, policies, challenges, or successes.[1] For the entire period of his kingship, no specific events are mentioned, no individuals are described, and no interactions are reported. The only dates in the last thirty-seven chapters occur in that one anomalous section, where Nephi notes that sometime between the thirtieth and fortieth year after their flight from Jerusalem he was commanded to write a second version of his personal history, one that highlighted spiritual matters (2 Ne. 5:28–34). As a result, most of his record consists of undated, contextless excerpts, along with reflections on how his religious experiences relate to the remote past and the distant future. (The contrast with the strict chronological march through Nephite history in the portion of the book narrated by Mormon is striking, though one wonders what Nephi's original account from the Large Plates—in the pages lost by Martin Harris—might have looked like.)

This means that trying to understand Nephi from his writings is something like interpreting the *Confessions*. Augustine's spiritual autobiography also begins with chapters of narrative (books 1–9), and those include the stories that most readers remember. Yet we cannot come to know the man as a whole without figuring out why he finishes his memoir with meditations on the nature of memory and time and a commentary on the opening chapter of Genesis (books 10–13). Similarly, we have to ask what Nephi was trying to accomplish with his own non-narrative chapters. What points does he want to make? What conflicts is he attempting to resolve? Why is he so fascinated with ancient prophecies, especially since by his own account he had direct access to God through revelations? Perhaps because of the disappointments he had experienced, Nephi seems driven to discover the meaning of his journey to a promised land not in the lives of his immediate relatives but rather from the much broader perspective of the history of the House of Israel.

In the revised version of his autobiography, Nephi appears oddly disconnected from the present. He is willing to share details of two or three decades earlier, when Lehi was leading the family through the wilderness, but he shows little interest in more recent events, the people he rules over, or even his own family members.[2] As mentioned earlier, his wife and children are virtually absent from his account, much to the frustration of those who would like to read modern Mormon family values back into the Book of Mormon.[3] Nephi seems obsessed with the past. We have already observed how he uses allusions to link his personal history to the biblical stories of Joseph and Moses; indeed, he sees Lehi's clan as reenacting sacred history as they deal with sibling rivalries and are led by God to the Promised Land.[4] Yet Nephi, as portrayed in the Book of Mormon, is not so much a storyteller as a writer. He allows us to observe him composing, editing, and revising as he tries to imagine who his future audience might be.

Even more remarkably, in the postnarrative chapters we come to know Nephi as a reader—poring over ancient texts, offering alternative interpretations, interweaving his own revelations with the words of past prophets, reading himself back into existing scripture, and envisioning himself as the author of future scripture. This sort of literary activity tends to be solitary, intellectual, introspective, time-consuming, and frustrating (Nephi complains in 2 Ne. 33:1 of his weakness in writing). The mature Nephi is something of a tragic figure, cut off from his culture, despairing of his descendants, and alienated from his own society (even though he is the king). Imagine, for a moment, his situation. He was educated in Jerusalem and literate at a time when such training was rare. He seems to have been fascinated by books and records. And then in his teenage years he was suddenly taken from the culturally rich and intellectually stimulating environment of Judah's capital to live in a distant land, in the company of only his relatives, with a single text (the Brass Plates) to read for the rest of his life. No one else in Nephi's family seems much interested in close readings and creative interpretations. Lehi and Jacob receive revelations, but they appear to be primarily oral prophets rather than reading-and-writing prophets.[5] In fact, Jacob was born after the family left Jerusalem; he had no firsthand knowledge whatsoever about the traditions and culture of the Jews. And in any event, the Brass Plates seem to have been written not in Nephi's native language, Hebrew, but rather in an odd form of Egyptian, or at least in an Egyptian script (1 Ne. 1:2; Mosiah 1:3–4; Morm. 9:32–33).

Nephi professes a love for these writings—"my soul delighteth in the scriptures, / and my heart pondereth them, / and writeth them for the learning and the profit of my children" (2 Ne. 4:15; cf. 2 Ne. 11:2, 8), and he copies long passages from Isaiah into his personal record (we are meant to picture him laboriously engraving the words into metal plates), but being completely cut off from his homeland means that Hebrew literature is no longer a living tradition for him or his descendants. He is keenly aware that most of the tradition will die with him, and that the decay has already started:

> Isaiah spake many things which were hard for many of my people to understand; for they know not concerning the manner of prophesying among the Jews. For I, Nephi, have not taught them many things concerning the manner of the Jews; for their works were works of darkness, and their doings were doings of abominations. (2 Ne. 25:1–2)

Nephi is obviously still bitter about the way that he and his father were treated in Jerusalem, but he is not hostile to Jewish scholarship. He believes that the Jews have been and will continue to be excellent stewards of their sacred writings (1 Ne. 13:24–25), and his admiration is evident as he speaks of their knowledgeable interpretations:

> My soul delighteth in the words of Isaiah, for I came out from Jerusalem, and mine eyes hath beheld the things of the Jews, and I know that the Jews do understand the things of the prophets, and there is none other people that understand the things which were spoken unto the Jews like unto them, save it be that they are taught after the manner of the things of the Jews. But behold, I Nephi, have not taught my children after the

manner of the Jews: but behold, I, of myself, have dwelt at Jerusalem,
wherefore I know concerning the regions round about. (2 Ne. 25:5–6)

He sees himself as a participant in a distinctive, Jewish mode of exegesis, though he
is the last one among his people. His infrequent (and generalized) references to his
children are usually in passages where he writes of preserving the scriptures, but
one senses that they do not share his enthusiasm for the ancient writings. He passes
on his precious spiritual history to his brother rather than a son, and by the time it
is inherited by the next generation (Jacob's son Enos), the tradition has dissipated.
Enos never quotes or even refers to scripture, and the entire corpus of his literary
efforts is just over two pages. He is nothing like his uncle, at least in terms of literary
interests and abilities.

Updating Isaiah

Nephi has one particular story—a prophetic interpretation of world history—that
he is anxious to communicate to his readers. He comes back to it again and again,
approaching it from different perspectives, even allowing other characters to offer
their versions. We first hear it in 1 Nephi 10, where after reporting Lehi's dream of
the tree, for the most part in Lehi's own words, Nephi paraphrases his father's
prophecies. In this brief synopsis we learn that:

1. The Jews will someday escape captivity in Babylon and return to
   Jerusalem.
2. After many centuries a messiah or savior will appear among them and be
   slain.
3. The House of Israel will be scattered among many nations (this process
   had in fact begun much earlier and included the flight of Lehi's family to
   the New World).
4. The fulness of the gospel will be revealed to the Gentiles, who will then
   assist in gathering the House of Israel back to their lands of inheritance
   and converting them to Christianity.

Nephi signals the importance of this comprehensive prophecy with an editorial interruption. He had concluded his account of Lehi's dream rather decisively
with the words "And after he [Lehi] had preached unto them [Laman and Lemuel],
and also prophesied unto them of many things, he bade them to keep the commandments of the Lord; and he did cease speaking unto them" (1 Ne. 8:38). Nephi
next writes of the two sets of plates and the fact that what we are reading is actually
the second, more spiritual record (1 Ne. 9), and then he goes back to his father's

telling of the dream and its accompanying prophecies: "For behold, it came to pass after my father had made an end of speaking the words of his dream, and also of exhorting them [the brothers] to all diligence, he spake unto them concerning the Jews" (1 Ne. 10:2). This is where we find the four prophecies outlined above. In other words, after his interruption Nephi returns to his narrative at a point earlier than where he left it—presumably because he missed some crucial spiritual information that needed to be included—and thus Lehi ends his remarks twice, once at 1 Ne. 8:38 and again at 1 Ne. 10:15.

Even more strikingly, Nephi immediately follows with his own, much elaborated rendition of the prophecy as he recounts how he prayed for a personal knowledge of the things his father had seen, and then received a dramatic revelation (1 Ne. 11–14). An angel leads him on a visionary tour of the future that includes many more details about the life of Jesus (including his postmortal ministry in the Americas), the eventual destruction of Nephi's descendants at the hands of the Lamanites (who subsequently forget their origins as a scattered branch of the House of Israel), and religious conditions at the time the gospel is restored among the Gentiles. Nephi omits the return from Babylon, and he adds information about the fulfillment of covenants and the emergence of new scriptures—including the Book of Mormon itself—but the basic story is the same. (Richard Bushman has observed that the American republic makes only "a cameo appearance" in the Book of Mormon: "The Book of Mormon allots just nine verses to the deliverance of the Gentiles [from English rule], and the rest of the book concentrates on the deliverance of Israel.")[6]

This message seems to be of critical importance to Nephi since he compulsively returns to the same prophetic overview of God's dealings with the House of Israel four more times: when he explains his father's prophecies to his brothers (1 Ne. 15:12–20), in his interpretation of Isaiah 48–49 (1 Ne. 22), when his brother Jacob comments on Isaiah 50–51 (2 Ne. 10), and after he quotes Isaiah 2–14 (2 Ne. 25–33). In fact, if we include the Isaiah quotations that complement Nephi's own prophecies, most of the non-narrative portions of First and Second Nephi are devoted to explicating Nephi's ideas of how the grand sweep of Nephite history fits into the even broader context of God's providential design for the children of Israel. He explains how Lehi's family was only one of several groups the Lord led away from Jerusalem, how this scattering was prophesied long ago, and how the failure of the Nephites to keep the commandments or even to survive will be offset by the preservation of their records, which in turn will be crucial to bringing the Gentiles to an awareness of their obligations to the scattered remnants of Israel around the world.

Nephi's recurring attention to the overall history of the House of Israel—a story that takes in several thousand years—gives him a distinctive voice; no one else in the Book of Mormon shares his obsession to place the Nephite experience within a world-historical perspective (though Mormon mentions the idea in passing and Jesus incorporates it into his teachings to the Nephites; see Morm. 5:8–24 and 3 Ne. 16, 20–22). Similarly, no one else is so focused on ancient Hebrew texts. One might assume that an angelic annunciation, as seen in 1 Nephi 11–14, might provide sufficient authority for Nephi's vision of the future, but over and over we see him attempting to connect his own revelations with what earlier prophets had foretold, and in particular with the writings of Isaiah. Nephi was the only Book of Mormon author to receive a classical Hebrew/Egyptian education (whatever that may have been in 600 BC), so it is not surprising that he remains the most literate and book-learned of the Nephite prophets. Indeed, he structures his teachings in a way that suggests he is working from written documents, as can be seen at 1 Nephi 22 and 2 Nephi 26–27.

Toward the end of First Nephi, he reports that "I did read many things to them [his brothers], which were engraven upon the Plates of Brass, that they might know concerning the doings of the Lord in other lands, among people of old" (1 Ne. 19:22), and as an example he quotes Isaiah 48 and 49 in full. We are left to imagine whether or not his brothers greeted this history lecture with rapt attention, but when they admit they do not understand his point, he responds with a prophecy of his own at 1 Nephi 22, which reiterates the familiar scenario of the House of Israel being scattered among all nations (the exiles include Lehi's family and their descendants in the Western Hemisphere). Eventually the Gentiles—presumably modern Americans—will be instrumental in restoring the Jews and the Lehite descendants to a full knowledge of the Christian gospel and its covenants, and they will assist in gathering the chosen people back to the "lands of their inheritance." An indeterminate period of warfare and religious strife follows, which will then give way to Christ's millennial reign.

Clearly the events foreseen refer to developments in Joseph Smith's day, but what makes 1 Nephi 22 striking from a literary perspective is the way that Nephi interlaces his original prophecy with phrases from the scriptural chapters he has just quoted (this can most easily be seen in the *Reader's Edition*, where key words from Isaiah that reappear in 1 Ne. 22 are set in italics). Not only does he provide an explicit interpretation for expressions such as "they shall bring thy sons in their arms, / and thy daughters shall be carried upon their shoulders" (Isa. 49:22 || 1 Ne. 21:22, 22:6–8), but he also works in distinctive phrases in less obtrusive ways, as when he writes, "Yea, the more part of all the tribes have been led away; and they are scattered *'to and fro' 'upon the isles of the sea'*; and whither they are none of us knoweth, save that we know that they have been led away" (1 Ne. 22:4, quoting Isa. 49:21, 8 || 1 Ne. 21:21, 8).[7] The Book of Mormon frequently employs biblical phrasing, but here Nephi's use of Isaiah is deliberate, an integral component of a particular individual's writing habits rather than just part of the general style of the book. (He employs the same type of commentary—which places familiar phrases into new contexts and thus reinterprets as it explains—in a slightly more diffuse form at 2 Ne. 25–33, following his lengthy citation of Isa. 2–14.)

Nephi gives the impression of someone who has read and reread Isaiah, trying to discern precedents for his experiences, eager to literally connect his own prophecies with those of his predecessor.[8] The most significant example of Nephi's reworking of a biblical prophecy comes in 2 Nephi 26–27, where he manages to reproduce the first half of Isaiah 29, in order, within a much longer discourse by inserting phrases here and there. We sometimes speak of "reading between the lines," but here Nephi is "writing between the lines." If we italicize the words of Isaiah starting in 2 Nephi 26:15–16 (a fairly dense example), it looks like this:

> After my seed and the seed of my brethren shall have dwindled in unbelief, and shall have been smitten by the Gentiles; yea, after the Lord God shall have *camped against them round about*, and shall have *laid siege against them with a mount*, and *raised forts against them*; and after they *shall have been brought down* low in the dust, even that they are not, yet the words of the righteous shall be written, and the prayers of the faithful shall be heard, and all those who have dwindled in unbelief shall not be forgotten. For those who shall be destroyed *shall speak unto them out of the ground, and their speech shall be low out of the dust, and their voice shall be as one that hath a familiar spirit*; for the Lord God will give unto him power, that he may whisper concerning them, even as it were *out of the ground; and their speech shall whisper out of the dust.*

Now compare those highlighted words with Isaiah 29:3–4:

> I will camp against thee round about, and will lay siege against thee with a mount, and I will raise forts against thee. And thou shalt be brought down, and shalt speak out of the ground, and thy speech shall be low out of the dust, and thy voice shall be, as of one that hath a familiar spirit, out of the ground, and thy speech shall whisper out of the dust.

One might be tempted to regard this close correspondence as coincidental, were it not for the fact that Isaiah 29:5–12 keeps coming, piece by piece, through the rest of this chapter and the next, with Isaiah 29:13–24 being quoted directly at the end of 2 Nephi 27.[9]

The significance of the phrases, however, has shifted, for the context is no longer Sennacherib's invasion of Judah in 701 BC (as it was for Isaiah); instead, Nephi is using the ancient words as a framework for his own prophecy of the eventual destruction of the Nephites and the coming forth of the Book of Mormon in the early nineteenth century. He does not deny the validity of the original, historic meaning of Isaiah's warnings ("I have made mention unto my children concerning the judgments of God, which have come to pass among the Jews, unto my children, according to all that which Isaiah hath spoken, and I do not write them," 2 Ne. 25:6), but he virtually ignores the original setting in favor of reinterpreting the words so that they apply to his own predictions of the distant future ("but behold, I proceed with mine own prophecy, according to my plainness, in the which I know that no man can err," 2 Ne. 25:7). So even though he has just quoted chapters concerning Assyria's attack on Israel and Judah—warnings that had been fulfilled more than a century earlier—he still believes that in some sense Isaiah's visions are as yet unrealized ("in the days that the prophecies of Isaiah shall be fulfilled, men shall know of a surety, at the time when they shall come to pass," 2 Ne. 25:7).

Nephi's general pattern for interpreting scripture is to follow a direct quote—often rather lengthy—with a discussion that incorporates a few key phrases but does not provide a comprehensive or detailed commentary. Instead, the phrases fit into a fresh prophecy that recontextualizes and expands the meaning of the original, always with particular reference to his own people. The self-referential nature of his approach is apparently deliberate since he introduces both sections of extensive Isaiah quotations with an acknowledgment that he wants to "liken all scriptures unto us" (1 Ne. 19:23–24; 2 Ne. 11: 2, 8), but at the same time he does not assert that his own situation was the primary focus of Isaiah's visions. Nephi believes that prophecies are capable of multiple fulfillment; hence, Isaiah's predictions concerning people "on the isles of the sea" apply to other branches of scattered Israel as well as the Nephites: "these things have been prophesied concerning them, and also concerning all those who shall hereafter be scattered" (1 Ne. 22:5–6). Or in the words of his brother Jacob (who learned nearly all he knew from Nephi):

> The Lord has made the sea our path, and we are upon an isle of the sea.
> But great are the promises of the Lord unto them who are upon the isles
> of the sea; wherefore as it says "isles," there must needs be more than
> this, and they are inhabited also by our brethren. For behold, the Lord
> God has led away from time to time from the House of Israel, according
> to his will and pleasure. And now, behold, the Lord remembereth all
> them who have been broken off, wherefore he remembereth us also.
> (2 Ne. 10:20–22)

As a fellow prophet, Nephi may have considered himself capable of providing creative reinterpretations of Isaiah's words that may never have occurred to the eighth-century BC seer but which were nevertheless divinely inspired and authoritative.[10]

The Puzzle of the King James Version

Nephi's exegetical methods are intriguing, and it might be interesting to compare them to nineteenth-century sermonizing, which often began from a scriptural passage and included key phrases;[11] to popular theology such as Ethan Smith's *View of the Hebrews*, which also cited Isaiah to assert a connection between Native Americans and the ancient Israelites;[12] to New Testament readings of the Hebrew Bible, which uncovered Christian meanings in the ancient prophets; to Jewish Targums, which elaborated and interpreted as they translated the Bible scriptures into Aramaic;[13] or even to the pesharim of the Qumran community, which consisted of authoritative commentaries that demonstrated to the followers of the Teacher of Righteousness that the predictions of the prophets were being fulfilled in their own lives.[14] Indeed, more parallels could be cited—it is not unusual for religious traditions that revere particular texts to update the meanings of those writings so that they continue to be relevant in the lives of believers in successive eras—yet it is important to try to understand what Nephi himself thought he was doing within the context of the Book of Mormon narrative. Before we continue, though, there is another issue that needs to be addressed: the Book of Mormon's long quotations from Isaiah inevitably raise questions about the translation/writing process. As we imagine Joseph looking into his seer stone and dictating to his scribes Nephi's autobiography, it is reasonable to ask why there is so much Isaiah in this part of the Book of Mormon, and in particular why it appears in the language of the King James Bible.

For readers who see Smith as the author, the easiest explanation is that the eighteen chapters of Isaiah in First and Second Nephi are filler, employed when his creativity flagged or because he felt the need to pad the narrative so that its size was roughly equivalent to the 116 pages lost by Martin Harris.[15] Believers, on the other hand, often see the Isaiah portions as preserving a version of Isaiah older and more accurate than anything else available today.[16] Yet there are puzzling features of Nephi's patterns of quotation that suggest that both of these explanations are too simplistic.

In the first place, unlike nearly everyone else in his religious environment, Joseph Smith is not simply quoting Isaiah from the Authorized Version; rather, he presents a modified form of the text. About half the quoted verses read differently from the King James Bible. However, it does not appear that these changes are always the result of intentional revision. Some are indeed inserted clauses or substituted phrases that clarify or expand Isaiah's words, but there are also a great number of variants that make little or no difference to the meaning. These include substituted relative pronouns, transposed words, changes in number, alternative verb forms, omitted articles, and added conjunctions (such as *for* and *yea*).[17] For instance, both significant and trivial changes can be seen in comparing Isaiah 13:15–18 with 2 Nephi 23:15–18 (following Royal Skousen's reconstruction of the original text).[18] (Underlining indicates substituted phrases, bold type marks insertions, and the italics are those occurring in the King James Bible that indicate phrases added by the translators.)

ISAIAH 13 (KING JAMES VERSION)	2 NEPHI 23
15. Every one that is <u>found</u> shall be thrust through; and every one that is joined *unto them* shall fall by the sword.	15. Every one that is <u>proud</u> shall be thrust through; **yea**, and every one that is joined <u>to the wicked</u> shall fall by the sword.
16. Their children also shall be dashed to pieces before their eyes; their houses shall be spoiled, and their wives ravished.	16. Their children also shall be dashed to pieces before their eyes; their houses shall be spoiled, and their wives ravished.
17. Behold, I will stir up the Medes against them, which shall not regard silver; and *as for* <u>gold</u>, they shall not delight in it.	17. Behold, I will stir up the Medes against them, which shall not regard silver <u>or gold</u>, **nor** they shall not delight in it.
18. *Their* bows <u>also shall</u> dash the young men to pieces; and they shall have no pity on the fruit of the womb; their <u>eye</u> shall not spare children.	18. Their bows <u>shall also</u> dash the young men to pieces; and they shall have no pity on the fruit of the womb; their <u>eyes</u> shall not spare children.

It is difficult to know what to make of all this. Some of the changes appear to be deliberate revisions (as in verse 15, where the two changes work in tandem, equating the "proud" and the "wicked," making it less likely that *proud* for *found* is a copying error), others seem to be the sorts of changes that might occur when citing a text from memory, and there are sentences such as verse 17 that have been rendered less grammatical. It is also significant that a large percentage of the changes (Skousen estimates about one-third) are associated with the italicized words of the King James Version.[19]

It is possible that when Joseph Smith felt the need to quote Isaiah, he opened his Bible and read the chapters aloud, making whatever changes he deemed necessary. Yet this explanation does not account for the irregularities that we see—some of the alterations increase parallelism or make Isaiah easier to understand, while others fragment the text or make it more obscure (sometimes in ways that later editors of the Book of Mormon had to remedy, as when italicized forms of the *be* verb are dropped, making the grammar difficult to follow).[20] If Joseph thought it better to omit words in italics—easy enough if he had been working directly from the Bible—he did so inconsistently: in 2 Nephi 12–24 || Isaiah 2–14, italicized *its* are sometimes dropped and sometimes kept, and twenty-seven of thirty-seven instances of italicized *is* are retained.[21] In addition, many of the revisions work together to reflect a well-thought-out reinterpretation of Isaiah, while others are trivial and serve no obvious purpose. The situation is further complicated by the fact that Joseph's wife, Emma, asserted that he never worked from a book or manuscript (which would have included the Bible), and there are no reports of Joseph having the kind of prodigious memory that would allow him to quote scripture by the chapter.[22]

It is striking that even though Joseph Smith sees the Authorized Version as authoritative, at the same time he appears comfortable modifying sacred writ. Equally remarkable is the fact that Nephi clearly expects that his writings will become scripture, with equal weight to Isaiah's words. There is a demarcation between the quoted Isaiah passages and Nephi's own prophecies, but this is not the sort of canon/commentary distinction common in the postbiblical world; Nephi is offering a new prophecy that is based on or responding to Isaiah. If some of what he says fits Joseph Smith's nineteenth-century environment (such as the distinction made at 1 Ne. 22:1–3 between spiritual and temporal interpretations), it is nevertheless surprising how little attention Nephi gives to standard Christological readings.[23] He tells us that he is citing Isaiah because Isaiah "saw my Redeemer, even as I have seen him" (2 Ne. 11:2, cf. 1 Ne. 19:23), yet even though the chapters he reproduces include famous references such as Isaiah 7:14 ("a virgin shall conceive") and 9:6 ("for unto us a child is born"), Nephi never mentions these verses in his comments. It is almost as if he does not recognize them as referring to Jesus.

Some Latter-day Saint scholars, despite Emma's testimony, have accepted the hypothesis that Joseph Smith dictated the Isaiah chapters directly from an open Bible, with the proviso that his modifications were inspired by God and better reflected his ancient source.[24] Others believe that Joseph read from the seer stone a translation that had been previously prepared by God or his angels.[25] Yet in either case, the connection with any early Hebrew version of Isaiah is somewhat tenuous, and not merely because Nephi tells us that he only had access to an Egyptian transcription on the Brass Plates. Clearly the Book of Mormon Isaiah chapters, as we have them today, are based on the King James Bible, and as David Wright notes, "The alternative claim that the BM [Book of Mormon] is a translation but follows the KJV [King James Version] when the KJV is correct cannot be maintained since this cannot explain the preoccupation with italicized words, variants based on English polysemy, inconsistencies with Hebrew language and style and the persistence of KJV errors in the BM text."[26] The Book of Mormon generally does not offer solutions to textual difficulties in the Hebrew, and readings from early manuscripts found since the time of Joseph Smith, such as the Dead Sea Scrolls, do not provide much support for the variants he introduced.[27]

For non-Mormon scholars, imagining the Brass Plates (ostensibly Nephi's source) as a historic artifact from 600 BC is made even more difficult by the presence in the Book of Mormon of chapters from Second Isaiah (Isa. 40–55), which scholarly consensus for more than a century has attributed to the time of the Exile or even later (though, interestingly enough, the Book of Mormon never cites Third Isaiah [chs. 56–66]). Latter-day Saints sometimes brush such criticism aside, asserting that such interpretations are simply the work of academics who do not believe in prophecy, but this is clearly an inadequate (and inaccurate) response to a significant body of detailed historical and literary analysis.[28] William Hamblin has suggested that the problem might be alleviated if we regard Second Isaiah as a prophet contemporary with Nephi, but even this is not an entirely satisfactory solution.[29] Recent Isaiah scholarship has moved away from the strict differentiation of the work of First and Second Isaiah (though still holding to the idea of multiple authorship) in favor of seeing the book of Isaiah as the product of several centuries of intensive redaction and accretion. In other words, even Isaiah 2–14 would have looked very different in Nephi's time than it did four hundred years later at the time of the Dead Sea Scrolls, when it was quite similar to what we have today.[30] A more promising avenue for the faithful, it seems, is to acknowledge that we probably know less about what constitutes an "inspired translation" than we do about ancient Israel. Once one accepts the possibility of divine intervention, the theology can accommodate the (always tentative) results of scholarship.[31]

However one chooses to account for the parallel passages in the Book of Mormon and the Bible, it is clear that the former offers something of a midrash (to use an anachronistic term) on Isaiah. From the time of Ezra through the first centuries AD, Jewish rabbis developed a method of scriptural interpretation that sought to explain sacred writ though creative reinterpretation, clever wordplay, metaphor, and allegory. They wanted to uncover meanings that were not apparent in a surface reading. In so doing they placed emphasis on particular phrases and juxtapositions of events, and they tried to fill in the gaps of scripture imaginatively. These rabbis were not especially concerned with discovering the import of the words in their original ancient contexts (this is the task claimed by modern academic scholarship); rather, they were interested in updating the scriptures and reading their own circumstances and lives back into the text. The Oxford Dictionary of the Jewish Religion defines midrash as "the discovery of meanings other than literal in the Bible; derived from the root darash (inquire), [it] denotes the literature that interprets scripture in order to extract its full implications and meaning. These interpretations often formed a response to the need of a particular age or environment."[32]

This could easily describe Joseph Smith's use of the King James Bible, but it also is true of Nephi's reinterpretations of Isaiah. Skeptical readers may want to jump from the obvious dependence of the Book of Mormon on the Authorized Version right to the sensibilities of Joseph Smith—"There is no reason why Nephi should quote such a lengthy extract from Isaiah . . . so we need to look to Smith," writes Dan Vogel—but this represents a failure of imagination.[33] Smith is not offering to the world his own commentary on Isaiah; everything in First and Second Nephi is depicted as coming through the mind of Nephi, and the appeal of the Book of Mormon is due in large part to the construction of Nephi as a unique and compelling voice.

Like unto Us

So within the context of the narrative, why does Nephi quote Isaiah? As we saw in the last chapter, Nephi's life was one of general disappointment. He referred to his first, original history as a record of the "wars and contentions and destructions of my people" (1 Ne. 19:4), which does not give the impression of a pleasant, successful reign. Despite the extraordinary revelations granted him, his powers of persuasion could not keep the family together, prevent his brothers from trying to kill him, or convince his people to forgo establishing a monarchy (over his explicit objections; 2 Ne. 5: 1–6, 18). He does briefly mention prosperity—right before he speaks of weapons and hatred (2 Ne. 5:13–14); and he writes of living "after the manner of happiness"—followed by a notice of "wars and contentions" (2 Ne. 5:27, 34). Life in the Promised Land had not turned out as he had expected.[34]

In his psalm, Nephi reveals his hopes concerning his second, revised memoir, how this time he would "write the things of my soul, and many of the scriptures which are engraven upon the Plates of Brass. For my soul delighteth in the scriptures, / and my heart pondereth them, / and writeth them for the learning and the profit of my children." Yet at the same time, he is overwhelmed with disappointment and frustration: "Nevertheless, notwithstanding the great goodness of the Lord in showing me his great and marvelous works, my heart exclaimeth: 'Oh wretched man that I am!' / Yea, my heart sorroweth because of my flesh; / my soul grieveth because of mine iniquities" (2 Ne. 4:15, 17). The Small Plates of Nephi— that is, the account we have been reading all along—come out of this crucible of contraries. This is the general context for Nephi's turn to Isaiah.

Back at 1 Nephi 19, when he was remembering a time before Lehi had died, before the family had divided, before he had "a people," Nephi reported a conversation with his brothers:

Now it came to pass that I, Nephi, did teach my brethren these things;
and it came to pass that I did read many things to them, which were
engraven upon the Plates of Brass . . . but that I might more fully
persuade them to believe in the Lord their Redeemer I did read unto
them that which was written by the prophet Isaiah; for I did liken all
scriptures unto us, that it might be for our profit and learning. Wherefore, I spake unto them, saying:
"Hear ye the words of the prophet,
  ye who are a remnant of the House of Israel,
  a branch who have been broken off;
hear ye the words of the prophet,
  which were written unto all the House of Israel,
  and liken them unto yourselves,
that ye may have hope as well as your brethren from whom ye have been
broken off; for after this manner has the prophet written." (1 Ne.
19:22–24)

In this way he introduces his lengthy quotation of Isaiah 48 and 49 in 1 Nephi 20–21.
What do these two chapters have to say about hope, the Redeemer, and the future
of the House of Israel? And, just as importantly, how might Nephi have applied
Isaiah's words to the difficult circumstances of his natal family, and in doing so
found consolation for the sorrows of his later years?[35]

If we look at Isaiah 48 and 49 from Nephi's perspective (and in his slightly
modified version of the King James Bible found at 1 Ne. 20–21), the following
themes stand out:

(48:1–2) Isaiah 48 begins with a warning against hypocrisy, aimed at those
who "swear by the name of the Lord . . . [but] not in truth nor in righteousness"
and specifically criticizes people who have more loyalty to the city of Jerusalem
than to its God. Our suspicion that Nephi had Laman and Lemuel in mind is
strengthened by the addition of a negative. The KJV denounces those who in self-
deception "call themselves of the holy city, and stay themselves on the God of
Israel"; the Book of Mormon sharpens the condemnation by railing against those
who "call themselves of the holy city, but they do *not* stay themselves upon the
God of Israel."[36]

(48:3–8) The Lord asserts that the purpose of prophecy is to persuade the obstinate; he reveals future events beforehand so that when they come to pass, people
will not be tempted to give credit to other gods. Still, there are always those who
will not hearken, and God's foreknowledge extends even to them: "for I knew that
thou wouldst deal very treacherously, and wast called a transgressor from the

womb." Of course, the most divisive issue in Nephi's family was the validity of prophecy, in particular Lehi's prediction of an attempt on his life and the impending destruction of Jerusalem. When we imagine Nephi reading these chapters from Isaiah to his brothers, we may hear a certain edge in his voice. Despite his evocation of "hope" and "profit and learning" when he introduced the Isaiah passages, he is here once again playing the role of a condemning younger brother. (By the way, 2 Nephi 1 opens with Lehi declaring that Jerusalem has indeed been destroyed, just as predicted, but because this knowledge came through a vision, Laman and Lemuel may not have been convinced.)

(*48:9–11*) God, however, will defer his anger and not "cut off" the offenders because "I have refined thee, I have chosen thee in the furnace of affliction." By this point in the narrative, Nephi has described his family's hardships in the wilderness as "afflictions" half a dozen times, and there is an echo here of his first revelation, in which God warned that "inasmuch as thy brethren rebel against thee, they shall be cut off from the presence of the Lord" (1 Ne. 2:22). At the time when Nephi was first quoting these chapters to his brothers, they still had a chance to repent; decades later, when Nephi was actually composing this account, their fate had been decided. God's long-deferred anger had found its mark.

(*48:12–19*) The Lord proclaims his love for a chosen prophet whom he has sent to declare his word. Nephi probably saw himself in these verses, and surely he saw his brothers in the conclusion, which laments, "O that thou hadst hearkened to my commandments— / then had thy peace been as a river, / and thy righteousness as the waves of the sea." There is a certain irony here when we recall that our first introduction to Laman and Lemuel was Lehi's hopeful expression: "O that thou mightest be like unto this river, / continually running into the fountain of all righteousness!" (1 Ne. 2:9). The family as a whole had experienced divine guidance through the wilderness, from "the Lord thy God . . . who leadeth thee by the way thou shouldst go."

(*48:20–22*) The Israelites are warned to flee from Babylon and are promised that God would protect them as he led them through the deserts. This might be read as a prediction of the future return of the Jews from Exile, but the Book of Mormon adds a line at the end of Isaiah 48 that places these events squarely in the past: "And notwithstanding he hath done all this, and greater also . . ." At this point in the narrative, Nephi and his family had traveled for eight years in the desert. And finally, in what Laman and Lemuel would have perceived as another inappropriate rebuke from their younger brother, Isaiah 48 concludes: "'There is no peace,' saith the Lord, 'unto the wicked.'"

It is possible to read any number of life situations into the words of Isaiah, and one might question whether Nephi (or Joseph Smith) was using the ancient prophecies quite as explicitly as I have outlined in my paraphrases. There is, in fact, specific evidence for a particular, deliberate reinterpretation of Isaiah, and this can be found in the changes made to the King James text. As noted in the previous section, not all of the modifications seem purposeful, but there is a consistent twist given whereby the focus of Isaiah 48 falls on the messengers of the Lord and their predictions. Compare these phrases, with additions in bold:

ISAIAH 48 (KING JAMES VERSION)	1 NEPHI 20
3 I did them suddenly . . .	3 I did **show** them suddenly . . .
7 even before the day	7 even before the day
when thou heardest them not;	when thou heardest them not
	they were declared unto thee,
lest thou shouldest say . . .	lest thou shouldst say . . .
14 which among them	14 who among them
hath declared these things?	hath declared these things **unto them**?
The Lord hath loved him:	The Lord hath loved him;
	yea, and he will fulfill his word which he hath declared by them;
he will do his pleasure on Babylon,	he will do his pleasure on Babylon,
15 yea, I have called him:	15 yea, I have called him **to declare**,
I have brought him . . .	I have brought him . . .
16 from the time that it was,	16 from the time that it was
there am I; and now the Lord	**declared have I spoken**. And the Lord
God, and his spirit, hath sent me.	God, and his Spirit, hath sent me.
17 Thus saith the Lord . . .	17 Thus saith the Lord . . .
	I have sent him.
I am the Lord thy God	The Lord thy God
which teacheth thee to profit,	who teacheth thee to profit,
which leadeth thee by the way	who leadeth thee by the way
that thou shouldest go.	thou shouldst go,
	hath done it.

The servant of God in Isaiah 48:12–17 is usually identified by scholars as Cyrus of Persia (who was mentioned by name in Isa. 44:28 and 45:1), but Nephi's changes to the text deflect this interpretation, so the words more readily apply to Nephi and his family. The key issue is no longer the Persian conquest of Babylon and the return of the Jews to Jerusalem; rather, it is Nephi's own predictions about the much more distant gathering of other branches of the House of Israel, including the descendants of Lehi. He is doing just what he proposed in his introduction when he urged his brothers to "liken them [these prophecies] unto yourselves" (1 Ne. 19:24). The variants that appear in the Book of Mormon may have little to do with the textual history of Isaiah (indeed, they clearly use the English KJV as a base text), but the way that Nephi transforms scripture is rather interesting from the perspective of scriptural interpretation in general.

The sort of glossing and reworking that we see here—which appeals to the authority of the text while at the same time modifying it—is similar to the process that scholars attribute to the prophets and scribes who redacted early Hebrew writings before they were fixed in their final canonical forms. Academics, recognizing Joseph Smith as the most successful producer of new scripture in the last few centuries, may find it useful to examine the ways that Nephi interacts with holy writ. Smith himself later offered a revised version of the Bible, though in that case he was clearly working from an open copy of the Authorized Version rather than dictating from a seer stone.[37] Latter-day Saints, on the other hand, can profit from imagining how Nephi fits into the evolving tradition of prophecy at the time of the Exile, when there was an increased emphasis on repentance, hope in the face of disaster, eschatology, apocalypticism, written communication, and an established canon (concerns that characterize much of Nephi's writings).[38]

If Nephi was able to read his troubled relationships with his brothers back into Isaiah 48 (particularly by emphasizing the role of prophets and prophecy), when he turned to chapter 49 he encountered a predicted figure—a spokesman of God— who would overcome the sorts of disappointments and apparent failures that he himself had experienced:

> And he hath made my mouth like a sharp sword;
>> in the shadow of his hand hath he hid me,
> and made me a polished shaft;
>> in his quiver hath he hid me;
> and said unto me: 'Thou art my servant, O Israel,
>> in whom I will be glorified.'"
> Then I said, "I have labored in vain,
>> I have spent my strength for naught and in vain;
> surely my judgment is with the Lord,
>> and my work with my God."
> And now saith the Lord—
>> that formed me from the womb that I should be his servant,
>> to bring Jacob again to him;
>>> though Israel be not gathered,

yet shall I be glorious in the eyes of the Lord,
and my God shall be my strength— (1 Ne. 21:2–5 ‖ Isa. 49: 2–5)

Latter-day Saints have interpreted this passage as referring to idealized Israel, or Jesus, or even Joseph Smith,[39] but it seems to me that Nephi would have seen himself in these words. He too had a "mouth like a sharp sword" (cf. 2 Ne. 1:26), but had "labored in vain" to bring his brothers to repentance; he continued to trust in God despite a keen awareness of the dispersion of Israel and even the fragmentation of his own family. Nephi adds an introductory verse to the King James Version that addresses this prophecy to a branch of the House of Israel that is "broken off," "driven out," and "scattered abroad" (1 Ne. 21:1), and he inserts a phrase into verse 8 ("O isles of the sea") to make it clear that these promises were specifically made to exiles from Jerusalem—in other words, Nephi and his kin. Certainly, his interpretive comments and expanded prophecy of 1 Nephi 22 (presented as answers to his brothers' questions) do not focus on the mortal Jesus as the fulfillment of these verses; rather, they explore the future of the House of Israel: how the Jews would be scattered both before and after the coming of Christ, and then eventually gathered—including the descendants of Lehi—with the assistance of the Gentiles in the last days. Nephi is the spokesman delivering this message, and he refers to a "marvelous work among the Gentiles, which shall be of great worth unto our seed" (1 Ne. 22:8). In so doing, he seems to present himself as filling the role of the servant in Isaiah 49.[40]

As usual, there is a double perspective at work here. Nephi is reporting a conversation with Laman and Lemuel that predated the death of their father; at the same time, he is composing this account several decades after the fact, and he has selected these two chapters out of many more that were originally discussed (1 Ne. 19:22–23). Whatever he may have thought of Isaiah 49 during that initial conversation, by the time he is writing this version he has developed a new understanding of his mission, and in particular of his role in facilitating the partnership between the Gentiles and scattered Israel: the "marvelous work" would be set in motion by the book he was now composing—the second, revised version of his history. Through his literary efforts, his failures among his own family would be redeemed by the lasting impact of his book, and his life would be justified. True, this would happen only posthumously, but it was all foreseen by Isaiah:

And he [the Lord] said:
"It is a light thing that thou shouldst be my servant
    to raise up the tribes of Jacob,
    and to restore the preserved of Israel.
I will also give thee for a light to the Gentiles,

that thou mayest be my salvation unto the ends of the earth." (1 Ne.
21:6 || Isa. 49:6)

The realization, however, that Nephi's true prophetic calling was to speak to remnants
of the House of Israel in the far distant future—rather than to his contemporaries or
the next generation—and by so doing to become "a light to the Gentiles," seems to
have come to him only gradually.

Nephi, Joseph, Isaiah, and a Book

The recounting of Nephi's vision at 1 Nephi 11–14 is an impressive piece of writing.
These chapters describe a revelation that came to Nephi in response to his asking
God about the meaning of his father's dream. What was originally seen as a family
drama among Lehi's children is now understood as an allegory of everyman faced
with the choice between the tree representing the "love of God" (according to
the key provided by the angel) and the great and spacious building that signified
"the vain imaginations and pride of the children of men," with the promise of the
"word of God" as a guiding rod of iron (1 Ne. 11:21–22, 25, 12:18). In addition, the
angel leads Nephi though a tour of the future, in which the allegorical elements of
the dream are combined with yet-to-be-fulfilled historical events,[41] all within
a narrative structure that fits John Collins's classic definition of an apocalypse:

> An apocalypse is a genre of revelatory literature with a narrative frame-
> work, in which a revelation is mediated by an otherworldly being to a
> human recipient, disclosing a transcendent reality which is both tempo-
> ral, insofar as it envisages eschatological salvation, and spatial, insofar as
> it involves another, supernatural world.[42]

In fact, several elements of Nephi's vision echo the most famous of Christian apocalypses—the book of Revelation. These include a character described as "the
mother of harlots, which is the great and abominable church of all the earth" (1 Ne.
14:17; Rev. 17:5), a great pit (1 Ne. 14:3; Rev. 20:1–3), and Jesus referred to as the
"Lamb" (of sixty-five such references in the Book of Mormon, fifty-seven are in
these four chapters). Nephi explains the connection at the end, when he is shown
the future apostle John and informed by the angel that this man would be charged
with writing the definitive account of the end of the world, presumably based on a
vision similar to that seen by Nephi himself (1 Ne. 14:18–30).[43]

In this wide-ranging revelation, the world-historical counterpart to the iron
rod is a future book that Nephi sees among the Gentiles—clearly the Bible (1 Ne.
13:20–23)—though he also observes that many things have been left out of that

volume of scripture, resulting in widespread religious confusion. The solution is another book:

> "For behold," saith the Lamb [according to the words of the angel], "I will manifest myself unto thy seed, that they shall write many things which I shall minister unto them, which shall be plain and precious; and after thy seed shall be destroyed, and dwindle in unbelief, and also the seed of thy brethren, behold these things shall be hid up, to come forth unto the Gentiles, by the gift and power of the Lamb." (1 Ne. 13:35)

The truths in this new book will supplement and support the witness of the Bible: "and the words of the Lamb shall be made known in the records of thy seed, as well as in the records of the twelve apostles of the Lamb; wherefore they both shall be established in one" (1 Ne. 13:41). From the perspective of readers, the angel is obviously speaking of the Book of Mormon, but Nephi, at this point, gives no indication that he recognizes the visionary volume as including a history that he himself would someday compose. Over the course of the revised version of his memoirs (that is, First and Second Nephi, as we now have it), he demonstrates a growing sense of an audience, a readership more than two millennia in the future. The question is, when does Nephi come to realize that the book he is writing is actually the same book he saw in vision several decades earlier?

Before we track this increasing awareness, however, we should note that Nephi knows of yet another prophecy of a future, world-changing book. In the third chapter of Second Nephi, he records Lehi's last words to his youngest son, Joseph. This is an important chapter whose significance is highlighted by its anomalous nature: this is the only time that Lehi quotes from the Brass Plates, and it is also the only passage in the Book of Mormon in which Nephi's brother Joseph receives direct attention (or is even mentioned apart from his brother Jacob). Lehi tells his son that the biblical Joseph saw their day and their family, and that the plates contained a prophecy in which the Lord had promised him that

> the fruit of thy loins shall write; and the fruit of the loins of Judah shall write; and that which shall be written by the fruit of thy loins, and also that which shall be written by the fruit of the loins of Judah, shall grow together, unto the confounding of false doctrines . . . and bringing them to the knowledge of their fathers in the latter days, and also to the knowledge of my covenants. (2 Ne. 3:12–13)

Most of this prophecy actually concerns the seer—always understood by Mormons to be Joseph Smith—who would bring forth this record in the last days, but here again is a prediction of a scripture, written by some of Joseph of Egypt's descendants (in this context clearly referring to the Nephites), that would at some future date stand alongside the Bible. This, of course, is another prediction of the Book of Mormon, but Nephi does not explicitly identify this book with his own literary labors. He does, however, follow his father's speech with an unusual affirmation—the only time he inserts an editorial comment into the four chapters of Lehi's last teachings:

> And now, I, Nephi, speak concerning the prophecies of which my father hath spoken, concerning Joseph, who was carried into Egypt. For behold, he truly prophesied concerning all this seed. And the prophecies which he wrote, there are not many greater. And he prophesied concerning us, and our future generations; and they are written upon the Plates of Brass. (2 Ne. 4:1–2)

Why does he make such an issue of this, other than possibly as a reminder that if it were not for his faithfulness, the family never would have obtained the Brass Plates? Perhaps it has to do with his evolving sense of his own contribution to the now doubly foretold book and an awareness of the readership for whom he was ultimately writing.

From the beginning, Nephi had some audience in mind ("Therefore, I would that *ye* should know . . . But behold, I, Nephi, will show unto *you* . . ."; 1 Ne. 1:18, 20). At first, these intermittent personal references seem directed to his people (1 Ne. 7:1, 19:3, 5, 18; 2 Ne. 5:32, 11:2), and he is writing either as a king or as an ancestor, despite one somewhat tentative appeal "unto all the House of Israel, if it so be that they should obtain these things" (1 Ne. 19:19). But by the time he begins to comment in 2 Nephi 25–33 on his long quotation of Isaiah 2–14, he is addressing a second audience as well. In the first few verses, Nephi complains to us (his latter-day readers) that his people do not understand Isaiah, and then he proceeds to report a speech given at some point to his subjects: "Hearken, O my people . . . because the words of Isaiah are not plain unto *you* . . . I give unto *you* a prophecy" (2 Ne. 25:4). Along the way, he says that he will "confine the words unto mine own people; for I know that they shall be of great worth unto them in the last days; for in that day shall they understand them; wherefore, for their good have I written them" (2 Ne. 25:8).

A reference to his people "in the last days" comes as a surprise, since Nephi is well aware that his direct descendants will all be destroyed (a point reiterated in the next chapter, at 2 Ne. 26:10); hence either he must have in mind the posterity of his brothers (with whom his descendents had intermingled) or he is claiming the entire House of Israel as his kin. In either case, this is his first acknowledgment that his prophecies will be more intelligible to a distantly removed audience, who will eventually become his primary readership. Nephi confides to his contemporaries that the Lord has promised him that "these things which I write shall be kept and preserved . . . from generation to generation as long as the earth shall stand," and that "the [Gentile] nations who shall possess them shall be judged of them according to the words which are written" (2 Ne. 25:21–22).

One of the main themes of this speech is the future of the record of the Nephites—how it will fulfill the prophecy of a sealed book in Isaiah 29, how it will someday have an authority equal to that of the Bible, and how it will be the means of converting many of the Gentiles (2 Ne. 26:14–17, 27:6–23, 29:1–14, 30:3).[44] By this time, Nephi clearly expects that his own writings will eventually find their place in that book—the same one that he and Isaiah and Joseph had seen in vision—and contribute to its destined role in God's plan for the House of Israel in the last days. Finally, in the last chapter of Second Nephi, he steps back from reporting his words to his people in order to address his ultimate, much wider audience. He begins with a writer's apology and continues by confessing to us his hopes:

> And now I, Nephi, cannot write all the things which were taught among
> my people; neither am I mighty in writing, like unto speaking . . . but I,
> Nephi, have written what I have written, and I esteem it as of great
> worth, and especially unto my people.
> 　　For I pray continually for them by day,
> 　　　　and mine eyes water my pillow by night, because of them;
> 　　and I cry unto my God in faith,
> 　　　　and I know that he will hear my cry. (2 Ne. 33:1, 3)

He concludes with a direct appeal to his future readers, whom he embraces with the same affectionate term he has been using for his contemporaries: "And now, my beloved brethren, all those who are of the House of Israel and all ye ends of the earth, I speak unto you as the voice of one crying from the dust" (2 Ne. 33:13). In this last phrase he explicitly connects his writings with the sealed book of Isaiah 29:4 ("thy speech shall whisper out of the dust," 2 Ne. 26:16) and with Joseph's predicted record ("and it shall be as if the fruit of thy loins had cried unto them from the dust," 2 Ne. 3:19).

There are more connections. Nephi introduces 2 Nephi 25–33 as an explanation of his lengthy quotation of Isaiah 2–14—"Now I, Nephi, do speak somewhat concerning the words which I have written, which have been spoken by the mouth of Isaiah" (2 Ne. 25:1)—but what he provides is not a detailed commentary. He uses phrases from those chapters, as well as from elsewhere in Isaiah, to present a new prophecy about the relationship of the Jews, the Gentiles, and the descendants of Lehi in the last days. One of his major concerns is the visionary book—the Book of Mormon—and how it will be received (as we have seen, Isaiah 29 plays an integral role in this discussion). At the same time, key terms from Joseph's Brass Plates prophecies are reintroduced into these chapters:

2 NEPHI 3	2 NEPHI 25–33
[The seer] shall do a work . . . which shall be of *great worth unto them* (7)	I know that they shall be of *great worth unto them* in the last days (25:8 + 28:2, 33:3)
unto him will I give power to *bring forth my word* unto the seed of thy loins (11)	I *bring forth my word* unto the children of men (29:7 + 25:18)
the fruit of thy loins shall write, and *the fruit of the loins of Judah shall write* (12)	I shall speak unto *the Jews* and they *shall write it*; and I shall also speak unto *the Nephites* and they *shall write it* (29:12)
unto the confounding of *false doctrines* (12)	all those who preach *false doctrines* (28:15 + 28:9, 12)
bringing them to the *knowledge of their fathers* (12)	they shall be restored unto the *knowledge of their fathers* (30:5)
when *my work shall commence* among all my people, unto the *restoring* thee, O House of Israel (13)	the Lord God *shall commence his work* among all nations . . . to bring about the *restoration* of his people (30:8)
their *words shall proceed forth out of my mouth* (21)	the *words* of your seed *should proceed forth out of my mouth* (29:2, 33:14)
the *weakness of their words will I make strong* (21)	the *words* which I have written in *weakness will be made strong* (33:4)

These do not seem to be random hits, nor are they simply the result of the pervasive biblical diction in the Book of Mormon. For the most part, these phrases are clustered in these two sections of Second Nephi. For instance, outside of these chapters, "false doctrine(s)" appears only once (at Alma 1:16), and both "bring forth my word" and "knowledge of their fathers" never occur anywhere else. In addition, in at least one passage (focusing on his own writings), Nephi tells us explicitly that he has Joseph's prophecy in mind: "the Lord God promised unto me that these things which I write shall be kept and preserved, and handed down unto my seed, from generation to generation, that the promise may be fulfilled unto Joseph, that his seed should never perish" (2 Ne. 25:21), which is a reference to 2 Nephi 3:16 ("the Lord hath said unto me, 'I will preserve thy seed forever'").

All this indicates that Nephi's concluding discourse in 2 Nephi 25–33 is not simply an academic commentary on Isaiah 2–14.[45] Rather, it represents a deliberate, creative synthesis of his own revelations, the writings of Isaiah, and the prophecy of Joseph.[46] In this case, the form of Nephi's writing reflects his theology. Just as the multiple witnesses of the visionary, future book—which will testify clearly of the Christian gospel in the last days—come together at the conclusion of Second Nephi, so also at the end of the world the record of the Nephites will combine with other holy texts testifying of God's dealings with branches of his chosen people scattered throughout the earth:

> For I [the Lord] command all men, both in the east and in the west, and in the north and in the south, and in the islands of the sea, that they shall write the words which I speak unto them; for out of the books which shall be written I will judge the world . . . For behold, I shall speak unto the Jews and they shall write it; and I shall also speak unto the Nephites and they shall write it; and I shall also speak unto the other tribes of the House of Israel, which I have led away, and they shall write it; and I shall also speak unto all nations of the earth and they shall write it. And it shall come to pass that the Jews shall have the words of the Nephites, and the Nephites shall have the words of the Jews; and the Nephites and the Jews shall have the words of the lost tribes of Israel; and the lost tribes of Israel shall have the words of the Nephites and the Jews. And it shall come to pass that my people, which are of the House of Israel, shall be gathered home unto the lands of their possessions; and my word also shall be gathered in one. (2 Ne. 29:11–14)[47]

This is a remarkably expansive notion of divine providence, but can such prophecies be relied upon? For Nephi, there are two strong pieces of evidence for authentic revelation. The first is multiple attestation. It is significant that Joseph, Isaiah, and Nephi all said the same thing (similarly, the rapid juxtaposition in Second Nephi of his brother Jacob's sermon [2 Ne. 6–10], Isaiah's writings, and his own final discourse was not accidental; the three men are explicitly named as witnesses of Jesus at 2 Ne. 11:2–3). The second evidence is "argument from fulfilled prophecy." That is to say, the fact that so many of the predictions in Isaiah 2–14—the details of the Syro-Ephraimite War of 743 BC and the Assyrian conquest of

Israel in 722 BC—had been fulfilled long before Lehi's family journeyed into the wilderness lends credibility to those prophecies of Isaiah that have yet to come to pass. Indeed, Nephi seems interested in Isaiah 2–14 for what those chapters reveal about the phenomenon of prophecy in general; he does not provide the kind of specific Christological or eschatological readings that Latter-day Saints have come to expect from modern Mormon commentaries on Isaiah.

Toward the end of his life, after decades of pondering how what he had read in the Brass Plates was connected to what he himself had experienced, Nephi appears to have discovered a satisfying resolution to his religious frustrations. Though he was bitterly aware of the disappointments of his lifetime and the unhappy fate of his descendants in the Promised Land, he nevertheless found solace in the assurance that his writings would someday be instrumental in the restoration of the House of Israel and the conversion of the Gentiles. His was the consolation of prophecy. The Lord had revealed to him that there would be an appreciative audience waiting for him far in the future. In other words, Nephi's mission from God was *not* to unite his family in faithfulness but rather to be a means of "restor[ing] the preserved of Israel," to "be a light to the Gentiles" in bringing salvation "unto the ends of the earth" (1 Ne. 21:6 || Isa. 49:6), and all this would be accomplished through his writing. God had shown Nephi and his book to both Joseph and Isaiah long ago. As Nephi pored over Isaiah 49 and 29, he could say to himself, *I am not a failure; it was part of the plan from the beginning,* or to quote Isaiah (quoting God), "I have even from the beginning declared to thee; before it came to pass I showed them thee" (1 Ne. 20:5 || Isa. 48:5). In this way Nephi situates himself within a community of seers and scripture readers that transcends the linearity of history:

> For behold, I have workings in the spirit, which doth weary me even that all my joints are weak, for those who are at Jerusalem; for had not the Lord been merciful, to show unto me concerning them [the people at Jerusalem], even as he had prophets of old, I should have perished also. And he surely did show unto the prophets of old all things concerning them [the inhabitants of Jerusalem]; and also he did show unto many concerning us [the family of Lehi]; wherefore, it must needs be that we know concerning them [the ancient prophets] for they are written upon the Plates of Brass. (1 Ne. 19:20–21)

Indeed, the concept of time itself can become slippery for someone who is more sure of the future than of the present; for example, untangling exactly what is past, present, and future can be a challenge when faced with a statement such as "And when these things have passed away, a speedy destruction cometh unto my people; for notwithstanding the pains of my soul, I have seen it; wherefore, I know that it shall come to pass" (2 Ne. 26:10). And it is odd to hear of events more than two thousand years in the future as coming "speedily" (1 Ne. 22:23–24; 2 Ne. 28:16, 30:10). Yet with the blurring of temporal distinctions comes a reassuring universality (here expressed by Nephi in language reminiscent of the New Testament):

> For [God] is the same yesterday, today, and forever,
>> and the way is prepared for all men from the foundation of the world,
>> if it so be that they repent and come unto him.
> For he that diligently seeketh shall find;
>> and the mysteries of God shall be unfolded unto them by the power
>>> of the Holy Ghost,
>> as well in these times as in times of old,
>> and as well in times of old as in times to come;
> wherefore, the course of the Lord is one eternal round. (1 Ne. 10:18–19)

These are some of the central themes of the Book of Mormon. The promises of God are to everyone equally; what is done now has been done before and will recur; prophets have foreseen it all; everything takes its place within God's plan.

This is a vigorous, even exhilarating theological perspective, and it is one that Nephi himself has not fully assimilated. He is blind to gender issues (though he notes that God "denieth none that come unto him, black and white, bond and free, male and female . . . all are alike unto God"; 2 Ne. 26:33). And despite his emphasis on descendants and ethnicity (in particular the role of the House of Israel in God's economy), he is forced to admit that ultimately righteousness is more significant than tribal affiliation: "as many of the Gentiles as will repent are the covenant people of the Lord" (2 Ne. 30:2; see also 1 Ne. 17:32–40 for a reinterpretation of the conquest of Canaan that puts morality rather than ethnicity at the forefront). In his comprehensive scheme of world history, it is not always obvious whether salvation is to be understood collectively or individually, or why God speaks with clarity to some and more obscurely to others (Nephi himself seems to struggle between a love for literary, artistic complexity and his awareness of the necessity of plain speaking).

When we read First and Second Nephi with "resistance and imagination," as James O'Donnell says of his own study of Augustine, a character emerges that is more complex and interesting than many readers first assume.[48] Not only does Nephi shape his narratives with particular ends in mind, but he also interprets scripture in intricate ways. We have seen long quotations followed not by detailed commentaries but by fresh prophecies that expand on particular themes by adopting and reinterpreting key phrases. For whatever reason, Nephi (as presented in the English-language Book of Mormon) had a complicated relationship with the King

James Bible. Whole chapters are quoted, but in slightly modified form, sometimes with glosses or interpolations directly related to Nephi's characteristic concerns. Indeed, Nephi deliberately rereads the Bible with his own situation in mind, and he finds himself in Isaiah's ancient prophecies. He introduces extrabiblical writings of Joseph, and he follows that material (more than twenty chapters later) with specific allusions and prophetic reworkings of those prophecies. He believes that his own writings are scriptural, and eventually he comes to realize that his work will some-day stand alongside the Bible when it reaches its ultimate audience of Gentiles and descendants of Israel in the last days. All the while, Nephi is using these scriptural interpretations to assuage deep personal frustrations and resolve theological diffi-culties that he only hints at in his narrative.

Clearly, there is an active mind at work here, one that is colored by his experi-ences, his sense of audience, and his desire for order. Readers will always be divided on whether that mind is ultimately Nephi's or Joseph Smith's, but it is possible to recover from the text a coherent personality within the multiple time frames, the different levels of narrative, and the extensive intertextual borrowings. There is enough consistency and craft in Nephi's writings that when we encounter anoma-lies, it is not unreasonable to look first for answers in his life and ambitions.[49] We can ask: How would Nephi have perceived these events or teachings? How does each story, prophecy, sermon, or biblical exegesis show "that the tender mercies of the Lord are over all those whom he hath chosen, because of their faith, to make them mighty even unto the power of deliverance" (1 Ne. 1:20)? How do they per-suade readers to "believe in Christ and to be reconciled to God" (2 Ne. 25:23)? When these questions have been satisfactorily answered, we can then move on to determine how Nephi's reading of scripture can be a model for Latter-day Saints, or how it might be connected to Joseph Smith's own complicated relationship with the Bible.[50]

Some of Nephi's theological concerns are picked up by other figures in the Book of Mormon, but a fair amount of what occupies his attention is unique; he has a distinct voice. The next major narrator, Mormon, never includes contextless sermons and has little to say about the House of Israel or the last days. Mormon does not focus on his own life or reinterpret scriptures creatively, and most of all, he is not a visionary. From the beginning, Nephi was interested in direct spiritual knowledge: "And it came to pass that I, Nephi, being exceedingly young . . . and also having great desires to know of the mysteries of God, wherefore, I did cry unto the Lord" (1 Ne. 2:16). Unfortunately, what he comes to know is not always pleas-ant. Even before he arrives in the Promised Land, he learns to his dismay that his descendants will have no long-term future there, while the posterity of his wicked brothers will continue on. Toward the end of his writings, he finally has to concede that most people are not like him:

And now, I, Nephi cannot say more; the Spirit stoppeth mine utterance, and I am left to mourn because of the unbelief, and the wickedness, and the ignorance, and the stiffneckedness of men; for they will not search knowledge, nor understand great knowledge, when it is given unto them in plainness, even as plain as word can be. (2 Ne. 32:7)

Prophetic knowledge can offer hope for eventual justification, but it can be a tremendous burden as well.

After his vision of the Tree of Life, Nephi reports that when he returned to camp he found his brothers arguing about the meaning of their father's dream (in a now familiar verse):

And now I, Nephi, was grieved because of the hardness of their hearts, and also because of the things which I had seen, and knew they must unavoidably come to pass because of the great wickedness of the children of men. And it came to pass that I was overcome because of my afflic-tions, for I considered that mine afflictions were great above all, because of the destruction of my people, for I had beheld their fall. (1 Ne. 15:4–5)

What he had learned by revelation—specifically, about the future fate of his and his brothers' descendants—was difficult to bear, though that bitter instruction seems to have been the result, at least in part, of Nephi's particular propensities. At a key moment, Nephi opted for knowledge, and that decision helps us make sense of another literary puzzle in his writings.

His vision in 1 Nephi 11 (which he received shortly after his family left Jerusa-lem) began with him being taken up by the Spirit of the Lord to an unfamiliar mountain. The two converse briefly and the Spirit shows him "the tree which bore the fruit which thy father tasted" (1 Ne. 11:7). A few verses later, the Spirit leaves and an angel takes over as Nephi's guide and interlocutor. Why the shift in personnel? What happened at that juncture? Here is the transitional passage:

And it came to pass after I had seen the tree, I said unto the Spirit, "I behold thou hast shown unto me the tree which is precious above all."
    And he said unto me, "What desirest thou?"
    And I said unto him, "To know the interpretation thereof." (For I spake unto him as a man speaketh; for I beheld that he was in the form of a man; yet nevertheless, I knew that it was the Spirit of the Lord; and he spake unto me as a man speaketh with another.)
    And it came to pass that he said unto me, "Look!" And I looked as if to look upon him, and I saw him not; for he had gone from before my presence. . . .

And it came to pass that I saw the heavens open; and an angel came down and stood before me; and he said unto me, "Nephi, what beholdest thou?" (1 Ne. 11:9–14)

Recall that Lehi had described this tree as one "whose fruit was desirable to make one happy," and he had continued by saying, "I did go forth and partake of the fruit thereof; and I beheld that it was most sweet above all that I ever before tasted . . . and as I partook of the fruit thereof, it filled my soul with exceedingly great joy" (1 Ne. 8:10–12). When the Spirit showed Nephi the same tree and asked what he wanted, it would not have been unreasonable to respond, *I want to taste the fruit; I want to experience that exceedingly great joy.* In fact, as readers, we have been set up to expect Nephi to respond in exactly this way (see 1 Ne. 8:13–16). Instead, he asks for knowledge: "to know the interpretation thereof" (1 Ne. 11:11). The Spirit leaves, an angel takes over, and in the end Nephi is wiser but not happier. For the rest of his life, and through the entirety of his literary labors, Nephi works through the implications of that choice.

The correlation of knowledge and suffering is, of course, the stuff of Greek tragedy, though perhaps a more pertinent example can be found in Milton's *Paradise Lost*, when Adam sees in vision the destruction of his posterity in the Flood:

> How didst thou grieve then, Adam, to behold
> The end of all thy offspring, end so sad,
> Depopulation; thee another flood,
> Of tears and sorrow a flood thee also drowned,
> And sunk thee as thy sons; till gently reared
> By th' Angel, on thy feet thou stood'st at last,
> Thou comfortless, as when a father mourns
> His children, all in view destroyed at once;
> And scarce to th' Angel utter'dst thus thy plain:
>   "O visions ill foreseen! better had I
> Lived ignorant of future, so had borne
> My part of evil only, each day's lot
> Enough to bear . . ." (XI, 754–66)

Who would have thought that the Book of Mormon might also have something to say about this timeless moral and spiritual dilemma? "O the pain, and the anguish of my soul for the loss of the slain of my people! For I, Nephi, have seen it, and it well nigh consumeth me before the presence of the Lord; but I must cry unto my God, "Thy ways are just" (2 Ne. 26:7).

PART II

Mormon

4

Mormon's Dilemma

Competing Agendas

After Nephi bids his readers farewell, his younger brother Jacob takes over the record. Jacob was born after the family left Jerusalem, and nearly everything he knows of the Old World would have come through either Lehi or Nephi. This makes his poetic closing summary, with its yearning for Jerusalem, somewhat unexpected:

> The time passed away with us,
>   and also our lives passed away
> like as it were unto us a dream;
> we being a lonesome and a solemn people,
>   wanderers, cast out from Jerusalem,
>   born in tribulation,
>   in a wild wilderness,
>   and hated of our brethren, which caused wars and conten-
>   tions;
> wherefore, we did mourn out our days. (Jacob 7:26)[1]

Jacob is an interesting figure but not a major narrator—at least not compared with Nephi. His book consists of just seven chapters, which include a sermon (Jacob 2–3), an address to modern readers incorporating Zenos' extended allegory of the olive tree (taken from the Brass Plates; Jacob 4–6), and a confrontation with a heretic named Sherem (Jacob 7).[2] From there the Small Plates rapidly trail off; three narrators write about two pages each, and the other four write only single paragraphs.

And then, suddenly, we find ourselves at the Words of Mormon. For someone reading the Book of Mormon for the first time, this brief section comes as something of a surprise. After nearly 150 pages of narrative—in which attentive readers will have learned to distinguish between Nephi the character and Nephi the memoirist—it turns out that there is another mind at work in the text. In this two-page editorial interruption, we discover that everything up to this point was part of a relatively brief document—the Small Plates of Nephi—that was specially chosen for inclusion by Mormon, a prophet/historian who lived nearly a thousand years after Nephi. The Book of Mormon will soon resume its chronological advance through Nephite history, but the Words of Mormon is an urgent time capsule from the future dropped into the narrative at about 200 BC. With no warning, we read, "And now I, Mormon, being about to deliver up the record which I have been making into the hands of my son Moroni, behold, I have witnessed almost all the destruction of my people, the Nephites. And it is many hundred years after the coming of Christ" (W. of M. 1:1–2).

Mormon goes on to explain that after he had written the history of his people from Lehi to King Benjamin (that is, from ca. 600 to 120 BC), he discovered the Small Plates among the many records in his possession. He was so taken by its prophecies of Christ (many of which had been fulfilled) that he incorporated those plates into his own history as an addendum of sorts. From the Words of Mormon on, most of the text is Mormon's edited abridgment of the primary record of the Nephites, the Large Plates of Nephi. As Mormon apologetically explains, "I cannot write the hundredth part of the things of my people" (W. of M. 1:5), a lament he repeats regularly (see Hel. 3:14; 3 Ne. 5:8, 26:6). The somewhat late introduction of a new major voice—an editor working at the end of Nephite civilization—means that everything that follows has to be interpreted from the perspective of Mormon. Careful readers must constantly ask, "Why would Mormon choose to include this? What might he have omitted? Is there any significance in the way he arranges events or tells particular stories? And who is Mormon anyway?"

The Book of Mormon does not yield answers to these questions easily. The Words of Mormon gives only the briefest introduction to the mind that will dominate the rest of the text. We know his name, his time period, and his general situation. In addition, he tells us that he is a Christian who cares about records, prophecy, and prayer, and that he hopes his writings will someday benefit the descendants of the Lamanites. Then, as the book of Mosiah begins, he steps into the background. Mormon addresses readers every now and again through the rest of his history—adding a comment, an explanation, or an interpretation—so we are regularly reminded that we are getting his particular perspective, a guided tour, so to speak, of Nephite civilization, but the details of his life are not revealed until his own book appears some three hundred pages later. We come to know Mormon only gradually and, for the most part, indirectly.

Clearly Mormon shares some of Nephi's concerns—deliverance, faith, revelation, and Christian theology—but his narrative style is distinct. Stories and sermons are set within a thick historical framework and strict chronology, with years ticking by like clockwork. He does not offer much scriptural exegesis, and he has little interest in House of Israel connections or messiah theology—the word *messiah* occurs twenty-three times in Nephi's writings but only twice in Mormon's work (and never in Moroni's).[3] Mormon is more attuned to narrative theology, that is, in showing how theological points are manifest or illustrated in particular events, and his fascination with prophecy is not so much reading himself into past revelations as using prophecies and their fulfillments to persuade his readers that God is directing history.

Yet perhaps the most striking difference between Nephi and Mormon is how much the latter sees himself as a historian, with a responsibility to tell the story of his civilization comprehensively and accurately. It may have been that Nephi's first version of his life story was equally concerned with the details of political and social change ("the wars and contentions and destructions of my people"; 1 Ne. 19:4), but what we see in First and Second Nephi is as much meditation as memoir. It is a spiritual reflection rather than a conventional historical narrative. Mormon's historiographical impulse, by contrast, is manifest in his meticulous attention to chronology and geography. There are passages, however, in which his urge to make clear moral points or create elegant narratives conflicts with his desire to tell the whole story, and Mormon feels himself caught between the competing roles of historian, artist, and moral guide.

Again we can turn to Meir Sternberg, who has observed that biblical narrative is characterized by three principles, which he identifies as historiographical, aesthetic, and ideological. The first can be seen in a concern for dates, genealogies, and historical details that do not lend themselves to easy moralizing or exemplary lessons. Aesthetics is evidenced in the delight that biblical narrators take in a well-told tale that might include "symmetry, repetition, wordplay, verbal chains, shifts in perspective or from prose to verse." And the ideological principle asserts a strong religious worldview where prophecies and ethical injunctions are echoed by pointed stories of sin, retribution, and deliverance. Although these tendencies, to some degree, are rivals pulling the narrative in different directions, Sternberg argues that in the Bible they are coordinated in their efforts, and good readings need to be cognizant of all three.[4]

The three Book of Mormon narrators also balance these functions, but they do so in distinctive ways. Mormon struggles the most with these competing agendas because he believes that history, fairly and objectively written, will provide an adequate demonstration of God's providence and design. Yet that does not stop him from adding specific moral commentary or shaping narratives into aesthetically pleasing patterns when the facts themselves do not quite convey his points. Nephi and Moroni, by contrast, give less weight to history than they do to visions of the distant future (in the case of the former) or the witness of the Spirit (in the latter). The trouble is that as a conscientious historian, Mormon provides us with enough extraneous details that we can sometimes see where he has trimmed his narratives in order to make them more faith-promoting. In reading the text against itself, we can identify his anxieties and biases as well as his assumptions and beliefs. In fact, Mormon's character is most clearly revealed as he tries to negotiate the divergent demands of being an accurate record keeper, a literary artist, and a moral guide. After a basic overview of Mormon's life and works, we will take up each of these roles in turn.

Meeting Mormon: First Impressions

If you were to read the Book of Mormon straight through, you would discover the details of Mormon's personal history only after several hundred pages of his edited narrative. It would be like first encountering Virgil as the guide in Dante's *Inferno* and only afterward learning of his life and achievements in the Roman world. My book, however, is not as subtle as the Book of Mormon, so we will work backward starting from Mormon's autobiography. Nevertheless, in order to provide new readers with the basic background, here is an outline of his account of the Nephites in a single paragraph:

> Mormon relates Nephite history from about *200 BC to AD 35 in some detail,*
> *especially with regard to events in the capital city, Zarahemla. He tells the*
> *story of a failed Nephite colony in Lamanite territory whose members*
> *miraculously escaped bondage, and he recounts how one of their leaders,*
> *Alma$_1$, established a church and founded the lineage that would provide its*
> *leaders for the next two centuries.[5] Mormon writes of religious renewals,*
> *missionary journeys, political intrigues, and protracted warfare. He*
> *describes the rise of organized robbers who terrorized both Nephites and*
> *Lamanites, a sudden reversal in which the Lamanites became more*
> *righteous than the Nephites, and then the dissolution of both religious and*
> *civil society just before Jesus made a postresurrection appearance in the New*
> *World. After a scene of cataclysmic destruction, the climax of his history is*
> *Christ's visit to the Nephites. Mormon quotes extensively from Jesus'*
> *sermons, but the next three hundred years—including two centuries of*
> *righteousness and peace—are covered in a short book of only four pages,*
> *Fourth Nephi.*

Finally, after three hundred pages with Mormon as our guide, we meet the man himself in the book of Mormon (with a lowercase *b*, to distinguish that section from the Book of Mormon as a whole). It turns out that Mormon is living at a time of general wickedness, when the resurgence of the ancient antagonisms between Nephites and Lamanites masks the fact that both groups are equally wicked (4 Ne. 1:35–46). The religious records had been buried for safekeeping by Ammaron, who had told Mormon (at the age of ten) to recover them and complete the Plates of Nephi when he turned twenty-four (Morm. 1:2–4). In the meantime, Mormon's family had moved south, he had attempted to preach to his people but was forbidden by God, and he had become a military leader (at fifteen) during the escalating warfare. After a series of defeats, it looked for a time as though the Nephites might repent, but in an entry dated about AD 344 Mormon writes:

> My joy was vain, for their sorrowing was not unto repentance, because of
> the goodness of God; but it was rather the sorrowing of the damned,
> because the Lord would not always suffer them to take happiness in sin. . . .
> And it came to pass that my sorrow did return unto me again, and I saw
> that the day of grace was passed with them, both temporally and spiritually,
> for I saw thousands of them hewn down in open rebellion against their
> God, and heaped up as dung upon the face of the land. (Morm. 2:13, 15)

The Nephites gather their people together and flee northward, fighting as they go, and Mormon is thirty-five before he can get back to the hiding place of the records to fulfill Ammaron's charge to add a detailed history of his own time period to the Large Plates of Nephi, as its last installment.

As with Nephi, what we are currently reading is not Mormon's full history but rather a later, shorter version. It is not exactly clear when or why Mormon decided to create this synopsis of the Large Plates. Perhaps this information was spelled out in the introductory material of the book of Lehi (part of the 116 pages lost by Martin Harris), but from comments elsewhere we gather that Mormon's abridgment presented his personal, inspired view of Nephite history ("I make it according to the knowledge and the understanding which God has given me"; W. of M. 1:9); that he saw his record as eventually going to Gentiles and remnants of the House of Israel in the latter days (3 Ne. 26:8, 29:1; Morm. 3:17–19, 5:9–10); that he was commanded by God to include and omit certain details (3 Ne. 26:6–12, 28:25, 30:1); and that he wrote it toward the end of his life as a portable summary so that the archival records themselves could remain safely hidden (Morm. 6:6). In addition, he saw his abridgment as honoring a heritage of faith:

> And it hath become expedient that I—according to the will of God, that
> the prayers of those who have gone hence, who were the holy ones,

should be fulfilled according to their faith—should make a record of
these things which have been done; yea, a small record of that which
hath taken place from the time that Lehi left Jerusalem, even down until
the present time. (3 Ne. 5:14–15)

This reflects a strikingly personal connection to history: Mormon's editorial labors
will directly fulfill the prayers of the earlier prophets he writes about, and thus vin-
dicate their faith. Yet at the same time he also reaches toward the future. Like
Nephi, Mormon failed in his efforts to bring his contemporaries to repentance, and
he consequently redirects his preaching into writings intended for an audience
many centuries later.

For the forty years following Mormon's initial updating of the Large Plates,
the Nephites are on the verge of extermination, sometimes battling to a stalemate,
but more often losing people and territory and retreating further north. Mormon
is one of the few who remain true to the Christian faith, and when he preaches
repentance he has very little success. At the age of fifty-three he refuses to continue
his command of the Nephite armies. Ten years later, as the end draws near, he
reluctantly agrees to lead them once again and they manage to hold off the Lamanites for another decade before nearly everyone is killed at the last great battle in 384.
Mormon, now age seventy-four, laments:

> Ye fair ones
>> how is it that ye could have fallen!
> But behold, ye are gone,
>> and my sorrows cannot bring your return. (Morm. 6:19–20)

Mormon does not spend nearly as much time on his own life as he does on
earlier prophets such as Alma$_2$—his autobiography consists of just seven chapters—but he reveals enough to give us an idea of his sensibilities and concerns.
He appears as a tragic figure, a witness to the self-destruction of his people, yet
powerless to stop it. Like Nephi, he hopes for their repentance but at some point
recognizes that it will not come (we can track the development of his despair in
the sermon and two letters that Moroni copied into his own book at Moro. 7–9).
Several prophets, including Jesus himself, had provided a fairly precise count-
down of the final destruction, predicting that it would occur four hundred years
after Jesus' visit to the New World, in the fourth generation (1 Ne. 12:12–15; 2 Ne.
26:9–10; Alma 45:10, 12; Hel. 13:5, 9–10; 3 Ne. 27:32), yet Mormon never mentions
this prophecy in his autobiography (which is quite at odds with his usual approach
to reporting prophecies and their fulfillments). He seems to be in a state of denial,
perhaps hoping that the prophecy would turn out to be conditional or reversible.
In the end, he confesses that though he poured out his soul to God on behalf of

his people, "it was without faith, because of the hardness of their hearts" (Morm. 3:12), and he was "without hope, for [he] knew the judgments of the Lord which should come upon them" (Morm. 5:2). Yet even without faith and hope, he never loses the third element of the Pauline trinity of virtues, love: "notwithstanding their wickedness I had led them many times to battle, and had loved them, according to the love of God which was in me, with all my heart" (Morm. 3:12; it is apparent from Moro. 7:1 that Mormon was quite familiar with this traditional Christian formula).

His love also extends to his future audience, as when he expresses concern for their tender feelings (note the "ye" at the end of the following quotation; he is speaking directly to his readers):

> And now, behold, I, Mormon, do not desire to harrow up the souls of
> men in casting before them such an awful scene of blood and carnage as
> was laid before mine eyes; but I, knowing that these things must surely
> be made known, and also that all things which are hid must be revealed
> upon the house-tops, and also that a knowledge of these things must
> come unto the remnant of these people, and also unto the Gentiles . . .
> therefore I write a small abridgment, daring not to give a full account of
> the things which I have seen, because of the commandment which I have
> received, and also that ye might not have too great sorrow because of the
> wickedness of this people. (Morm. 5:8–9)

Having seen the destruction of the Nephites, Mormon knows that the primary readership for his abridged version of Nephite history would consist of Gentiles and descendants of the Lamanites in the latter days.[6]

Mormon's account of his own era is fairly sparse (Morm. 1–7). There are few detailed descriptions of significant people or events, and what we are left with seems to be a quick summary of one defeat after another (even when reporting the occasional Nephite victory, Mormon sustains the grim trajectory of his narrative: "[We] did beat them; nevertheless, the strength of the Lord was not with us"; Morm. 2:26). The only causation highlighted by Mormon is military and spiritual; we learn little of social or economic factors. This narrow focus on general wickedness and warfare is sufficient for his purposes here; when he speaks directly to his readers, he pleads with them to prepare for the final judgment day (Morm. 3:20–22, 5:22, 7:6–7, 10), which apparently will come upon them as suddenly and surely as destruction fell upon the Nephites. Nevertheless, Mormon's historiographical urge for precision is still evident; despite the radically constricted viewpoint of these seven chapters, he notes twenty-two specific years in passing and gives the names of ten different cities that were lost to the Lamanites, in chronological order.

Another possible reason for a truncated version of his life is that it was simply too painful to recount again. At least that is the impression he gives at Mormon 2:18–19:

> And upon the Plates of Nephi I did make a full account of all the wickedness and abominations; but upon these plates I did forbear to make a full account of their wickedness and abominations, for behold, a continual scene of wickedness and abominations has been before mine eyes ever since I have been sufficient to behold the ways of man. And wo is me because of their wickedness; for my heart has been filled with sorrow because of their wickedness all my days; nevertheless, I know that I shall be lifted up at the last day.

In this passage, a brief reference to the judgment day provides some relief to Mormon's troubled spirit, but unlike Nephi, who found consolation in contemplating ancient prophecies and the future destiny of the House of Israel, Mormon mainly escapes from his bitter present by immersing himself in the study of history. His turn to the past is a literary response to national tragedy.

After reading Mormon's own story, several features of the preceding narrative take on new meaning. For instance, when describing the way in which Alma₁ first founded a Christian church and introduced the rite of baptism among the Nephites, Mormon becomes uncharacteristically effusive:

> And now it came to pass that all this was done in Mormon,
>   yea, by the waters of Mormon,
>   in the forest that was near the waters of Mormon;
> yea, the place of Mormon,
>   the waters of Mormon,
>   the forest of Mormon,
> how beautiful are they to the eyes of them
> who there came to the knowledge of their Redeemer;
>   yea, and how blessed are they,
>   for they shall sing to his praise forever. (Mosiah 18:30)

There are a lot of references here to a place called Mormon; the mesmerizing, almost incantatory repetition seems to indicate that our narrator would rather have been living with Alma₁'s people than with his own hard-hearted contemporaries. (Much later in the book, he reveals that he was named after this location: "I am called Mormon, being called after the land of Mormon, the land in which Alma did establish the church among the people"; 3 Ne. 5:12.) Similarly, his observations that "there never was a happier time among the people of Nephi . . . than in the days of [Captain] Moroni" (Alma 50:23) and—speaking of the first generation after Christ's visit—"surely there could not be a happier people among all the people who had been created by the hand of God" (4 Ne. 1:16) sound plaintive rather than descriptive.

Hearing Mormon's Voice

In addition to the Words of Mormon and his autobiographical book, Mormon's voice—sorrowful, humane, moralistic, and precise—can be heard in three sorts of passages. The first is in the short editorial interruptions that are scattered throughout his abridgment of the Large Plates, beginning with the first chapter of Mosiah: "and many more things did King Benjamin teach his sons, which are not written in this book" (Mosiah 1:8). This may not be a particularly revealing remark, but it does show Mormon as a deliberate, conscientious editor.[7] Other comments connect the narrator to his readers more directly with phrases such as "I will show unto you . . ." or "I would that ye should see . . ." There are more than a hundred such interruptions, distributed evenly throughout Mormon's history, and they can be categorized as follows (with two or three examples of each type):

1. Comments dealing with the editorial process
   A. Omissions
      "for he [King Limhi] spake many things unto them and only a few of them have I written in this book"—Mosiah 8:1
      "Samuel, the Lamanite, did prophesy a great many more things which cannot be written"—Hel. 14:1

   B. Editorial promises
      "an account of their baptism shall be given hereafter"—Mosiah 21:35
      "and more of this Gadianton shall be spoken hereafter"—Hel. 2:12

   C. Notes on sources
      "and thus ended the record of Alma, which was written upon the Plates of Nephi"—Alma 44:24
      "and now it came to pass that according to our record, and we know our record to be true, for behold, it was a just man who did keep the record . . ."—3 Ne. 8:1

   D. Resumptions
      "we will return to the account of Aaron and his brethren"—Alma 22:1
      "and now I return to an account of the wars between the Nephites and the Lamanites"—Alma 43:3

2. Summaries

"their wars never did cease for the space of many years with the Lamanites, notwithstanding their much reluctance"—Alma 48:22

"and thus they had had wars, and bloodsheds, and famine, and affliction, for the space of many years"—Alma 62:39

3. Explanatory details

"now it was the custom of the people of Nephi to call their lands, and their cities, and their villages . . . after the name of him who first possessed them"—Alma 8:7

"now these are the names of the different pieces of their gold, and of their silver, according to their value"—Alma 11:4

"behold, I have somewhat to say concerning the people of Ammon, who in the beginning were Lamanites"—Alma 53:10

4. Notices of fulfilled prophecies

"yea, all this was done that the word of the Lord might be fulfilled"—Mosiah 21:4

"the words which came unto Nephi were fulfilled, according as they had been spoken"—3 Ne. 1:15

5. Narrative foreshadowing

"I will show unto you that they were brought into bondage, and none could deliver them but the Lord their God"—Mosiah 23:23

"but behold, we shall see that his promise which he made was rash"—Alma 51:10

"now behold, I will show unto you that they did not establish a king over the land"—3 Ne. 7:1

6. Intensifying exclamations

"now was not this exceeding joy?"—Alma 27:18

"and now surely this was a sorrowful day"—Alma 28:6

"great and terrible was the slaughter thereof, insomuch that there never was known so great a slaughter among all the people of Lehi since he left Jerusalem"—3 Ne. 4:11

7. Moral generalizations

"and thus we can plainly discern, that after a people have been once enlightened . . . and then have fallen away into sin . . . their state becomes worse than though they had never known these things"—Alma 24:30

"and thus we see that the devil will not support his children at the last day, but doth speedily drag them down to hell"—Alma 30:60

"thus we may see that the Lord is merciful unto all who will, in the sincerity of their hearts, call upon his holy name"—Hel. 3:27

The second place where we can recognize Mormon's voice is in several extended comment sections. These begin with Alma 48:11–20 and are *not* evenly distributed, becoming more frequent as Mormon moves toward the culmination of his history: Alma 50:19–23; Hel. 4:11–16, 12:1–26; 3 Ne. 5:8–26, 10:11–19, 26:6–14, 28:13–30:2. In these passages, Mormon begins to develop a comprehensive theory of historical change, as we see at Hel. 12:2–3:

> Yea, and we may see at the very time
>   when he doth prosper his people,
> yea, in the increase of their fields,
>   their flocks and their herds,
> and in gold and in silver,
>   and in all manner of precious things of every kind and art;
> sparing their lives,
>   and delivering them out of the hands of their enemies;
> softening the hearts of their enemies
>   that they should not declare wars against them;
> yea, and in fine, doing all things for the welfare
>   and happiness of his people;
> yea, then is the time that they do harden their hearts
>   and do forget the Lord their God,
>   and do trample under their feet the Holy One—
> yea, and this because of their ease,
>   and their exceedingly great prosperity.
> And thus we see that except the Lord doth chasten his people
>   with many afflictions,
> yea, except he doth visit them with death and with terror,
>   and with famine and with all manner of pestilence,
> they will not remember him.[8]

In addition, these longer comments allow Mormon to reveal more of his mind as he shares with readers his circumstances and his intentions. In 3 Ne. 5:12, he first identifies himself by name, and thereafter at 3 Ne. 26:12, 28:24, and 4 Ne. 1:23, we encounter the phrase "I, Mormon." Even so, he is a historian rather than a memoirist, so this usage is minimal compared with the eighty-eight times we read "I, Nephi" in First and Second Nephi.[9]

It is reasonable to ask why Mormon's persona becomes more pronounced later in his abridgment of Nephite history. It may be that Joseph Smith, as the author, was developing a clearer conception of this character as he went along, but it is striking that the level of direct narrator comment increases just at the time when the strong parallels exhibited in the narratives of the books of Mosiah and

Alma diminish (there will be more on this in Chapter 6). Susan Taber noticed this transition from more literary to more didactic presentations and suggested that political turmoil was the cause: "It seems likely that the conditions under which Mormon lived and wrote became so threatening that he no longer had the time or the inclination for the craftsmanship he employed in Mosiah. He seems concerned now with getting his story told by the quickest possible method," even as "he no longer trusts the impact of the narrative alone to carry his message."[10] There are other possible explanations—it may be that the closer Mormon's history got to the self-destruction of the Nephites, the more urgent he felt his message to be, or perhaps some of the literary shaping of his narratives was adapted from his underlying sources and he was simply following their lead, or he shifted his focus from parallels within Nephite history to parallels with the future events—but in any case, regardless of whether one looks for explanations within or without the framework of the narrative, constructing a coherent picture of the narrator is a crucial step in understanding the Book of Mormon.

The third and final place where Mormon's voice is prominent is in the material added by his son Moroni. At each of the major transitions in the Book of Mormon, readers gain a new, broader perspective on the portion of the text they have just finished, as if we were clicking on the "zoom out" function of an interactive map. First and Second Nephi turn out to be an addition to the primary history; through Mormon's editorial comments and autobiography we come to know much better the voice that first intruded into the narrative at the Words of Mormon; and Moroni includes sermons and letters of his father that offer an expanded view of Mormon's life and concerns. In this last section, we discover that Mormon speaks differently to his contemporaries and to his son than he does to us. The rhetoric of persuasion to which we have become accustomed (arguments based on historical events, fulfilled prophecies, and moral generalizations) gives way to theological analysis, impassioned exhortation, appeals to revelation, and despairing assessments of contemporary conditions.

Much like Nephi, Moroni neglects to tell us exactly when and where Mormon originally delivered his sermon on faith, hope, and charity (Moro. 7), but we do know that he was speaking to believers. This is the reason, perhaps, that when he talks of faith, he is more interested in its effects than in how one might acquire it in the first place. Through faith, he says, believers can "lay hold upon every good thing" (Moro. 7:25). In this address, Mormon never cites specific historical events in an attempt to persuade his listeners to believe. Although he makes a general reference to the influence of angels and prophets (Moro. 7:22–25), he ends up arguing that angelic visitations and miracles are as much the result of faith as its cause (Moro. 7:37). He then goes on to explore the relationship between faith, hope, and charity, arguing that the latter two virtues are natural products of true faith. His main concern seems to be teaching his hearers how to distinguish between good and evil—a topic for which concrete examples might have been useful—but he argues from general theological principles rather than from historical examples, and his only quotations are from the words of Jesus (vv. 33–34).

The first letter to Moroni (Moro. 8), on the folly of infant baptism, similarly eschews historical analysis for personal revelation ("immediately after I had learned these things of you I inquired of the Lord concerning the matter"), for theological argument ("little children are alive in Christ . . . if not so, God is a partial God . . . for how many little children have died without baptism!"), direct exhortation ("behold, I speak with boldness, having authority from God"), and blunt condemnation ("Wo unto such [preachers of false doctrines], for they are in danger of death, hell, and an endless torment"; Moro. 8:7, 12, 16, 21). Nevertheless, in his closing comment we hear a brief, familiar theme (on prophecy) from the Mormon that we have come to know from his historical editing: "And after rejecting so great a knowledge, my son, they must perish soon, unto the fulfilling of the prophecies which were spoken by the prophets, as well as the words of our Savior himself" (Moro. 8:29).

If these two chapters show Mormon as a formal theologian (a role we have not so far seen him in), the second letter (Moro. 9) reveals him to be an astute observer of politics and current events. In this personal correspondence he names names, specifies locations, and identifies his sources, much as we observed him doing in his historical abridgment, but Mormon takes a different tone here than when he is writing for latter-day readers. He does not delicately spare his son the gruesome details of slaughter, rape, and cannibalism (as he did for us; see Morm. 5:8–9), nor does he try to persuade Moroni of anything. Moroni is already a believer and already knows how bad things have become. Consequently, Mormon expresses his dismay ("How can we expect that God will stay his hand in judgment against us?") and suggests that the Nephites may be destroyed like the Jaredites (Moro. 9:14, 23), but he draws no "thus we see" moral generalizations and he never refers to fulfilled prophecies. He is simply reporting the latest news. Yet even here his aesthetic urge for eloquence is evidenced by his use of repetitions ("how can a people like this . . ."; vv. 11 and 13), allusions (compare v. 15 with 3 Ne. 9:5, 7, 8), and contrasts (compare his recommendations in vv. 21–22).

Mormon's direct assertions in his comments, sermon, and letters offer the easiest, most direct access to what he believes. There is no mistaking the meaning of a statement such as this:

My son, be faithful in Christ; and may not the things which I have
written grieve thee, to weigh thee down unto death; but may Christ lift
thee up, and may his sufferings and death, and the showing his body

unto our fathers, and his mercy and longsuffering, and the hope of his
glory and of eternal life, rest in your mind forever. (Moro. 9:25; note the
fine contrast between "weigh thee down" and "lift thee up")

Yet we may learn just as much about his character by watching him balance the
competing agendas implicit in his historiography, making the choices that editing
a history requires.

Mormon's narrative style is characterized by three distinct impulses: as a historian, he needs to present an overview of Nephite history that is true to his sources; as
a writer, he wants to construct a narrative that is aesthetically pleasing and compelling;
and as a moralist, he takes responsibility for teaching correct doctrine and providing
spiritual guidance. Unfortunately, the demands of historical accuracy, literary excellence, and moral clarity do not always fit well together, and if we read closely we can
see Mormon struggling to reconcile them. Yet throughout his abridgment (and in
contrast with the items added by his son)—whether he is borrowing from earlier
records, summarizing, rewriting, or commenting directly—his basic orientation is
one of persuasion. Mormon does not simply want to inform or delight or inspire;
rather, he wants to convince his future readers to believe certain things and take particular actions. Through his use of historiographical conventions, he establishes his
credentials as a reliable narrator, and then in his comments he tells us what lessons we
should gain from our study of Nephite history. Yet these two functions do not exhaust
his intentions; whether from his own artistic ambitions or for instrumental purposes
(since a well-crafted narrative can keep people reading and even rereading), he
arranges his stories in complex ways that highlight parallels and contrasts. There is
naturally some overlap among these impulses—for instance, an inserted primary
source document might be eloquent and ethically astute, in addition to being histori-
cally accurate—but here follows a list of some of the major techniques by which Mormon fashions his narrative, arranged according to their dominant mode.

Mormon as Historian

Geography, Genealogy, and Chronology

Mormon's historiographical inclination is most evident in the way he organizes his
narrative within clear spatial, familial, and temporal coordinates. In his abridgment, he includes more than four hundred references to over a hundred distinct,
named locations.[11] Although it is difficult to make concrete correlations with modern maps, the internal geography of the Book of Mormon is almost perfectly consistent, even to the extent that travel to certain places is always "up" or "down." (The
only two geographical mistakes occur at Alma 51:26, where "city of Nephihah" seems

to be an error for "city of Moroni," and Alma 53:6, which places the city of Mulek in the southern land of Nephi while Alma 51:22–27 implies that it was actually on the eastern coast).[12] Over the duration of Nephite history, the center of the action gradually shifts northward, but Mormon alludes often enough to specific places that it is fairly easy to distinguish events occurring in the land of Nephi in the south, the land of Zarahemla in the middle, or the land Desolation in the north. Similarly, there are more than two hundred named individuals in the text, many of whom are related to each other in complex but significant ways. And the fact that so many share the same names (e.g., there are four Lehis, four Nephis, and three Zorams) complicates the situation even further. Nevertheless, Mormon's editorial markers are clear and consistent enough that readers, if they were so inclined, could construct geographical and genealogical tables of Book of Mormon history.[13] Mormon's fastidiousness as a historian can also be seen in his careful use of nomenclature; for example, after the people of Anti-Nephi-Lehi change their name in Alma 27:26 to the "people of Ammon," Mormon never again refers to them by their former title.[14]

Unlike Nephi and Moroni, Mormon employs an explicit, strict chronology, particularly after the end of the monarchy in 91 BC, when events are precisely dated according to "the X year of the reign of the judges" (though stories taking place in Lamanite territory have many fewer chronological markers; e.g., Mosiah chs. 9–24 and Alma chs. 17–27). Almost every year is mentioned individually, even if Mormon does not give them equal coverage. Sometimes nothing of note seems to have happened and a year is passed by in a sentence or less. Often, however, the dates come in pairs as Mormon indicates both the beginning and ending of a particular year. These references can be separated by only a few verses, but frequently they are several chapters apart (e.g., 83 BC, the eighteenth year of the reign of the judges, begins at Alma 35:13 and ends at 44:24). Most of the time, readers who are paying attention will know exactly when a particular incident took place, and there is a sense of momentum that builds when the year markers come faster as the narrative gets closer to Jesus' appearance among the Nephites.[15]

Given the comprehensive chronological framework of the Book of Mormon, it is always interesting when Mormon presents things out of sequence. For instance, at Helaman 5:5–13, Mormon quotes a speech by Helaman₃ not at the time it was originally given but instead by having his two sons remember it many years later (perhaps not coincidentally, the subject of that discourse was remembrance). The regular march of time is also interrupted when the same event is told more than once, as in Helaman 4:10 and 17, where the sixty-first year of the judges ends twice. This might seem like a mistake, but verses 11–17 offer a recapitulation or summary in which the military achievements of the year are reinterpreted in spiritual terms—one of the examples of Mormon commenting directly when he felt that the religious meaning of a story was insufficiently clear. (Alternatively, the connection between vv. 10 and 16–17 could be regarded as an example of resumptive repetition.)

Simultaneous Stories

Narratives that follow multiple characters often have to deal with the problem of how to clearly convey events that happened at about the same time in different locations. One of the most impressive examples in the Book of Mormon occurs during the Amalickiahite Wars, when the Lamanites expand their invasion into a second front in Alma 52 and Mormon has to help readers keep straight the geography and chronology during simultaneous campaigns in the both the west and the east. In this case, he uses a letter from Helaman$_2$, a general in the west, recounting the events of the previous four years (Alma 56–58). But he handles the two most extensive instances of simultaneous narratives through flashbacks. In the first, a search party locates a long-lost Nephite colony in Lamanite territory (Mosiah 7–8). The history of that colony—some eighty years' worth—is told in a lengthy flashback that extends from Mosiah 9:1 to 21:27 and ends with a second account of the arrival of the searchers, but this time told from the point of view of the colonists. At that point Mormon's secondary narration returns not only to the main narrative sequence but even to the same conversation that had been interrupted thirteen chapters earlier. Mormon then tracks two more simultaneous narrative strands— the escape of Limhi's people from bondage (Mosiah 22) and the escape of Alma's people (Mosiah 23–24), with the Lamanite army jumping from the first narrative to the second at Mosiah 22:16/23:30. Finally, at Mosiah 25 both groups are reunited with the main body of Nephites and the focus of the narrative shifts back to the Nephite capital of Zarahemla, from which the search party had left not long before.

The second major flashback occurs after an account of the Nephite Reformation from 91 to 77 BC. The main character in that narrative, Alma$_2$, is on a journey and runs into his old friends the sons of Mosiah, who are themselves returning from a fourteen-year mission among the Lamanites. Alma 17:5–27:15 then recounts what had happened to them during those same years before returning to the scene of the unexpected reunion. There is also a subsidiary flashback in Alma 21 explaining just how Aaron and his brethren had come to be imprisoned (Ammon rescues them at 20:30, where the flashback begins, and then again at 21:14, when it ends). The primary flashback also allows for the retelling of another crucial event—the destruction of the border city of Ammonihah by the Lamanites—from two perspectives (Alma 16:1–11/25:1–2), but I will have more to say about this at the end of the chapter. Although these twists and turns of narrative may seem quite complicated, Mormon handles them smoothly (and the added headings and foot-notes in my *Reader's Edition* make his guidance even clearer).

Embedded Documents

Mormon regularly inserts primary sources into his narrative. These include a memoir by Zeniff (Mosiah 9:1–10:22); an edict of King Mosiah (Mosiah 29:5–32); six letters—by Moroni$_1$ (Alma 54:5–14, 60:1–36), Ammoron (Alma 54:16–24), Helaman$_2$ (Alma 56:2–58:41), Pahoran (Alma 61:2–21), and Giddianhi (3 Ne. 3:2–10); and speeches by King Benjamin (Mosiah 2:9–4:30) and Alma$_2$ (Alma 5:2–62, at Zarahemla; Alma 7:1–27, at Gideon; Alma 9:8–33, at Ammonihah; Alma 36:1–37:47, to Helaman$_2$; Alma 38:1–15, to Shiblon; Alma 39:1–42:31, to Corianton). The transi-tion to embedded documents is usually marked by a clear introduction and a shift from third-person to first-person voice. The origins of speeches are sometimes dif-ficult to ascertain since the Book of Mormon includes a considerable amount of direct discourse, and even historians as careful as Thucydides have been known to write dialogue and orations for their characters (based on available evidence and appropriate to the setting, of course).[16] Mormon tells us directly that the speeches above were all taken from previously existing records authored by the speakers themselves (Mosiah 2:8–9; Alma 35:16; headnotes at Alma 5, 7, 9). There are, how-ever, several additional major speeches in Mormon's writings, which may have been either reported verbatim or significantly edited or even reconstructed by Mormon, including another by Alma$_2$ (Alma 32:8–33:23, at Antionum), as well as those given by Abinadi (Mosiah 12:25–16:15), Amulek (Alma 10:2–23, at Ammoni-hah; Alma 34:2–41, at Antionum), King Anti-Nephi-Lehi (Alma 24:7–16), Ammon (Alma 26:1–37), Samuel the Lamanite (Hel. 13:5–15:17), and the resurrected Jesus (three distinct discourses found at 3 Ne. 12–28).[17]

Turning the narrative over to another voice is a dramatic editorial move, and such cases deserve careful scrutiny. Why doesn't Mormon simply paraphrase a speech or a letter and then describe the reactions of the original recipients? And why these particular documents rather than others in his possession (e.g., we know that Alma$_2$ preached at four cities during the Nephite Reformation, but we have sermons from only three [see Alma 8:3–5]); a paraphrased letter can be seen at Alma 59:3–4).[18] Here all three of Mormon's roles come into play. The inclusion of primary sources certainly adds historical value and authenticity to an account of the past. From the perspective of aesthetics, direct discourse enhances the drama of the narrative—even villains such as Korihor and Ammaron get to present their ideas in their own words—and Mormon seems to have admired the literary quali-ties of speeches he preserves, which suggests at least a partial explanation of why we have so many of Alma$_2$'s sermons. As a moralist, Mormon may have wanted his readers to experience crucial moments of testimony and exhortation for themselves as they read the actual words of Benjamin, Alma$_2$, Amulek, and Jesus in real time. For instance, Alma's sermon at Zarahemla (Alma 5) included more than fifty rhetorical questions intended to provoke his listeners (and Mormon's readers) into reflecting on the state of their souls.

Mormon as Literary Artist

Large Narrative Units

Mormon's abridgment of Nephite history covers a great many people and years, but for the most part his narratives focus on one major event after another. For instance, the longest book—that of Alma—divides fairly neatly into seven sections: the Amlicite Rebellion (Alma 2:1–3:19), the Nephite Reformation (4:6–16:21), the Missionary Journeys of the Sons of Mosiah (17:5–27:15), the Mission to the Zoramites (31:1–35:14), Alma's Testimony to His Sons (35:15–42:31), the Zoramite War (43:1–44:24), and the Amalickiahite Wars (46:1–62:41). These lengthy, coherent, fairly discrete narrative blocks represent a rather advanced style of storytelling, one that is cognizant of readers' needs for interconnections, explanations, and followability, and in addition incorporates several primary sources.

As is so often the case in the Book of Mormon, we are not left to make our own subjective judgments; Mormon frequently assists his readers in demarcating major segments of the text by providing headnotes, transitional comments, chronological markers, indications of shifts in source materials, introductions to embedded documents, and so forth. At times he uses resumptive repetition as a framing device. For instance, Alma 28 begins: "And now it came to pass that after the people of Ammon were established in the land of Jershon . . .," which is nearly identical to the opening of chapter 30: "Behold, now it came to pass that after the people of Ammon were established in the land of Jershon . . ." The material in between consists largely of Alma$_2$'s comments on contemporary events, suggesting that these chapters be read as a literary unit. Mormon shapes his text not only for clarity but also to highlight meaning, and he appears to exercise considerable control over this material.

We can see Mormon employing several of these devices to delineate the boundaries of the Amalickiahite Wars in the latter half of Alma. The headnote to Alma 45 informs us that what follows is *the account of the people of Nephi, and their wars and dissensions, in the days of Helaman, according to the record of Helaman, which he kept in his days,* and this overt declaration is accompanied by an observation that "Helaman and his brethren went forth to establish the church again in all the land" (Alma 45:22). Within a few verses the Amalickiahite Wars begin, and they continue until Alma 62, where we read once again that "Helaman and his brethren went forth and . . . did establish again the church of God throughout all the land" (Alma 62:45–46). Less than half a page later, Helaman dies, which necessitates another change in Mormon's sources—a transition he obliquely references when he notes that Helaman's brother Shiblon "took possession of those sacred things [including the Large Plates of Nephi] which had been delivered unto Helaman by Alma" (Alma 63:1). We are meant to read Alma 45–62 as a coherent unit, and once we recognize it as such, we can compare it to other wars or similar episodes.

Selective Attention

H. D. F. Kitto once wrote of Thucydides that, given the amount of source material available to him, "one of his chief preoccupations must have been to leave things out."[19] The Book of Mormon similarly asks us to imagine Mormon poring over piles of ancient records, able only to incorporate "a hundredth part" into his abridgment (W. of M. 1:5; Hel. 3:14; 3 Ne. 5:8, 26:6). Consequently, what he leaves out is often as important as what he chooses to include (even if there is an element of hyperbole in his repeated assertion). Determining what is not there can be a delicate business, but it is clear that Mormon gives more attention to some periods and themes than others. For instance, when he shifts the focus of his history to the people of Zeniff—a Nephite colony in the midst of Lamanite territory—we learn almost nothing of the contemporaneous reign of King Mosiah in Zarahemla, which was apparently very successful. This is in keeping with Mormon's general disinclination to provide details about periods of social harmony—other examples include the mass conversion of the Lamanites in Helaman 5:50–52 (which led to a complete transformation of their society and indeed was much more miraculous than anything accomplished by the Sons of Mosiah in the eleven chapters devoted to their missionary labors), as well as the two centuries of peace that followed Jesus' appearance among the Nephites (dispensed with by Mormon in just twenty-one verses; see 4 Ne. 1:1–21). Either Mormon is not interested in the economy, politics, sociology, or religious practices of these periods or he doesn't think this is what his readers most need to hear.

Actually, the choice to dwell on dysfunctional eras seems odd in a book whose point is to urge readers to embrace the Christian gospel. We might expect inspirational accounts of the glorious existence possible for nations who repent and come to Christ; instead we get extensive narratives only from contentious and self-destructive periods. The bulk of the text is devoted to the two hundred years that precede Jesus' visit, and if Mormon's narrative has a central focus, it is the church founded by Alma₁ at the Waters of Mormon (Mormon follows this institution and its leaders—all descendants of Alma₁—more closely than the central government, making the Book of Mormon almost a lineage history) and the military exploits of

Captain Moroni₁ fighting on behalf of that church (Alma 43:16–63:3).[20] Mormon has a personal connection to both stories, since he informs us that he was named after the place where the church originated (3 Ne. 5:12), and he apparently named his own son after Moroni₁. (Strangely enough, Mormon himself is not a member of the lineage he chronicles; after eight generations within the same family line of church leaders, the Plates of Nephi are entrusted by Ammaron to Mormon, an outsider whose pedigree is obscure [Morm. 1:1–5; though he does describe himself as "a pure descendant of Lehi" at 3 Ne. 5:20].)

Some of Mormon's omissions were commanded by God—"I was about to write them all, which were engraven upon the Plates of Nephi, but the Lord forbade, saying, 'I will try the faith of my people'" (3 Ne. 26:11)—while others seem to have been his own decision, but in general, Mormon chooses details that reflect his characteristic concerns: divine design, human agency, and the tension between them; religious and political dissidents; the dangers of social inequality and government corruption; secret societies and bands of robbers; ecclesiastical history; religious conversions; charismatic leaders; argument from fulfilled prophecy; and warfare. In addition, there are some significant omissions in the *way* he writes. As a military man himself, Mormon never speaks of war figuratively or makes it a metaphor for Christian living. There is no mention of putting on the armor of God, the good fight of faith, or spiritual warfare against temptation (in contrast to some recent Latter-day Saint readings of the war chapters in Alma).[21] And although Mormon occasionally quotes people who identify certain things or events as "types," typological thinking is *not* a major factor in his own understanding of history. The only time he himself refers to types, he is describing the beliefs of others: "they did look forward to the coming of Christ, considering that the law of Moses was a type of his coming" (Alma 25:15). By contrast, Moroni does offer an explicitly typological interpretation in his own voice at Ether 13:6–7.[22]

Meaningful Phrases

Many of the Book of Mormon's distinctive phrases (especially those borrowed from the Bible) occur throughout the text in unrelated contexts and seem simply to be part of its generic vocabulary. For instance, "pervert the right ways of the Lord" (Acts 13:10) shows up, with variations, some 12 times, and "the spirit of prophecy" (Rev. 19:10) appears 18 times; "as the Lord liveth" occurs 27 times in the Old Testament and 17 times in the Book of Mormon; "from the foundation of the world" is used 6 times in the New Testament and 22 times in the Book of Mormon; and there are 22 uses of "the children of men" in the Old Testament and 129 in the Book of Mormon. Yet there are also phrases whose distribution is irregular in potentially meaningful ways. Variations of "keep [God's] statutes and commandments" appear

24 times in the Old Testament and 8 in the Book of Mormon, but never after Jesus' visitation, when adherence to the Mosaic law was no longer required of believers (4 Ne. 1:12). The sudden loss of this idiom, after we have seen it in the books of Mosiah, Alma, and Helaman (3 times in combination with "according to the law of Moses"), is an indication of Mormon's care in getting the details right.

There are also dozens and dozens of passages where phrases are used exclusively in similar situations, signaling a deliberate allusion to an earlier event. For example, when the Lord reveals to Alma's people that he will deliver them from bondage, he says, "I know of the covenant which ye have made unto me . . . and this will I do that ye may stand as witnesses for me hereafter" (Mosiah 24:13–14), referring to the covenant they made at baptism when they promised, among other things, to "stand as witnesses of God at all times and in all things, and in all places" (Mosiah 18:8–10). The formula "stand as witnesses" occurs only in these two verses in all of the Book of Mormon. Similarly, when surveying the aftermath of the last great battle of the Nephites, Mormon mourns for the many "fair sons and daughters" who had fallen (Morm. 6:19). In using this locution, he brings to mind the only previous occasion we have encountered it, that is, when a voice from heaven enumerated the cataclysmic destructions at the time of Christ's death, lamenting "the slain of the fair sons and daughters of my people" (3 Ne. 9:2).[23]

When the converted Lamanites known as the Anti-Nephi-Lehies are unsure of whether they should seek refuge with Nephites—fearing that their former enemies would kill or enslave them rather then welcome them—the Lord says, "*Get this people out of this land*, that they perish not; for Satan has great hold on the hearts of the Amalekites, who do stir up the Lamanites to anger against their brethren to slay them; *therefore get thee out of this land*" (Alma 27:12; emphasis added). Alert readers may notice that the only other verse in the Book of Mormon that uses similar language is when God told Alma₁ to flee with his followers: "Haste thee and *get thou and this people out of this land*, for the Lamanites have awakened and do pursue thee; *therefore get thee out of this land*" (Mosiah 24:23). Although it is conceivable that the Anti-Nephi-Lehies knew of this precedent and its indication of God's tender mercies, attentive readers can certainly gain insight by connecting the broader contours of the former episode with the latter. The fact that both accounts are told by the same narrator makes such allusions possible; the observation that in this case both verses include a double injunction to "get out of this land" makes an intentional allusion more likely. There will be more such examples in the chapters that follow.

In analyzing significant phrases, it is important to keep the conventions of the text in mind. For instance, at Alma 48:11–18, Mormon interrupts his narrative to insert a highly unusual, resounding endorsement of Captain Moroni₁'s spiritual stature. It is a good thing he does so, because otherwise readers might get the wrong idea from the narratives that follow. Moroni₁ is stubborn and hot-tempered, he is never depicted as praying for assistance or relying solely upon God, and—justified though it may be—he ends up with a lot of blood on his hands. Mormon's comment helps us read Moroni's story in a particular way, and it is remarkable what lengths he goes to in order to ensure that. The culmination of Mormon's praise is the assertion "Yea, verily, verily I say unto you, if all men had been, and were, and ever would be, like unto Moroni, behold the very powers of hell would have been shaken forever" (Alma 48:17). This is as strong a statement as Mormon can possibly make; the only other instances of "verily, verily I say unto you" in the Book of Mormon are spoken by the resurrected Christ himself.[24]

Parallel Narratives

Mormon's literary ambitions can also be seen in the organization of his narratives. While theological implications are never far away, the exact meaning to be gained from comparing similar stories is often left to readers, while Mormon's skill (and delight) in constructing narratives is clearly evident. Large-scale parallel narratives are most pronounced early in Mormon's abridgment, with the dual deliverances of Alma's and Limhi's peoples in the book of Mosiah and the preaching of Alma$_2$ among the Nephites and the sons of Mosiah among the Lamanites in the first half of Alma (these examples will be taken up in detail in Chapter 6). Yet it seems that many of the major narratives in the Book of Mormon come in pairs, such as the preaching of Alma and Amulek at Ammonihah (Alma 8–15) and then at Antionum (Alma 31–35), the missionary adventures of Ammon (Alma 17–20) and Aaron (Alma 21–22), the political subversions of the King-men (Alma 51) and the men of Pachus (Alma 62–63), or the mass conversions of Lamanites in Alma 23–24 and Helaman 5–6 (both episodes include a ceremonial burying of weapons, at Alma 24:15–19 and Hel. 5:51, with a later reference at Hel. 15:9). Narratives can also be parallel by contrast. The righteous Lamanites known as the Anti-Nephi-Lehies defect to the Nephites in a way that mirrors the movement of Nephite dissidents in the other direction, and in both cases ethnic tensions are exacerbated (compare Alma 27–28 with chs. 35, 43 [Zoramites], or 46–47 [Amalickiah]). In addition, a contrast between physical and spiritual deliverance can be seen in the experiences of Alma$_1$ and Alma$_2$ (Mosiah 24 and Alma 36; the latter story includes direct references to the former).

The above parallels all take the form of fairly extensive narratives, with numerous structural and verbal correspondences. One might also contrast specific individuals, as Susan Taber does with the kings Benjamin and Noah and the prophets Abinadi and Alma$_1$. Mormon may have meant for his readers to make these comparisons, but it is harder to be sure of his intentions here—one can always draw distinctions between good and bad kings, or between successful prophets and martyrs.[25] Nevertheless, the sheer abundance of specific narrative repetition in Mormon's abridgment suggests not only deliberate selection and shaping but also that, in the working out of God's will, certain kinds of events are likely to recur. Hence there are two confrontations between prophets and Antichrists (Alma 1 and 30, with a precedent at Jacob 7), two chief judges who give up their offices to devote themselves to preaching (Alma 4 and Hel. 5), two cases where a pair of prophets are cast into prison and then miraculously escape (Alma 14, Hel. 5), three accounts of prophets facing legal confrontations (Mosiah 12–17, Alma 10–14, Hel. 7–9), three prophets who are commanded by God to return to preach in cities where they had been previously rejected (Mosiah 12, Alma 8, Hel. 13), and so forth.[26]

In light of Mormon's artistic structuring of his account with deliberate editing, parallel narratives, and specific verbal connections, Latter-day Saints may want to rethink their long-held assumption that the circumstances of Mormon's life forced him to write hurriedly. The intentionality implicit in the literary aspects of his history suggest that, from a believer's perspective, he did not compose as he engraved, but rather transmitted to the plates a text previously written and carefully revised, a process that can thereby explain the many intricate interweavings separated by long passages of text. For outsiders, there will naturally be a higher threshold of skepticism for the identification of large-scale patterns and deliberate allusions— repetitions can always be ascribed to Joseph Smith's limited vocabulary and imagination—but that imagination may turn out to be more expansive than is generally assumed.

Mormon as Moral Guide

Direct Editorial Comments

As noted above, from Mosiah to Fourth Nephi there are over a hundred passages in which Mormon interrupts his narrative to speak directly to his readers. Most of these are relatively brief comments explaining his editorial decisions and sources or noting the fulfillment of prophecies, but he also provides summaries, adds explanatory details, offers explicit judgments, and points out universal moral principles. Longer comments appear more frequently as his history proceeds, and consequently we get a sense of gradual self-disclosure. When we finally come to Mormon's autobiographical book, we can return to the beginning of his record to compare his persona as editor with his persona as memoirist. Given the disappointments and tragedy of his own life, it is easy to read a larger background into comments such as that at Alma 46:8, where he reflects on a sudden turn in Nephite history by noting, "Thus we see how quick the children of men do forget the Lord their God, yea, how quick to do iniquity, and to be led away by the evil one."

It is this sort of moralizing that most accounts for our sense of the Book of Mormon as a didactic text, and indeed Mormon's role as spiritual guide takes precedence in these passages. But it is interesting that at times he uses this technique preemptively, to shape our perceptions of an ensuing narrative that might otherwise be hard to explain. For instance, his basic premise of "the wicked suffer while the righteous prosper" is threatened when the blameless followers of Alma₁ are enslaved by the Lamanites. Consequently, he introduces that episode by suggesting that it is an aberration that will, in the end, turn out well: "The Lord seeth fit to chasten his people; yea, he trieth their patience and their faith. Nevertheless, whosoever putteth his trust in him, the same shall be lifted up at the last day. Yea, and thus it was with this people. For behold, I will show unto you that they were brought into bondage, and none could deliver them but the Lord their God" (Mosiah 23:21–23). Mormon is also enough of a historian that he occasionally includes details that allow us to critically reevaluate the points he is making, as when he works hard to convince his readers that the martyrdom of more than a thousand believers was actually a good thing (Alma 24:20–27), or that Captain Moroni₁, an impetuous and sometimes brutal military commander, was in reality a paragon of Christian virtue (Alma 48:11–18).

Prophecy and Fulfillment

Many of Mormon's direct comments point out explicitly where prophecies have been fulfilled, but other features of Mormon's editing also reinforce this theme, from the contents of the embedded documents he chooses to include to the allusive wording he employs in telling stories. For instance, in the prophet Abinadi's preaching, shortly before his martyrdom, to the Nephite colony established by Zeniff, there are at least seven instances where his predictions are picked up later in the narrative:

> Mosiah 11:21—"except this people repent . . . they shall be brought into bondage"; fulfilled at Mosiah 19:13–15, 25–28
>
> Mosiah 11:24–25—"when they shall cry unto me I will be slow to hear their cries"; fulfilled at Mosiah 21:15
>
> Mosiah 12:2—"this generation, because of their iniquities . . . shall be smitten on the cheek; yea, and shall be driven by men, and shall be slain"; fulfilled at Mosiah 21:3, 8, 11, 12
>
> Mosiah 12:3—"the life of King Noah shall be valued even as a garment in a hot furnace" (also at Mosiah 17:18); fulfilled at Mosiah 19:20
>
> Mosiah 12:5—"they shall have burdens lashed upon their back; and they shall be driven before like a dumb ass"; Mosiah 21:3–4

Mosiah 13:10—"what you do with me, after this, shall be as a type and a shadow of things which are to come"; fulfilled at Mosiah 19:20 and Alma 25:9–10

Mosiah 17:15, 18—"thy seed shall cause that many shall suffer even the pains of death by fire . . . and in that day ye shall be hunted, and ye shall be taken by the hand of your enemies"; fulfilled at Alma 25:11–12

In the last three references Mormon adds a personal comment explicitly noting the connections, but the other cases of prophetic fulfillment are equally clear. In addition, Abinadi's main message included a detailed prophecy of the coming of Christ, which modern readers will recognize as fulfilled in the New Testament. Even characters within the story recognize the significance of his predictions— Mormon reports a Nephite leader named Gideon saying, in a direct quote, "For are not the words of Abinadi fulfilled, which he prophesied against us?" (Mosiah 20:21).

Prophecies provide connections between larger episodes, and even between books, as when Mormon spends considerable effort in Alma 3 demonstrating how the Amlicites' adornment for battle fulfilled predictions made by Nephi several centuries earlier (Alma 3:13–18; 2 Ne. 5:22–23), or when he explains Ammon's miraculous preservation by referring to a previous revelation from God given to his father, King Mosiah (Alma 17:35; Mosiah 28:7). In addition, prophecies are often integral to the stories themselves: the destruction of major cities is always preceded by recent prophetic warnings, prophets occasionally foretell the movements of enemy troops (Alma 16:4–8, 43:23–24; 3 Ne. 3:19–21), and the story of Nephi$_3$ hinges upon his accurate prediction of the reaction of a chief judge's murderer (Hel. 9). There is a double climax to Mormon's history, both elements of which were prophesied about extensively. The first is the coming of Jesus to Palestine, with unmistakable signs in the New World of his birth and death, quickly followed by a dramatic postresurrection appearance of Christ to the Nephites. The second culmination of prophecy occurs with the destruction of the Nephites as a people some four hundred years later.

If the chronology forms the backbone of Mormon's history, prophecy is the ligament that holds it together. We should also note that Mormon has a vested interest in linking prophecies and their realizations; the Book of Mormon presents an extended "argument from fulfilled prophecy," that is, readers are assured that if all of these predictions have come to pass as foretold, so too will those that are as yet unfulfilled, including many that concern their own lives at the time when the Book of Mormon would be published (e.g., Mormon's prophecies at 3 Ne. 29 and Mormon 5:8–24), as well as in the final judgment day. (Perhaps surprisingly, Jesus' Second Coming and the Millennium are almost never mentioned in Mormon's writings.)[27]

Spiritual Interpretations of History

Mormon sees his narrative as reflecting two additional historical patterns, but their use is more limited than the pervasive prophecy/fulfillment sequence and he does not try to organize his entire history around them. The first has its classic statement in Lehi's words at 2 Nephi 1:20: "Inasmuch as ye shall keep my commandments ye shall prosper in the land; but inasmuch as ye will not keep my commandments ye shall be cut off from my presence." Variations of this promise appear eight more times in the Small Plates and eleven times in Mormon's writings, with the last three occurrences coming in Mormon's direct editorial comments (Alma 48:15, 25, 50:20).[28] We can imagine a history of the Nephites arranged to illustrate this thesis from beginning to end, but after Alma 50, the "prosper"/"cut off" dichotomy is dropped as an organizing principle.

What seems to take its place is a somewhat more complex cyclical theory of historical development in which people are blessed with prosperity and as a result become proud and divisive. Their contentiousness leads to political troubles, and when things get bad enough, the people humble themselves, repent, and call upon the Lord, who then delivers them and blesses them with renewed prosperity. There is a regular ebb and flow of obedience and wickedness though the book of Alma, but with the book of Helaman this particular cycle becomes even more pronounced as the transitions come more regularly and frequently. We see a complete cycle at Helaman 3–4, with Mormon's explicit interpretations at Hel. 4:11–17. The same basic sequence is evident again at Helaman 5–12 and 3 Nephi 6–10. After Christ's visit, however, the pride cycle seems no longer operative; the wicked are prosperous (4 Ne. 1:46) and upturns in fortune can occur without repentance (Morm. 3:1–10). In the last generation, Mormon asserts that "the pride of this nation, or [of] the people of the Nephites, hath proven their destruction, except they repent" (Moro. 8:27), but they do not avail themselves of that opportunity. Nephite history has become linear rather than cyclical.

Watching Mormon at Work: Alma 16

I have been speaking of Mormon as if he were a historical figure (which to Latter-day Saints, of course, he is). Outsiders, however, may find it useful to compare Mormon's presence in the text with that of another famous character, Cide Hamete Benengeli, the purported author of *Don Quixote*. In the ninth chapter of Cervantes' novel, just after the episode with the windmills, readers are informed that the rest of the book is a translation of a history of Quixote written in Arabic by Benengeli, which Cervantes claims to have discovered in the Alcaná market at Toledo. Cervantes takes great delight in this conceit and mentions Benengeli several dozen times over the course of parts I and II, sometimes praising him, but also blaming him for various inconsistencies and incongruities in the narrative. For example, at the beginning of Part II, chapter 10, we read:

> When the author of this great history [Benengeli] came to recount what is recounted in this chapter, he says he would have preferred to pass over it in silence, fearful it would not be given credence, for the madness of Don Quixote here reached the limits and boundaries of the greatest madnesses that can be imagined, and even passed two crossbow shots beyond them. But finally, despite this fear and trepidation, he wrote down the mad acts just as Don Quixote performed them, not adding or subtracting an atom of truth from the history and not concerning himself about the accusations that he was a liar, which might be made against him; and he was right, because truth may be stretched thin and not break, and it always floats on the surface of the lie, like oil on water.[29]

Yet Cervantes' references to "the original author" are sporadic (though they become more frequent in part II), and in the end we do not have enough information to form a coherent picture of Benengeli as a writer. He never gets a chance to explain his life and motivations directly; instead we know him mostly through Cervantes' criticisms (in a way that Joseph Smith never comments on Mormon).[30] The Book of Mormon may not be as much fun to read as *Don Quixote*, but at least in this one respect, it is more thoroughly composed. However readers may conceptualize Mormon, part of the interest of the book is observing the way he interacts with and shapes his material.

So a broad overview of Mormon's editorial techniques may be helpful, but only as a preliminary step to the careful reading of individual passages, where we can see how Mormon actually handles his competing objectives. Alma 16 provides a convenient example. This chapter, relating the destruction of the wicked city of Ammonihah, comes at the conclusion of Alma's preaching in Alma 4–16, which I refer to in my *Reader's Edition* as the "Nephite Reformation." The eight chapters immediately preceding (Alma 8–15) formed a subunit that told the story of Alma$_2$ and Amulek's mission to Ammonihah and described how, despite limited success, they were eventually rejected and thrown into prison. Then, in an act of terrible brutality, the people of Ammonihah drove Alma's male converts from the city and burned to death their defenseless wives and children. In time Alma and Amulek were miraculously delivered from prison by an earthquake (our scrupulous narrator notes that it was "on the twelfth day, in the tenth month, in the tenth year of the reign of the judges over the people of Nephi"; Alma 14:23), and they made their way to the city of Sidom, where they found the now familyless refugees. Alma and

Amulek converted many in Sidom and organized a church there before returning to Zarahemla at the end of the year.

Alma 16 begins as follows:

> And it came to pass in the eleventh year of the reign of the judges over the people of Nephi, on the fifth day of the second month, there having been much peace in the land of Zarahemla, there having been no wars nor contentions for a certain number of years, even until the fifth day of the second month in the eleventh year, there was a cry of war heard throughout the land. For behold, the armies of the Lamanites had come in upon the wilderness side, into the borders of the land, even into the city of Ammonihah, and began to slay the people and destroy the city. And now it came to pass, before the Nephites could raise a sufficient army to drive them out of the land, they had destroyed the people who were in the city of Ammonihah, and also some around the borders of Noah, and taken others captive into the wilderness. (Alma 16:1–3)

Mormon continues his tale by recounting how the Nephite armies, with the assistance of Alma (who as high priest could receive revelations concerning enemy troop movements) defeated the Lamanites and rescued the captives. At this point, Mormon wants to make the moral of his story absolutely clear. His editorial summary emphasizes, in nonstandard grammar, that "there was not one soul of them had been lost that were taken captive," while "the people of Ammonihah were destroyed; yea, every living soul of the Ammonihahites was destroyed . . . and the carcasses were mangled by dogs and wild beasts of the wilderness" (Alma 16:8–10). The alternatives are clearly distinguished, and the good things that happen are truly wondrous, while the bad things are terrible indeed. In this way, our editor offers a striking illustration of God's justice, by which the righteous are saved while the wicked are punished.

But something is wrong with this picture. The innocent bystanders are all rescued, and the wicked Ammonihahites are all destroyed, but there is a third group not mentioned at all in Mormon's summary. These are the people "around the borders of Noah" who were also killed in the Lamanite raid. What exactly had happened to them? Why did they die, in contrast to their neighbors who were taken captive and then safely returned? We do not know, for they have dropped entirely out of Mormon's history and are never referred to again. Mormon obviously had some information about them—after all, he noted them in his initial account—but he chose not to elaborate upon their fate. Why? It seems that these inhabitants of the borderlands did not fit into the pattern of "the righteous prosper, the wicked suffer"; they complicated the moral message of his history. Nevertheless, it is significant that Mormon's urge for historical accuracy compelled him to mention them in the first place. The Book of Mormon is not exclusively dedicated to illustrating moral principles, though Mormon often simplifies or streamlines the facts to emphasize what he saw as transcendent spiritual realities.

Alma 16 also provides an intriguing example of multiple lines of causation, where we can see Mormon thinking through historical incidents both spiritually and politically. The first verse is remarkable for Mormon's insistence that this Lamanite raid was absolutely unexpected and unprovoked: "there having been much peace in the land of Zarahemla, there having been no wars nor contentions for a certain number of years." Given the juxtaposition of this event with the gross wickedness of the people of Ammonihah in the preceding chapters, the meaning is clear: an act of God destroyed the Ammonihahites in retribution for their arrogance, brutality, and rejection of his prophets.

Mormon reinforces this reading by framing the destruction with a prophecy. His editorial summary includes this observation: "Their great city [was destroyed], which they said God could not destroy, because of its greatness. But behold, in one day it was left desolate" (16:9–10). Here Mormon is referring to an exchange that took place much earlier in this particular narrative unit. Several chapters previously, the people of Ammonihah had rejected Alma's message: "We will not believe thy words if thou shouldst prophesy that this great city should be destroyed in one day." At that point Mormon commented, "Now they knew not that God could do such marvelous works, for they were a hard-hearted and a stiffnecked people" (Alma 9:4–5). In retrospect, Mormon suggests that the crowd had challenged not just Alma but God himself, and though Alma never quite said, *A single day will do it for you,* his warnings were nevertheless quite pointed: "[I]f ye persist in your wickedness . . . the Lamanites shall be sent upon you; and if ye repent not they shall come in a time when you know not, and ye shall be visited with utter destruction; and it shall be according to the fierce anger of the Lord" (Alma 9:18). Mormon's summary, which picks up a key phrase from the crowd at Ammonihah, alerts readers to the fact that everything that happened was a fulfillment of prophecy. Clearly, Ammonihah's destruction, as described in Alma 16, was a wondrous work of God manifesting his divine power and justice. God himself had sent the Lamanites upon them.

However, a little later in the book of Alma, chapter 25 offers an alternative explanation. The end of Ammonihah is recounted again, but this time it comes near the conclusion of another narrative unit, one that relates the missionary adventures of the sons of Mosiah among the Lamanites (Alma 17–27). It turns out that the city of Ammonihah was not destroyed as if by lightning from heaven. There was a perfectly natural sequence of causes and effects that led to the Lamanite raid, and this series of events was set in motion by Ammon and his brothers.

After the sad demise of Ammonihah, Alma and Amulek are traveling in the south (between the cities of Gideon and Manti, according to Mormon) when they meet Ammon and the other sons of Mosiah returning to Zarahemla after an absence of fourteen years. Alma 17 begins a lengthy flashback that recounts the events of those years. We learn that after an uncertain beginning marked by afflictions and miraculous deliverances, these missionaries enjoyed a decade of tremendous success during which they converted thousands of Lamanites, who took the name Anti-Nephi-Lehies and entered into a diplomatic relationship with the Nephites. Other Lamanites, incited by Nephite dissenters, were furious and took up arms against their newly converted brethren. These pacifist Anti-Nephi-Lehies chose to die rather than fight, and more than a thousand were killed.

We can turn now to Alma 25:

> And behold, now it came to pass that those Lamanites were more angry
> because they had slain their brethren; therefore they swore vengeance
> upon the Nephites; and they did no more attempt to slay the people of
> Anti-Nephi-Lehi at that time. But they took their armies and went over
> into the borders of the land of Zarahemla, and fell upon the people who
> were in the land of Ammonihah, and destroyed them. And after that,
> they had many battles with the Nephites, in the which they were driven
> and slain.

Here the flashback parallels the main narrative, but it does not entirely catch up until Alma 27:16, which continues the story from 17:5 and unites the two narratives. Such flashbacks and multiple accounts are complex editorial maneuvers, but Mormon handles them adroitly. Nevertheless, there are still evidences of extensive editing. For example, the "many battles" of Alma 25:3 and 27:1 do not quite correspond to the account in 16:6–9, where the Lamanites were driven back after one great battle, but this may be another example of Mormon trying not to unduly burden his narrative with unnecessary details that might distract readers from more important spiritual truths.

So in Alma 8–16 and 17–25, we find two separate narrative strands that both culminate in the destruction of Ammonihah, but the explanations given in each version are different. One is spiritual (due to God's justice) and one political (due to Lamanite aggressions in the aftermath of Anti-Nephi-Lehi conversions). Nevertheless, both seem equally valid; apparently God's will is sometimes manifest through ordinary historical means, and Mormon, as a historian as well as a moral guide, is interested in promoting both perspectives. Multiple explanations might seem to undermine an easy didacticism (as historical details often do), so Mormon gives the spiritual causation a bit of emphasis by telling that version first, and he also adds a later comment in which he reiterates that "the Lamanites had destroyed it [the city of Ammonihah] once because of the iniquity of the people" (Alma 49:3), even though the political causes have already been laid out for all to see.

Yet even here, a closer look reveals that Mormon is deliberately shifting his gaze away from other types of analysis for which he had evidence. He mentions Ammonihah again in Alma 49 because at that time, some eight years later, the Lamanites came back once more to attack Ammonihah, which had since been rebuilt. As I just noted, Mormon resumes his spiritual mode of interpretation when he reports their motives: "Because the Lamanites had destroyed it once because of the iniquity of the people, they supposed that it would again become an easy prey for them" (v. 3). There is an odd mix of perspectives here—even though Mormon is reporting Lamanite thoughts, they probably did not attribute their previous victory to being the instruments of God's wrath upon the wicked. In any case, their new offensive was turned back and the disappointed Lamanite armies moved on to the city of Noah (home of our edited-out unfortunates). However, in this passage Mormon offers a tactical, military explanation for the Nephites' earlier losses there: "The city of Noah had hitherto been the weakest part of the land" (v. 15). Apparently Mormon did know more about why so many of the inhabitants of Noah had met their deaths, but he chose not to share that information in Alma 16, because there it would have disrupted the clear moral point that he was trying to make. The fact that these parallel narratives and flashbacks, with their interlocking story lines and causes, are so deftly negotiated says something about Mormon's abilities as an editor/narrator.[31]

Even in this brief chapter survey we can see the tensions implicit in Mormon's historiographical project. He tries to portray himself as a careful editor who pays close attention to sources, accuracy, and historical details. Yet the situation is complicated by his ambition to write literature—to create complex, interlocking narratives that invite us to see more than he explicitly comments on, that are open to multiple interpretations, and that will repay repeated readings. At the same time, he wants his readers to draw particular moral lessons from his work. To that end, he guides them step by step through a much abbreviated account, deliberately choosing which facts to include or omit, suggesting appropriate emotional responses, and even occasionally telling them exactly how they should interpret specific events. Balancing his three agendas can be a delicate enterprise.

Generally Mormon is a practitioner of narrative theology; that is, he relies on stories to convince readers of the power of God, the consequences of sin, the reality of prophecy, and so forth. He certainly has a hand in fashioning his narratives for didactic and aesthetic purposes, but he cannot distort the history too much since the cogency of his argument depends on the accuracy of his facts: we should believe certain things because they are demonstrated by actual events of the past. (This appeal to history is keenly felt by Latter-day Saints today who believe that reading the Book of Mormon as myth or fiction would seriously compromise its authority and power to persuade.) In each of the three chapters that follow, as we work our way through Mormon's writings, we will explore in more detail one of the techniques listed above, taken from each of Mormon's three editorial roles: historian, literary artist, and moral guide. Then, as we approach the conclusion of the book of Third Nephi, we will see how the different components of Mormon's agenda are transcended when the direction of his project takes an unexpected turn.

5

Other Voices

Embedded Documents

The Book of Mormon, with its multiple records, plates, writers, and editors, is anything but a naive, straightforward narrative.[1] This makes it something of a puzzle. If Joseph Smith had intended to author a religious morality tale, either to gain converts or to make money, he could have written something much simpler. Latter-day Saints regard the integrated complexity of the text (especially in light of its oral dictation) as evidence of both its divine transmission and the contingencies of its origins as an actual historical record. Skeptics might point to the precedents of early modern novels by authors such as Aphra Behn, Samuel Richardson, Laurence Sterne, Jean-Jacques Rousseau, and Mary Shelley that similarly incorporated letters, memoirs, and diaries. Or they might note that Gothic novels of the eighteenth and nineteenth centuries offered a profusion of fictions framed as discovered-manuscript stories, including works by Hugh Walpole, Ann Radcliffe, Charles Maturin, and Edgar Allan Poe.[2] In any case, the Book of Mormon's use of embedded documents increases its verisimilitude, and though this was a literary device used in novels, it has also been one of the techniques by which historians have presented the past. Classical historians tended to focus more on speeches than documents, but both Thucydides and Josephus quote letters, and Ezra-Nehemiah includes memoirs, letters, royal decrees, and archival materials.[3] In fact, the book of Acts is something of a composite text, with stories, speeches, dialogues, and letters, but the unnamed narrator is much less of a presence than Mormon is in his history of the Nephites.

In his indispensable study of books that include accounts of their composition and transmission, Bernard Duyfhuizen introduced the term "hybrid narratives" to describe "texts that are patchworks of different documents that an extradiegetic narrator has pieced together to frame a coherent narrative."[4] The Book of Mormon fits this category with its three major sections comprising Nephi's memoirs, Mormon's edited history, and Moroni's additions. Furthermore, each of the major narrators includes documents within their contributions. In Nephi's writings, we saw entire chapters of Isaiah inserted into the narrative. These lengthy quotations tell us something of Nephi's relationship with scripture, particularly when he comments on, responds to, and reinterprets Isaiah's words so that they more clearly apply to his own situation and prophecies. Mormon uses embedded documents as well, but for different purposes (it is worth noting that he never inserts extended passages from scripture).[5] His abridgment of the Large Plates includes two chapters of a memoir by Zeniff, an edict of King Mosiah, a revelation to Alma$_1$, and six letters.[6] He also inserts as many as sixteen sermons into his history, depending on how one counts them, of which seven are explicitly identified as having been copied directly from preexisting sources.[7] Moroni's work includes five short liturgical items, two letters and a sermon from Mormon, and—in the most remarkable instance of textual appropriation in the Book of Mormon—an edited revision of a pre-Nephite chronicle from the Jaredite people (see Chapter 8 below).

All of this adds considerable interest to the narrative. As Duyfhuizen has noted, "To engage a text of hybrid narrative transmission is to engage a narrative matrix that connects different voices and different acts of writing within what appears to be a unified whole, yet such hybrid texts also enact a competition for priority among the linked, enclosed, or alternated narrations."[8] In the last chapter we saw Mormon working through some of the conflicts implicit in his desire to simultaneously serve history, literature, and theology. Here the tensions increase as various characters pull the narrative in different directions when they give voice to their own literary impulses. Nevertheless, the competition is never such that it throws into question the ultimate meaning of the work; Mormon is always the final arbiter, the editor who is using the words of others for his own ends. Our task, as readers, is to try to ascertain those ends, despite the fact that Mormon generally does not specify exactly why he is inserting particular documents. The only exception comes in the Words of Mormon, when he tells us that he added the Small Plates because they were "pleasing" to him, because they contained "prophesyings and revelations" (some of which had already been fulfilled), and, most importantly, because God told him to do so (W. of M. 1:4–7). For all the other embedded documents, we have to guess at Mormon's motives; or, rather, we get a chance to exercise our interpretive creativity and then test

our hypotheses against close readings of the text at hand. In this way, we gradually construct a coherent picture of our narrator by observing how he handles
his sources.

Some possibilities come to mind. From Mormon's perspective, the inclusion
of letters, sermons, and other writings might give his readers a better sense of the
past or more immediate access to events and personalities of long ago. Presenting
their voices directly could add variety and drama to his account. Inserted documents could also increase the historical value of his work and give it more of an
air of authenticity. Mormon simply may have admired the literary qualities of particular speeches and hesitated to substitute his own paraphrase for their original
eloquence. Or perhaps he wanted to give his audience a chance to respond directly
to the pleas and teaching of past prophets. And certainly such insertions slow down
the narrative and give emphasis to particularly significant incidents. These sorts of
motivations probably apply across the board, but examining a few specific instances
will give us a better sense of exactly why and how Mormon inserts documents into
his narrative.

Memoirs: The Record of Zeniff

In Daniel Defoe's *Robinson Crusoe*, the narrator—some fifty pages into his
story—tells how he found writing materials in the shipwreck and started to make
a record: "I began to keep my Journal, of which I shall here give you the Copy
(tho' it will be told all these Particulars over again) as long as it lasted, for having
no more Ink I was force'd to leave it off."[9] He then reproduces several months'
worth of short entries, though he gradually begins to add reflective comments
(marked by the refrain "But I return to my Journal . . ."), and then he eventually
drops the device of quoting from his diary entirely, presumably because, as we
were warned, at some point in his island sojourn he ran out of ink. It is a remarkable device, which allows Defoe to perform some complex literary maneuvers.
According to Michael Seidel:

> By making the journal an entry of sorts into the larger narrative, Defoe
> can write time in two senses, the mimetic time of the experience and the
> reflective time that writing produces or encourages. The process reveals
> to the reader the kinds of transformations that take place between the
> recording of events in a story and the understanding of events that
> constitute the novelistic telling of that story. Mimetic journal time is
> documentary, dating the action; reflective narrative time is retrospective,
> patterning the action.[10]

A similar narratological transition can be found at Mosiah 9–10 when Mormon inserts the first-person memoirs of Zeniff, yet the disjunction is even greater than in *Robinson Crusoe* since the document was written by someone else, the demarcation of document and narration is sharper, and the shift in chronological perspective is measured in centuries rather than decades. Nevertheless, we see the same distinction between the immediate time of the original experience and Mormon's much later reflective time.

Mormon had mentioned in the previous chapter that Limhi (the king of the Nephite colony) had brought out the records of his people so that Ammon$_2$ (the leader of the rescue party from the Nephite capital, Zarahemla; *not* Ammon$_3$, the missionary to the Lamanites a generation later) could read them, and then, quite suddenly, we ourselves are reading those same records.[11] In the middle of Limhi and Ammon's conversation, we encounter a brief heading: "*The Record of Zeniff—An account of his people, from the time they left the land of Zarahemla until the time that they were delivered out of the hands of the Lamanites*" (Mosiah 9: headnote). These editorial guideposts occur regularly in the Book of Mormon, and they were part of the original dictation rather than later additions to the text. The subject of this particular heading encompasses thirteen and a half chapters, from Mosiah 9:1 to 21:27, where the conversation between the two men, Limhi and Ammon, is resumed, yet even within this block of material, chapters 9 and 10 constitute a distinct unit. Without much warning, we hear the voice of Zeniff, writing almost five hundred years before Mormon: "I, Zeniff, having been taught in all the language of the Nephites..." Third-person narration returns at the beginning of chapter 11, when Zeniff's kingship ends: "And now it came to pass that Zeniff conferred the kingdom upon Noah, one of his sons."

Mormon, of course, knows how Zeniff's attempt to found a Nephite colony in Lamanite territory will turn out (i.e., not happily; hence the need for Ammon to rescue the enslaved people of King Limhi), but the fact that Zeniff does not have the same knowledge allows readers to imaginatively reexperience the hope and promise and gradual realizations of that initial generation firsthand. It is much like the way that Defoe captures the adventure, wonder, and anguish of Crusoe's first months on the island by reproducing his protagonist's journal, written at a time when the shipwrecked man had no idea whether he would survive, let alone return to civilization.

Perhaps the most striking thing about Zeniff's personal record is its introduction of a character who does not seem to follow the rules of Book of Mormon narration. In order to communicate their theological principles clearly, both Mormon and Nephi present morally unambiguous figures. Notwithstanding momentary lapses such as Lehi's murmuring (1 Ne. 16:20) or Nephi's self-recriminations

(2 Ne. 4:17–29), it is rarely difficult to distinguish the heroes from the villains, and even those individuals who are transformed by conversion, such as Alma$_2$ and Zeezrom, are often catapulted from extreme wickedness to extreme righteousness. (Remarkably, there are no stories like the biblical accounts of Saul or David about good men who fall; all the tragedy in the Book of Mormon happens on a national rather than a personal level.)

Zeniff, by contrast, resists easy categorization. He is a basically decent fellow, yet despite his good intentions nearly everything he attempts turns out disastrously. Indeed, he seems to subvert the regular pattern of "righteousness leads to prosperity." His morally indeterminate status, along with the self-reflection that leads him to write candidly about his mistakes and weaknesses, makes him one of the most intriguing personalities in the Book of Mormon, at least according to modern sensibilities. What follows is a reading of his story, as set within the Book of Mormon's internal historical framework.

Initial Attempt to Regain the Land of Nephi (Mosiah 9:1–2)

We first meet Zeniff as a rather ineffective spy, whose talents in espionage and reconnaissance are undermined by a virtue—compassion:

> I, Zeniff, having been taught in all the language of the Nephites, and
> having had a knowledge of the land of Nephi, or of the land of our fathers'
> first inheritance, and having been sent as a spy among the Lamanites that
> I might spy out their forces, that our army might come upon them and
> destroy them—but when I saw that which was good among them I was
> desirous that they should not be destroyed. (Mosiah 9:1)

Zeniff has a remarkable ability to see the good in others, for earlier record keepers such as Enos and Jarom found nothing of value in Lamanite culture (compare Enos 1:20 and Jarom 1:6–7).[12] Yet Zeniff, as a man of peace, argues that the Nephites should make a treaty with the Lamanites and regain the land of their inheritance through negotiation rather than by conquest.

This might seem a laudable, ethically superior approach, but unfortunately most of Zeniff's companions shared the more traditional attitudes of hostility and suspicion toward the Lamanites and would hear none of it. Zeniff, however, was a persuasive speaker, and he swayed so many of the troops that their commander felt that his mission (and perhaps his authority) was in danger of being compromised. He accordingly ordered Zeniff's summary execution. The Book of Mormon provides two accounts of what happened next. The first is from the book of Omni, in the Small Plates (the speaker is a minor narrator named Amaleki):

> And now I would speak somewhat concerning a certain number who went up into the wilderness to return to the land of Nephi; for there was a large number who were desirous to possess the land of their inheritance. Wherefore, they went up into the wilderness. And their leader being a strong and mighty man, and a stiffnecked man, wherefore he caused a contention among them; and they were all slain, save fifty, in the wilderness, and they returned again to the land of Zarahemla. (Omni 1:27–28)

Zeniff also places the blame for their failed expedition on this unnamed leader, but he does not neglect to mention his own role in the disaster:

> Therefore, I contended with my brethren in the wilderness, for I would that our ruler should make a treaty with them; but he, being an austere and a blood-thirsty man, commanded that I should be slain; but I was rescued by the shedding of much blood; for father fought against father, and brother against brother, until the greater number of our army was destroyed in the wilderness; and we returned, those of us that were spared, to the land of Zarahemla, to relate that tale to their wives and their children. (Mosiah 9:2)

Zeniff's moral arguments won him supporters (note that it was not just his family members who came to his rescue; he explicitly states that these issues overpowered family loyalties), and yet there is a terrible irony here, for an admirable desire to show kindness to one's enemies has directly led to the slaughter of one's allies and relatives.

Both accounts clearly fix the blame on an obstinate, unreasonable leader, but moral vindication does not bring back the dead, and Zeniff acknowledges the tragedy of the situation in his last sentence. We might expect those who had narrowly escaped such a harrowing and unexpected catastrophe to return gratefully to their own wives and children, but Zeniff does not say, *We related this tale to* our *wives and* our *children*. Rather, he indicates that it was the sad duty of the survivors to try to explain the terrible turn of events to the dependents of the men whom they themselves had killed. Ever consistent, in this way Zeniff once again demonstrates a humane compassion for his enemies, and we're able to make these sorts of engaging interpretations precisely because Mormon left this document intact; a paraphrase would not have communicated with the same level of detail and nuance.

Second Attempt to Regain the Land of Nephi (Mosiah 9:3–9)

One can imagine how Zeniff might have advertised the next expedition—promising that this time things would be different, that they would be committed to peaceful means from the beginning, that he would be a different kind of leader—but it is hard to understand why he still wanted this particular territory so badly. He himself frankly admits that he was "over-zealous to inherit the land of our fathers" (Mosiah 9:3), and the same phrase was later used by his grandson King Limhi (Mosiah 7:21). Apparently this explanation was the one that became enshrined in family tradition.[13] Whatever his motivations might have been, Zeniff was certainly aware that they would be reliving sacred history in the very place where it had first occurred some four hundred years earlier—this second attempt at establishing a settlement, unlike their earlier experience but similar to that of Lehi, would include women and children.

In his record, Zeniff manages to combine time-honored scriptural themes with his own unique sensibilities:

> After many days' wandering in the wilderness [*just like Lehi*] we pitched our tents in the place where our brethren were slain [*why revisit that terrible site? for a moment of reflection? a memorial service?*], which was near to the land of our fathers [*this proximity makes the failure of the last attempt all the more poignant: they almost made it*].[14] (Mosiah 9:4)

This time Zeniff's plan is carried through smoothly. Instead of relying on the force of arms to conquer their enemies, they negotiate a treaty with the Lamanite king (who rather callously expels his own people from the territory in question), and Zeniff's colonists are able to "possess the land in peace" (Mosiah 9:5). They immediately set about tilling the earth and rebuilding the very cities in which Nephi and Jacob had once lived. Indeed, it looks as if Zeniff's peaceful, principled tactics have carried the day. Unfortunately, what we have here is a slow-motion disaster in the making, for within two generations Zeniff's people will be enslaved by the very Lamanites who now appear so accommodating and reasonable.

First War with the Lamanites (Mosiah 9:10–10:5)

Toward the end of his life, when Zeniff was writing his personal history, he realized that he had been overly optimistic, even naive. He saw then what he could not see at the time, that "it was the cunning and the craftiness of King Laman, to bring my people into bondage, that he yielded up the land that we might possess it" (v. 10). Apparently this realization came with Zeniff's gradual maturation as a leader.

The king of the Lamanites had made an investment, banking on the industriousness of the colonists and the simmering resentment of his own displaced people, and from the beginning he planned to reconquer the Land of Nephi just as soon as Zeniff's people had made it productive (vv. 10–12). The Lamanites attacked in the thirteenth year of Zeniff's reign, and Zeniff responded admirably, showing himself to be a resourceful, humane leader. When his people appealed to him for protection, he organized them and armed them with "all manner of weapons which we could invent" (Mosiah 9:16), and then led them to battle himself. He describes the conflict in scriptural terms:

> Yea, in the strength of the Lord did we go forth to battle against the
> Lamanites; for I and my people did cry mightily to the Lord that he
> would deliver us out of the hands of our enemies, for we were awakened
> to a remembrance of the deliverance of our fathers. (v. 17)

Once again Zeniff is aware of reliving sacred history, and this time he explicitly draws our attention to the parallels. As in earlier, now legendary times, the Lord "did hear [their] cries and did answer [their] prayers" (v. 18; cf. 2 Ne. 4:23–24; Jacob 7:22), and on this occasion they were able to drive the Lamanites completely out of their land.

Zeniff ends his narrative of this first war with a body count, and not surprisingly (from his own providential point of view), more than ten times as many Lamanites as Nephites lost their lives in the fighting. Zeniff takes care to provide exact, uneven numbers of the dead, including the dead Lamanites—3,043—but he does not exult over his slain foes. We might suspect that his careful counting is evidence of his concern for his enemies as individuals, and this conjecture seems to be borne out by his sad comment, "And I, myself, with mine own hands, did help to bury their dead" (v. 19). Not *our* dead, but *their* dead.

Despite the Nephites' miraculous victory, there is nevertheless a sense of loss here. Zeniff's youthful enthusiasm has been transformed by his encounter with the concrete conditions of the world. He had assumed that reasonableness, moral principles, and hard work were all that he needed to achieve his ambitions, and he had counted on the integrity and honor of others. In this he was sorely disappointed. His assessment of Lamanite culture in verse 12 is fairly harsh ("lazy," "idolatrous," eager to "glut themselves with the labors of our hands"), and when he surveys the results of his policies, it is with "sorrow and lamentation" (v. 19). Reluctantly, the man of peace has become a man of war. Yet he seems to have retained his faith in God, his connection to his heritage, and his compassion.

Chapter 10 begins with an acknowledgment of the compromises involved in his new, sadder but wiser perspective: "We again began to possess the land in peace. And I caused that there should be weapons of war made of every kind" (v. 1). It is a painful but necessary juxtaposition. Although he speaks of "continual peace" (v. 5) for the next nine years, both he and his people know that sooner or later the Lamanites will be back.

Second War with the Lamanites (Mosiah 10:6–22)

A change in leadership among the Lamanites provided the impetus for renewed conflict. King Laman's son, undoubtedly impatient with his father's defeat and withdrawal, came to the throne and immediately launched another round of fighting. Zeniff and his people were prepared this time, in part because Zeniff had seen fit to send out spies (the same activity that had gotten him into so much trouble in his younger days; Mosiah 9:1).

In his memoirs, Zeniff describes the advance of the Lamanites (attacking from the opposite direction this time; compare Mosiah 9:14 and 10:8), as well as their weapons and their fearsome appearance. He recounts the mass mobilization of the colonists and their attempts to hide their women and children, and then he writes:

> And it came to pass that we did go up to battle against the Lamanites;
> and I, even I, in my old age, did go up to battle against the Lamanites.
> And it came to pass that we did go up in the strength of the Lord to
> battle. (v. 10)

At this point readers might reasonably expect an account of the battle and its outcome, but Zeniff keeps us in suspense. In fact, he does not resume his narrative until verse 20.

Modern scholars of literature have identified a rhetorical pattern that they have labeled "suspension." This is where a speaker or an author will build to a climax, but just before that moment, when he has the audience's full attention, he backs off and makes them wait just a bit. This has the effect of heightening the suspense, but it also allows the author to slip in something of importance while he has his readers at the edge of their seats.[15] This is exactly what Zeniff does in this case, and the intervening material is remarkable, for it is nothing less than an explanation of the war—*from the Lamanites' perspective.*

The problem, as Zeniff explains, is that the Lamanites have been deceived by the traditions of their fathers. He then proceeds to offer the Lamanite version of history:

> Believing that they were driven out of the land of Jerusalem because of
> the iniquities of their fathers, and that they were wronged in the wilder-
> ness by their brethren, and they were also wronged while crossing the
> sea; and again, that they were wronged while in the land of their first
> inheritance, after they had crossed the sea . . . (vv. 12–13)

In fact, some of what the Lamanites say makes sense. Nephi did usurp the leadership positions of his elder brothers, he did take the Brass Plates (family property) when he abandoned his kin, and perhaps King Laman did see his plot to enslave the colonists as a just recompense for hundreds of years of Nephite insults and slights.

Zeniff goes on to point out that this alternative version of Book of Mormon history is flawed because it does not take into account Nephi's faithfulness and the ignorance and rebelliousness of Laman and Lemuel, but it is extraordinary that he both knows the Lamanites' point of view and takes it seriously enough to offer a reply—in prime time, as it were. There is no comparable passage in the rest of the Book of Mormon.[16] Zeniff might have simply chosen to tell us of his sympathy for his benighted foes, but instead he *shows* us through the literary organization of his narrative (and Mormon takes advantage of this well-crafted rendition by quoting it directly, as an embedded document).

This digression turns out in verse 19 to have been part of Zeniff's exhortation to his men before they went into battle, and this also is worthy of comment, for one might expect a commander to demonize his enemies rather than suggest that they are fundamentally decent men who have been defrauded by their leaders. Apparently Zeniff continues to believe that reason and compassion are appropriate responses to evil, even though in the end he is forced to acknowledge that he himself, through his gullibility, is responsible for their current predicament: "For this very cause has King Laman, by his cunning, and lying craftiness, and his fair promises, deceived me, that I have brought this my people up into this land, that they may destroy them" (v. 18).

After all this, the description of the battle itself is somewhat anticlimactic, taking only a single verse: "And it came to pass that we did drive them again out of our land; and we slew them with a great slaughter, even so many that we did not number them" (v. 20). The fact that the Nephites did not bother to count the dead this time may be an indication of Zeniff's weariness and dwindling idealism. Two more verses finish Zeniff's record: his people return to their peaceful occupations, and Zeniff himself confers the kingdom on one of his sons with the concluding words, "And may the Lord bless my people. Amen" (v. 22).

And Back to Mormon

At the end of his reign, Zeniff could view his well-intentioned decisions as the cause of a great deal of death and disappointment—"we have suffered these many years in the land" (Mosiah 10:18)—but the settlement was still intact and its inhabitants had been protected by God. What Zeniff could not see was how quickly all of this would fall apart after his death. As Mormon picks up the story in Mosiah 11, it is clear that Zeniff's final act perpetuated the unhappy pattern of his life, for his last disaster was his son, who in LDS Sunday school classes is usually referred to as "wicked King Noah." Noah's evil example corrupted his people, lost for them the favor of the Lord, and led to their enslavement by the Lamanites after they had rejected and executed the prophet Abinadi. Zeniff had been so anxious to see the good in everyone, and so unrealistic in his assessments of crucial situations, that perhaps even as a father he was excessively lenient and long-suffering, at least with this particular son.[17]

What in the end are we to make of Zeniff? His life is punctuated by a series of disasters, which are all the more pitiable because they are at least partly the result of his good impulses. The very qualities that we might most admire in him—tenacity, adherence to moral principles, compassion—are easily seen as faults when his plans go awry, and he is consequently remembered as being over-zealous, naive, and a poor judge of character. Yet these mistakes seem to be something less than sins, and we may feel that Zeniff got less from life than he deserved.

As Mormon resumes his third-person narration, it is reasonable to ask why he chose to insert Zeniff's memoir as an intact document. John Paul Riquelme, in an article on James Joyce's *Portrait of the Artist as a Young Man*, has observed how literary techniques such as inserted diary entries "interrupt and disrupt the semblance of a continuous flow of narrative" and "draw attention to the text's artifice, to its status as art, and to themselves as relatively independent of the text in which they are found."[18] The Record of Zeniff is an unexpected, disrupting presence within Mormon's history, yet its inclusion was obviously the result of a conscious editorial decision, which must have been intended to communicate something particular. Mormon, however, barely registers the transition and does not provide any explicit explanation. Zeniff does not seem to have been particularly eloquent, even though his account—with its poignant details, nicely timed disclosures, contrasts, and repetitions—makes for a coherent, well-constructed narrative.[19] He also never mentions Jesus or Christian theology, unlike most of the rest of Mormon's embedded documents. Yet Zeniff does have an engaging and distinctive voice, which Mormon conveys directly to his readers.

It may be that Mormon was impressed by Zeniff's example of faith despite unexpected hardships, his devotion to his people, and his compassion for his enemies. He undoubtedly identified with Zeniff's predicament of trying to protect his outnumbered people from imminent destruction by the Lamanites, and Mormon could have wondered about the wisdom of the treaty he himself had negotiated—the only other treaty, besides Zeniff's, mentioned in the Book of Mormon (Morm. 2:28; cf. Mosiah 7:21, 9:2). Yet perhaps the most likely reason Mormon slowed down and particularized his narrative at Zeniff's founding of a colony was because it was a pivotal moment in Nephite history. Even though the colony eventually failed (something that Zeniff feared but did not live to see), Mormon knew that this settlement was the origin of both the Nephite Christian church and a line of prophets who would dominate the years leading up to the coming of Christ. These leaders included the two Almas, the two Helamans, and the two later Nephis.

Sermons: Benjamin and Alma

By reproducing the Record of Zeniff as part of his account of the Nephite colony in the (Lamanite-held) Land of Nephi, Mormon was able to introduce his readers to a particular voice and sensibility. For other embedded sources, however, there is no question that Mormon inserted them verbatim because of their significance as founding, or even canonical, documents. One example is the speech that King Benjamin delivered when he appointed his son Mosiah$_2$ as the new king over the combined peoples of the Nephites and Mulekites (Mosiah 2–6). Everyone gathered at the temple in Zarahemla for the occasion and a written transcript was made (2:1–8). Benjamin's discourse appears to be an attempt to unify his people along religious lines at a time when political tensions would have been high. In the previous generation, Benjamin's father, King Mosiah$_1$, had led a group of Nephites to the land of Zarahemla, where they had discovered the Mulekites, another party who had come from Jerusalem to the Americas several hundred years earlier, but who had quickly lost their memory of Hebrew culture—the narrator explains that this was because "they had brought no records with them" (Omni 1:17). The two groups merged, and although the Mulekites were more numerous, they adopted the Nephite language and scriptures, and they accepted Mosiah as their king (Omni 1:14–19). It has been suggested that there were Mulekites who still resented their loss of status, and if so, a transfer of power—endeavoring to keep it firmly in Nephite hands—would have been a delicate political maneuver.[20]

On this occasion, Benjamin spoke of the future coming of Jesus into the world (according to prophecies that were given to him by an angel) and then invited his subjects to think of themselves as "children of Christ," an alternative identity that would supersede old ethnic divisions. This new status was confirmed by both a covenant and a roster:

> And now, King Benjamin thought it was expedient, after having finished
> speaking to the people, that he should take the names of all those who
> had entered into a covenant with God to keep his commandments. And
> it came to pass that there was not one soul, except it were little children,

but who had entered into the covenant and had taken upon them the name of Christ. (Mosiah 6:1–2)

Nearly a century later people were still talking about this day of national significance—Helaman says, "Remember, remember, my sons, the words which King Benjamin spake unto his people" (Hel. 5:9; cf. Mosiah 3:17)—and in the intervening years there had been many more oblique references to it.

Three years after Benjamin's speech, when Ammon discovered the remnants of Zeniff's colony, he "rehearse[d] unto them the last words which King Benjamin had taught them" and put them under the same covenant (Mosiah 8:3, 21:32). In the next generation, Alma$_2$ attempted to renew the covenant in Zarahemla with a speech that reiterated many of Benjamin's key terms, such as experiencing a "mighty change" of heart (Alma 5:14 || Mosiah 5:2) and being spiritually begotten or born of God (Alma 5:14 || Mosiah 5:7). When Amulek tried to bring the dissident Zoramites back into the Nephite mainstream, he taught them in the language of King Benjamin. Compare Amulek's warning that "ye have become subjected to the spirit of the devil, and he doth seal you his; therefore, the Spirit of the Lord hath withdrawn from you, and hath no place in you . . . and this I know, because the Lord hath said he dwelleth not in unholy temples" with Benjamin's original words: "[I]f ye should . . . withdraw yourselves from the Spirit of the Lord, that it may have no place in you . . . [the Lord] dwelleth not in unholy temples" (Alma 34:35–36; Mosiah 2:36–37). An even more ominous contrast is with a later section of Benjamin's speech, where he had promised the righteous that it would be Christ (rather than the devil, as in Amulek's admonition) who would "seal you his" (Mosiah 5:15). Of course, we can perceive these kinds of repetitions, contrasts, and variations only because Mormon chose to insert Benjamin's discourse into his history as an intact document.[21] And if problems later appeared with "many of the rising generation that could not understand the words of King Benjamin, being little children at the time he spake unto his people" (Mosiah 26:1), Mormon wanted to be sure to give his readers an opportunity to experience the full power of Benjamin's words, so that they too might have an opportunity to covenant to accept Christ and "impart of [their] substance to the poor" (Mosiah 4:26), a phrase that Mormon himself uses in recounting Alma's preaching at Zarahemla (Alma 4:13), along with "retaining a remission of sins" (Alma 4:14 || Mosiah 4:12, 26)

In the absence of explicit citations, however, we might wonder if verbal parallels indicate deliberate quotations and allusions, or whether they might best be explained as due to the common language and phrasing of Joseph Smith, either as translator or as author. Yet there are many instances where the correspondence between phrases is unique, or nearly so. To take just a few examples from the previous paragraph, the idiom "change of heart," with all its variations, appears nine times in the Book of Mormon, seven of which are in Mosiah 5 (Benjamin's speech) and Alma 5 (Alma's speech at Zarahemla).[22] "Seal you his" is found only twice, "no place in you" occurs in just three verses (those cited above, plus Alma 30:42), and "retaining a remission of sins" (including all variations) appears only in Alma 4 and Mosiah 4. In such cases, it seems reasonable to conclude that the speakers of these distinctive terms do indeed have King Benjamin's earlier words in mind. It would be interesting to track various phrases throughout the Book of Mormon to determine which Nephite prophets were particularly influenced by which of their predecessors (for instance, Alma$_2$ shows an affinity for the words of Abinadi), but it is nevertheless immediately evident that Mormon himself is quite impressed with Alma$_2$.[23] Of the seven sermons that he quoted directly from his sources, six are attributed to this man (often called "Alma the Younger" by Latter-day Saints, though that appellation never appears in the Book of Mormon; for the remainder of this chapter, the name "Alma" will refer to Alma$_2$ unless otherwise noted).

Alma is, in fact, one of the most compelling figures in the Book of Mormon. As a rebellious son, he shared the name but not the religious sensibilities of his father, Alma the Elder, who had founded a Christian church amongst the Zeniffite colonists about 150 BC (earlier prophets had preached of Christ, but Alma the Elder seems to have been the first to organize institutionalized worship and begin baptizing). Both Alma$_1$'s people and the people of King Limhi escaped from Lamanite bondage and returned to the main body of Nephites at Zarahemla. This story of deliverance is not, however, a happy ending because Alma the Younger (along with the four sons of King Mosiah) spent his days undermining the very church his father was trying to cultivate. Nevertheless, after a dramatic encounter with a reproving angel, he changed his ways and later became both the chief judge of the Nephites and high priest of the church.

A Composite Portrait Through Documents

When we first meet Alma, he is introduced as "a man of many words [who] did speak much flattery to the people; therefore he led many of the people to do after the manner of his iniquities" (Mosiah 27:8). After his miraculous conversion, he turns those same skills to reclaiming souls, and his speeches are remarkable for their variety, argument, doctrinal clarity, and audience specificity. These qualities can be seen in three back-to-back sermons that he delivered to three different cities in quite distinct spiritual situations—Zarahemla (wavering between good and evil), Gideon (righteous), and Ammonihah (wicked)—as part of the Nephite Reformation (Alma 4–16). (Mormon tells us in passing that Alma's preaching tour included two more cities, Melek and Sidom, and that Alma enjoyed success in both places, but we do not learn anything about his sermons there, not even in a quick paraphrased summary, perhaps because they would not have fit into Mormon's expository scheme; see Alma 8:3–5, 15:13–14.) By including so many of Alma's own words, Mormon makes it possible for us to form a fairly clear picture of the man and his personality.

The three sermons are stylistically varied, but the general messages are similar, and several of the same themes and even phrases recur.[24] All three discourses include a command to repent and be baptized, a caution that time is short, quotations of angels or the Spirit, references to deliverance and redemption through Christ, appeals to spiritual knowledge, and a warning that the wicked cannot "inherit the kingdom of God/heaven." Two of the three sermons highlight the need to remember the captivity of their fathers (5:4–6, 9:8–11, 22), hold forth the hope of someday sitting down in the kingdom of God/heaven (5:24, 7:25), and employ the phrases "bands of death" (5:7–10, 7:12), "only Begotten of the Father, full of grace . . . and truth" (5:48, 9:26), and "born again" (5:49, 7:14). Much of this may seem generic to the Book of Mormon (especially the New Testament concepts and phrases), but several of these items are in fact characteristic of Alma's speech patterns. That is to say, rather than being part of Joseph Smith's general religious vocabulary, they show up in the Book of Mormon in very specific contexts; they seem to be indicative of the way that Alma views the world.

Take, for instance, "only Begotten of the Father, full of grace . . . and truth." The expression is derived from John 1:14 and occurs only three times in the Book of Mormon, each time in the words of Alma (the additional reference is Alma 13:9). "Sit down . . . in the kingdom of God/heaven" originates with Matthew 8:11 and Luke 13:29, but the phrase is not pervasive in the Book of Mormon; rather, it seems to have been a favorite of Alma's (Alma 5:24, 7:25, 29:17, 38:15).[25] "Bands of death" (not in the Bible) appears twelve times in the Book of Mormon: once in Mormon's account of why Alma began his preaching journey (Alma 4:14), four times in Alma's sermons, once in Amulek's defense of Alma (Alma 11:41), and five times in Abinadi's words. This means that "bands of death" is almost exclusively associated with Alma and Abinadi, who was the prophet Alma cited at 5:11: "[D]id not my father Alma believe in the words which were delivered by the mouth of Abinadi?"[26] This close connection between the two prophets (which we have already noted above) makes sense in terms of the story, in which recalling Abinadi and his words is precisely what Alma is encouraging his listeners to do.

Random variation might be a possible explanation for patterns like this, but three of Alma's distinctive expressions follow the logic of the narrative exactly:

(1) At Zarahemla, Alma asks his audience if they have "sufficiently retained in remembrance the captivity of [their] fathers" (Alma 5:6); at Ammonihah he

similarly asks, "Do ye not remember that our father, Lehi, was brought out of Jerusalem by the hand of God . . . have ye forgotten so soon how many times he delivered our fathers out of the hands of their enemies," later reminding them how their fathers had been "brought out of bondage time after time" (Alma 9:9–10, 22). At Alma 29:12 he exclaims, "Yea, I have always remembered the captivity of my fathers." When counseling his son Helaman (in another embedded document), he says, "I would that ye should do as I have done, in remembering the captivity of our fathers, for they were in bondage, and none could deliver them except [God]" (Alma 36:2). And then, not very surprisingly, after two dozen verses he again picks up the theme: "Yea, and he has also brought our fathers out of the land of Jerusalem; and he has also, by his everlasting power, delivered them out of bondage and captivity from time to time even down to the present day. And I have always retained in remembrance their captivity; yea, and ye also ought to retain in remembrance, as I have done, their captivity" (Alma 36:29).[27] No one else in the Book of Mormon speaks like this.[28]

(2) In both Alma 5 (his speech at Zarahemla) and 7 (at Gideon), Alma uses the familiar phrase "born again." He is the only person in the Book of Mormon to do so. Similarly, the term "born of God" appears nine times in the Book of Mormon, and eight of those are in quotations from Alma.[29] Although several Nephite prophets preach about becoming children of God, these particular terms are nearly unique to Alma.

(3) All three sermons share the idea that the wicked cannot "inherit the kingdom of God/heaven," phrasing that is found in both First Corinthians and Galatians. In the Book of Mormon the expression occurs nine times, six of which are spoken by Alma (and two other occurrences—within a single sentence—are in the words of his missionary companion Amulek).[30]

What is striking about these characteristic speech patterns is that they were all central to Alma's conversion story. As recounted by Mormon in Mosiah 27, an angel reproached Alma for his wickedness and commanded: "Now I say unto thee, Go, and *remember the captivity of thy fathers* in the land of Helam [Alma₁'s settlement in the wilderness], and in the land of Nephi; and remember how great things he has done for them; *for they were in bondage, and he has delivered them*" (v. 16). Alma fell to the earth and was in a comalike state for three days. When he awoke he declared himself a changed man, saying:

> I have repented of my sins and have been redeemed of the Lord; behold I
> am born of the Spirit. And the Lord said unto me, "Marvel not that all
> mankind, yea, men and women, all nations, kindreds, tongues and
> people, must be *born again*; yea, *born of God*, changed from their carnal
> and fallen state, to a state of righteousness, being redeemed of God,
> becoming his sons and daughters. And thus they become new creatures;

and unless they do this, *they can in nowise inherit the kingdom of God.*"
(Mosiah 27:24–26)[31]

The nonrandom appearances of these phrases in the Book of Mormon are an indication of how deeply Alma was affected by this experience; he spent the rest of his days urging his people to remember the captivity of their fathers and to receive the same spiritual transformation that he had undergone.[32] Mormon highlights the coherence of Alma's life's work by providing the documents that allow us to correlate his message with the story of his conversion, at least in the version that Mormon originally narrated at the end of the book of Mosiah.

A Second Account of Alma's Conversion

In addition to the transcripts of sermons at Zarahemla, Gideon, and Ammonihah that Mormon works into his account of the Nephite Reformation, he similarly inserts into his history the texts of three speeches that Alma directed toward each of his sons (Alma 36–42), "according to his own record" (Alma 35:16). The first of these includes another detailed recital of his conversion (Alma 36:1–30), even though Mormon has already told this story at Mosiah 27:8–31, and we might ask what this second version contributes to our understanding (a third, abbreviated account, again in Alma's voice, appears at Alma 38:6–8, and there is a fourth at Alma 26:17–20).[33] To return once again to Mormon's three agendas, copying Alma's account verbatim allows Mormon to claim historical specificity (i.e., *this is how Alma actually came to understand his own experience, with no tendentious paraphrases or prejudicial phrasing on my part*), spiritual immediacy (in one of the most compelling expositions of the effects of the atonement to be found anywhere in the Book of Mormon), and literary quality (as will be seen in the care with which Alma has structured his account). Alma 36 is a remarkable piece of writing, and it is not surprising that Mormon chose to embed it whole into his narrative.

Alma is speaking to his oldest son, Helaman, and in verse 3 he offers a theological proposition: "Whosoever shall put their trust in God shall be supported in their trials, and their troubles, and their afflictions, and shall be lifted up at the last day." He claims firsthand knowledge of this principle and then tells a story that explains the origins of his certainty. What follows here is a rather lengthy quotation, but Alma's eloquent account deserves to be read in its entirety rather than in a quick paraphrase (verse numbers appear at the left margin):

5   "Now, behold, I say unto you, if I had not been born of God I should
       not have known these things; but God has, by the mouth of his holy
       angel, made these things known unto me, not of any worthiness of myself.

6   "For I went about with the sons of Mosiah, seeking to destroy the church of God; but behold, God sent his holy angel to stop us by the way.

7   And behold, he spake unto us, as it were the voice of thunder, and the whole earth did tremble beneath our feet; and we all fell to the earth, for

8   the fear of the Lord came upon us. But behold, the voice said unto me,

9   'Arise.' And I arose and stood up, and beheld the angel. And he said unto me, 'If thou wilt of thyself be destroyed, seek no more to destroy the church of God.'

10   "And it came to pass that I fell to the earth; and it was for the space of three days and three nights that I could not open my mouth, neither had I

11   the use of my limbs. And the angel spake more things unto me, which were heard by my brethren, but I did not hear them; for when I heard the words 'If thou wilt be destroyed of thyself, seek no more to destroy the church of God,' I was struck with such great fear and amazement lest perhaps I

12   should be destroyed, that I fell to the earth and I did hear no more. But I was racked with eternal torment, for my soul was harrowed up to the greatest degree and racked with all my sins.

13   "Yea, I did remember all my sins and iniquities, for which I was tormented with the pains of hell; yea, I saw that I had rebelled against my

14   God, and that I had not kept his holy commandments. Yea, and I had murdered many of his children, or rather led them away unto destruction; yea, and in fine, so great had been my iniquities, that the very thoughts of coming into the presence of my God did rack my soul with inexpressible

15   horror. 'Oh,' thought I, 'that I could be banished and become extinct both soul and body, that I might not be brought to stand in the presence of my

16   God, to be judged of my deeds.' And now, for three days and for three nights was I racked, even with the pains of a damned soul.

17   "And it came to pass that as I was thus racked with torment, while I was harrowed up by the memory of my many sins, behold, I remembered also to have heard my father prophesy unto the people concerning the coming of one Jesus Christ, a Son of God, to atone for the sins of the

18   world. Now, as my mind caught hold upon this thought, I cried within my heart, 'O Jesus, thou Son of God, have mercy on me, who am in the gall of bitterness, and am encircled about by the everlasting chains of

19   death.'

"And now, behold, when I thought this, I could remember my pains no more; yea, I was harrowed up by the memory of my sins no more. And

20   oh, what joy, and what marvelous light I did behold; yea, my soul was filled

21   with joy as exceeding as was my pain! Yea, I say unto you, my son, that

there could be nothing so exquisite and so bitter as were my pains. Yea, and again I say unto you, my son, that on the other hand, there can be

22   nothing so exquisite and sweet as was my joy. Yea, methought I saw, even as our father Lehi saw, God sitting upon his throne, surrounded with numberless concourses of angels, in the attitude of singing and praising

23   their God; yea, and my soul did long to be there. But behold, my limbs did receive their strength again, and I stood upon my feet, and did manifest unto the people that I had been born of God.

24   "Yea, and from that time even until now, I have labored without ceasing, that I might bring souls unto repentance; that I might bring them to taste of the exceeding joy of which I did taste; that they might also be

25   born of God, and be filled with the Holy Ghost. Yea, and now behold, O my son, the Lord doth give me exceedingly great joy in the fruit of my

26   labors. For because of the word which he has imparted unto me, behold, many have been born of God, and have tasted as I have tasted, and have s een eye to eye as I have seen; therefore they do know of these things of which I have spoken, as I do know; and the knowledge which I have is of God."[34]

This is a vivid, memorable account of conversion that completely overwhelms the rather generic doctrinal point ("trust in the Lord") that it was intended to support. In addition, although it features the appearance of an angel and an earthquake, the focus is on Alma's psychological state rather than on the miraculous nature of his experience; throughout the Book of Mormon angels are described in a fairly matter-of-fact manner. The heavenly messenger here does not symbolically or metaphorically stand in for something else; he is just part of the story, and that is at least part of what makes this a "realistic" or "history-like" narrative, despite its supernatural elements.

It would be easy at this point to become distracted by issues of fact and historicity, even apart from the appearance of an angel. One might casually regard this tale as a simple reworking of Paul's transformation on the road to Damascus (though there are significant differences as well as similarities),[35] or speculate on how it might reflect Joseph Smith's own conversion experience,[36] or observe how it mirrors other evangelical conversion narratives of the day,[37] or note the presence of key phrases from the King James Bible.[38] Latter-day Saints, however, have been eager to demonstrate that what makes this particular account remarkable—and distinct from other retellings of Alma's conversion story—is the way that Alma 36 is organized chiastically (as John Welch first noted in the

1960s); that is, key elements from the first half appear in reverse order in the second:

A. "born of God," personal knowledge (v. 5)

   B. an angel warns Alma not to "destroy the church of God" (vv. 6–9)

      C. he loses "the use of my limbs" (v. 10)

         [vv. 11–13 are a description of his fears and mental anguish]

         D. he is horrified at the thought of "coming into the presence of my God" (vv. 14–15)

            E. he is racked with "the pains of a damned soul" (v. 16)

               F. he is "harrowed up by the memory of my many sins" (v. 17)

                  G. he remembers a prophecy of "Jesus Christ, a son of God" (v. 18)

                  G. he prays to "Jesus, thou Son of God" for mercy (v. 18)

               F. he is "harrowed up by the memory of my sins no more" (v. 19)

            E. he experiences a joy as intense as his former "pains" (vv. 20–21)

         D. his soul longs to be in the presence of God (v. 22)

      C. his "limbs did receive their strength again" (v. 23)

   B. he describes his missionary labors (vv. 24–25)

A. "born of God," personal knowledge (v. 26)

The narrative contour of the chapter follows a trajectory that mirrors the chiastic arrangement of particular words and phrases. Alma starts by noting the captivity and deliverance of his ancestors (Alma 36:1–2); then he moves to the circumstances of his own life (vv. 3–10), followed by his interior about-face and vision of God (vv. 11–22), his postconversion activities (vv. 23–28a), and another recital of national history (vv. 28b–29). In this way, his account moves from public to personal to private and then back again (with a striking juxtaposition of physical and spiritual deliverance). It is noteworthy, however, that God is present in every phase. Indeed, the order and purposeful design of Alma 36 suggest a world in which God—like the writer—is in control, where the lives of individuals fit into some overarching (though perhaps not always immediately perceptible) plan. Mormon obviously believed that such a perspective was worth presenting directly to his readers.

A chiasmus like this, Latter-day Saint scholars assert, is evidence that the Book of Mormon is an authentic example of ancient Hebrew literature.[39] Readers might argue over how chiastic the passage really is (not all the elements fit neatly, though the overall pattern is unmistakable), whether this sort of repetition is indeed characteristic of Hebrew literature, whether nineteenth-century Americans were aware of biblical chiasmus, and so forth.[40] But most of these debates would be about Joseph Smith—what did he know and when could he have known it?—rather than about the Book of Mormon.

Within the framework of the narrative, which includes both Alma as the author of this document and Mormon as the general editor, this is a well-written, powerful account. Alma draws on direct experience to show us the anguish of the wicked, the crisis moment of conversion, and the joy of the redeemed. He demonstrates how to repent, how to call on Jesus, how to make amends through a life of service, and how to gain a personal knowledge of God. He describes a transition that is available to all readers, though perhaps on a less dramatic scale (minus the intervention of an angel or three days of physical paralysis). Alma tells this story because he wants his son to follow his example, and by inserting this tale as an embedded document, Mormon wants to pass the same message on to his readers.

It is true that Mormon could have communicated these ideas through a paraphrased rendition (as he did at Mosiah 27), but by presenting Alma's testimony in full, we can appreciate its form as well as its content. Whether or not it represents valid evidence for ancient origins, Alma 36 does reflect a careful, deliberate arrangement of the story. The reversing, balanced halves indicate that Alma had spent some time and effort organizing his memories of an event twenty years earlier into a rhetorically compelling, aesthetically pleasing form. This experience obviously meant a great deal to him, and at the end of his career, when trying to provide guidance and counsel to his oldest son, he gives the story its most definitive, literary rendering. Just as his conversion to Christianity marked a major turning point in his life, so also his appeal to Jesus in verse 18 is, quite literally, the pivotal moment in his narrative.[41]

Along with a distinctive structure, Alma's language is evocative. He speaks of being "harrowed up" and "racked with torment," of pain and joy that were equally "exquisite," and of a happiness so acute that he could taste it.[42] This is not a dispassionate recitation of fact; rather, it is a lyrical mode of expression meant to engage his son—and whoever else might read his transcript—emotionally; he wants them to imagine themselves in his situation, to stir in them a desire to feel what he has felt. He also emphasizes the intensely personal nature of his experience. After one sentence from the angel, he loses contact with the outside world and the only direct quotations that follow are of his own voice, in his own mind. This effectively downplays the fervent prayers on his behalf described in Mosiah 27 and even the appearance of the angel (who has much more to say in Mormon's earlier version)— apparently a provocative word from anyone, at just the right moment, might be enough to propel a hearer on an inner spiritual journey toward redemption.

Letters: Helaman

Mormon includes six letters in his abridgment, and all but one of these appear within a block of eight chapters at the end of the book of Alma (chs. 54–61).[43] Each was either written by or to Helaman$_2$ or Captain Moroni (that is, Moroni$_1$— not to be confused with the narrator, Moroni$_2$, his namesake who lived about five centuries later). These embedded documents once again add vividness and variety to Mormon's account, as we hear the voices of major characters directly and get a chance to imagine how we might have responded to receiving such epistles. And it is worth noting that information concerning Helaman's campaigns on the western front is conveyed nearly entirely through his correspondence, which includes the story of the two thousand stripling warriors whose courage and faith have inspired generations of Latter-day Saint youth (Alma 56–58). Yet the fact that almost all these epistolary sources occur in a fairly tight cluster raises questions. Why in this section of his history—and only here—does Mormon tell his story primarily through letters? (Again, some readers may find my descriptions of Mormon and Helaman jarringly historical, but the point is to make sense of the narrative from within its own parameters—a task not entirely foreign to close readings of fiction.)

The urgency of Alma's chiastic retelling of his conversion story at Alma 36 may make us wonder about his relationship with Helaman, the original recipient of those remarks. Helaman was Alma's oldest son and successor as high priest, yet this was the one son he did not take with him on his missionary journey to the Zoramites at Antionum (Alma 31:6–7). Perhaps Helaman had other obligations that kept him at home, but there may have been spiritual concerns as well. It sounds as if Alma desperately wanted Helaman to take his words to heart, and Alma 36 is the most complete account of his conversion we have, as well as the one that focuses most intently on both the pains and joys that he felt. By contrast, we see only an abbreviated version in his words to his second son, Shiblon, along with an acknowledgment of Shiblon's faithfulness and diligence (Alma 38:2–3; there is no similar praise for Helaman in chs. 36–37).[44] The rest of Alma's lecture to Helaman is a charge to receive, safeguard, and update the sacred records in his possession (Alma 37), so it comes as something of a surprise when we learn some fourteen chapters later, after Alma's death, that Helaman had not been his first choice to be the next keeper of the records:

> And it came to pass that in the same year that the people of Nephi had peace restored unto them, that Nephihah, the second chief judge, died, having filled the judgment-seat with perfect uprightness before God. Nevertheless, he had refused Alma to take possession of those records and those things which were esteemed by Alma and his fathers to be most sacred; therefore, Alma had conferred them upon his son, Helaman. (Alma 50:37–38)

Perhaps Alma had a premonition about the literary abilities of this particular son. Helaman seems to have gotten off to a reasonable start—at least Mormon gives him some credit when he inserts a headnote at the beginning of Alma 45: "*the account of the people of Nephi . . . according to the record of Helaman, which he kept in his days*"—but once he is swept up in the traumatic events of the Amalickiahite Wars as a major participant, it appears that he gets behind in his historiographical responsibilities. Consequently, rather than abridging Helaman's record for the years 66–62 BC, Mormon instead has to piece together the sequence of events himself, based on the primary sources, mainly letters, that he had at hand. In other words, Helaman may have assembled notes and documents, but in the four years between the end of the war and his own death, when he was busy preaching and rebuilding the church (Alma 62:44–47), he apparently never got around to finishing his portion of the Large Plates of Nephi. (This would also explain why, contrary to convention in the Book of Mormon, Alma 45–62 was not made into a separate literary unit called "the First Book of Helaman"—it seems that the underlying source had been too meager and incomplete to stand on its own).[45] Helaman is certainly an adequate letter writer, but the war chapters of the book of Alma, for which Helaman's record would have been the source, have struck many readers as being relatively dry and uninspiring (though as we shall see in Chapter 6, Mormon manages to make something wonderful of them).

A final indication of the unfinished nature of Helaman's book is that he seems to have failed in his most important responsibility as record keeper—to ensure the smooth transmission of the plates in his possession. By this time in the Book of Mormon, we have seen numerous instances of how this was supposed to be done: before his death, Nephi entrusted his records to his brother Jacob, with words of counsel and warning (Jacob 1:1–5), and Jacob did the same with his own son (Jacob 7:27), as did Enos, Jarom, Omni, Amaron, Amaleki, Benjamin, Mosiah, and Alma.[46] By contrast, Helaman dies before he makes the traditional and proper arrangements (presumably because he still had more work to do): "And Helaman died in the thirty and fifth year of the reign of the judges over the people of Nephi. And it came to pass in the commencement of the thirty and sixth year . . . that Shiblon took possession of those sacred things which had been delivered unto Helaman by Alma" (Alma 62:52–63:1).

This is the only time in the Book of Mormon when the records go into probate, as it were, and a relative is forced to step in and take over the transmission process on his own authority. Mormon is quick to add that Helaman "was a just man, and he did walk uprightly before God, and he did observe to do good continually" (Alma 63:2), but it is hard to miss the implicit comparison a few verses later when Shiblon, though only an interim figure, still manages to get the pattern right: "it became expedient for Shiblon to confer those sacred things, before his death, upon the son of Helaman, who was called Helaman, being called after the name of his father" (v. 11). And again, for added emphasis: "these things were to be . . . handed down from one generation to another; therefore, in this year, they had been conferred upon Helaman [that is, Helaman$_3$], before the death of Shiblon" (v. 13). Helaman's son finally gets the records, but only after a detour through an uncle. Helaman$_2$ may have been a good, even great man, but he was not a great record keeper, and Mormon's inclusion of letters at the end of the book of Alma seems to be an attempt to fill in the historiographical gaps that Helaman had left.

Integrating Sources

So far we have seen how embedded documents add variety and verisimilitude to Mormon's abridgment. The sources he copied directly into his account seem to have been chosen on the basis of historical significance, literary quality, and theological clarity, though there may be considerable overlap between these categories. For instance, the seven sermons of King Benjamin and Alma that were reproduced from written transcripts all emphasize the Christological nature of Nephite society before the birth of Jesus. These constitute better historical evidence for pre-Christian Christianity than any paraphrase could, because Mormon—writing in the fourth century AD—might be suspected of either intentionally or inadvertently coloring his own descriptions with later, more developed Christian concepts or interpretations.

Similarly, Mormon is keen to demonstrate the rationality of faith by citing the successful fulfillment of prophecy. For this type of argument to be persuasive, it is important that the original predictions be authentic—a quality that can best be inferred when prophecies are presented within embedded documents, with particular details, in the voice of the prophet himself, before their fulfillment. Predictions that were remembered or reconstructed after the fact, in the words of the narrator, would not carry the same evidentiary weight. Nevertheless, Mormon is not above helping his readers make connections by referring to or even quoting the original prophecy at the time it comes to pass, or using parallel language to record the fulfillment of a prediction. For instance, Abinadi warns his executioners that "ye shall *suffer, as I suffer, the pains of death by fire*" (Mosiah 17:18); later Mormon reports that "they were angry with the king, and caused that he should *suffer, even unto death by fire*" (Mosiah 19:20; cf. Alma 25:9, 11).[47]

This last example can serve as a reminder that there is more to the subject of embedded documents than just noting where Mormon incorporates such sources and speculating as to which of their inherent characteristics most impressed him. To do so is to reduce his editorial efforts to a simple either/or decision: *Should I include this document or not?* But it is also instructive to track *how* he integrates documents into his narrative—where he places them, how he sets the scene for firsthand accounts or follows up on them later, whether they move forward or disrupt particular story lines, and whether they reinforce or call into question themes in the main narrative. Mormon reveals a great deal about his historiographical inclinations through his handling of primary sources, and we can see how he employs this technique to strengthen the coherence of his history, to avoid discussing certain subjects, or to highlight a resonant implication.

Coherence

Mormon hopes that the primary sources he inserts will have an effect upon his readers, but they also influence his own writing. There are nearly two hundred instances in which his narration incorporates phrases he has picked up from embedded documents. We see this, for instance, when the sons of Mosiah preach to the Lamanites. Through phrasal allusions, Mormon tells us indirectly that the converted Lamanites were taught these things:

• The moral principles enunciated by King Benjamin, since the Lamanite king's proclamation (in Mormon's paraphrase) that his people "*ought not to murder, nor to plunder, nor to steal, nor to commit adultery, nor to commit any manner of wickedness*" (Alma 23:3) matches both the elements and order of Benjamin's assertion that he had not permitted his subjects to "*murder, or plunder, or steal, or commit adultery, nor even have I suffered that ye should commit any manner of wickedness*" (Mosiah 2:13; cf. Alma 30:10).

• The same understanding of the law of Moses that Abinadi had taught the priests of Noah. In Mormon's narration, it reads, "For *it was expedient that they should keep the law of Moses as yet*, for . . . [it] was *a type of his coming*" (Alma 25:15). Abinadi's original language is, "*It is expedient that ye should keep the law of Moses as yet* . . . all these things were *types of things to come*" (Mosiah 13:27, 31).

• The doctrine of resurrection, again as explained by Abinadi. In Mormon's narration, the newly converted Lamanites had a "hope . . . of . . . the resurrection; therefore, *death was swallowed up* to them by the *victory of Christ* over it" (Alma 27:28). In Abinadi's language: "there is a resurrection, therefore the grave hath no *victory*, and the sting of *death is swallowed up in Christ*" (Mosiah 16:8; with an echo of 1 Cor. 15:54–55).[48]

In a different sort of allusion, at 3 Nephi 6:17–18 Mormon reverses an earlier phrase. He informs us that about AD 30 the Nephites "were in a state of awful wickedness. Now *they did not sin ignorantly, for they knew the will of God concerning them*," which relies for its chilling effect upon readers recalling the words of the angel that King Benjamin reported in his speech: "[Christ's] blood atoneth for the sins of those . . . who have died *not knowing the will of God concerning them, or who have ignorantly sinned*" (Mosiah 3:11). The clear implication of the familiar language is that the Nephites have set themselves up to receive the full justice of God; that is, their deliberate, knowing disobedience has made them fully responsible for their actions, and if they do not repent, they will surely suffer the consequences (which is exactly what happens just two chapters later). We may wonder whether Mormon (or Joseph Smith) could have reasonably expected readers to notice this verbal parallel, but these are the only two instances of the phrase "ignorantly sin(ned)" in the entire book, so it seems like a conscious allusion.[49] The impression it leaves is of Mormon as a careful editor, in full control of his sources, who is able to make sweeping connections over hundreds of pages of text.

The Book of Mormon features a profusion of characters, many of whom speak and write. There is a great deal of direct discourse as well as numerous plates and records, and the embedded documents represent the most extensive examples of giving readers direct access to historical personalities. One result is that the sheer number of disparate voices can tend to disintegrate or fragment the unity of the text. Mormon helps us keep everything straight through headers and colophons, but in addition, he often incorporates phrases from embedded documents into adjacent narratives by way of preview or summary (in the former case, we must imagine that Mormon knew the contents of his sources before he copied them into his history). In this way he strengthens the overall coherence of his account. Some representative examples include the following:

Mormon's preview: "And it came to pass that the Lord began to bless them, insomuch that they *brought many to the knowledge of the truth*; yea, they did *convince many* of their sins, and *of the traditions of their fathers, which were not correct*" (Alma 21:17).

Embedded document (Ammon's testimony): "For they said unto us, 'Do ye suppose that ye can *bring the Lamanites to the knowledge of the truth*?

Do ye suppose that ye can *convince the Lamanites of the incorrectness of the traditions of their fathers?'"* (Alma 26:24).

Mormon's preview: "they [the stripling warriors] *took their weapons of war, and they would that Helaman should be their leader*" (Alma 53:19).

Embedded document (Helaman's letter): "two thousand of these young men have *taken their weapons of war, and would that I should be their leader*" (Alma 56:5). (Note also that the narrative gap in Helaman's letter at Alma 56:8–9—i.e., how exactly did those two thousand boys happen to enlist?—has been provided for in advance by Mormon's explanation at Alma 53:16–18.)[50]

Embedded document (Alma's sermon at Zarahemla): "Come ye out from the wicked . . . behold, *their names shall be blotted out, that the names of the wicked shall not be numbered among the names of the righteous*" (Alma 5:57).

Mormon's summary: "And it came to pass that whosever did belong to the church that did not repent of their *wickedness . . . their names were blotted out, that their names were not numbered among those of the righteous*" (Alma 6:3).

Embedded document (Alma's sermon at Zarahemla): "it has thus been *revealed unto me that the words which have been spoken by our fathers are true, even so according to the spirit of prophecy which is in me . . .* and now I say unto you that this *is the order after which I am called*" (Alma 5:47, 49).

Mormon's summary: "Alma went and began to declare the word of God . . . according to the *revelation of the truth of the word which had been spoken by his fathers, and according to the spirit of prophecy which was in him . . .* and *the holy order by which he was called*" (Alma 6:8).

Embedded document (Jesus' instructions to the Twelve): "more blessed are ye [his three disciples], for ye shall *never taste of death . . .* and again, ye shall *not have pain* while ye shall dwell in the flesh, *neither sorrow save it be for the sins of the world*" (3 Ne. 28:7, 9).

Mormon's summary: "that they might *not taste of death* there was change wrought upon their bodies, that they might *not suffer pain nor sorrow save it were for the sins of the world*" (3 Ne. 28:38).

The regular interplay between embedded documents and narrative paraphrase makes the Book of Mormon more than just a compilation of primary sources; it shows Mormon as a thoughtful, engaged editor who is consciously responding to and adapting the material at hand.

Avoidance

Occasionally there is tension between Mormon's desire to tell an edifying story and his commitment to accuracy. He believes the facts of history will demonstrate moral principles, but the messy details of the past can get in the way of clear, unambiguous lessons. Embedded documents offer one way of avoiding inconvenient truths while at the same time fulfilling his obligations as a historian. They allow him to present a few significant particulars without having to comment upon them directly. For instance, Mormon greatly admires the courage and spirit of Captain Moroni. He praises him so extravagantly at Alma 48:11–18 that any subsequent criticism would be inconsistent. Nevertheless, there are indications that Moroni had his faults and could have been a difficult man to work with—or at least this is the conclusion that readers can draw for themselves from reading his letters reproduced at Alma 54 and 60. In the former letter, it is hard to see how the accusation "thou art a child of hell" (54:11) might have been a successful opening for negotiations, and in the latter Moroni claims (inaccurately, as it turns out) a revelation suggesting that the governor has "transgress[ed] the laws of God" and needs to repent of his "sins and iniquities" (60:33; see Chapter 6 for more details).

We have already considered the chiastic version of Alma's conversion story at Alma 36, which was part of an embedded document originally directed toward his son Helaman, but we have not yet noted that Mormon inserts this primary source at a strategic position in his narrative. Just two years after the sons of Mosiah returned from their missionary journeys, Alma—perhaps wishing to replicate the astonishing success they had had among the Lamanites—proposes a joint preaching tour into another political hotbed, the city of Antionum, which was inhabited by the Zoramites, a group of hostile Nephite dissenters:

> Now the Nephites greatly feared that the Zoramites would enter into a correspondence with the Lamanites, and that it would be the means of great loss on the part of the Nephites. And now, as the preaching of the word had a great tendency to lead the people to do that which was just—yea, it had had more powerful effect upon the minds of the people than the sword, or anything else which had happened unto them— therefore Alma thought it was expedient that they should try the virtue of the word of God. (Alma 31:4–5)

What follows are a pair of sermons, one by Alma and the other by Amulek, with the result that many of the poorer Zoramites repent and are consequently expelled from the city. They make their way to the land of Jershon, where they are welcomed and given land (Alma 32:1–5, 35:1–7). The Zoramites are so angered by the hospitality of the Nephites in Jershon that they form an alliance with the Lamanites to attack them (the very scenario that Alma's preaching was intended to prevent). Next we read that "thus commenced a war betwixt the Lamanites and the Nephites, in the eighteenth year of the reign of the judges; and an account shall be given of their wars hereafter" (Alma 35:13; note that the combined Zoramite/ Lamanite forces are now simply referred to as "Lamanites").

Mormon quickly observes that Alma and his companions returned home to Zarahemla and that their new converts were forced to take up arms to defend themselves (35:14), and then he begins a rather lengthy digression: "Now Alma, being grieved for the iniquity of his people, yea for the wars, and the bloodsheds, and the contentions which were among the people, and having been to declare the word . . . among all the people in every city . . . therefore, he caused that his sons should be gathered together, that he might give unto them every one his charge" (35:15–16). After seven chapters copied from Alma's personal record— consisting of Alma's eloquent speeches of counsel to his three sons—Mormon tells us that Alma and his sons went out to preach again, and then he brings us back to the war that had begun so many pages earlier: "And now I return to an account of the wars between the Nephites and the Lamanites . . . therefore, in the commencement of the eighteenth year, the people of the Nephites saw that the Lamanites were coming upon them" (Alma 43:3–4; observe that once again the conflict has been reduced to Nephites vs. Lamanites, further obscuring the cause of the invasion).

In other words, Mormon inserts Alma's instructions to his sons in the middle of the Zoramite War, where it represents a significant break in the narrative.[51] But since the war itself takes place entirely within the eighteenth year, with no discernible impact from the new round of preaching, Mormon could have recounted the Zoramite affair from beginning to end and then added Alma's document without upsetting the chronology at all. In fact, under this arrangement, Alma's teachings would have concluded his term as record keeper (Alma 44:24) and would have led quite naturally into his last words and death (Alma 45), the place where we typically would expect final words of fatherly wisdom (as in 2 Ne. 1–4). The surprising placement seems designed to disrupt a smooth reading of the Zoramite story, which, taken as a whole, did not go so well. By the time readers get back to the war, they may have forgotten the rather awkward truth that Alma's preaching to the Zoramites not only did not prevent hostilities but was itself a major catalyst for the fighting (upon his return to the main narrative, Mormon quickly adds additional factors; see Alma 43:5–8). Yet all the facts are there, even if the sequence of causation is obscured. Technically, Mormon has acquitted himself as an honest historian, but he has also managed to divert our attention from some awkward details.

Resonance

Finally, the way that Mormon integrates embedded documents can sometimes draw attention to things that are left unsaid in the original sources. After Alma's stirring speech at Zarahemla in Alma 5, he heads to the city of Gideon, where he is delighted to find that the people are still faithful. Indeed, the sermon there is the only document from Alma's hand in which he does not urge his listeners to remember the captivity of their fathers. Perhaps he does not need to mention it, since they are living in a city named for the martyred hero most responsible for the deliverance of the Zeniffite colonists from bondage (Mosiah 22; Alma 1:8):

> And now it came to pass that when Alma had made these regulations [in Zarahemla] he departed from them, yea, from the church which was in the city of Zarahemla, and went over upon the east of the river Sidon, into the valley of Gideon, there having been a city built, which was called the city of Gideon, which was in the valley that was called Gideon, being called after the man who was slain by the hand of Nehor with the sword. And Alma went and began to declare the word of God unto the church which was established in the valley of Gideon. (Alma 6:7–8)

Note, for later, how many times Mormon in this introduction refers to "the valley of Gideon."

Alma begins his remarks by observing that this is "the first time that I have spoken unto you by the words of my mouth, I having been wholly confined to the judgment-seat, having had much business that I could not come unto you" (Alma 7:1), but in fact it was *not* the first time he had been in the area. The city of Gideon was located in a valley of the same name, where Alma had led troops in the most significant battle of the Amlicite Rebellion, which had been fought four years earlier with more than nineteen thousand casualties (Alma 2:16–20, 26–38). Not only had Mormon described the aftermath of that conflict in terms of the men who had died, but he also had recounted how "many women and children had been slain with the sword, and also many of their flocks and their herds; and also many of their fields of grain were destroyed" (3:2). It is therefore a striking reversal when Alma closes his sermon at Gideon with this invocation: "May the peace of God rest upon you, and upon your houses and lands, and upon your flocks and herds, and all that you possess, your women and your children, according to your faith and good works, from this time forth and forever" (7:27). And when he gives thanks that "the Lord in much mercy hath granted that I should come unto you" (7:2), he may have had in mind a very specific instance of divine intervention—at the moment he had fought face-to-face with Amlici, somewhere near the valley of Gideon, he had prayed, saying, "O Lord, have mercy and spare my life, that I may be an instrument in thy hands to save and preserve this people" (2:29–30).

The key connection made by Mormon between Alma's sermon and the grim wartime scenes of four years earlier is the phrase "the valley of Gideon," an expression that Alma himself never uses. (The place name appears twice at Alma 2, with a note on its origin—"the valley being called after that Gideon who was slain by the hand of Nehor with a sword"—and then three times in Alma 6; there are no other occurrences in the entire Book of Mormon.) Everyone within the sound of Alma's voice would have been very familiar with the recent horrific events, and many may have been directly affected by them, having lost loved ones and property. It is an indication of Alma's sensitivity that he does not mention such things directly. And Mormon, not wanting to spoil the effect, also refrains from explicit comment, though the multiple references to the valley of Gideon in his two-verse introduction should be enough to remind alert readers what was at stake in this delicate visit, fraught with political meaning, to a people still in need of spiritual assurance and healing. Mormon's subtle employment of the phrase sets up a resonance between a primary source and its broader historical background. As we saw above, the documents that Mormon inserts into his history can offer significant clues as to his intentions and sensibilities, but the way he integrates these sources can also reveal both his mind and his command of his material.

6

Providential Recurrence

Parallel Narratives

The Book of Mormon will always be a difficult book for outsiders to read. Not only is the language somewhat off-putting, but the tone is as well. When Mormon offers an integrated, abridged version of Nephite history, he simply assumes that we will accept his account as factual. He makes no accommodations for those who might consider the book's Christology anachronistic or its lack of archaeological support troubling. It would probably be easier for some readers to find value in or even enjoy the Book of Mormon if it were a wisdom text or a collection of aphorisms like the Daodejing, the Dhammapada, or the Gospel of Thomas. These classics can be, and often have been, decontextualized and dehistoricized in ways that allow them to transcend cultural and even religious differences; their lack of specificity makes it possible for them to speak universally. So also the Book of Mormon might have reached a wider audience had its narratives been more obviously mythological or archetypal. Yet it stubbornly resists being read in ecumenical, postmodern (or even modern) ways. Hence a lovely allegory such as Lehi's dream—which has probably been the subject of so many artistic representations precisely because of its universal appeal—is soon encumbered by pointed prophecies about Columbus and the American Revolution (1 Ne. 13:12, 17–19). King Benjamin's moving observation that "when ye are in the service of your fellow beings, ye are only in the service of your God" (Mosiah 2:17) is found within a politically fraught sermon that is said to have taken place in the Nephite capital about 121 BC.

One response to the Book of Mormon's thick historical context is to read it looking for nineteenth-century elements or possible correlations with ancient Mesoamerican cultures, to insistently assess its veracity or meaning in light of academic sources of knowledge. Yet to do so is to disregard the book's organizing principles, to wrench it out of its own framework and consequently miss what Mormon is trying to accomplish. To understand this man (either as an ancient prophet or as a fictional character), we must enter into his world. In the end, we may view his project of persuading future readers through the marshaling of historical evidence as naive or misguided, but we should at least start with his own conception of what he was about. As Hans Frei has suggested with regard to the Bible, there is value in acknowledging the "realistic" or "history-like" nature of the text, even if most readers can no longer approach scripture as history plain and simple. While not denying the validity of historical criticism, he argued that narratives can be understood by their own logic and on their own terms rather than by constant reference to external standards of truth. Whether one believes them or not, "miraculous accounts are history-like or realistic if the depicted action is indispensable to the rendering of a particular character, divine or human, or a particular story."[1] The Book of Mormon, like the Bible, constantly refers to angels, prophecies, and miraculous deliverances. Although these elements will pose difficulties for many (in addition to the lack of independent verification of its basic claims), an essential perspective is lost when readers are "interested not in the text as such but in some reconstructive context to which the text 'really' refers and which renders it intelligible."[2]

Mormon has constructed his account as a continuous plot in which various episodes are contextualized, temporally sequenced, causally connected, thematically intertwined, and moved forward by interactions of characters and events that lead toward a recognizable conclusion. In short, it is the sort of narrative that we generally encounter in both historical writing and fiction, and Mormon shows considerable literary skill in the way he fashions and shapes his narrative.[3] What is not so familiar to modern readers, however, is the way in which he refuses to draw a sharp distinction between the sacred and the secular. It turns out that Mormon does want to get at universal truths, but he believes the best approach is through the particularities of history (his attachment to exact dates, locations, and written sources demonstrates a different sort of historical consciousness from that found in the Hebrew Bible, or even in the Gospels). In Mormon's eyes, history and theology are inseparable.

Mormon tells stories with unmistakable spiritual meanings, he presents characters as moral exemplars, and he identifies patterns such as "[God's] arm is extended to all people who will repent and believe on his name," "the Lord worketh in many ways to the salvation of his people," and "the devil will not support his children at the last day, but doth speedily drag them down to hell" (Alma 19:36, 24:27, 30:60). Yet each of these three observations comes at the conclusion of a specific tale, and is prefaced by "thus we see that . . ." It is crucial to Mormon's understanding of the world and his own role as moral guide that the lessons he conveys to readers actually come from the details of history. Properly interpreted, history itself reveals religious truths, and in fact the totality of human experience offers sufficient evidence to demonstrate God's divine plan and influence in earthly affairs. Or at least this is what Mormon believes. What makes his book interesting is watching how he selects, adapts, and arranges his material, particularly when his sources do not seem to adequately illustrate spiritual verities on their own. Mormon is not free to simply create stories; he is constrained by what he perceives as the facts of history. But through his editing he often highlights certain features or encourages readers to see events in a particular light.

One of the most characteristic features of Mormon's writing is his use of parallel narratives. This is so ubiquitous that, as Richard Rust has observed, "it seems that every important action, event, or character type is repeated." Rust continues with a list (which also includes a few episodes from the Small Plates):

> For instance, two wealthy men (Lehi and Amulek) lose their riches as they pursue prophetic callings. Kings Benjamin and Limhi each assemble their people in order to speak to them. Two sons of kings (Ammon and his brother Aaron) speak with kings (Lamoni and his father). Alma the Younger and Lamoni fall into trances in which they appear to be dead. Two detailed accounts are given of prophets threatened within a prison (Alma and Amulek, Nephi and Lehi). Two Lamanite leaders (who also are brothers) are killed by a spear within their tents. And prophets (Abinadi, Alma, and Samuel) are cast out of cities and then return at the Lord's bidding. Further, prophet-leaders (Lehi, Zeniff, and Mosiah) gather people to read records to them. Antichrists (notably Sherem, Korihor, and Nehor) lead people to follow their iniquities. A man named Ammon, living in the time of King Mosiah, is captured and taken before King Limhi—and ends up helping Limhi's people escape from captivity; Mosiah's son Ammon is captured and taken before the Lamanite king Lamoni and helps save Lamoni's people both spiritually and physically. And three prophets, Alma the Younger, Nephi the son of Helaman, and Samuel the Lamanite, depart out of the land and are "never heard of more," with the implication that Alma is translated and does not taste death.[4]

This is only a partial list, yet even so, the degree of narrative repetition is remarkable. One might attribute these sorts of parallels to Joseph Smith's limited imagination, but from within the parameters of the narrative—giving full play to Mormon's narration—the repetitions take on a broader significance. When Mormon underscores the commonalities of different episodes to this extent, he runs the risk of tediousness or accusations of contrivance. Rust suggests that Mormon deliberately employs parallelism as an aid to comprehension or remembrance, to "teach, emphasize, and confirm," and he sees it as akin to the biblical "type-scenes" brilliantly analyzed by Robert Alter.[5] What we see in the Bible, however, are narrative conventions, stock situations such as "the annunciation . . . of the birth of the hero to his barren mother; the encounter with the future betrothed at a well; the epiphany in the field; the initiatory trial; danger in the desert and the discovery of a well or some other source of sustenance; the testament of the dying hero," all recounted with subtle variations that testify to the consummate storytelling art of the anonymous narrators.[6] Mormon, by contrast, seems to be more constrained by his sources. Similarities in the Book of Mormon often look like historical coincidences rather than cultural conventions or archetypes. In the Bible, meaning can be discovered in the "minute and often revelatory changes that a given type-scene undergoes as it passes from one character to another."[7] In the Book of Mormon, the significance lies in the literal repetition of actual events rather than in the ways they are recounted, even if Mormon's editing sometimes is intended to draw our attention to earlier precedents or later reenactments.

In Mormon's world, similar experiences are not necessarily random or coincidental; historical repetition is evidence of God's engagement with humankind. That is to say, certain types of events tend to recur regularly because God is constant: his will is unchanging, his plans are set, and he responds in the same way to similar situations. Thucydides famously asserted that his history was useful because it explained "events which happened in the past and which (human nature being what it is) will, at some time or other and in much the same ways, be repeated in the future."[8] Mormon would only amend this to say, *Divine nature being what it is . . .* His task as an editor, then, is to make the hand of God manifest by deftly emphasizing (not creating) patterns that were already present in past events. He uses selection, arrangement, and phrasal repetition to indicate the parallel nature of certain episodes, and through such means he cumulatively constructs an elaborate argument for the rationality of belief, documenting God's intervention in Nephite history and, by extension, in human history at large.

It appears that Mormon writes on two levels. On a first reading, his work is quite didactic. He is an active narrator who makes judgments, inserts comments, and proclaims moral principles. He provides the first round of interpretation so that the basic message of the text is unmistakable. Yet at the same time, through his editing and phrasing, Mormon subtly suggests to his audience that certain figures and events should be read in light of each other. Without specifying exactly what we should find, he nevertheless directs our attention toward avenues that will reward deeper reflection and more nuanced approaches. A truly didactic text only has to be read once to grasp its full meaning, but editorial strategies such as parallel narratives make it possible to read the Book of Mormon again and again with increasing insight and pleasure.[9] There is a fair degree of variation in how Mormon employs selection, arrangement, and phrasing to construct parallel narratives—the better to demonstrate through history the working out of God's will—but a few examples can provide an introduction. Those that follow are categorized according to the relationship between the two plots.

Abinadi: Simple Parallels

In Genesis, when Joseph's brothers travel to Egypt for grain and then run into difficulties (at the hand of Joseph himself, though they do not recognize him), they immediately start talking among themselves about a painful incident from their past: "And they said one to another, We are verily guilty concerning our brother, in that we saw the anguish of his soul, when he besought us, and we would not hear; therefore is this distress come upon us" (Gen. 42:21). This quick emergence of regret makes us wonder how many times in the preceding years any setback has reopened that particular wound of conscience. Similarly, when Ammon and his fifteen companions from Zarahemla appear at Limhi's court, the king spontaneously brings up a terrible mistake that had weighed upon his people for more than two decades (the fact that he shifts here into third-person discourse is an indication of the uncomfortable, unresolved nature of the matter): "And a prophet of the Lord have they slain; yea, a chosen man of God, who told them of their wickedness and abominations . . . therefore, who wondereth that they are in bondage, and that they are smitten with sore affliction?" (Mosiah 7:26–28).[10] Mormon soon begins a flashback that will retrace the history of Limhi's colony, beginning with the memoirs of Zeniff, and eventually we come to realize that the unnamed prophet was Abinadi. The story of his preaching, trial, and execution by fire in the days of King Noah (Limhi's father and Zeniff's son) is related at Mosiah 11–17.

Like other Nephite prophets, Abinadi taught about the coming of Christ and warned that destruction would overtake the people unless they repented, but Mormon makes no specific comment on the story other than to observe that Abinadi was "put to death because he would not deny the commandments of God, having sealed the truth of his words by his death" (Mosiah 17:20). Of course, no reader could miss the point that the martyred Abinadi was a paragon of faithfulness, and when Mormon later interrupts his narrative to note when Abinadi's predictions were fulfilled (Mosiah 21:4; Alma 25:9, 11; Morm. 1:19; cf. Mosiah 20:21), the authenticity of his revelations and God's justice are also confirmed. These sorts of lessons belong to the first, didactic level of the text. Yet Mormon also shapes his account to suggest that the narrative of Abinadi's life and death could be profitably read as a parallel to other stories, where similarities and differences might yield additional meaning. In fact, one of the messages Mormon hereby conveys is that some of these recurring patterns are at God's initiative and are not simply the result of his own editorial choices.

Abinadi as a New Moses

Abinadi's trial is a well-constructed episode in which seemingly diverse elements come together in the end. After prophesying of the misery that would afflict the Nephite colonists, Abinadi is arrested and brought before King Noah. He is interrogated by the king's priests, who ask him to explain the meaning of Isaiah 52:7–10, which speaks of the joy and comfort afforded by prophets who bring "good tidings of good." Their question is not so much a request for an interpretation as a taunting challenge to his legitimacy as a prophet; his message has been anything but good news. Abinadi responds by quoting the Ten Commandments and then citing and commenting on Isaiah 53 as a prophecy of Christ. When he comes to the phrase "he shall see his seed" (Isa. 53:10), Abinadi explains that this is an allusion to "all the holy prophets who prophesied of the coming of the Lord" (Mosiah 15:11), and he identifies these messengers as those who "bring good tidings of good." In this way, his discourse comes full circle as he finally answers the question originally put to him four chapters earlier. He quotes the same verse they quoted to him, adds an explication of Christian redemption (thereby placing himself within what he sees as the prophetic tradition extending back to Moses; Mosiah 13:33), and then concludes with "Therefore, if ye teach the law of Moses, also teach that it is a shadow of those things which are to come—teach them that redemption cometh through Christ the Lord" (Mosiah 16:14–15). His explicit references to Moses correspond with the way that Mormon has structured the narrative.

The tale of Abinadi includes a number of parallels to the Exodus story, beginning with God's command "Go forth and say unto this people, 'Thus saith the Lord . . .'" (Mosiah 11:20). The injunction to "say (un)to [someone], 'Thus saith the Lord'" is fairly common in the Hebrew Bible, where it recurs more than fifty times, but the first—and most memorable—usages are in the story of Moses' confrontation with Pharaoh at Exodus 4:22, 8:1, 20, and 9:13. Although King Noah may unwittingly play the part of Pharaoh, Mormon recognizes the pattern and narrates accordingly, though it was God himself who first spoke to Abinadi in the same language he had used long before with Moses. It appears that both Mormon and God want us to perceive Abinadi's preaching not just as a doctrinal discourse but as a reenactment of sacred drama—Abinadi is a new Moses, giving the law once again (as when he recites the Ten Commandments) and standing up to a recalcitrant, faithless ruler. The verbal correspondences become more distinctive as the story progresses, though it adds yet another layer of complexity to note that the narrator never reports God's words directly; we always hear them as quoted by Abinadi.[11]

Mosiah 11:22 (God): "And it shall come to pass that they shall know that I am the Lord their God, and am a jealous God, visiting the iniquities of my people."

> *shall know that I am the Lord:* a key phrase in Exodus, where it appears five times (elsewhere it occurs once in First Kings and fifty-one times in Ezekiel). In the Book of Mormon we find it only in speeches by Abinadi, here and at Mosiah 12:3: "King Noah . . . shall know that I am the Lord."

> *a jealous God, visiting the iniquities:* a famous line in the second of the Ten Commandments, found in the Bible only at Exodus 20:5 and Deuteronomy 5:9. It occurs only here in the Book of Mormon, in addition to Abinadi's quotation of the first of the Ten Commandments at Mosiah 13:13 (a quick comparison will show that Abinadi is quoting the Exodus rather than the Deuteronomy version of the Ten Commandments).

Mosiah 11:27 (King Noah): "Who is Abinadi, that I and my people should be judged of him, or who is the Lord, that shall bring upon my people such great affliction?"

> *who is the Lord, that . . . :* an impudent question that appears in the Book of Mormon only here, and in the Bible only at Exodus 5:2, where Pharaoh demands of Moses: "Who is the Lord, that I should obey his voice to let Israel go?" As soon as King Noah utters these fateful words, skilled readers will recognize the allusion and know that he is doomed.[12]

Mosiah 11:29 (Mormon): "Now the eyes of the people were blinded; therefore they hardened their hearts against the words of Abinadi, and they sought from that time forward to take him. And King Noah hardened his heart against the word of the Lord, and he did not repent of his evil doings."

> *hardened heart(s):* a common formula in the Book of Mormon, but in the Hebrew Bible it is overwhelmingly associated with the confrontation between Moses and Pharaoh in Exodus (sixteen out of eighteen occurrences).[13]

Mosiah 12:2 (God): "Stretch forth thy hand and prophesy, saying . . ."; also Mosiah 16:1, "after Abinadi had spoken these words, he stretched forth his hand and said . . ."

> *stretch(ed) forth [someone's] hand:* a regular expression in both the Bible and Book of Mormon that would not carry much weight were it not for the fact that here it is part of a distinctive cluster of allusions. The expression is found five times in the Moses/Pharaoh story, where it received considerable prominence because Moses (or Aaron) is directly commanded by the Lord to perform this prophetic gesture, just as Abinadi is.

Mosiah 12:2 (God): "Yea, wo be unto this generation! . . . It shall come to pass that this generation, because of their iniquities, shall be brought into bondage."

> This would appear to be a contrast with the Exodus story since Moses was attempting to deliver his people from slavery rather than threatening them with it, but Abinadi's quotation of God's words in this verse indicates that he is adapting the Exodus account for his own purposes. The Second Commandment included the warning that "I the Lord thy God am a jealous god, visiting the iniquity of the fathers upon the children unto the third and fourth generation of them that hate me" (Ex. 20:5). When Abinadi began his preaching, he echoed these words, but shortened them to "[I] am a jealous god, visiting the iniquities of my people" (Mosiah 11:22). If his audience felt an ominous undertone in the omission of the expected phrase "unto the third and fourth generation," this verse makes it unmistakable. Abinadi is prophesying immediate consequences that will overtake "this generation."

Mosiah 12:6–7 (God): "And it shall come to pass that I will send forth hail among them, and it shall smite them; and they shall also be smitten with the east wind; and insects shall pester their land also, and devour their grain. And they shall be smitten with a great pestilence—and all this will I do because of their iniquities and abominations."

> *hail, east wind, insects, pestilence:* these threats never materialize in the history of Noah's people (though the fulfillments of other items in Abinadi's prophecies are meticulously recorded), and, given the cluster of Exodus phrases, they make more sense as allusions to the plagues of Egypt rather than as critical elements of the Nephite narrative. "Hail" (seventeen times in Ex. 9–10) is mentioned just once more in the Book of Mormon; "east wind" (three times in Ex.) appears only in Abinadi's prophecies; and even though "insects" (only here in the Book of Mormon) and "pestilence" do not match the exact words of Exodus, they are nevertheless key components of the story of the plagues, which included lice (or gnats), flies, locusts, and illnesses of both cattle and humans.

As the narrative of Abinadi unfolds, it becomes clear that the Book of Mormon account is not a simple retelling in a different guise. Abinadi, unlike Moses, is executed; the people of Noah are indeed brought into bondage by the Lamanites; and a new figure, Alma₁, takes over in the role of deliverer of his people.[14] Nevertheless, when Abinadi confronts a stubborn monarch and delivers the Mosaic law (or at least the Ten Commandments), his resemblance to Moses is unmistakable, and

Mormon himself makes a direct comparison at Mosiah 13:5: "his face shone with exceeding luster, even as Moses' did while in the mount of Sinai, while speaking with the Lord." Through these connections, Mormon can affirm the continuity of the Nephite prophetic tradition with that of the Hebrews, and also establish the righteousness and authority of Abinadi. Yet when we examine the verbal associations between the two tales, it is striking that it is God himself who orchestrates the parallelism through a provocative allusion to Moses in his first command to Abinadi. Readers are to understand here that although Mormon recognizes and highlights this particular reenactment, he seems to be following God's lead rather than imposing a pattern of his own devising.

Abinadi as a Precedent

Just as Abinadi reprised the role of Moses, so also Alma$_2$ and Amulek at Ammonihah relive the same sort of trial that Abinadi underwent. There are significant common narrative elements, including prophets who start to leave when their words are rejected only to receive a directive to return and deliver a final warning; a dramatic confrontation with the authorities; a challenge to interpret scripture; the deliberate misconstruing of the prophet's words; imprisonment; a single, named convert who pleads for the prophet and then is himself driven out (Alma$_1$ in the first case and Zeezrom in the second); and martyrdom by fire. Each of these components was selected and integrated into the narrative by the editor, and the parallels are by no means always necessary to the tale—Zeezrom was not nearly as important a figure as Alma the Elder, for example. Rather, the similarities are often indicative of Mormon's editorial interests.

God once again initiates the parallels by issuing similar commands—"Say unto this people . . . except they repent I will visit them in mine anger . . . yea, in my fierce anger will I visit them" (Mosiah 11:20, 12:1; Alma 8:29)—but most of the verbal allusions are provided by the narrator or the characters:

ABINADI	ALMA AND AMULEK
"they stood forth and attempted to lay their hands on him, but he withstood them"—Mosiah 13:2	"they stood forth to lay their hand on me; but behold, they did not"—Alma 9:7
"except they repent, I will utterly destroy them from off the face of the earth"—Mosiah 12:8	"he has commanded you to repent, or he will utterly destroy you from off the face of the earth"—Alma 9:12
"they began to question him, that they might cross him"—Mosiah 12:19	"they began to question Amulek, that thereby they might make him cross his words"—Alma 10:16

"the very Eternal Father of heaven and of earth"—Mosiah 15:4	"the very Eternal Father of heaven and of earth"—Alma 11:39
"God himself shall come down among the children of men and shall redeem his people"—Mosiah 15:1[15]	"he shall come into the world to redeem his people"—Alma 11:40
"what meaneth the words which are written . . .saying . . ."—Mosiah 12:20	"what does the scripture mean, which saith that . . ."—Alma 12:21
"[Abinadi] has reviled the king"—Mosiah 17:12	"they also said that Amulek . . . had reviled against their law and also against their lawyers and judges"—Alma 14:2
"if you slay me ye will shed innocent blood, and this shall also stand as a testimony against you at the last day"—Mosiah 17:10	"the blood of the innocent shall stand as a witness against them . . . at the last day"—Alma 14:11

Several of the shared expressions are rather distinctive. For instance, the phrase "very Eternal Father of heaven and of earth" occurs only in the two verses cited above.[16] The idea of God visiting people in his anger (perhaps related to Job 35:15) appears seven times in the Book of Mormon. Of those instances, two are in Abinadi's preaching, one is the voice of the angel telling Alma to return to Ammonihah, and two more are included in his sermon there (Mosiah 11:20, 12:1, Alma 8:29, 9:12, 9:18). Similarly, Abinadi is partial to the concept of hardening one's heart against the word(s) of God or his prophets, an image he uses three times (Mosiah 11:29, 12:1); the only other occurrences in the Book of Mormon are in Alma's preaching at Ammonihah (at Alma 9:30 and 12:13). Finally, it is Abinadi who first introduces the term "bands of death," which he repeats five times. Alma is also fond of this phrase—five of the remaining seven instances in the Book of Mormon are in his words—but it is only at Ammonihah that anyone explains exactly what it means (Alma 11:41–45).

Once we recognize the parallel nature of the stories of Abinadi at King Noah's court and Alma and Amulek at Ammonihah, it may come as a surprise that the denouements of the two narratives differ so strikingly (especially if we did not register Mormon's editorial heading that the latter two prophets would be "*delivered by the miraculous power of God which was in them*"; headnote to Alma 9). Abinadi, of course, was burned as a martyr, while Alma and Amulek walk unscathed out of a prison that dramatically collapsed around them, killing all their guards and accusers. Such divergent outcomes in narratives that have been told in parallel fashion challenge readers to look more closely for ways in which God's guidance of events is nevertheless constant.

Perhaps the most likely connection is Abinadi's declaration that God would spare him as long as his mission remained uncompleted: "Touch me not, for God shall smite you if ye lay your hands upon me, for I have not delivered the message which the Lord sent me to deliver . . . therefore, God will not suffer that I shall be destroyed at this time" (Mosiah 13:3). After his discourse ended, however, this divine protection was withdrawn. Alma and Amulek, by contrast, still have more to do at the end of their story: "Our work is not finished; therefore they burn us not" (Alma 14:13). Still, the murderous rage of the crowd at Ammonihah, equal to that of the priests of King Noah, was vented upon the wives and children of Alma's converts, and the martyrdom—by fire—of those innocents seals the fate of the city.

What is interesting, from a narratological perspective, is that although Abinadi reenacts Moses, and Alma and Amulek reenact Abinadi, the latter two do not reenact Moses.[17] We are dealing here not with typologies but rather with specific events that work out similarly in some ways and quite distinctly in others. Abinadi and Alma, like Paul and other early Christians, were familiar with the concept of types, by which a historical person, event, or object could symbolize or represent something in the future (usually Christ). Thus Abinadi speaks of the requirements of the Mosaic law as "types of things to come" (Mosiah 13:31), and Alma refers to the priesthood as being "a type of [Christ's] order" (Alma 13:16). There is usually an intensification from the sign (or type) to the thing that is signified (the antitype); that is, the second element fulfills or completes the first. Yet it makes little sense to read the story of Moses as somehow prefiguring Abinadi, or Abinadi's experience as being fulfilled in Alma and Amulek. There are shared identities, but the meaning of one story is not subsumed in the other. Instead, Mormon's use of parallel narratives suggests that similar situations will tend to recur over time; these are the kinds of tribulations that prophets of the Lord will always face.[18]

Nephi$_2$ and Lehi$_4$: Complex Parallels

Although Mormon is a pervasive editor and a didactic one, he seldom explicitly identifies relationships between various plots and subplots (with the large exception of his insistent comments on fulfilled prophecies). He only rarely says, *I am reminded here of an earlier incident* or *This happened in much the same way as that.* One example occurs at Helaman 2:13–14, where Mormon draws a parallel between the Gadianton Robbers of the first century BC and secret combinations in his own day, the fourth century AD. A little later, at Helaman 6:15–30, he connects these groups to the secret societies among the Jaredites a millennium earlier, though in this particular case he explicitly denies any direct historical causation; instead, he provides a supernatural explanation—Satan inspired these groups in similar ways (see Alma 37:26–32 and Hel. 6:25–26). But this sort of thing is unusual. More often Mormon indicates parallelism (and thus encourages his readers to make comparisons) through his editing and wording. The parallel narratives we have examined thus far have taken the relatively simple form of "X is like Y," but there are other, more complicated patterns in which the parallel elements point toward more than one analogous narrative or feature unexpected correlations.

When Mormon tells the story of how Nephi$_2$ and his brother Lehi$_4$ were thrown into prison in 30 BC as they were preaching to the Lamanites, he informs us that they were in "the same prison in which Ammon and his brethren were cast by the servants of Limhi" (Hel. 5:21). This is one of the few explicit connections between narratives that Mormon makes, but the two incidents do not actually exhibit many parallels. In the earlier case, which had occurred nearly a century beforehand, Ammon and his companions were incarcerated for only two days and set free as soon as King Limhi realized who they were (Mosiah 7:7–16; cf. Mosiah 21:23–24). In Helaman 5 the two brothers are in prison for a long time and they are released only after a miraculous spiritual manifestation. The two incidents are so different that it is difficult to compare them. Indeed, Mormon's note appears to be an antiquarian's excited observation of geographical coincidence rather than a hint at thematic relevance. Or it may have been intended to throw off our expectation that this account would be parallel to the story of Alma and Amulek's imprisonment at Ammonihah about 82 BC (Alma 14:14–29).

Such an expectation is not unreasonable since, at first glance, there seem to be a number of commonalities between the experiences of Alma and Amulek on the one hand and Nephi$_2$ and Lehi$_4$ on the other, including a pair of missionary-prophets in prison, harsh treatment for "many days," the withholding of food, an earthquake, and a dramatic deliverance (though in the first instance the guards all die; in the second they are converted). Mormon's reference to Ammon's detention, however, can cause a sort of double take, and when we look at the episode in detail, what is surprising is that there are even more connections between the Helaman 5 prison narrative and the coming of the resurrected Jesus in Third Nephi, at least in terms of distinctive narrative elements and key phrases (though of course we cannot know this until later, after we are well into Third Nephi; this is an interpretation accessible only to rereaders of the text, and it entails a shift in their perception of exactly which narratives exhibit the most significant parallels):

JESUS' VISIT TO THE NEPHITES	NARRATIVE ELEMENTS/PHRASES	NEPHI AND LEHI IN PRISON
3 Ne. 8:6	the earth shook "as if it were/was about to divide asunder"	Hel. 5:33
3 Ne. 8:19–22	a cloud or vapor of darkness	Hel. 5:28–34

3 Ne. 10:9	the darkness disperses	Hel. 5:43
3 Ne. 11:3–5	a voice comes three times	Hel. 5:29–33
3 Ne. 11:3	it was not a loud voice, but rather one that was "still" or "small" and "it did pierce . . . to the very soul"	Hel. 5:30
3 Ne. 11:5	they look up to see "from whence the voice/sound came"	Hel. 5:48
3 Ne. 11:8	angels/Jesus came down "out of heaven"	Hel. 5:48

As always, the first question to ask when presented with such a list is, "Are these parallels intentional or are the connections coincidental?" In this particular case, even though one could readily point out differences between the narrative contours of the two stories, there does seem to be an intriguing overlap of distinctive elements. And some of the phrases are uniquely shared: "as if it were about to divide asunder" occurs only in Helaman 5:33 and 3 Nephi 8:6 (though 1 Ne. 17:45 is similar), while Helaman 5:30 and 3 Nephi 11:3 are the only two verses in all of scripture that include the formula "pierce . . . to the very soul" (perhaps with an echo of Luke 2:35).[19]

The second question is, "If Mormon has indeed worded his narratives so that readers are supposed to recognize parallels, what might that mean?" It appears that the deliverance of Nephi and Lehi and those with them in the prison is a foreshadowing of the more extensive deliverance of the Nephites at Bountiful from the darkness and destruction preceding Christ's coming. The prison story functions as a physically enacted, dramatized prophecy that points forward to Christ, but it also testifies of a God who speaks to individuals in the depths of darkness and fear (in this respect, Hel. 5 may have typological potential). In any case, both Helaman 5 and 3 Nephi 11 are extraordinary chapters. The arrival of Jesus at Bountiful is the climax of Nephite religious history, while the prison experience of Nephi and Lehi sets in motion the most astonishing conversion in the entire book—a majority of the Lamanites accept the gospel, to the extent that they renounce war and return occupied territories to the Nephites (Hel. 5:45–52). (Incidentally, this is only time when Nephite dissenters are reconverted [see vv. 17, 27, 35–39], as an exception to the general principle articulated by Mormon at Alma 24:30.) In both chapters, the power of Christ's redemption is manifest in a spectacular fashion.[20]

There is one more connection to notice when comparing this prison episode with the postresurrection visitation of Jesus. As we shall see in Chapter 7, Jesus came to the New World not only to show himself to the Nephites and teach them the gospel but also to give them the gift of the Holy Ghost. When we come to two key passages in Third Nephi, they will sound very similar to a description we have already encountered in Helaman 5:

(Hel. 5:43, 45, 48) Behold, they saw that they were *encircled about*, yea, every soul, by a pillar of *fire*. . . . *the Holy Spirit of God did come down from heaven* . . . and they were *filled as if with fire* . . . And now, when they heard this they *cast up their eyes* as if to behold from whence the voice came; and behold, *they saw the heavens open*; and the *angels came down out of heaven and ministered unto them*.

(3 Ne. 17:24) And as they looked to behold, they *cast their eyes towards heaven*, and *they saw the heavens open*, and they saw *angels descending out of heaven* as it were in the midst of fire; and they came down and *encircled* those little ones *about*, and they were *encircled about with fire*; and the angels did *minister unto them*.

(3 Ne. 19:13–14) The *Holy Ghost did fall upon them*, and they were *filled with* the Holy Ghost and with *fire*. And behold, they were *encircled about as if it were by fire*; and it *came down from heaven* . . . and *angels did come down out of heaven and did minister unto them*.

In other words, when the Nephites receive the Holy Ghost, they will do so in much the same manner as the Lamanites had experienced earlier.

Thus far, it is clear that Helaman 5 exhibits parallels with several other incidents. Mormon makes a specific reference to earlier events in the same prison at Mosiah 7; the basic story is reminiscent of Alma and Amulek's incarceration at Alma 14; there are a number of verbal connections to 3 Nephi 8–11, even though the two narratives are quite dissimilar (a miraculous prison deliverance is hardly comparable to Jesus' appearance to the Nephites after his resurrection); and there is a remarkable link to the Nephite children and disciples receiving the Holy Ghost at the time of Christ's visit. Indeed, this last parallel is affirmed by the Lord himself. When the risen Jesus speaks from heaven in 3 Nephi 9:20, he alludes to events at Helaman 5: "Whoso cometh unto me with a broken heart and a contrite spirit, him will I baptize with fire and with the Holy Ghost, even as the Lamanites, because of their faith in me at the time of their conversion, were baptized with fire and with the Holy Ghost, and they knew it not" (Moroni will make the same connection later at Ether 12:14).

Modern readers are familiar with the phrase "baptize with fire and with the Holy Ghost" from the biblical account of John the Baptist (Matt. 3:11; Luke 3:16), but it may not have been commonly known among the Nephites.[21] They were, however, well aware of the precedent of martyrdom by fire, and given that Christ speaks shortly after a widespread conflagration (including the incineration of Zarahemla), the implications could have been both puzzling and frightening. For this reason, Jesus explains the phrase with a reference to Nephi and Lehi in prison. Mormon has prepared his readers for this moment by telling the earlier story in a manner that anticipated Jesus' bestowal of the Spirit, so we recognize and understand Christ's allusion.

If we can only grasp the larger significance of Mormon's narration of Nephi and Lehi's prison experience later in the text, we can take comfort in the fact that the Lamanites themselves did not yet fully understand what was happening at that time either. As Jesus noted, "They were baptized with fire and with the Holy Ghost, *and they knew it not.*" Actually, we have a significant advantage over any Lamanite in the story because, as Meir Sternberg has observed with regard to a biblical character, "he directly confronts a world that we receive through the mediation of an artful teller and text. He exercises interpretation on the world of objects; we, on a web of words that project such a world."[22] All of the phrasing in common between the prison episode and Jesus' arrival in the New World occurs in the words of the narrator; it is Mormon's descriptions that make the incidents parallel, which means that connections will be more obvious to us than to the actors themselves. Or, again with Sternberg, "the poetics of the narrative is reserved for the reader's viewpoint and interpretive operations."[23]

Competence Versus Blessedness: Contrastive Narratives in a Series

Thus far, we have seen how Mormon shapes single narratives to highlight the ways in which they parallel earlier precedents, or so that they themselves can be reenacted in later events. There are, however, larger narrative patterns that can be discerned over the course of his abridgment. Sometimes parallels occur in series, and though the connections are more subtle, the repetition is enough to indicate intentionality. Such large-scale structuring represents a remarkable level of editorial control or even literary achievement, though Mormon would undoubtedly disavow his own creativity, claiming instead merely to be making manifest the moral principles of history. A fine example of this occurs in a series of three pairs of contrasting stories in the books of Mosiah and Alma, each reiteration of which makes a distinction between faithful, ordinary competence and miraculous, blessed achievement. Mormon sees both modes of action as virtuous and acceptable to God. He never makes this point in so many words, but the message is implicit in the structure of his history. Through his patterning of the past, he demonstrates how the Lord rewards those who serve him with their best efforts, and how he pours out extraordinary blessings upon those who trust him beyond their abilities.

The idea that meaning can be implicit in the configuration of a narrative was explored by Hunter Rawlings in his *Structure of Thucydides' History*. Rawlings argued that Thucydides deliberately fashioned his history of the Peloponnesian War as two parallel ten-year wars, with the incidents in the first books corresponding to those in the second half of his work. The Greek historian brought order to the events he recounted through the techniques of "selection, emphasis, and juxtaposition," where emphasis could be gauged by the level of dramatic portrayal employed, as indicated by the presence of detailed and highly charged narratives, formal dialogue, indirect dialogue, a speech, a set of paired speeches, and so forth.[24] Thucydides bases his account solidly on the information available to him, and then he "arranges and characterizes the facts in a manner that brings out or even creates their essential meaning." Rawlings continues, "The historian who masters this method is more than a recorder of facts—he is an artist."[25] Thucydides was a much more secular historian than Mormon, who is eager to discover and convey to his readers the workings of divine providence, but their narrative techniques share at least a few elements.

The Deliverances of Limhi's People and Alma₁'s People (Mosiah 22 and 23–24)

The Deliverances of Limhi's People and Alma₁'s People
(Mosiah 22 and 23–24)

By the time Ammon's search party arrived at the Nephite colony originally established by Zeniff, the colonists had divided into two groups. The larger population, led by King Limhi, was in bondage to the Lamanites (as predicted by Abinadi) and, having unsuccessfully attempted to free themselves by armed rebellion on three occasions, they were decimated and demoralized (Mosiah ch. 7, 21). The other group, the original Nephite church organized by King Noah's former priest Alma₁, was prospering in an independent settlement in the wilderness.

As soon as contact with representatives from the capital city of Zarahemla had been made, "Ammon and King Limhi began to consult with the people how they should deliver themselves out of bondage" (Mosiah 22:1). They settled on a plan proposed by a senior advisor, Gideon, who had proved his reliability in the past, by which they would gather the people with their flocks and herds, deliver an extra-large tribute of wine to the Lamanite guards—knowing it would result in drunkenness that night—and then, once the guards were thoroughly inebriated and asleep, slip out by "the back pass, through the back wall, on the back side of the city" (Mosiah 22:6). Somewhat amazingly, this strategy proved successful, despite the fact that the Lamanites sent an army in pursuit, and the people of Limhi made their way to Zarahemla, where they were reunited with the main body of the Nephites. The Lamanite army, on the other hand, became lost in the wilderness and eventually stumbled upon the people of Alma₁, whom they promptly enslaved. We might note here that the people of Limhi seem to have been able to "deliver themselves out of bondage" (Mosiah 22:1) through fairly ordinary means.

Alma₁'s people, now in need of deliverance, suffer involuntary servitude and harsh treatment for some time because, as Mormon writes at the beginning of this section, "the Lord seeth fit to chasten his people; yea, he trieth their patience and faith" (Mosiah 23:21). In fact, Mormon is uncomfortable enough with this seemingly unjust turn of events that he works hard to shape his readers' impression of what they are about to hear:

> Nevertheless, whosoever putteth his trust in him, the same shall be lifted up at the last day. Yea, and thus it was with this people. For behold, I will show unto you that they were brought into bondage, and none could deliver them but the Lord their God, yea, even the God of Abraham and Isaac and of Jacob. And it came to pass that he did deliver them, and he did show forth his mighty power unto them, and great were their rejoicings. (Mosiah 23:22–24)

This is a fair summary of what is about to transpire. The people of Alma₁ do not, and perhaps cannot, come up with a plausible escape plan; instead, they appeal to the Lord for aid. At first, in response to their faith, the Lord lightens their burdens, and then sometime later he tells Alma₁ that he will deliver them the next day. During the night, they gather the people with their flocks and grain, and in the morning God causes "a deep sleep to come upon the Lamanites" (Mosiah 24:19). Alma₁'s followers simply walk out with no interference at all. They set up camp after a day's travel, thanking God in recognition that "none could deliver them except it were the Lord their God," but the Lord tells Alma₁ to keep moving, "for the Lamanites have awakened and do pursue thee." Nevertheless, he assures Alma₁, "I will stop the Lamanites in this valley that they come no further in pursuit of this people" (Mosiah 24:21–23). And with that, they make the trip safely back to Zarahemla.

The fact that Mormon tells these stories one right after the other encourages us to think of them as a pair, as does some of the distinctive language he employs. In both cases, we read how they "gather(ed) their flocks together," "depart(ed) . . . into the wilderness," and "after being many/twelve days in the wilderness . . . they arrived in the land of Zarahemla . . . and (King) Mosiah received them with joy" (Mosiah 22:10, 11, 13, 14; Mosiah 24:18, 20, 25). In addition, the idea that none could deliver them but God appears only four times in the Book of Mormon, each time associated with the peoples of Limhi and Alma:

Mosiah 11:23: "except this people repent and turn unto the Lord their God, they shall be brought into bondage; *and none shall deliver them, except it be the Lord the Almighty God*" (Abinadi's initial prophecy to Noah's people)

Mosiah 23:23: "For behold, I will show unto you that they were brought into bondage, *and none could deliver them but the Lord their God*, yea, even the God of Abraham and Isaac and of Jacob" (Mormon's cautious editorial foreshadowing)

Mosiah 24:21: "they poured out their thanks to God because he . . . had delivered them out of bondage; for they were in bondage, *and none could deliver them except it were the Lord their God*" (Mormon's narrative summary)

Alma 36:2: "I would that ye should do as I have done, in remembering the captivity of our fathers; for they were in bondage, *and none could deliver them except it was the God of Abraham, and the God of Isaac, and the God of Jacob*" (Alma₂'s sermon to his son Helaman)

There is thus a similarly happy outcome for both groups, but also a significant difference: extraordinary faith begets extraordinary results. The second deliverance (brought about through a divinely induced sleep) is obviously more miraculous than the first (which depended on the effects of alcohol). Gideon becomes something of a national hero, with a city named in his honor (Alma 6:7), and while there is never a city that bears the name of Alma₁ (so far as we know), he is allowed to establish branches of the church through the land of Zarahemla. As we observed in Chapter 4, this church of Christ provides a focal point for Mormon's narrative. He ignores a great many details of political and social history so that he can concentrate his attention on the fortunes of this particular organization and its leaders, even though it generally encompasses only a minority of the Nephite population.[26]

Yet part of Alma₁'s divine commission is to try to convince all the Nephites to adopt a proper religious perspective. It is intriguing that as soon as everyone is reunited in Zarahemla and King Mosiah has welcomed the new arrivals, Mosiah

> desired that Alma should also speak to the people. And Alma did speak unto them, when they were assembled together in large bodies, and he went from one body to another, preaching to the people repentance and faith on the Lord. And he did exhort the people of Limhi and his brethren, all those that had been delivered out of bondage, that they should remember that it was the Lord that did deliver them. (Mosiah 25:14–16)

This message of divine providence is directed particularly to the people of Limhi, who otherwise might be tempted to think that they had delivered themselves through their own cunning (in fact, God was never mentioned in Mosiah 22). The contrast that appears in Mormon's telling of the two accounts remains, but he softens the edges just a bit here, allowing us to wonder how exactly an army might have lost the tracks of a large, slow-moving party that included women and children as well as animals (Mosiah 22:8, 15–16). Was there a torrential downpour? A washed-out bridge? A deadly altercation within the Lamanite army? A significant injury or illness? Perhaps God was involved in some way or another (later, at Alma 1:8, Gideon is described by the narrator as someone "who was an instrument in the hands of God in delivering the people of Limhi out of bondage"), but Mormon does not provide any more details. He simply moves on with his history, having made his point that God's purposes can be accomplished through both ordinary competence and miraculous intervention.

The Parallel Preaching of Alma₂ and the Sons of Mosiah (Alma 4–16 and 17–27)

As we have noted before, two of the major narrative blocks in the book of Alma consist of the preaching tour of Alma₂ (the son of Alma₁; hereafter referred to simply as Alma) through the territory of the Nephites and the missionary labors of the sons of King Mosiah in Lamanite lands. Both of these are marked off by Mormon's headings:

> Alma 5, headnote: *"The words which Alma, the High Priest according to the holy order of God, delivered to the people in their cities and villages throughout the land"*
>
> Alma 17, headnote: *"An account of the sons of Mosiah, who rejected their rights to the kingdom for the word of God, and went up to the land of Nephi to preach to the Lamanites; their sufferings and deliverance—according to the record of Alma"*[27]

Alma and the sons of Mosiah were close friends who shared similar backgrounds (elite social class, wayward younger years, conversion by an angel), but they followed different paths after they turned to God. Alma became the high priest and first chief judge of the Nephites, while his companions renounced their royal station and undertook a fourteen-year mission to the Lamanites. Their proselytizing and Alma's preaching (the Nephite Reformation) both take place during the same time period (ca. 91–77 BC).

Alma is disturbed by increasing wickedness within the church—pride, costly apparel, worldly desires, inequality, and hearts set on riches—which had given rise to "envyings, and strife, and malice, and persecutions" (Alma 4:9). He therefore resigns his position as chief judge and commences a preaching tour that starts at Zarahemla and takes him to Gideon, Melek, Ammonihah, Sidom, and elsewhere. He was first introduced in the narrative as a skilled orator (even though he was then using his gifts for evil; Mosiah 27:8), and his rhetorical style impressed Mormon enough that he included several of his sermons verbatim. Alma is good at this sort of preaching—as readers can see for themselves—and he enjoys a fair amount of success. Ammonihah, of course, was entirely wiped out, but otherwise "the establishment of the church became general throughout the land" (Alma 16:15–16).

Although priests continued to denounce "all lyings, and deceivings, and envyings, and strifes, and malice, and revilings, and stealing, robbing, plundering, murdering, committing adultery, and all manner of lasciviousness" in following years (Alma 16:18; a list quite similar to the problems that Alma started with, but longer), Mormon concludes his account of Alma with the church "having got the victory over the devil, and the word of God being preached in its purity in all the land, and the Lord pouring out his blessings upon the people" (Alma 16:21). Alma has worked hard, utilizing his talents to the best of his ability, and he has seen reasonable results.[28]

The sons of Mosiah, by contrast, seem to have enjoyed extraordinary success. Their experiences are constantly characterized by miraculous turns of events. Ammon$_3$ (not the same Ammon who led the search party a century earlier) single-handedly took on more than a dozen bandits, killing seven and cutting the arms off several more (Alma 17:38); Lamanite kings and queens were converted, sometimes as a result of falling into spiritual trances (this never happens in response to any of Alma's sermons); "thousands were brought to the knowledge of the Lord" by "the power of God working miracles in them"; and "as many of the Lamanites as . . . were converted unto the Lord, never did fall away" (Alma 23:5–6). More than a thousand of these new church members—the Anti-Nephi-Lehies—chose to perish rather than break their covenant never to take up arms again, and as a result, even more Lamanites accepted the gospel (Alma 24:20–27). At the end of their mission, the sons of Mosiah returned home accompanied by several thousand Lamanite converts who wished to join with the Nephites.

It would be difficult to compare the numbers won by Alma and those converted by the sons of Mosiah since we never get even round figures for Alma's tour, but many had believed that converting any Lamanites at all was an impossible task (see Alma 17:14–16 and 26:23–27). Ammon can scarcely contain himself when he reflects on their unexpected achievements:

> My brothers and my brethren, behold I say unto you, how great reason have we to rejoice; for could we have supposed when we started from the land of Zarahemla that God would have granted unto us such great blessings? And now, I ask, what great blessings has he bestowed upon us? Can ye tell? Behold, I answer for you—for our brethren, the Lamanites, were in darkness, yea, even in the darkest abyss, but behold, how many of them are brought to behold the marvelous light of God! . . . Behold, thousands of them do rejoice, and have been brought into the fold of God. (Alma 26:1–4)

Even Alma is impressed at "the success of my brethren [the sons of Mosiah], who have been up to the land of Nephi. Behold, they have labored exceedingly, and have brought forth much fruit; and how great shall be their reward!" (Alma 29:14–15; see also 37:9).

When he reflects upon his own labors, Alma feels a sting of disappointment at his limitations:

> O that I were an angel,
>   and could have the wish of mine heart,
> that I might go forth and speak with the trump of God,
>   with a voice to shake the earth,
> and cry repentance unto every people! (Alma 29:1)

Here we might detect a hint of envy at the astonishing accomplishments of his friends, who were actually treated by the Lamanites "as though they were angels sent from God to save them from everlasting destruction" (Alma 27:4).[29] Yet in the end Alma is reconciled to an appreciation of his own task and his own gifts: "Behold, I am a man, and do sin in my wish; for I ought to be content with the things which the Lord hath allotted unto me. . . . Now, seeing that I know these things, why should I desire more than to perform the work to which I have been called? Why should I desire that I were an angel, that I could speak unto all the ends of the earth?" (Alma 29:3–7).

Mormon's editing emphasizes the contrast between Alma's faithful but conventional achievements and the extraordinary triumphs of the sons of Mosiah in several ways. First, he makes the two narrative units structurally parallel, providing accounts that are roughly similar in length and scope (despite the fact that Alma's preaching takes place over two years while the sons of Mosiah are gone for fourteen years). Each unit contains three major incidents of teaching in three different locations. In Alma's section, the preaching is done primarily through formal sermons and lengthy speeches delivered at Zarahemla, Gideon, and Ammonihah (Alma 5, 7, and 9–14). The teaching among the Lamanites, mostly portrayed through dialogue and interspersed with much more action, is conducted by Ammon in the land of Ishmael, by Aaron in Jerusalem, and by Aaron again in the land of Nephi (Alma 17:18–20:30, 21:1–17, 22–24). The third episode in each sequence is more extensive and includes a lengthy digression (on the Nephite monetary system at Alma 11 and on geography at Alma 22) as well as an account of martyred innocents (the families of believers in Ammonihah and the Anti-Nephi-Lehies; Alma 14 and 24).

Second, after providing basic equivalence for the two narrative blocks, Mormon devotes more than half of his account of the Nephite Reformation to the people of Ammonihah's disastrous rejection of Alma's words—a move that dampens our perception of his success. It does not help that this is the last city of his preaching tour for which we have an extended account, and hence it seems to constitute a sad culmination to his efforts (his subsequent labors in Sidom, described only briefly, are easy to overlook [Alma 15:1–14]). Even so, Mormon concludes his account with another pointed reference to the "hard-hearted" people in Ammonihah who "repented not of their sins" (Alma 15:15).

Third, Mormon seriously underplays the political costs of Ammon's idea of bringing thousands of Lamanite converts back to Nephite lands. Whether out of a desire for revenge or the fear that current power relationships would be destabilized, the Lamanites immediately pursued the newly Christianized Anti-Nephi-Lehies (later called the people of Ammon) as they traveled through the wilderness, and consequently encountered a Nephite army. The result was "a tremendous battle; yea, even such an one as never had been known among all the people in the land from the time Lehi left Jerusalem; yea, and tens of thousands of the Lamanites were slain and scattered abroad. Yea, and also there was a tremendous slaughter among the people of Nephi" (Alma 28:2–3). Mormon quotes Alma as acknowledging the sorrow that this caused, but then passes quickly on, noting that "while many thousands . . . truly mourn for the loss of their kindred, yet they rejoice and exult in the hope, and even know, according to the promises of the Lord, that they are raised to dwell at the right hand of God, in a state of never-ending happiness" (Alma 28:12).

Finally, although both Alma and the sons of Mosiah are described as operating by "the spirit of revelation and prophecy" (Alma 4:20, 8:24 and 17:3, 23:6), what this means in their day-to-day affairs varies significantly. According to details provided by Mormon, Alma preaches from professional expertise and confidence as the former chief judge, who retains his current position as high priest of the church (Alma 4:18, 20, 5:3, 7:1–2). His plan is to "pull down . . . all the pride and craftiness . . . [of] his people" by "bearing down in pure testimony against them" (Alma 4:19) as he speaks from a privileged position to those under his authority. It is only when he gets to Ammonihah, where the people question his jurisdiction over them, that he runs into trouble (see Alma 8:11–12). In general, his sermons are polished and eloquent, and presumably they were delivered to large audiences.

The sons of Mosiah, on the other hand, are enthusiastic but nervous about their missions. They are going among their longtime enemies—who are described as "a wild and a hardened and a ferocious people; a people who delighted in murdering the Nephites" (Alma 17:14)—where they may be particularly vulnerable as sons of the Nephite king. They face challenges in both language (Mosiah 24:4) and culture in trying to convert hostile audiences who share neither their religious vocabulary nor their political traditions (Alma 18:24–39, 20:13, 22:7–13). In anticipation of the task before them, they "fasted and prayed much" and "the Lord did visit them with his Spirit," comforting them and promising that they would be "an instrument . . . in my hands" (Alma 17:9–11; this designation is acknowledged by both the narrator and Ammon in Mosiah 27:36 and Alma 26:3, 15).[30] Rejecting any special treatment that might come to them as Nephite princes (Alma 17:24, 20:23), they find an audience by humbling themselves, offering themselves as servants (Alma 17:25, 22:3), and suffering many afflictions (Alma 20:30, 21:12–14). Their preaching takes the form of conversations, and much more than Alma, they appear to be moving forward step by step, not knowing what might come next, or, as Mormon puts it, being "led by the Spirit" (Alma 21:16, 22:1, 4). The general effect of all this is a pair of narratives in which Alma's accomplishments are substantial but those of the sons of Mosiah are extraordinary.

The Simultaneous Military Campaigns of Captain Moroni and Helaman₂ (Alma 52–62)

Captain Moroni is a complex, somewhat problematic character. Mormon obviously admires him and goes to great lengths to encourage readers to see him in the most positive light possible, yet there is much in his actions and personality that may strike some observers as less than sympathetic. This is a case when some space opens up between what Mormon says and what he actually shows us.

We first meet Moroni at the commencement of the Zoramite War, when he is twenty-five years old and the new chief captain of the Nephite armies. To have so much responsibility at such a young age probably implies that he came from a well-connected family, but he quickly proves his abilities by outmaneuvering the Lamanite invaders.[31] He has prepared his troops with armor, he asks Alma to seek a revelation from God as to where their defensive forces might best be deployed, he sends out spies (a move that Mormon feels compelled to justify; see Alma 43:29–30), and he sets an ambush by which he is able to defeat an army twice the size of his own. In the heat of the battle he rallies his men with "thoughts of their lands [and] their liberties" (Alma 43:48), and when he finds that the Nephites have the upper hand, he allows Lamanites who are willing to surrender their weapons and renounce violence a chance to return home to their own lands.

All in all, it is a heroic performance, and Moroni comes across as a skilled and humane commander. This man will dominate the last third of the book of Alma, but even at this point there are hints of difficulties to come. Despite Moroni's extensive preparations and decisive handling of military affairs, Mormon concludes his account of the war by admitting that victory came at a high cost: "Now the number of [the Lamanite] dead was not numbered because of the greatness of the number; yea, the number of their dead was exceedingly great, both on the Nephites and on the Lamanites" (Alma 44:21). He has also described Moroni as "angry" (Alma 44:17), a trait that will show up several more times in subsequent chapters. And although Moroni uses the cause of religion to justify his actions and threaten his enemies (Alma 44:2–5), we never actually see him engage in personal acts of faith. For instance, he never prays for aid or guidance (though his men certainly do; see Alma 43:49).[32] In short, Moroni conducts himself with a certain professionalism. His patriotism and love of liberty include religion, and he is a believer, to be sure, but he is not portrayed as a particularly religious man. This is something new in the Book of Mormon, at least with regard to a major character.

These patterns continue through the twelve years of the Amalickiahite Wars (ca. 73–61 BC). The trouble starts, apparently, as a schism within the church (Alma 45:22–46:1, 7, 10, 48:24), which becomes a political movement to restore the monarchy. Captain Moroni, "angry with [their leader] Amalickiah" (Alma 46:11), raises a militia of believers—evidently quite separate from the army under his command—that he rallies around the "Title of Liberty," a banner of his own devising. He and his followers pursue the fleeing Amalickiahites and summarily execute those who refuse to join with them (Alma 46:34–35, though Mormon hastens to assure us that these killings were not extralegal). Amalickiah escapes to the Lamanites and, while he is stirring up trouble there, Moroni makes extensive military preparations for the invasion he knows is coming.

At this point Mormon fudges things a bit, telling us that "Moroni planted the standard of liberty among the Nephites . . . and thus they did maintain peace in the land until nearly the end of the nineteenth year of the reign of the judges" (Alma 46:36–37). This sounds like a considerable achievement unless readers are keeping track of the chronology themselves, in which case they realize that we are already well into year nineteen, so this peace lasts only a matter of months. But even more surprisingly, Mormon inserts a paean to Moroni that is unlike anything else in the Book of Mormon:

> And Moroni was a strong and a mighty man; he was a man of a perfect understanding; yea, a man that did not delight in bloodshed; a man whose soul did joy in the liberty and the freedom of his country and his brethren from bondage and slavery; yea, a man whose heart did swell with thanksgiving to his God for the many privileges and blessings which he bestowed upon his people; a man who did labor exceedingly for the welfare and safety of his people. Yea, and he was a man who was firm in the faith of Christ, and he had sworn with an oath to defend his people, his rights, and his country, and his religion, even to the loss of his blood. (Alma 48:11–13)

Mormon keeps this up for a few more verses and then concludes with:

> Verily, verily I say unto you, if all men had been, and were, and ever would be, like unto Moroni, behold, the very powers of hell would have been shaken forever; yea, the devil would never have power over the hearts of the children of men. Behold, he was a man like unto Ammon,

the son of Mosiah, yea, and even the other sons of Mosiah, yea, and also Alma and his sons, for they were all men of God. (Alma 48:17–18)

Again, this is remarkable. Not only does Mormon employ language elsewhere reserved for deity ("verily, verily I say unto you"), but the rarity of these sorts of direct comparisons makes one sit up and take notice. Nevertheless, a little reflection may suggest that Moroni is not, in the end, very much like Ammon and the sons of Mosiah, who were missionaries rather than warriors, renounced power, humbled themselves, suffered willingly, and reached out to the Lamanites. Moroni brings a very different temperament and set of skills to the challenges of his own day and circumstances. If they are all "men of God," it must be because God has rather eclectic tastes; he seems to honor very different types of people.[33]

Over the next fourteen chapters we see Moroni at war—defending, maneuvering, strategizing, threatening, and attacking. We could cite several passages where his actions seem questionable. During a lull in the fighting he clears out Lamanite villages and establishes fortified cities in their stead (Alma 50:7–16), a particularly aggressive form of keeping the peace, which seems contrary to the articulated ideal of engaging only in defensive warfare (Alma 43:46–47, 48:14). (This is the moment that Mormon, somewhat jaw-droppingly, pronounces to be the happiest in all of Nephite history; see Alma 50:23.) At one point Moroni slaughters some four thousand of his political opponents, thus "breaking down the wars and contentions among his own people, and subjecting them to peace and civilization"(!) (Alma 51:17–22). His negotiating skills are a bit weak. When he responds to a Lamanite offer of a prisoner exchange, his letter starts out well, but his temper gets the best of him by the end ("I am in my anger, and also my people; ye have sought to murder us, and we have only sought to defend ourselves"; Alma 54:13). In such situations, it is generally not a good idea to refer to the commander of the opposing forces as "a child of hell" (Alma 54:11). Ammaron, the Lamanite leader in question, is offended, not surprisingly, but he nevertheless agrees to the conditions Moroni sets forth. Unfortunately, by this time Moroni is so exercised that he breaks off negotiations entirely. (Mormon thoughtfully includes the two letters as embedded documents so that we can get a better feel for the personalities involved.)

The most dramatic example of Moroni's temper comes in a letter to Pahoran, the chief judge in Zarahemla responsible for sending provisions, arms, and reinforcements, none of which had arrived. Moroni begins "by way of condemnation" (Alma 60:2) and over the course of his epistle he becomes more and more sure that he has been betrayed by the civilian government. He accuses them of neglect, indifference, and slothfulness. He wonders if they have become "traitors to [the] country" (Alma 60:18) and threatens to overthrow them unless things change fast (60:25–27). By the end he boldly asserts, "[Y]e know that ye do transgress the laws of God, and ye do know that ye do trample them under your feet" (60:33; perhaps an allusion to Mosiah 29:22), and he claims a revelation to that effect: "Behold, the Lord saith unto me, 'If those whom ye have appointed your governors do not repent of their sins and iniquities, ye shall go up to battle against them'" (60:33). It turns out that Moroni was mistaken in this. Pahoran had not been able to send supplies because there had been a coup against him and he was now heading a government in exile. He is actually quite gracious in the face of such unjust criticism, responding, "And now, in your epistle you have censured me, but it mattereth not; I am not angry, but do rejoice in the greatness of your heart" (Alma 61:9). He even offers a face-saving reinterpretation for Moroni's off-the-mark revelation: "I was somewhat worried concerning what we should do, whether it should be just in us to go against our brethren. But ye have said, except they repent the Lord hath commanded you that ye should go against them" (Alma 61:19–20).

On the other hand, there are also instances where Moroni can be seen giving quarter to his enemies (Alma 52:37, 55:18–19, 62:16–17, 27–29) and proving that he was indeed a reluctant warrior (Alma 48:22), one who "did not delight in bloodshed" (Alma 48:11, 55:19). Mormon seems quite sincere in his admiration of Captain Moroni, even though his account of the Amalickiahite Wars is uncharacteristically secular. God and religion are mentioned in the quoted letters, but hardly at all by the narrator, who seems content to explain causation in naturalistic terms. Perhaps this is the respect of one professional soldier for another. Whatever success the Nephites have at this time is credited to Moroni's skill as a general. If his blunt manner, quick temper, aggressive posture, and hasty suspicions would have made him a poor missionary, they are nevertheless qualities that serve him well on the battlefield. (Even so, Mormon's account glosses over the fact that under Moroni, the Nephites lost a whole string of heavily fortified cities, including, for a time, the capital Zarahemla itself; Alma 51:11, 22–28, 52:12.)

Because the Book of Mormon is primarily a religious history, we are accustomed to seeing religious virtues—humility, self-sacrifice, kindness, and relying upon the Lord. Mormon never criticizes Moroni for his lack of such qualities, but he does provide a counterexample of a very different type of military leader, one who boasts no particular martial skills or background. This is Helaman$_2$ (the son of Alma$_2$), the high priest over the church. During the first years of the conflict, Helaman and his brothers do their part for the Nephite cause by preaching (Alma 48:19–20, 49:30). When the people of Ammon (the converted Lamanites known earlier as the Anti-Nephi-Lehies) want to support the war effort by breaking their oath of nonviolence, he talks them out of it, but two thousand of their sons—who had been too young to take the original vow—swear just the opposite: "they covenanted that they . . . would fight in all cases to protect the Nephites and themselves from bondage" (Alma 53:17), and they asked Helaman to be their leader (Alma 53:19).

Moved by their sincerity and uprightness, he marches at their head to the western front, apparently knowing next to nothing about warfare.

We learn the fate of these young men, whom he refers to as his "stripling soldiers" (Alma 53:22), from a long, retrospective letter that Helaman wrote to Moroni several years later (Alma 56–58).[34] There he describes narrow escapes, clever stratagems, and surprising victories, but success comes from God's intervention rather than his own expertise. He marvels at the faith of his soldiers—"As I had ever called them my sons (for they were all of them very young) even so they said unto me, 'Father, behold our God is with us, and he will not suffer that we should fall; then let us go forth'" (Alma 56:46)—and reports that they fought with "miraculous strength" (Alma 56:56). In their first battle not one of them fell (Alma 56:56). In their second encounter the results were even more marvelous: "There were two hundred, out of my two thousand and sixty, who had fainted because of the loss of blood; nevertheless, according to the goodness of God, and to our great astonishment, and also the joy of our whole army, there was not one soul of them who did perish; yea, and neither was there one soul among them who had not received many wounds," despite the fact that a thousand of the other troops with them had been killed (Alma 57:25–26).

Over and over we hear of their faith (Alma 57:21, 27, 58:40) and prayers (58:10), how they trusted in the Lord (58:33, 37), and how they have been preserved by the "miraculous power of God" (57:26) or the "goodness of God" (57:25, 36). They too suffer from a shortage of supplies, but Helaman has a better sense of the situation than Moroni ("we fear that there is some faction in the government"; 58:36). Nevertheless, Helaman and his stripling soldiers continue to retake cities on the western front that had been captured by the Lamanites in their initial invasion, usually with minimal bloodshed on either side. At the same time, the army of Moroni lost one of the biggest prizes in the east, the city of Nephihah (Alma 59:5–13)—a turn of events that led Moroni to "be exceedingly sorrowful, and [he] began to doubt, because of the wickedness of his people" (Alma 59:11).

Thus once again we see a contrast between ordinary success—the result of diligent effort and personal skills—and the sort of miraculous accomplishments that can occur when humble people put their trust in God. Both types of service are praiseworthy and acceptable (which may be an interesting lesson for a modern church that relies on a lay ministry in which members are sometimes asked to assume responsibilities for which they have no prior experience or formal training). Indeed, in this last case, Mormon goes out of his way to ensure that his readers do not quickly dismiss Moroni's very human strivings. *If only everyone could be like Moroni*, he tells us. Perhaps for this reason he is particularly drawn to Moroni's achievements, and he lavishes fourteen chapters on his career. In the next generation, a similar Lamanite invasion conquers vast tracts of Nephite territory (including again the capital, Zarahemla), and another army, led by Moroni's son, retakes about half of their lost possessions, city by city. This five-year conflict is recounted in just six verses (Hel. 4:5–10, with another seven verses of spiritual reinterpretation of these same political events). So also, one of the most remarkable occurrences in all of Nephite history is passed by in a single verse: the rest of the lost Nephite lands are simply returned by the Lamanites after they are converted to the gospel. "And as many as were convinced did lay down their weapons of war, and also their hatred and the tradition of their fathers. And it came to pass that they did yield up unto the Nephites the lands of their possession" (Hel. 5:51–52; the missionaries in this case were the Lamanite guards from the prison where Nephi$_2$ and Lehi$_4$ were freed by divine intervention).

Based on an analysis of form—taking into account Mormon's selection, arrangement, and phrasing—it appears that what interests him is not mundane events or astonishing miracles so much as the contrast between these two modes of existence. Over the course of two hundred pages, Mormon constructs a repeating sequence of three sets of parallel stories, organizing them into narrative blocks of similar size and importance, one right after the other. Even though the two tales within each set take place at nearly the same time—so the narrative order is a matter of choice—the second story is always the more miraculous. What is more, the second tale connects with the next set: the church founded by Alma$_1$, whose members escape to Zarahemla, is the same organization that Alma$_2$ attempts to reform and that the sons of Mosiah take to the Lamanites; the converts made by the sons of Mosiah, who join with the Nephites, are the parents of Helaman's stripling soldiers. It is a clever design that highlights Mormon's literary craftsmanship, but such large-scale patterns are easy to miss. Mormon himself does not draw attention to them; instead he simply professes that "I know the record which I make to be a just and a true record" (3 Ne. 5:18). His message is that God will respond in predictable ways both to those who serve him competently and also to those who seek blessings beyond their capacities. Mormon suggests that the facts of history demonstrate this, even if the point is a little clearer when he is the one telling the stories.

In Mormon's abridgment, the meaning of any individual story is plain enough; it is, after all, a very didactic text. Yet there are additional insights to be gained from comparing and contrasting related narratives, and this process allows for much more open-ended and evocative readings. Occasionally Mormon encourages this sort of analysis through direct references, but more often he signals connections through the use of common phrases or narrative elements, or through repeated plotlines that arguably are distinctive and persistent enough to be intentional. In this way Mormon provides opportunities for reflection and rereading. Although the clever arrangement of his material could be taken as evidence for his ingenuity as a storyteller or his aesthetic sensibilities, he tends to deflect attention away from himself when he implies that God speaks and acts in regularly recurring patterns.

7

The Day of the Lord's Coming

Prophecy and Fulfillment

It seems obvious that the climax of the Book of Mormon is Christ's three-day visit to the Nephites. Jesus is the central figure of the book's theology, and his earthly ministry and redemptive sacrifice had been prophesied, discussed, and anticipated among the Nephites since the time of Lehi. Moreover, his dramatic appearance in the Americas presents a stark contrast to his rather quiet birth in Bethlehem, which, according to the gospels, was noted mainly by a few shepherds and foreign priests. In the Book of Mormon, Christ appears as a resurrected god, descending from heaven very publicly at the temple in Bountiful shortly after widespread destruction by storms, whirlwinds, lightning fires, earthquakes, landslides, and flooding, as well as three terrifying days of total darkness.[1] His advent is accompanied by a voice from heaven proclaiming, as at his baptism and transfiguration, "Behold my Beloved Son, in whom I am well pleased" (3 Ne. 11:7), and then he himself announces, "Behold, I am Jesus Christ, whom the prophets testified shall come into the world" (3 Ne. 11:10).[2]

With such a buildup, it is easy for readers to be disappointed in what follows. If archaeologists in Palestine discovered a previously unknown account of Jesus' teachings dating back to the first or second century, the world would hardly be able to contain its excitement (such was the case with the Gospel of Thomas in 1945), yet our desire for novelty and fresh insight is thwarted in the Book of Mormon when Jesus delivers a lightly revised version of the Sermon on the Mount to the Nephites, followed by extended quotations from Isaiah, Micah, and Malachi.[3] True, he instructs his twelve disciples, heals the sick, prays, administers the Eucharist, and blesses children, but the narrative is very repetitive—each of these actions occurs more than once—and, at least at first glance, it appears that there is not much in Third Nephi that we have not already seen in the New Testament. Latter-day Saints will recognize the importance of making it absolutely clear that the Jesus who visited the Nephites was the same figure who ministered to the Jews, and that he taught the same gospel in both the Old and New Worlds. To non-Mormons, however, it may seem as if Joseph Smith's scripture-creating hubris reached its limit when it came to writing lines for the Lord himself, and instead he fell back into plagiarism and filler.

Third Nephi often amplifies the miraculous aspects of the gospels, but it never reaches the fantastic heights of Buddha's sermon in the Lotus Sutra—when before an audience of hundreds of thousands of both mortal and heavenly beings, flowers rained down from heaven, perfume filled the air, the earth shook, and the Buddha emitted a ray of light that illuminated eighteen thousand worlds, in each of which another Buddha was preaching.[4] Instead, the Book of Mormon generally stays close to the parameters of biblical supernaturalism as it literalizes and expands upon familiar stories. For instance:

• Jesus persuaded doubting Thomas by allowing him to touch the wounds on his hands and side; at Bountiful he invited twenty-five hundred Nephites to do the same (John 20:24–29; 3 Ne. 11:13–17, 17:25).

• John the Baptist promised that his successor would "baptize with the Holy Ghost and with fire"; when the Nephite disciples were "filled with the Holy Ghost and with fire," they "were encircled about as if it were by fire, and it came down from heaven, and the multitude did witness it" (Matt. 3:11, Luke 3:16; 3 Ne. 19:13–14).

• At the Transfiguration, Jesus' "face did shine as the sun and his raiment was white as the light"; in the New World, this heavenly glow was transferred to his twelve disciples as well: "the light of his countenance did shine upon them, and behold they were as white as the countenance and also the garments of Jesus" (Matt. 17:2, Mark 9:2–3, Luke 9:29; 3 Ne. 19:25).

• Jesus said of one Roman centurion, "I have not found so great faith, no, not in Israel"; but of the entire Nephite multitude he marveled, "so great faith have I never seen among all the Jews" (Matt. 8:10, Luke 7:9; 3 Ne. 19:35).

• In Palestine, Jesus miraculously multiplied five loaves to feed five thousand people; in the Americas he fed even greater numbers by producing bread out of nothing (Matt. 14:15–21, Mark 6:30–44, Luke 9:10–17, John 6:1–14; 3 Ne. 20:1–8).

• The New Testament reports that Jesus once thanked the Father because "thou hast hid these things from the wise and prudent, and hast revealed them unto babes"; in Bountiful Jesus "loosed [the] tongues" of Nephite infants, so that "even babes did open their mouths and utter marvelous things" (Matt. 11:25, 21:16; 3 Ne. 26:14–16).

- There is a hint in the gospel of John about Jesus granting one apostle an extraordinary life span; at the end of Third Nephi three disciples were unambiguously transformed so that they would "never taste of death" (John 21:20–23; 3 Ne. 28:1–40).

- In the Bible Jesus alludes to several Old Testament verses; in the Book of Mormon he recites entire chapters.

In light of all this, it may be tempting to write off the Book of Mormon's account of Jesus' coming to the New World as merely derivative, especially when one recognizes that the scriptures he quotes are all adapted from the King James Version.

Although the Book of Mormon contains some three dozen prophecies of Christ's coming, the vast majority concern his life in Palestine—that he would be born, receive baptism, work miracles, be slain for the sins of the world, and then rise from the dead. Only five passages indicate that his ministry would include a postresurrection visit to the New World. Nephi had spoken plainly on the subject (1 Ne. 12:4–7; 2 Ne. 26:1–9, 32:6), but these prophecies apparently did not have wide distribution. As late as 83 BC Alma explicitly states that he does not know whether Jesus will come to the Nephites (Alma 7:8), though he later receives a revelation that this would be the case (Alma 45:10), and Mormon reports that other prophets at the time "taught that he [Christ] would appear unto them after his resurrection" (Alma 16:20).[5] Some have seen in this disjunction evidence that Joseph Smith was inventing the story as he went along, with Nephi's predictions being so much clearer because his words were dictated after Third Nephi had already been written. In any case, there was not a strong expectation of Christ's coming to the New World on anyone's part, even after the time of Alma.[6]

Just before the book of Third Nephi begins, Samuel the Lamanite offers very specific prophecies about signs in the Americas of Jesus' birth and death (with the former being predicted to occur in only five years' time), yet he never mentions Christ's visit.[7] In fact, some of his listeners complain that they are being asked to believe in a figure who will live "in a land which is far distant," and they wonder, "Why will he not show himself unto us as well as unto them who shall be at Jerusalem?" (Hel. 16:18, 20).[8] Forty years later, as righteous survivors gather in Bountiful, they too are caught by surprise—when they hear a voice proclaim "Behold my Beloved Son" and see a celestial being descending from heaven, they "wist not what it meant, for they thought it was an angel that had appeared unto them." Only after this personage proclaims, "I am Jesus Christ," do they remember that "it had been prophesied among them that Christ should show himself unto them after his ascension into heaven" (3 Ne. 11:8–12). In short, the Book of Mormon story is *not* structured around a straightforward expectation of Jesus' postresurrection appearance among the Nephites that is satisfied and brought to an unambiguous conclusion; the workings of prophecy and God's providence are portrayed as being a bit more enigmatic.

So also, events that follow the book of Third Nephi lack detailed connection with what transpired at the time of the Savior's visit. It appears that there was an astonishing social transformation, for Mormon reports that the next two centuries were a time of miracles when everyone joined the church, shared their possessions, and prospered. There was no crime, no economic inequality, no ethnic divisions, and no contention. But Mormon recounts all this in just twenty-three verses (4 Ne. 1:1–23), which makes it assertion rather than history—and with no narrative or causal analysis, it is hard to understand what happened. There is little in Mormon's report of Jesus' teachings that points the way. Christ establishes a church, but the organizational details are missing. He offers no critique of social conventions, customs, or government (despite serious problems in the system established by Mosiah, which included a susceptibility to corruption and apparently no outlet for dissent except violence). He declares that the Mosaic law is fulfilled and therefore no longer applicable, but he offers little in its place other than the broad principles of the Sermon on the Mount.

There are still other ways in which the Book of Mormon's report of Jesus' visit does not match our expectations. He clearly came as the Redeemer, introducing himself as the one who had "glorified the Father in taking upon me the sins of the world" (3 Ne. 11:11), but he does not clarify what this means or how it came about— the word *atonement* is never used and he nowhere mentions Adam, Gethsemane, Golgotha, or the empty tomb. He never even explains how he received the wounds he invites the multitude to examine.[9] Jesus announces that he has come to fulfill prophecy, but the scriptures he cites are all from Old World prophets; he does not explicitly quote the predictions of Nephi, Alma, or Samuel the Lamanite.[10] And a great deal of his preaching concerns events of the distant future, when the Gentiles would aid in the final gathering of Israel. As wondrous as this might be, it would only take place some two thousand years later. One might have thought that the Nephites, in the aftermath of terrible destructions or facing the challenge of completely rebuilding their society, would have had more pressing concerns.

Yet if Third Nephi seems disappointing or frustrating, it may be that our expectations are at odds with Mormon's own objectives. It is easy to imagine how he might have shaped his story differently in order to provide an account that was more integrated either in historical terms (by explicitly connecting events and describing how people at the time understood and responded to them) or from a literary vantage (by building up the drama through clearer foreshadowing, anticipation, suspense, and then resolution). Mormon, however, seems to be after something else. As we saw in Chapter 4, both history and literature matter to him, but as he brings his record to its culmination, his main concern is increasingly theological. Because the narrator's theological priorities here converge with the words of Jesus himself, a comprehensive overview of Third Nephi offers a unique opportunity to identify and evaluate the main religious themes of the text. At its theological climax, what does the author (or authors) of the Book of Mormon most want to communicate?

In 1831, Alexander Campbell, one of the book's first critics (and certainly the first one to read it carefully), famously observed that it seemed to weigh in on all the popular religious questions of the day, including "infant baptism, ordination, the trinity, regeneration, repentance, justification, the fall of man, the atonement, transubstantiation, fasting, penance, church government, religious experience, the call to the ministry, the general resurrection, eternal punishment, who may baptize, and even the question of freemasonry, republican government, and the rights of man."[11] This is a fair list, and references to these topics—or their analogous counterparts—can be found throughout the Book of Mormon. Yet the danger of starting with nineteenth-century controversies and then mining the narrative for relevant verses is that such a procedure may distort and misrepresent what the book actually says; it ignores the underlying logic of the text.

In this chapter we will follow Mormon's narration of Third Nephi closely, paying attention to his direct comments as well as the way he organizes and edits his material, to see which themes are given the most prominence and explored in the most detail. This path will take us deep into the world of the text with its characteristic concerns and assumptions, which may seem like an odd place to be if one regards Mormon as a fictional construct, but reading the Book of Mormon from the inside out—rather than the reverse—is essential in distinguishing what is integral from what is merely peripheral. The one issue that most seems to connect the diverse parts of Third Nephi is prophecy and its fulfillment, particularly as it concerns the destiny of the House of Israel. As Mormon weaves his account around this overarching theme, he begins to insert longer comments into his narrative, which contrast with the quick observations about editing, sources, or ethical implications that we have seen throughout his writings. There are four substantial editorial interruptions in Third Nephi, and as we attempt to reconstruct Mormon's intentions, we will give them particular attention.[12]

Signs of Jesus' Birth and Death: The Vindication of Prophecy

As the book of Third Nephi opens with the year of Christ's birth, Mormon assigns a prominent role to prophecy: "And it came to pass in the commencement of the ninety and second year, behold, the prophecies of the prophets began to be fulfilled more fully" (3 Ne. 1:4). To understand the context of this, we must backtrack a few pages to the book of Helaman, where the previous fifty years in Nephite society had been characterized by rapid shifts between righteousness and wickedness. These swings were so sudden that they seem to reflect volatility rather than developed historical cycles (they also give the impression that the population was small and institutional continuity weak). Mormon notes that "in the eighty and sixth year [i.e., six years before Jesus' birth], the Nephites did still remain in wickedness, yea, in great wickedness, while the Lamanites did observe strictly to keep the commandments of God, according to the law of Moses," and he tells of the Lamanite prophet named Samuel who climbed up on the walls of Zarahemla and prophesied to the Nephites that "the sword of justice hangeth over this people; and four hundred years pass not away save the sword of justice falleth upon this people" (Hel. 13:1, 5).[13]

Over the next three chapters, Samuel offers additional information about the catastrophe scheduled for the late fourth century AD, along with warnings about false prophets and disappearing riches, intimations of destruction awaiting Zarahemla, and detailed predictions of the signs that would accompany both Jesus' birth (a new star in addition to a day, a night, and a day of uninterrupted light) and his death (tempests, earthquakes, and three days of darkness). These prophecies are something of a chronological jumble, with predictions of events in the next few years mixed with calamities still decades or even centuries away. It is hard to imagine that the Nephites of Zarahemla were overwhelmed by tidings of devastation for their distant posterity, though for those listening closely enough to remember later, these long-term prophecies may have provided hope for recovery when disasters struck at the time of Christ's death—while it may have seemed like the end of their civilization, believers would have been assured that their posterity would survive for several more centuries.

Again and again in Samuel's sermon, or at least in Mormon's rendition of it, the critical issue is prophecy, not just as a guide to the future but as a rationale for belief, a justification for punishment (of those who reject it), and an occasion for rejoicing:

> Christ . . . surely shall come into the world, and shall suffer many things and shall be slain for his people. And behold, an angel of the Lord hath declared it unto me, and he did bring glad tidings to my soul. And behold, I was sent unto you to declare it unto you also, that ye might have glad tidings; but behold, ye would not receive me. (Hel. 13:6–7)

> Wo unto this people, because of this time which has arrived, that ye do cast out the prophets, and do mock them, and cast stones at them, and do slay them, and do all manner of iniquity unto them, even as they did of old time. (13:24)

> In the days of your poverty ye shall cry unto the Lord . . . and lament and say, "O that I had repented, and had not killed the prophets, and stoned them, and cast them out." (13:32–33)

The Lord commanded me, by his angel, that I should come and tell this thing unto you; yea, he hath commanded that I should prophesy these things unto you. . . . For this intent I have come up upon the walls of this city, that ye might hear and know of the judgments of God which do await you because of your iniquities . . . that ye might know of the signs of his coming, to the intent that ye might believe on his name. (14:9, 11–12)

And the angel said unto me that many shall see greater things than these, to the intent that they might believe that these signs and these wonders should come to pass upon all the face of this land, to the intent that there should be no cause for unbelief among the children of men. (14:28)[14]

Unfortunately, Samuel was not particularly persuasive. The crowds who said to themselves, "If our days had been in the days of our fathers of old, we would not have slain the prophets; we would not have stoned them, and cast them out" (Hel. 13:25), are the same people who try to stone Samuel and drive him away.[15] A few believe, but the majority stubbornly hold out even when the signs and wonders begin, saying, "Some things they may have guessed right, among so many; but behold, we know that all these great and marvelous works cannot come to pass, of which has been spoken" (Hel. 16:16).

Samuel had predicted that the signs of Christ's birth would appear after "five years more cometh" (Hel. 14:2). In the sixth year, when it seemed that the time had passed, skeptics set a date to put to death those still foolish enough to believe in the failed prophecy. And then, in a story whose brevity belies its drama, Nephi$_3$ prays for help and is answered by the voice of the Lord, saying, "Lift up your head and be of good cheer; for behold, the time is at hand, and on this night shall the sign be given, and on the morrow come I into the world, to show unto the world that I will fulfill all that which I have caused to be spoken by the mouth of my holy prophets" (3 Ne. 1:13). When everything transpires exactly as foretold by Samuel, including a night without darkness, people fall to the ground in amazement (Hel. 14:3–7; 3 Ne. 1:15–16). Unbelievers are abashed and the majority of Nephites are converted and baptized. Clearly, prophecy is reliable and believers will be vindicated, even if some of the details appear problematic.

One might think that such a marvelous prediction of a unique event would bring an end to doubt (as Samuel had suggested it might; Hel. 14:11–12), and so it does, but only for a short while. We read that just three years later

the people began to forget those signs and wonders which they had heard, and began to be less and less astonished at a sign or a wonder from heaven, insomuch that they began to be hard in their hearts, and

blind in their minds, and began to disbelieve all which they had heard
and seen—imagining up some vain thing in their hearts, that it was
wrought by men and by the power of the devil, to lead away and deceive
the hearts of the people. (3 Ne. 2:1–2)

Soon the political situation devolves into yet another round of conflict between the
Gadianton Robbers and the combined forces of the Nephites and Lamanites. By
following the guidance of Gidgiddoni, a military leader who was also chief judge
and prophet (3 Ne. 3:19), the Nephites win a decisive battle in AD 21 with the result
that, according to Mormon's summary,

> *there was not a living soul among all the people of the Nephites who did*
> *doubt in the least the words of all the holy prophets who had spoken;* for
> they knew that it must needs be that they must be fulfilled. And they
> knew it must be expedient that Christ had come, because of the many
> signs which had been given, according to the words of the prophets; and
> *because of the things which had come to pass already, they knew that it*
> *must needs be that all things should come to pass according to that which*
> *had been spoken.* (3 Ne. 5:1–2, emphasis added)

The level of belief here seems even greater than that which resulted from the
miraculous signs of Jesus' birth, but it appears that there is something of a gap in
the narrative—some further explanation is needed for the overwhelming spiritual
response of the Nephites at this time, as opposed to other, earlier occasions when
they also enjoyed dramatic military victories under dire circumstances.[16] Nevertheless, this passage demonstrates the persuasive power of fulfilled prophecies: because
some of Samuel's predictions had come to pass, one could reasonably expect that
his other prophecies would be fulfilled as well (and not just Samuel's proclama-
tions, but "all things . . . which had been spoken" by "all the holy prophets").
Mormon follows up this climactic moment with an extended comment highlighting
his conscientiousness as a historian.

(*First editorial comment: 3 Ne. 5:7–26*) Arguments based on historical data are
only as good as the data itself, and Mormon begins his remarks with familiar historiographical issues, again reminding us of his radical selectivity—"this book cannot contain even a hundredth part of what was done among so many people"
(v. 8)—and his reliance upon written records. Then for the first time he identifies
himself by name and assignment: "Behold, I am called Mormon . . . I have been
called of him [Christ] to declare his word among his people, that they might have
everlasting life" (vv. 12–13).[17] Perhaps because, as we will learn later, Mormon was
not particularly successful at converting his contemporaries, he redefines his call to
preach as a divine injunction to write history: "it hath become expedient that I,

according to the will of God . . . should make a record of these things which have been done; yea, a small record of that which hath taken place from the time that Lehi left Jerusalem, even down until the present time" (vv. 14–15). He continues by emphasizing the accuracy of his history: "I know the record which I make to be a just and a true record" (v. 18), even if it is by necessity greatly abbreviated (v. 19). He claims direct-observer status for events of his own day (v. 17), but he also wants us to know that Nephi₃, his principal source for the material included in Third Nephi, was himself an eyewitness who authored a "shorter but true account" (v. 9; cf. 3 Ne. 7:15). He concludes this comment section with an affirmation of what the prophets had said concerning the House of Israel, or, as he consistently refers to it, the "House of Jacob" (an expression that only Mormon uses in the Book of Mormon, aside from Isaiah quotes and two verses in Third Nephi spoken by Jesus).[18] House of Israel theology has never before played a role in Mormon's writing, and in this case it seems to be prefiguring a major theme of Jesus' teachings to the Nephites.

Somewhat surprisingly, in light of Mormon's strong assertion, within a decade of military triumph and universal testimony—when "not a living soul . . . did doubt in the least"—disputations, inequality, and persecutions had returned. By the year 30, "the church was broken up" and the Nephites "were in a state of awful wickedness" (3 Ne. 6:14, 17). Mormon keeps the focus of his account on prophecy by informing us that prophets arose among the people, calling them to repentance and "testifying unto them of the redemption which the Lord would make for his people, or in other words, the resurrection of Christ" (6:20), but many of these seers were put to death secretly and illegally by those in power. In fact, in short order the chief judge was assassinated, the central government collapsed, and "the more righteous part of the people had nearly all become wicked" (7:7). Still, the prophet Nephi₃ kept testifying and working miracles until the end. Although his insistent preaching made numerous enemies, in the last year before Christ's coming "there were many . . . that were baptized unto repentance" (7:26). Some people began looking for the fulfillment of Samuel's prophecies of the signs of Jesus' death (even though there is no record of prophecies concerning how long he would live), particularly the three days of darkness, and "there began to be great doubtings and disputations among the people, notwithstanding so many signs had been given" (8:4). And then in the thirty-fourth year, a great storm arose, with earthquakes, fires, and floods that enveloped entire cities.

Here at last was evidence so terrible and final that it could not be denied. Samuel had preached that "signs and wonders" would be given "to the intent that there should be no cause for unbelief among the children of men," warning that "whosoever will believe might be saved, and that whosoever will not believe, a righteous judgment might come upon them; and also if they are condemned, they bring upon themselves their own condemnation" (Hel. 14:28–29). That day had arrived, and great multitudes perished, saying, "O that we had repented before this great and terrible day, and had not killed and stoned the prophets, and cast them out" (3 Ne. 8:25), just as Samuel had predicted: "then shall ye lament and say, 'O that I had repented, and had not killed the prophets, and stoned them, and cast them out'" (Hel. 13:32–33).

As this example illustrates, Mormon often draws an implicit connection between prophecies and their fulfillment by reporting events in the language of the original prediction. His chapter-long account of the destruction among the Nephites at the time of Jesus' death borrows heavily in its wording not just from Samuel's prophecies but also from Nephi's (1 Ne. 12, 2 Ne. 26) and Zenos' (1 Ne. 19).

3 NEPHI 8	ORIGINAL PROPHECY	PROPHET	PHRASES AND NARRATIVE ELEMENTS
v. 10	1 Ne. 19:11	Zenos	a "mountain" "carried up"
vv. 13, 17	2 Ne. 26:6	Nephi	"thunderings, and lightnings, and earthquakes"
	Hel. 14:21	Samuel	"thunderings and lightnings" and earthquakes
v. 13	Hel. 14:24	Samuel	"highways broken up"
v. 14	1 Ne. 12:4	Nephi	"many cities . . . sunk . . . burned" and collapsed
v. 14	Hel. 14:24	Samuel	"many cities [became] desolate"
v. 16	2 Ne. 26:5	Nephi	"whirlwinds shall carry them away"
v. 18	Hel. 14:21–22	Samuel	rocks "rent in twain . . . [and] were found in seams and in cracks, and in broken fragments upon the face of the whole earth/land"[19]
vv. 20–23	1 Ne. 19:10–11	Zenos	"vapor of darkness" lasting for three days
v. 22	Hel. 14:20	Samuel	no light from sun, moon, or stars for three days
v. 22	1 Ne. 12:4	Nephi	"mist(s) of darkness"

As the "thick darkness" comes (3 Ne. 8:20), a voice from heaven names sixteen destroyed cities, explaining that these disasters were divine punishment for abusing and killing the prophets (a charge repeated five times; 3 Ne. 9:5, 7, 8, 9, 10–11). And then, finally, the voice identifies itself, saying:

> Behold, I am Jesus Christ the Son of God. I created the heavens and the earth, and all things that in them are. I was with the Father from the beginning. . . . I came unto my own, and my own received me not. And the scriptures concerning my coming are fulfilled. . . . and in me is the law of Moses fulfilled. I am the light and the life of the world. I am Alpha and Omega, the beginning and the end. (3 Ne. 9:15–18)

With a flourish of New Testament phraseology, Jesus proclaims himself the culmination and fulfillment of prophecy. The emphasis on scriptural predictions is not just Mormon's personal interpretation of events; it is Christ's own characterization of what has happened. And much of the familiar biblical language takes on a heightened poignancy in the immediate physical context of three terrible days of death, destruction, and total darkness: "return unto me . . . that I may heal you" (3 Ne. 9:13), "if ye will come unto me ye shall have eternal life; behold, mine arm of mercy is extended towards you" (9:14), "I am the light and the life of the world" (9:18). Indeed, when Jesus says "I am the beginning and the end," many of the Nephites must have assumed that the end of the world had come. Yet Mormon's account concludes on a note of hope. After the darkness disperses and the aftershocks stop, "the weeping and the wailing of the people who were spared alive did cease; and their mourning was turned into joy, and their lamentations into the praise and thanksgiving unto the Lord Jesus Christ, their Redeemer" (3 Ne. 10:10).

It does not appear that those Nephites who were spared destruction expected anything beyond Jesus' verbal assurance of comfort and healing. Zenos had long before prophesied that "the Lord God surely shall visit all the House of Israel at that day, some with his voice, because of their righteousness, unto their great joy and salvation; and others with the thunderings and the lightnings of his power, by tempest, by fire, and by smoke, and vapor of darkness, and by the opening of the earth" (1 Ne. 19:11). All this had happened by 3 Nephi 10. Like the Israelites at Sinai, the righteous Nephites had heard the voice of God amidst "thunders and lightnings," fire, smoke, earthquake, and "thick darkness" (Ex. 19:16–18; Deut. 4:11–12). The Israelites, terrified at hearing the voice of God, requested that only Moses, as their representative, be brought into God's presence. In Third Nephi, however, the Nephites at Bountiful will soon transcend the Sinai precedent as they hear and then see and even touch their Lord. And like Moses, when they are with God he gives them a new law.

(*Second editorial comment: 3 Ne. 10:11–18*) This section, which demarcates the most important transition in Nephite history, is in many ways the culmination of Mormon's historical endeavors. In it, he summarizes what he considers his strongest evidence for the rationality of belief—that is, the argument from fulfilled prophecy.

He begins, following the lead of Jesus' proclamation from heaven at 9:16 ("the scriptures concerning my coming are fulfilled"), by observing that "thus far were the scriptures fulfilled which had been spoken by the prophets" (10:11). He notes again the natural disasters and catastrophes in the New World that heralded the death of Jesus in Jerusalem, and then places them within the context of long-term, multiple prophecies:

> And now, whoso readeth, let him understand; he that hath the scriptures, let him search them, and see and behold if all these deaths and destructions by fire, and by smoke, and by tempests, and by whirlwinds, and by the opening of the earth to receive them, and all these things, are not unto the fulfilling of the prophecies of many of the holy prophets. (v. 14)

He goes on to name men whose predictions had been vindicated by events up to this point—Zenos and Zenock (two extrabiblical Hebrew prophets), along with Jacob (Nephi's brother)—and he refers to the scriptures brought by Nephi from Jerusalem.[20] All of this seems to Mormon to constitute self-evident, overwhelming proof. Then follows a major editorial break, complete with a preview ("I will show unto you that . . ."), a promise ("an account of his [Jesus'] ministry shall be given hereafter"), a sign-off ("therefore for this time I make an end of my sayings"), and a headnote ("*Jesus Christ did show himself unto the people of Nephi*"), all within two verses (vv. 18–19). One age ends and another begins when Jesus appears in person to the Nephites in the next chapter (3 Ne. 11), in effect resetting the trajectory of their history. We will also see a shift in Mormon's relationship to his record and his audience.

Jesus' New World Ministry: Prophecies Fulfilled and Renewed

Mormon begins his account of Christ's visit to the Americas with a headnote: "*Jesus Christ did show himself unto the people of Nephi, as the multitude were gathered together in the land Bountiful, and did minister unto them; and on this wise did he show himself unto them.*" As in the past, this device signals the beginning of a discrete section of narrative, but rarely has the break been so thorough. The scene has shifted to the land Bountiful, a region that has thus far not played a prominent role in the story and about which we know little (other than that it was the site of battles described in Alma 51–52 and Hel. 1); Jesus' words and actions show few connections to what came before; and Mormon, usually a meticulous recorder, does not tell us exactly when Jesus appeared. We know the cataclysmic destructions occurred "in the thirty and fourth year, in the first month, on the fourth day of the month" (3 Ne. 8:5), but after his editorial interruption Mormon does not offer a date for the most momentous event in Nephite history, when the people in Bountiful were gathered at the temple, marveling at the extent of the devastation and talking of Christ, and then suddenly heard another voice from above and saw a heavenly figure descending. Although most Latter-day Saints have assumed that Jesus appeared right after the three days of darkness—as can be seen in LDS artistic depictions of the event—some have suggested that the destruction and the visitation could have been separated by several weeks or even months.[21]

The lack of a precise date means that it is hard to determine whether Jesus' sermons interrupted rescue operations, consoled bereaved survivors, or encouraged rebuilding efforts already under way. (When he healed all that were "lame, or blind, or halt, or maimed" [3 Ne. 17:7], was he repairing injuries that were sustained in the recent disasters?)[22] The resurrected Jesus never mentions the death and ruin that preceded his arrival, even though that would have been on everyone's mind, even months later. Rather than these types of narrative connections, what Mormon does provide are excerpts from two sermons that were delivered on two consecutive days. He informs us that "the Lord truly did teach the people for the space of three days" (3 Ne. 26:13), yet as we shall see, just as he is about to give details from Christ's second-day sermon concerning prophecies of the last days, he is stopped short by Jesus and obediently forbears. He goes on to describe how the people gathered expectantly the following day and their infants miraculously spoke (26:16), yet in this telling Jesus never again appears to the multitude and we, like the Nephites, are left waiting. In place of the anticipated third-day discourse, Mormon inserts an account of a later, undated appearance to the twelve disciples (3 Ne. 27–28).

Just as Mormon has, at Jesus' command, left readers wanting more content, so also we might wish for more clarity. Jesus' teachings are neither simple nor straightforward; instead they offer a series of puzzles that invite reflection and interpretive effort. One useful approach is to imagine Third Nephi as a sort of alternative history (or, if one prefers, a thought experiment or a Christian fantasy). How would things have been different if the Jews in Palestine had read the Hebrew prophets in the same way that early Christians did, as pointing toward a future savior figure? What if they had recognized Jesus as their Redeemer and joined the church en masse? What if they had understood the law of Moses to be a set of temporary requirements prefiguring the atonement of Christ? This is exactly the situation of the Nephites in Bountiful.

When Jesus appears, his first words affirm that he is indeed the promised savior: "Behold, I am Jesus Christ, whom the prophets testified shall come into the world," and he invites the multitude to feel the nail prints in his hands and feet "that ye may know that I am the God of Israel, and the God of the whole earth, and have been slain for the sins of the world" (3 Ne. 11:10, 14). After this positive identification, in which the people "did know of a surety and did bear record, that it was he, of whom it was written by the prophets, that should come" (11:15), they fall at his

feet and worship him. He responds by giving Nephi₃ and eleven others the authority to baptize, and then instructs them on how to perform this ordinance (with little
acknowledgment that efficacious baptisms had been practiced among the Nephites
since the days of Alma₁ other than mentioning prior "disputations" concerning the
rite; 3 Ne. 11:22, 28).[23] Thus the Nephites, who have been keeping the Mosaic law for
centuries even while anticipating a future messiah, immediately recognize the Lord
and prepare to be baptized into his church. The transition is much smoother than
what we see in the New Testament. There is no conflict between the Church
and Israel, or between Jewish Christians and Gentile Christians. Indeed, since all
the wicked have recently perished, the gospel is universally accepted.

Two major issues, however, remain for the Nephite multitude. The first per-
tains to the law of Moses—now that it has been fulfilled and its requirements done
away with, what is to take its place? How should believers worship? How should
they live? How are they to maintain a right relationship with God? The second concerns the Nephites' identity as Israelites—once the "God of Israel" is seen as "the
God of the whole earth" (3 Ne. 11:14), what advantage is there in claiming descent
from Abraham, Isaac, and Jacob? What will become of the covenants and prophecies made to the House of Israel? Paul took up these questions, within a Greco-
Roman context, in his Epistle to the Romans, where he developed the doctrine of
grace (a word that never occurs in Third Nephi). The resurrected Jesus, addressing
Nephites under very different circumstances, offers another set of answers.

The Fulfillment of the Law of Moses

Long before, Nephi had written that "notwithstanding we believe in Christ, we keep
the law of Moses, and look forward with steadfastness unto Christ, until the law shall
be fulfilled" (2 Ne. 25:24)—a principle reiterated by Abinadi, Amulek, and Mormon
himself (Mosiah 13:27–28; Alma 25:15–16, 30:3, 34:13–14). This doctrine was well
enough known that there was some confusion at the time when the Nephites saw the
signs of Jesus' birth. Some thought that "it was no more expedient to observe the law
of Moses," though they soon came to understand that their interpretations of scripture were in error, that "the law was not yet fulfilled," and that it would not be until
Christ's death (3 Ne. 1:24–25; cf. Alma 34:13–14). Thirty-four years later, Christ's
voice in the darkness announced that the long-anticipated day had finally arrived:

> By me redemption cometh, and in me is the law of Moses fulfilled . . . ye
> shall offer up unto me no more the shedding of blood; yea, your sacri-
> fices and your burnt offerings shall be done away, for I will accept none
> of your sacrifices and your burnt offerings. And ye shall offer for a
> sacrifice unto me a broken heart and a contrite spirit. (3 Ne. 9:17–20,
> echoing Ps. 51:17; cf. Ps. 34:18)

Yet the Mosaic law concerned more than just animal sacrifices; it was a comprehensive code that had guided the Israelites in matters ranging from prayer, the Sabbath, and defilement to circumcision, diet, and clothing, as well as marriage, inheritance, wages, and lending. The Nephites presumably lived by some sort of adaptation suited to the plants, animals, and social conditions of the New World (the Book of Mormon offers few details), and the announcement of the fulfillment of the law would have left them wondering what would take its place. It is therefore fitting that Jesus begins his public teachings among the Nephites with a rendition of the Sermon on the Mount, which took as one of its major themes the relationship between the old law and the new.

In strictly historical terms this is problematic since the Greek text of that discourse was not written until several decades after Jesus' resurrection and alleged visit to the New World (and the English King James Version, which the Book of Mormon follows very closely, obviously came much later still).[24] For some readers, this may be all the evidence one needs of Joseph Smith's nineteenth-century authorship, yet believers, viewing the Book of Mormon as a miraculous translation, have other options, including an extraordinary revelation or even an inspired but somewhat free translation by Joseph Smith.[25] In any case, because the Sermon on the Mount is often taken as the quintessential expression of Christian thought, one can hardly imagine a better way to assert that the personage who appeared in Bountiful was indeed the Christ of the New Testament and that he taught the same gospel in both the Old World and the New. John Welch has referred to the Third Nephi version of Matthew 5–7 as the "Sermon at the Temple," in part to buttress his own interpretation of the episode as a veiled synopsis of sacred ritual, and while we may hesitate in adopting that particular reading, the nomenclature is nevertheless useful and will be adopted in the following discussion.[26]

The first thing to notice is that even though the language of the Sermon on the Mount and the Sermon at the Temple is very similar, the latter has been substantially recontextualized so that the same words take on different meanings. It is almost like imagining, with Jorge Luis Borges, that *Don Quixote* had been rewritten word for word by an early twentieth-century French symbolist poet, Pierre Menard: "the Cervantes text and the Menard text are verbally identical, but the second is almost infinitely richer"; sentences that seemed conventional rhetoric in the seventeenth-century appear ironic and daringly countercultural when penned by "a contemporary of William James."[27] So also a very different setting casts the words of Matthew 5–7 in a new light. We can enumerate some of the distinctions that make a difference in how we interpret the familiar biblical phrases:

- In Third Nephi, Jesus is speaking as God, with maximal authority (he has descended from heaven in glory bearing signs of his crucifixion), not as a seemingly human reformer at the beginning of his public career. When Christ at the temple promises rewards in heaven or speaks of the judgment day or what the Father will do, these are more than expressions of faith—the Nephites recognize that he is in a position to make such things happen. Indeed, this may be an extreme case of performative language.

- Unlike in Galilee, the people at Bountiful all recognize and embrace Jesus as their Redeemer; they are awestruck to be with him. As a result, several of the beatitudes have an immediate rather than eschatological application. For instance, when Jesus affirms that the "pure in heart . . . shall see God" (Matt. 5:8 ‖ 3 Ne. 12:8), he is speaking to people who are at that very moment in God's presence.

- To a person, the Nephite audience is righteous and has just experienced (and survived) widespread, catastrophic destruction. The commands—and, coming from God himself, they are commandments rather than ethical suggestions (3 Ne. 12:20)—to be generous, to refrain from judging, to pray fervently, not to pursue material treasures, and to build on solid foundations are all relevant to their current situation. On the other hand, warnings about false prophets and persecutions seem to belong to an earlier era (or perhaps to centuries in the future); those at the temple already know firsthand about the broad way "that leadeth to destruction."

- They have just been commanded to defer to new leaders and be baptized. As Jesus begins to speak, he prefaces his sermon with three additional beatitudes: "*Blessed are ye if ye shall give heed unto the words of these twelve whom I have chosen from among you to minister unto you and to be your servants*; and unto them I have given power that they may baptize you with water; and after that . . . I will baptize you with fire and with the Holy Ghost; therefore *blessed are ye if ye shall believe in me and be baptized*, after that ye have seen me and know that I am. . . . Yea, *blessed are they who shall believe in your words . . . and be baptized*" (3 Ne. 12:1–2; emphasis added). This makes the Sermon at the Temple something like a charter for a newly formed religious community.

- Because of prophecies and Jesus' voice in the darkness, the Nephites at Bountiful know the law of Moses is fulfilled and they are anxious to understand the implications of this. Jesus' revisions to the requirements concerning murder, adultery, divorce, oaths, retribution, and love ("ye have heard that it hath been said . . . but I say unto you . . .") are indications that although Christian standards will be, in some ways, even more demanding, core principles remain unchanged.[28] In addition, the focus of moral behavior is now on Jesus Christ himself, and specific regulations are derived from the continuing revelation of his word. (As Nephi once prophesied: "After Christ shall have risen from the dead he shall show himself unto you, my children, and my beloved brethren; and the words which he shall speak unto you shall be the law which ye shall do," 2 Ne. 26:1; cf. 32:6.)

There are a few differences between the Sermon on the Mount and the Sermon at the Temple (the majority of which occur in the first chapter—Matt 5 ‖ 3 Ne. 12), and these textual variants tend to reinforce the contextual contrasts.[29] Krister Stendahl, former dean of the Harvard Divinity School, astutely observed that Jesus at Bountiful is not so much the synoptic "teacher of righteousness, basing his teaching on the law and the prophets," as he is "a Johannine Jesus, the revealed revealer who points to himself and to faith in and obedience to him as the message."[30] (Incidentally, like Jesus in the Gospel of John, the Christ of Third Nephi does not tell parables.) Stendahl's interpretation was based on variants such as the following—with substituted phrases underlined, insertions in bold, deletions in angle brackets, and italicized words in the KJV left in italics:

MATTHEW 5	3 NEPHI 12
3 Blessed *are* the poor in spirit: for theirs is the kingdom of heaven.	**Yea**, blessed are the poor in spirit **who come unto me**, for theirs is the kingdom of heaven.
6 Blessed *are* they <u>which</u> do hunger and thirst after righteousness: for they shall be filled.	**And** blessed are **all** they <u>who</u> do hunger and thirst after righteousness, for they shall be filled **with the Holy Ghost**.
18 For verily I say unto you, <Till heaven and earth pass>, one jot <u>or</u> one tittle <u>shall in no wise pass</u> from the law, <till> all <u>be fulfilled</u>.	For verily I say unto you, one jot <u>nor</u> one tittle <u>hath not passed away</u> from the law, **but in me it hath** all <u>been fulfilled</u>.
19 <Whosoever therefore shall break one of these least commandments, and shall teach men so, he shall be called the least in the kingdom of heaven: but whosoever shall do and teach *them*, the same shall be called great in the kingdom of heaven.>	**And behold, I have given you the law and the commandments of my Father, that ye shall believe in me, and that ye shall repent of your sins, and come unto me with a broken heart and a contrite spirit. Behold, ye have the commandments before you and the law is fulfilled. Therefore come unto me and be ye saved;**
20 For I say unto you, That except <your righteousness shall exceed *the righteousness* of the scribes and Pharisees>, ye shall in no case enter into the kingdom of heaven.	for **verily** I say unto you, that except **ye keep my commandments, which I have commanded you at this time**, ye shall in no case enter into the kingdom of heaven.

24 <Leave there thy gift before the altar, and> go thy way; first be reconciled to thy brother, and then come <and offer thy gift>.	Go thy way **unto thy brother, and** first be reconciled to thy brother, and then come **unto me with full purpose of heart, and I will receive you.**
46 <For if ye love them which love you, what reward have ye? do not even the publicans the same?>	**Therefore, those things which were of old time, which were under the law, in me are all fulfilled.**
47 <And if ye salute your brethren only, what do ye more *than others?* do not even the publicans so?>	**Old things are done away, and all things have become new** [in an echo of 2 Cor. 5:17].[31]
48 Be ye therefore perfect, even as your Father <u>which</u> is in heaven is perfect.	Therefore **I would that** ye **should** be perfect even as **I, or** your Father <u>who</u> is in heaven is perfect.

Again, we should bear in mind that most of the words in the two sermons are identical, but in the examples above we can see Third Nephi's distinctive emphasis on coming to Christ and developing faith in him, highlighting his role as the focal point of the law, both as the fulfiller of the old and as the giver of the new. Jesus' invitation to "come unto me"—which does not appear in the Sermon on the Mount—is inserted six times into his discourse at Bountiful (3 Ne. 12:3, 19, 20, 23, 24), and for people who have just been urged to personally inspect the wounds in his hands and feet, this is a literal rather than metaphorical invitation. Whereas in Matthew Jesus promised that the law will remain in force "till all be fulfilled" (5:18), here he unambiguously proclaims that the new age has arrived, that "in me it hath all been fulfilled." The phrase from the Lord's Prayer, "thy kingdom come," is omitted from the version in Third Nephi, presumably because God's kingdom *has* come to the righteous Nephites (3 Ne. 13:10), and Jesus' injunction not just to follow the example of the Father but "to be perfect even as I . . . [am] perfect" is a further affirmation of his glorified, postresurrection status.[32]

Jesus follows up his sermon by addressing the concerns of those who did not understand how exactly "old things had passed away," explaining that "I am he that gave the law . . . therefore, the law in me is fulfilled . . . therefore it hath an end," later reiterating that "the law which was given unto Moses hath an end in me" (3 Ne. 15:5, 8). In fact, going beyond what is asserted in the New Testament, Jesus flatly declares, "I *am* the law" (3 Ne. 15:9, emphasis added). He continues in that same verse, "Look unto me and endure to the end, and ye shall live; for unto him that endureth to the end will I give eternal life."

As these ideas are developed throughout his teachings to the Nephites, it becomes clear that Jesus himself will replace the statutes and commandments of the prior law. Through the sacrament (the LDS term for the Eucharist), prayer, communal worship, and especially the gift of the Holy Ghost, believers could continue in the same relationship to Christ that they were then experiencing in his presence. Their constant access to him would allow for ongoing instruction and guidance, and would serve as the foundation of a new covenant. In establishing his church and instituting new modes of worship, Jesus is directing the faithful toward a spiritual path focused on himself. We can see this, for example, in Mormon's account of the second day of Christ's ministry, which begins with the twelve disciples asking the assembled multitude to pray (crowds had gathered expectantly through the night, awaiting Jesus' promised return). The disciples are baptized by Nephi₃ and subsequently receive the Holy Ghost in a dramatic fashion: they are "encircled about as if it were by fire," angels come down from heaven, and finally Christ appears and "stood in the midst and ministered unto them" (19:15). The sequence functions as a concrete demonstration that the practices that had been taught on the first day—baptism, prayer, seeking the Spirit, communal worship—could indeed make Christ present in the lives of believers. Jesus administers the sacrament to the disciples and then directs them to give bread and wine to the multitude. Eventually the twelve will baptize the rest of the people, who will thereupon be "filled with the Holy Ghost" (26:17).

The details provided by Mormon underscore a pattern in which blessings come first to the disciples and then to the general population. We see this same progression when we compare two prayers given by Jesus in quick succession shortly after his appearance on the second day (with added emphases and obvious references to John 17):

Father, I thank thee that thou hast *given the Holy Ghost* unto these whom I have chosen; and it is because of their belief in me that I have chosen them out of the world. Father, I pray thee that thou wilt *give the Holy Ghost* unto all them that shall believe on their words . . . I pray unto thee for them, and also for all those who shall believe on their words, *that they may believe in me*, that I may be in them as thou, Father, art in me, that we may be one. (3 Nephi 19:20–23)

Father, I thank thee that thou hast *purified* these whom I have chosen, because of their faith, and I pray for them, and also for them who shall believe on their words, that they *may be purified* in me through faith on their words . . . I pray . . . for those whom thou hast given me out of the world, because of their faith, *that they may be purified in me*, that I may be in them as thou, Father, art in me, that we may be one. (3 Ne. 19:28–29)

A process is delineated here by which believers can follow the example of the disciples and move from enjoying the blessings of the Spirit to becoming purified.[33] Yet things are not always so straightforward. As we saw in Chapter 6, when the disciples receive the Holy Ghost ("encircled about as if it were by fire . . . and angels did come down out of heaven and did minister unto them"; 3 Ne. 19:14), they are only recapitulating what had happened on the first day to the little children whom Jesus had blessed—"they were encircled about with fire, and the angels did minister unto them" (3 Ne. 17:24)—or indeed what had occurred sixty-five years earlier to the Lamanites in the prison with Nephi$_2$ and Lehi$_4$: "they were filled as if with fire . . . and angels came down out of heaven and ministered unto them" (Hel. 5:45–48).[34] It is remarkable that within God's providential design, which includes a hierarchical church organization, there are nevertheless times when children, and even Lamanites, take precedence over God's chosen ones.

Similarly, although the House of Israel has long enjoyed an extraordinary measure of divine care and revelation, and will be the means through which the Lord will bless the entire world, Jesus also taught that there would be periods when priority would be given to the Gentiles. This does not mean, however, that the covenants and prophecies made to the House of Israel had been abrogated or nullified. Even as Jesus proclaims an end to the Mosaic law, he hastens to add, "I do not destroy the prophets, for as many as have not been fulfilled in me, verily I say unto you, shall all be fulfilled . . . for behold, the covenant which I have made with my people is not all fulfilled" (3 Ne. 15:6–8).

Prophecies Concerning the House of Israel

Christ had earlier reaffirmed to the Nephites the significance of their status as descendants of Israel, declaring that his visit to them was a fulfillment of his words to the Jews as recorded at John 10:16 ("Other sheep I have, which are not of this fold: them also I must bring, and they shall hear my voice") and indicating that there were other scattered branches of Israel elsewhere in the world that he would similarly visit (3 Ne. 15:11–16:3). On the second day, the role of the House of Israel in the new age is his dominant theme. In a lengthy discourse, he explains how the covenant made to Israel will eventually be fulfilled, and he outlines the Father's plan for the salvation of humankind:

(1) The Gentiles will accept Christ and receive the Holy Ghost, thereby gaining dominance over the Jews who do not acknowledge Jesus, as well as the benighted descendants of Lehi in the New World. They will oppress and scatter God's chosen people, but eventually most of the Gentiles themselves will fall into wickedness and unbelief.

(2) The Book of Mormon will come forth as a sign that God is about to fulfill his covenant with Israel (i.e., those aspects not fulfilled at the time of Jesus' coming to the Nephites).

(3) Through the words of Christ recorded in that book, some of the Gentiles will be converted, and they in turn will use the Book of Mormon to preach to the Lamanites (who are themselves a branch of Israel).

(4) Christ will establish his church among these converted Gentiles, and those who repent will be adopted into the House of Israel and receive the blessings of the covenant.[35]

(5) Remnants of the House of Israel throughout the earth will be gathered together, with the help of the Gentiles.

(6) Each branch of Israel will take possession of its particular promised land, with the Jews returning to Palestine and the Lehites receiving their inheritance in the New World, where they will build a New Jerusalem, again with Gentile support.

(7) Gentiles who do not repent will be afflicted by the newly resurgent House of Israel, just as they themselves had previously oppressed Israel.

(8) The House of Israel will be brought to a knowledge of Jesus Christ as their Redeemer.[36]

Yet the extraction and analysis of theological propositions does not do justice to Jesus' sermons to the Nephites (or to the Book of Mormon in general). The *way* that Jesus teaches is just as important as the doctrinal content of his discourses, and the clarity of my synopsis misrepresents the actual style of 3 Nephi 20–25, which is anything but a straightforward exposition. Indeed, Jesus preaches in a manner that thwarts ready understanding and forces multiple rereadings with close attention to interruptions, antecedents, repetitions, and reversals. For example, even with the addition of parentheses and some bracketed identifications, the following passage makes for slow going (note how the "you" addressed by Jesus shifts back and forth between the Nephites at Bountiful, the House of Israel as a whole, and the Lamanites in the latter days)[37]:

> And verily, I say unto you, I give unto you a sign, that ye may know the
> time when these things shall be about to take place—that I shall gather
> in, from their long dispersion, my people, O House of Israel, and shall
> establish again among them my Zion. And behold, this is the thing
> which I will give unto you for a sign—for verily, I say unto you that
> when these things which I declare unto you (and which I shall declare
> unto you hereafter of myself, and by the power of the Holy Ghost which
> shall be given unto you of the Father), shall be made known unto the
> Gentiles [as part of the Book of Mormon] that they may know

concerning this people who are a remnant of the House of Jacob, and
concerning this my people [the Lamanites] who shall be scattered by
them; verily, verily, I say unto you, when these things shall be made
known unto them of the Father, and shall come forth of the Father, from
them [the Gentiles] unto you (for it is wisdom in the Father that they
should be established in this land, and be set up as a free people by the
power of the Father, that these things might come forth from them unto
a remnant of your seed, that the covenant of the Father may be fulfilled
which he hath covenanted with his people, O House of Israel) . . . it shall
be a sign unto them [the Lamanites], that they may know that the work
of the Father hath already commenced unto the fulfilling of the covenant
which he hath made unto the people who are of the House of Israel.
(3 Ne. 21:1–4, 7)

Convoluted though it may be, this was the passage in the Book of Mormon
most often quoted by early Latter-day Saints, who certainly saw their new scripture
as a sign that God's work in the last days had commenced.[38] Readers can be thank-
ful that the Book of Mormon's prose is generally not characterized by this type of
convoluted syntax and ambiguous referents. Mormon's writing, in particular, is
usually much more clear and precise, which leads us to wonder what is happening
in these chapters. Jesus is conveying information here, but he is doing so in a way
that undermines readers' attempts to master the material. A discourse such as this
has to be read and reread with multiple perspectives in mind, working from the
whole to the parts and vice versa. For all readers, this type of writing presents a
challenge in identifying and interpreting major themes; for believers, such passages
are virtual invitations to ask for and receive further revelation. This, at least, was
the pattern of learning Jesus proposed at 3 Nephi 17:1–3, where he encouraged the
confused and overwhelmed multitude to return home and prepare for further revelation by "ponder[ing] upon the things which I have said, and ask[ing] of the
Father, in my name, that ye may understand." Reading Jesus' sermons in Third
Nephi is more like interpreting prophecy rather than following structured arguments or straightforward narrative.

Significantly, Jesus claims the title of prophet when he asserts that he was the
one foretold by Moses in Deuteronomy 18:15, 18–19: "Behold, I am he of whom
Moses spake, saying, 'A prophet shall the Lord your God raise up unto you of your
brethren, like unto me; him shall ye hear in all things whatsoever he shall say unto
you. And it shall come to pass that every soul who will not hear that prophet shall
be cut off from among the people'" (3 Ne. 20:23).[39] Given his relationship with his
Nephite audience, it hardly seems necessary for him to urge them to give heed to
his words. His point here, then, concerns prophecy—both its fulfillment and its

continuing validity. In the teachings that follow, he communicates his message through extensive quotations of scripture. This rhetorical strategy is somewhat surprising. Usually people cite holy writ when they need to bolster their authority. Jesus, descending from heaven as God, does not need any further proof of his power or legitimacy; it would have been obvious to everyone present on that occasion that his words *were* scripture. So the effect is just the opposite. He validates the ancient prophets by quoting their writings, thus demonstrating that even the arrival of the Lord himself will not annul or supplant the authority of the scriptures. The resurrected Christ does not just fulfill prophecies; he renews the promise of those that were as yet unrealized.

Jesus had opened his second discourse with an allusion to something he said on the first day with regard to Isaiah: "Ye remember that I spake unto you, and said that when the words of Isaiah should be fulfilled . . . then is the fulfilling of the covenant which the Father hath made unto his people" (3 Ne. 20:11–12, picking up the argument from 16:16–20, where he had quoted Isa. 52:8–10). As he continues his discussion of relations between the Gentiles and the descendants of Israel in the last days, he augments his words with lengthy quotations from the Hebrew prophets. He combines Micah 5:8–9 and 4:12–13, adding an interpretation that the rampaging lion and the charging bull both symbolize the way that remnants of Israel will eventually turn on unbelieving Gentiles. He quotes most of Isaiah 52 (placing vv. 8–10 at the beginning and omitting the prose interruption of vv. 4–5), a chapter that describes the joyful day when the Lord and his people will return to Jerusalem. From a biblical perspective, this would already have been fulfilled at the end of the Babylonian Exile in 538 BC, but at the verse "kings shall shut their mouths at him," Jesus interrupts to assert that some aspects of this prediction are still to come (3 Ne. 20:46).

Then follows the complex passage reproduced above, which also ends with "kings shall shut their mouths at him" (3 Ne. 21:8) and therefore serves as a commentary on Isaiah 52. After the discussion of the Book of Mormon as a sign in the last days, Jesus again cites Micah 5:8–9 (this time continuing the quotation to verse 15), and he quotes both Isaiah 54 and Malachi 3–4, the latter being new to the Nephites since it had not been included in the Brass Plates that Nephi and his brothers had brought from Jerusalem (3 Ne. 26:2).[40] These citations generally follow the King James Version, but they are not simply a matter of cutting and pasting. There are often interpretive insertions and substitutions that highlight the themes of Christ's discourse to the Nephites—just as in the Sermon on the Mount—as can be seen in the following excerpt (with deletions in angle brackets, insertions in bold, and substitutions underlined):

MICAH 4:12–13	3 NEPHI 20:18–19
<u>for he shall gather them</u> as <u>the</u> sheaves into the floor. [Arise and thresh, O daughter of Zion:] for I will make thine horn iron, and I will make thy hoofs brass: and thou shalt beat in pieces many people: and I will consecrate their gain unto the Lord, and their substance unto the Lord of the whole earth.	<u>And I will gather my people</u> **together** as **a man gathereth** <u>his</u> sheaves into the floor. **For I will make my people with whom the Father hath covenanted, yea,** I will make thy horn iron, and I will make thy hoofs brass. And thou shalt beat in pieces many people; and I will consecrate their gain unto the Lord, and their substance unto the Lord of the whole earth. **And behold, I am he who doeth it.**

Jesus' discourse is made even more dense and complex by his use of connecting catchphrases. His citation of Moses' prediction that "every soul who will not hear that prophet shall be *cut off from among the people*" (3 Ne. 20:23) follows his quotation of Micah 5:9 ("all thine enemies shall be *cut off*"; 3 Ne. 20:17) and is echoed again at 3 Nephi 21:11 ("it shall be done even as Moses said: they shall be *cut off from among my people*"), 21:13 (again quoting Micah 5:9), and 21:20 ("whosoever will not repent . . . will I *cut off from among my people*"). The phrase "tread(eth) down" appears at 3 Nephi 16:14, 15, 20:16, 21:12, and 25:3, often in biblical quotations or allusions (Micah 5:8; Mal. 4:3; Matt. 5:13). In addition, Jesus sometimes quotes the same scriptures with substantial differences, as can be seen when he doubles back and repeats Isaiah 52:8–10—a passage he had recited to the Nephites the day before:

3 NE. 16:18–20	3 NE. 20:32–35
<u>Thy</u> watchmen shall lift up <u>the</u> voice; with the voice together shall they sing; for they shall see eye to eye, [when the Lord shall bring again Zion].	**Then** shall <u>their</u> watchmen lift up <u>their</u> voice; **and** with the voice together shall they sing; for they shall see eye to eye.
	Then will the Father gather them together again, and give unto them Jerusalem for the land of their inheritance.
Break forth into joy, sing together, ye waste places of Jerusalem; for the <u>Lord</u> hath comforted his people, he hath redeemed Jerusalem.	**Then shall they** break forth into joy— Sing together, ye waste places of Jerusalem; for the <u>Father</u> hath comforted his people, he hath redeemed Jerusalem.

The <u>Lord</u> hath made bare his holy arm in the eyes of all the nations; and all the ends of the earth shall see the salvation of <u>God</u>.	The <u>Father</u> hath made bare his holy arm in the eyes of all the nations; and all the ends of the earth shall see the salvation of <u>the Father</u>, **and the Father and I are one**

At least some of the variations can be accounted for by the idea of multiple fulfillments—3 Nephi 16 refers more particularly to the latter-day Lamanites, while 3 Nephi 20 has the Jews as its primary focus—but the differences are nevertheless considerable, particularly the emphasis on "the Father" in the second rendition. Even as he reaffirms covenants made with Israel, Jesus in Third Nephi is also explicating a doctrine of deity.[41]

One further wrinkle in the text is Jesus' awareness of a dual audience comprising both the Nephites at Bountiful and also latter-day readers who would someday peruse Third Nephi. This double mindfulness is in striking contrast to other figures in the Book of Mormon, such as Alma$_2$ or Samuel the Lamanite, who when they spoke to the people of Zarahemla showed no awareness that their words would be meaningful to anyone other than the crowds at hand. We can see Jesus nodding toward that other, later audience when he tells the Nephites: "These scriptures [from Malachi], which ye had not with you, the Father commanded that I should give unto you; for it was wisdom in him that they should be given unto future generations" (3 Ne. 26:2).[42] And he speaks of the prophecies of Isaiah as having particular meaning for both his immediate audience and also the later Gentiles:

> A commandment I give unto you that ye search these things diligently, for great are the words of Isaiah. For surely he spake as touching all things concerning my people which are of the House of Israel; therefore, *it must needs be that he must speak also to the Gentiles.* And all things that he spake have been and shall be, even according to the words which he spake. Therefore give heed to my words; write the things which I have told you; and according to the time and the will of the Father they shall go forth unto the Gentiles. And whosoever will hearken unto my words and repenteth and is baptized, the same shall be saved. Search the prophets, for many there be that testify of these things. (3 Ne. 23:1–5, emphasis added)

Nevertheless, Jesus was obviously addressing the Nephites who had gathered to hear him, and it is important to determine what the prophecies he quoted would have meant to his original audience at the temple in Bountiful. Imagine, for example, how these sentences from Isaiah 54 (3 Ne. 22) would have been perceived in the context of the recent, massive destructions and Jesus' subsequent blessing of the Nephite children (3 Ne. 17:11–25):

For a small moment have I forsaken thee, but with great mercies will I gather thee. (v. 7)

In a little wrath I hid my face from thee for a moment. (v. 8)

The mountains shall depart and the hills be removed, but my kindness shall not depart from thee, neither shall the covenant of my peace be removed. (v. 10)

O thou afflicted, tossed with tempest, and not comforted! (v. 11)

All thy children shall be taught of the Lord; and great shall be the peace of thy children. (v. 13)

Indeed, Jesus' proclamation to the Nephites—"I am the God of Israel and the God of the whole earth" (3 Ne. 11:14)—was an allusion to Isaiah 54:5: "thy Redeemer the Holy One of Israel; The God of the whole earth shall he be called" (which is later quoted at 3 Ne. 22:5). The intentionality of the reference is suggested by the fact that the phrase "God of the whole earth" occurs only in these three verses in all of scripture.[43]

Through his editing, Mormon keeps the focus of Jesus' second discourse squarely on prophecies concerning the covenant with Israel. In so doing, he modifies standard Book of Mormon soteriology. Thus far in Mormon's writings, the mission of Jesus Christ has been explained in terms of individual salvation—that sinners who exercise faith in him can repent, accept baptism, and be forgiven through the effects of his sacrificial atonement, eventually being resurrected and pronounced clean at the final judgment. This basic message was taught by King Benjamin (Mosiah 3:16–23), Abinadi (Mosiah 15:1–9, 16:1–15), Alma$_1$ (Mosiah 18:7–16), Alma$_2$ (Mosiah 27:23–31; Alma 5:14–32, 12:22–37, 33:12–23, 42:1–28), and Amulek (Alma 34:1–16). The idea of personal redemption is not foreign to Third Nephi—baptism is mentioned regularly—but when Jesus speaks to the multitude at Bountiful, he most often emphasizes a different type of salvation: a corporate or collective redemption centered on the restoration of the House of Israel. What matters most, apparently, is one's place within that story (and baptism becomes the means by which Gentiles can be adopted into Israel; see 3 Ne. 21:6, 30:2). In the rest of the Book of Mormon, Christ is preeminently a personal savior whose atonement has made it possible for individuals to return to God, but as the resurrected Jesus defines his own role in Third Nephi, his primary task is to save a people, *his* people.

Jesus' extensive use of Hebrew prophecies in his teachings in the New World can sometimes make for remarkable acts of multiple appropriation. Malachi originally prophesied to listeners in postexilic Israel; his words were then quoted by Jesus to an audience of Nephites several centuries later, who would have understood his message from a quite different perspective (for instance, they would have felt free to pass over his injunction to keep the law of Moses with all its "statutes and judgments," Mal. 4:4 || 3 Ne. 25:4). Jesus' comments, in turn, were recorded by Nephi₃, whose account was the basis for Mormon's abridgment, in which he selected a few of Jesus' teachings for the benefit of modern readers, who themselves come to the text with very distinct concerns and experiences. From the perspective of the Book of Mormon, none of this is considered strange or strained. It is assumed that it was part of God's plan for prophecies to be multiply fulfilled and recurrently relevant.

When the Nephites at the temple in Bountiful first heard the words "the Lord whom ye seek shall suddenly come to his temple, even the messenger of the covenant, whom ye delight in" (3 Ne. 24:1 || Mal. 3:1), they must have thought they were witnessing the fulfillment of prophecy on that very day. After all, in his sermons and instructions to them, Jesus had presented himself principally as "the messenger of the covenant" (the word *covenant* appears more than twenty times in 3 Ne. 11–29) and, like Malachi's promise that God would "purify the sons of Levi," Christ had visibly purified his servants so they could administer his ordinances (24:3; cf. 3 Ne. 19:25–36). In addition, many more of Malachi's words would have seemed tragically apt to the survivors of the widespread devastation:

> Who may abide the day of his coming, and who shall stand when he appeareth? (3 Ne. 24:2)

> I will come near to you in judgment; and I will be a swift witness against the [wicked]. (24:5)

> Even from the days of your fathers ye are gone away from mine ordinances, and have not kept them. Return unto me and I will return unto you. (24:7)

> I will spare them as a man spareth his own son that serveth him. Then shall ye return and discern between the righteous and the wicked (24:17; compare 3 Ne. 9:13: "O all ye that are spared because ye were more righteous than they, will ye not now return unto me, and repent of your sins, and be converted, that I may heal you?")

> The day that cometh shall burn them [the wicked] up . . . but unto you that fear my name, shall the Son [Sun?] of Righteousness arise with healing in his wings. (25:1–2)[44]

So also, the attention given to prophecy in Jesus' sermons—with a reminder that "ye are the children of the prophets" (3 Ne. 20:25)—and the extensive discussion of the future destiny of the House of Israel, including the part that descendants of Lehi would play in that unfolding story, would have served to "turn the heart of the fathers to the children, and the heart of the children to their fathers" in a powerful, moving manner (3 Ne. 25:5 ‖ Mal. 4:5). It must have been reassuring for the Nephites to realize that everything that had happened to them was part of God's overall design, and that Malachi, a prophet long before, had unbeknownst to them foreseen and described it all.[45]

When Nephi₁ prophesied that Christ would show himself among the Nephites, he did so in terms that appear in the book of Malachi:

> After the Messiah shall come there shall be signs given unto my people of his birth, and also of his death and resurrection; and *great and terrible* shall that *day* be unto the wicked for they shall perish . . . Wherefore, *all those who are proud, and that do wickedly, the day that cometh shall burn them up, saith the Lord of Hosts, for they shall be as stubble* . . . but the *Son of righteousness* shall appear unto them; and *he shall heal them*, and they shall have peace with him until three generations shall have passed away, and many of the fourth generation shall have passed away in righteousness. (2 Ne. 26:3–9; emphasis added)

All of this came to pass exactly as Nephi had predicted, yet when Jesus begins to explain the meaning of Malachi 3–4, he speaks of events still to come, in the time of Mormon's future readers (3 Ne. 26:1–5).[46] Hence it appears that, at least in some aspects, Malachi's predictions were both fulfilled and still in effect; that is, prophecies could be applicable to several eras and might be realized more than once.

We have already seen an example of this in Christ's citation of Isaiah 52. A century and a half earlier, Abinadi had delivered a lengthy discourse on this same chapter, beginning with the exclamation "How beautiful upon the mountains are the feet of him that bringeth good tidings, that publisheth peace" and demonstrating how it pointed toward the life and death of Christ himself (Mosiah 12:20–16:15). When Jesus quotes the chapter, which in Abinadi's interpretation had been fulfilled in his coming, he shifts its significance further into the future, noting explicitly that "all these things shall surely come" (3 Ne. 20:46).[47] From this perspective, when Jesus praises Isaiah and observes that "all things that he spake *have been and shall be*" (3 Ne. 23:3, emphasis added), he does not necessarily mean that some of his prophecies have been fulfilled and others are yet to come; rather, some predictions are apparently germane to both the past and the future simultaneously.

(*Third editorial comment: 3 Ne. 26:6–12*) Just at this point, Mormon interrupts his narrative and reminds us again of his selective editing ("there cannot be written in this book even a hundredth part of the things which Jesus did truly teach unto the people"; v. 6). From everything we know of him, we expect a "thus we see" observation here—something about how Christ's coming to the New World fulfilled prophecies of Isaiah and Malachi, or how the faithful response of the Nephites could serve as an example to future readers, or how the accuracy of some predictions makes it reasonable to believe that other prophecies will likewise come to pass, or how Jesus' visit to the Americas might foreshadow his Second Coming. Indeed, this comment section comes right on the heels of one of the most provocative summaries in the entire book: "When Jesus had told these things [that is, recited Malachi 3–4], he expounded them unto the multitude . . . and he did expound all things, even from the beginning until the time that he should come in his glory—yea, even all things which should come upon the face of the earth, even until the elements should melt with fervent heat, and the earth should be wrapt together as a scroll" (3 Ne. 26:1, 3; cf. 2 Pet. 3:10, Isa. 34:4). These explications concerned events of the last days, the time period that presumably would be of most interest to Mormon's future audience.[48] As he seeks to engage and persuade those particular readers, it is hard to imagine any information better suited to the task; in fact, detailed predictions of the last days could function much like the signs proclaimed by Samuel—they would provide sure evidence, at the time of their fulfillment, such that "there should be no cause for unbelief" (Hel. 14:28). But even though Mormon is eager to transcribe a fuller account of Jesus' words as contained in his sources, he does not do so. Instead, his ambitions as a historian are suddenly deflected by a somewhat frustrating revelation.

In his remarks at 3 Nephi 26, Mormon describes how he heard the voice of the Lord directly, instructing him to take his history in a different direction. At this moment, Jesus becomes doubly present both in Mormon's life and in his text, not just as the central figure in his record of events of AD 34 but also as his contemporary in the late fourth century—his interlocutor and supervising editor. As Mormon explains:

> Behold, I was about to write them all, which were engraven upon the
> Plates of Nephi, but the Lord forbade it, saying, "I will try the faith of my
> people." Therefore I, Mormon, do write the things which have been
> commanded me of the Lord. (vv. 11–12)

In other words, Mormon's message and agenda are no longer of his own design; instead, he is speaking for God, as prophets do. He appears somewhat reluctant to assume this new role, which of course is part of the tradition. In this case, however, his qualms are not the result of fearfulness or concerns about personal inadequacies. Rather, his hesitancy stems from the fact that Jesus' methods are at odds with those he has been developing over the last three hundred pages. Mormon admits that he is editing against his own best judgment about how to meet his longstanding objectives. Indeed, he is confident that if his readers had access to everything he knew about Jesus' Nephite sermons, they would find his account persuasive or even compelling, but he nevertheless complies with the divine injunction. In 3

Nephi 28:33 we again sense his regret at mandated omissions: "And if ye had all the scriptures which give an account of all the marvelous works of Christ [i.e., those he was commanded not to pass on], ye would, according to the words of Christ, know that these things must surely come." As Mormon is transformed here from historian to prophet, he concludes his remarks with a sentence that, if read literally, marks the transition with some poignancy: "And now I, Mormon, make an end of *my sayings*, and proceed to write *the things which have been commanded me*" (v. 12, emphasis added).

From Historian to Prophet

Mormon's historical project reaches its culmination in Third Nephi. We have observed that 3 Nephi 1–10 is a relatively integrated account of predictions that came true, with Mormon inserting two extended comments that emphasize the reliability of his sources and the significance of his argument from fulfilled prophecy. His depiction of Jesus' New World ministry (3 Ne. 11–25) consists primarily of quoted excerpts from sermons, yet we can still see him editing in accordance with his characteristic concerns.

As a historian, Mormon adds a few brief comments intended to increase our confidence in his narrative—several times he tells us that disciples or the multitude "did bear record" of their experiences, he promises verifying details yet to come (3 Ne. 18:37), he incorporates an incident in which Jesus himself reviewed and corrected the official Nephite history (23:6–13), and he cautions us that his account is an extremely abbreviated version of what was contained in his sources (26:6–7).[49]

As a literary artist who shapes his chronicle of Christ's visit primarily through selection, editing, and brief descriptions, he nevertheless employs meaningful phrases to highlight connections between various incidents (such the bestowal of the Holy Ghost upon Lamanites, children, and the twelve disciples), he organizes his material around the themes of the fulfillment of the law and the destiny of the House of Israel, and he starts to suggest parallels between the coming of the Lord to the Nephites and Christ's second coming in the last days—at least until he is cut short.[50]

In his role as moral guide, Mormon seems content to stand back and let Jesus take the lead in theology and doctrine, though after so much attention to the issues of prophecy and covenants we expect some sort of summation or an exhortation to give heed to scripture or a declaration that the promises made to Israel are indeed the key to the spiritual interpretation of world history. In the end, however, Mormon does not simply draw our attention to significant lessons from the past; rather, he moves from telling stories about prophets to speaking as a prophet himself. It is a remarkable development, for as Arnaldo Momigliano once noted:

> The Hebrew historian never claimed to be a prophet. He never said, "The Spirit of the Lord God is upon me." But the pages of the historical books of the Bible are full of prophets who interpret the events because they know what was, is and will be. The historian by implication subordinates himself to the prophet, he derives his values from him.[51]

This would have been a fitting description of Mormon as well, until 3 Nephi 26.

Actually, Mormon's transformation is neither instantaneous nor complete; after all, he still has his history to finish. So after being directed away from what he himself had wanted to write (that is, additional details from the third day of Jesus' ministry), Mormon instead describes a later visitation of Christ to his twelve Nephite disciples when they were instructed concerning the proper name of the church and essentials of the gospel, and then each was granted the desire of his heart; nine asked to enter God's kingdom at the end of their lives, while the remaining three wished to escape death and continue their spiritual labors until the judgment day (3 Ne. 27:1–28:12). Perhaps out of habit, Mormon acknowledges the limits of his historical knowledge and his dependence on source documents: "And now, whether they [the three] were mortal or immortal, from the day of their transfiguration, I know not; but this much I know, according to the record which hath been given—they did go forth upon the face of the land, and did minister unto all the people" (3 Ne. 28:17–18). After a brief description of their efforts among the Nephites and the Lamanites, Mormon concludes Third Nephi with a final comment, full of revelation and prophecy.

(*Fourth editorial comment: 3 Ne. 28:24–30:2*) This section begins rather abruptly, with another instance of the resurrected Jesus dictating the contents of the record:

> And now I, Mormon, make an end of speaking concerning these things for a time. Behold, I was about to write the names of those who were never to taste of death [*again, his historian's inclination to detail, accuracy, and specificity*], but the Lord forbade; therefore I write them not, for they are hid from the world. But behold, I have seen them, and they have ministered unto me. (28:24–26)

Imagine, for a moment, what this would have meant for Mormon the historian. After a span of three and a half centuries, he has access to eyewitnesses who were actually present when Christ taught the Nephites, men whom he could question and press for explanations (cf. Morm. 8:10–11). But Mormon does not pursue this, and he never identifies them as the source for any particular details in his account. His focus is now on the future, and he prophesies of how these three Nephites will operate largely unrecognized among the Gentiles and Jews to perform "great and marvelous works" (28:31).

In the midst of these predictions, Mormon receives another revelation: "And now, behold, as I spake concerning those whom the Lord hath chosen . . . that I knew not whether they were cleansed from mortality to immortality—but behold, since I wrote, I have inquired of the Lord, and he hath made it manifest unto me that there must needs be a change wrought upon their bodies, or else it needs be that they must taste of death" (28:36–37).[52] This comment may provide a model of spiritual seeking and divine disclosure for readers to follow, but again, such a remark throws into disarray the cautions and limitations of historical research. Why would the past hold any mysteries at all for someone who could simply ask God to make up any gaps in the records? By this time, however, Mormon is in full prophetic mode: "[W]hen the Lord shall see fit, in his wisdom, that these sayings shall come unto the Gentiles according to his word, then ye may know that the covenant which the Father hath made with the children of Israel . . . is already beginning to be fulfilled" (29:1). He leaves behind historical generalizations such as "thus we see" and now pronounces the familiar prophetic formula "wo (be) unto him that . . ." (28:34, 29:5, 6, 7).

As Third Nephi concludes, Mormon is unambiguously imparting God's words in a manner of prophecy that is signaled elsewhere in scripture by the phrase "thus saith the Lord." The thirtieth chapter, in its entirety, reads:

> Hearken, O ye Gentiles, and hear the words of Jesus Christ, the Son of the living God, which he hath commanded me that I should speak concerning you, for behold, he commandeth me that I should write, saying:
> Turn, all ye Gentiles, from your wicked ways;
>   and repent of your evil doings,
> of your lyings and deceivings,
>   and of your whoredoms, and of your secret abominations,
> and your idolatries, and of your murders,
>   and your priestcrafts, and your envyings, and your strifes,
>   and from all your wickedness and abominations,
> and come unto me, and be baptized in my name,
>   that ye may receive a remission of your sins,
>   and be filled with the Holy Ghost,
>   that ye may be numbered with my people who are of the House of Israel.

This is *not* the measured language of a historian trying to make the best case possible based on his understanding of available sources. Mormon is now speaking in the name of the Lord, with prophetic authority, oriented to the future rather than the past, and directed by God as to exactly what he should say. He has moved from the historian's stance, knowing the beginning from the end, to the prophetic perspective, knowing the end from the beginning.

Mormon's new role as a prophet transcends his threefold agenda of history, literature, and morality, but it does not entirely supplant it. Jesus does not demean Mormon's efforts as a conscientious historian (keep in mind the story of Jesus' taking a personal interest in the accuracy of the Nephite records at 3 Ne. 23:6–14, where he instructed Nephi$_3$ to add a notation concerning a fulfilled prophecy of Samuel's that had been overlooked), but at the same time he decisively orders Mormon to cut his account short at 3 Nephi 26:11, suggesting that at this point the interests of the two audiences diverge, and for later readers a different approach was preferable.

It appears that the resurrected Jesus in Third Nephi is concerned less with conveying precise information than in inviting his listeners, both ancient and modern, to come into a particular sort of relationship with him. He told Mormon to omit certain details because he wanted to "try the faith of [his] people," but Mormon understands this to be a promise of knowledge yet to be revealed: "if it shall so be that they shall believe these things, then shall the greater things be made manifest unto them" (3 Ne. 26:9–11). The key is to ask. "Go ye unto your homes," Jesus urged the Nephites at the end of the first day, "and ponder upon the things which I have said, and ask of the Father, in my name, that ye may understand" (3 Ne. 17:3; cf. 18:20). The disciples in Jerusalem could have learned about the Nephites, he confides, if they had only "ask[ed] the Father in my name" (16:4). The bestowal of the gift of the Holy Ghost, who will manifest truth to inquiring believers, is a major theme of Jesus' teachings and is explicitly offered to latter-day Gentiles by Mormon—speaking the words of the Lord—at 30:2: "come unto me . . . and be filled with the Holy Ghost." The invitation in the Sermon at the Temple to "ask, and it shall be given unto you" (3 Ne. 14:7) is reiterated again by Christ at 27:28. In short, Jesus wants to engage his people in an ongoing dialogue, and Third Nephi is designed to be, among other things, a conversation starter.[53]

It is not clear whether Mormon ever realized the spiritual limitations of his historical project, but as we follow his abridgment through Third Nephi, the wisdom of an alternative approach becomes obvious. Mormon's method of persuasion seems vindicated in 3 Nephi 4:31–5:3 when the signs of Christ's birth and a miraculous military victory combine to bring the people to certain knowledge. They cry, "Hosanna to the Most High God . . . blessed be the name of the Lord," and Mormon reports that "there was not a living soul among all the people of the Nephites who did doubt in the least the words of all the holy prophets." It appears that his prescription for rational, evidence-based faith has succeeded stunningly, but within just a few years the people revert to their wicked ways. Mormon's emphasis was on *knowing*; nevertheless, as the sequence of events in his own narrative demonstrates, even if he was successful in his ambitions—if his readers were entirely convinced by the instances of prophecy and fulfillment that he lays out—it would still be possible for them to abandon their convictions. Jesus' prophetic pedagogy, on the other hand, aimed to produce a more resilient faith, a faith capable of withstanding doubts and temptations, one that transcends the historical moment. The situation is very different when the Nephites at Bountiful proclaim, "Hosanna! Blessed be the name of the Most High God!" (3 Ne. 11:17). These believers, having entered into a relationship with Christ, are permanently changed and never fall away (27:30–31).

Although Jesus' teachings in Third Nephi may appear derivative, when examined in detail they demonstrate a complicated interaction between Christ's ministering to the Nephites and his messages for latter-day readers; between Jesus' words, Nephi₃'s record, and Mormon's editing; between the predictions of ancient prophets and their multiple fulfillments; and between the exact wording of the Book of Mormon and the King James Bible. The narrators provide a controlling perspective that can bring together diverse incidents, voices, and documents in the service of major themes such as the nature of faith, the reliability of prophecy, and the role of Israel in God's providence (topics that each play a more significant role in the narrative than those listed by Alexander Campbell). Indeed, it is through the narrators that we are most likely to ascertain the primary message of the Book of Mormon. Nevertheless, the meaning of the text is neither unitary nor static. The editors/historians are portrayed as living, thinking individuals who develop as characters over the course of their writings. In addition, there are differences of approach between the narrators. Mormon and Moroni, in particular, appear to have quite distinct ideas about how to best persuade their readers.

After the end of Third Nephi, Mormon's prophetic impulse dissipates somewhat. He still receives revelations (Morm. 3:2, 14–15, 20; Moro. 8:7–9) and occasionally warns his readers of things to come (Morm. 3:17–22, 5:8, 24), but he is nonetheless committed to finishing his history as competently and precisely as possible. When he resumes his narrative in Fourth Nephi and his own book of Mormon, his writing is once again structured around a clear timeline, with careful identifications (as at Morm. 1:8–9), exact numbers, specific names and locations, and comments noting the fulfillment of particular prophecies (Morm. 1:19, 2:10). His historian's agenda of persuasion through valid evidence and logical reasoning still holds sway. His son Moroni, by contrast, views things differently. As we shall see in the next chapter, Moroni virtually abandons his father's careful exposition of facts and evidence; instead, his strategy is to rely almost entirely on the Spirit to convince readers of the truth of his words.

PART III

Moroni

8

Weakness in Writing

A Sense of Audience

Mormon's abridgment of Nephite history breaks off unexpectedly, in the middle of his autobiographical book. He describes the final battle of the Nephites in the late fourth century, after which only twenty-four soldiers survived (apart from a few stragglers), and he includes an emotional lament he had directed toward the dead at a time when thousands of corpses still littered the ground (Morm. 6:16–22). He next informs us that he wants to "speak somewhat unto the remnant of this people who are spared [the modern-day Lamanites], if it so be that God may give unto them my words" (Morm. 7:1), and then turns to address them directly, urging them to repent, accept Christ, believe the Bible, and embrace their identity as descendents of the House of Israel. His last words are: "If it so be that ye believe in Christ, and are baptized, first with water, then with fire and with the Holy Ghost, following the example of our Savior, according to that which he hath commanded us, it shall be well with you in the day of judgment. Amen" (Morm. 7:10).

Perhaps the Book of Mormon could have ended there, but it does not. After a chapter break (but not even a page turn in either the original or the current official edition), we find ourselves in the hands of yet another narrator. Chapter 8 of Mormon's book begins: "Behold, I, Moroni, do finish the record of my father, Mormon. Behold, I have but few things to write, which things I have been commanded by my father." And it dawns on us that Mormon has left the burden of concluding his lengthy history to his son. Apparently he died before he could complete his book; either that or Joseph Smith's literary exuberance and delight in creating new characters led him to continue the story just a little longer. In either case, Moroni has a distinctive voice and viewpoint. Certainly, his general perspective does not contradict that of Mormon or even Nephi—he also preaches the Christian gospel for the benefit of future readers—yet he takes an individualized approach to his historiographical task, and there are some surprises.

One is that Moroni appears to be a very reticent author. Mormon's last dated entry was in AD 384 (Morm. 6:5), but Moroni waits some sixteen years, until 400, before beginning his continuation of his father's account (Morm. 8:6). He writes two chapters and ends with a reference to the final judgment and an "Amen," which together constitute a conventional sign-off for Book of Mormon narrators (see 2 Ne. 33:15; Enos 1:27; Morm. 7:10; Moro. 10:34).[1] Then suddenly he begins a new book, that of Ether, which is his abridgment of the twenty-four gold plates found by the people of Limhi (Mosiah 8:7–12, 21:27, 28:11–19), containing an account of the Jaredites—pre-Nephite inhabitants of the Promised Land who, like the Nephites, had been destroyed. It is not clear exactly when Moroni made this abridgment or appended it to Mormon's shortened version of the Large Plates, but the next time he writes—admitting that he had not really intended to say anything further after "having made an end of abridging the account of the people of Jared" (Moro. 1:1)—we discover that another twenty years have slipped by (Moro. 10:1).

A lot can happen in thirty-six years; Moroni, however, tells us nothing of his life other than that he was a fugitive, always on the run or in hiding from the Lamanites (Moro. 1:1–3). Instead, the book of Moroni includes half a dozen brief liturgical items, two letters and a sermon written by his father, and one last farewell. As a result, Moroni's contribution to the Book of Mormon is much briefer than either Nephi's or Mormon's and he reveals much less about his own life, though stories and details from his decades of wandering alone undoubtedly would have proven quite interesting. He professes again and again that he has only a little to add: "I have but few things to write" and "I seal up these records, after I have spoken a few words by way of exhortation unto you" (Morm. 8:1; Moro. 10:2; cf. Ether 12:40 and Moro. 1:4). Indeed, Moroni neglects to provide the basic facts that readers might expect, such as a narration of his father's death. He merely mentions in passing that Mormon was "slain in battle" (Morm. 8:5)—hardly a satisfying send-off for the figure who has been our guide though more than five hundred years of Nephite history.

Reticence and Stumbling Over Words

In trying to reconstruct the mind of the third and last major narrator, the questions are clear, even if evidence is sparse. After the destruction of the Nephites, what was there still left to say? Why did it take Moroni so long to say it? Why did he find it so difficult to write? We can imagine a number of obstacles to becoming an author. There may be insufficient time or inclination; it is easy to be intimidated by earlier writers or discouraged by the effort required; a focused drive for self-expression or fame or understanding could be missing. But we do not have to guess in Moroni's case, because he explicitly identifies the roots of his writerly reticence in two passages, beginning with our first introduction to him:

> Behold, I, Moroni do finish the record of my father, Mormon. Behold, I have but few things to write, which things I have been commanded by my father.
>
> And now it came to pass that after the great and tremendous battle at Cumorah, behold, the Nephites who had escaped into the country southward were hunted by the Lamanites, until they were all destroyed. And my father also was killed by them, and I, even I, remain alone to write the sad tale of the destruction of my people.[2] But behold, they are gone, and I fulfil the commandment of my father. And whether they will slay me, I know not.
>
> Therefore I will write and hide up the records in the earth; and whither I go it mattereth not. Behold, my father hath made this record, and he hath written the intent thereof. And behold, I would write it also if I had room upon the plates, but I have not; and ore I have none, for I am alone. My father hath been slain in battle, and all my kinsfolk, and I have not friends nor whither to go; and how long the Lord will suffer that I may live I know not.
>
> Behold, four hundred years have passed away since the coming of our Lord and Savior. And behold, the Lamanites have hunted my people, the Nephites, down from city to city and from place to place, even until they are no more; and great has been their fall; yea, great and marvelous is the destruction of my people, the Nephites. And behold, it is the hand of the Lord which hath done it. And behold also, the Lamanites are at war one with another; and the whole face of this land is one continual round of murder and bloodshed; and no one knoweth the end of the war. (Morm. 8:1–8)

There is a note of resignation and passivity here that we have not encountered before in the Book of Mormon. At least four times Moroni confesses that he doesn't know or doesn't care. The overriding emotion is loss—he is alone, with no more space to write, no ore, no family, no friends, and no plan beyond finishing his father's record and burying the plates. Sixteen years after the final battle (though there have apparently been subsequent traumas), Moroni is still in shock. Both the physical and psychological challenges to writing are nearly overwhelming, though he *is* writing.

Sometime later, after he had evidently found some breathing space and ore enough to fashion additional metal tablets on which to inscribe his redaction of Jaredite history, he confesses to yet another set of challenges (directing his concerns to God):

> And I said unto him, "Lord, the Gentiles will mock at these things, because of our weakness in writing; for Lord, thou hast made us mighty in word by faith, but thou hast not made us mighty in writing; for thou hast made all this people that they could speak much, because of the Holy Ghost which thou hast given them; and thou hast made us that we could write but little, because of the awkwardness of our hands. Behold, thou hast not made us mighty in writing like unto the brother of Jared, for thou madest him that the things which he wrote were mighty even as thou art, unto the overpowering of man to read them. Thou hast also made our words powerful and great, even that we cannot write them; wherefore, when we write we behold our weakness, and stumble because of the placing of our words; and I fear lest the Gentiles shall mock at our words." (Ether 12:23–25)

The first thing to notice in this passage is the abundance of first-person plural pronouns (fourteen), which is unexpected from someone who has spent more than a decade utterly alone. Moroni seems to be speaking on behalf of the entire line of Nephite record keepers; the immediate antecedent to his worries was a reference to "my fathers [who] have obtained the promise that these things [the Book of Mormon] should come unto their brethren [the Lamanites] through the Gentiles" (v. 22). The second striking feature is the combination of frustration, self-consciousness, and anxiety that may strike a familiar chord with anyone who has tried to put his or her thoughts on paper for public display. Moroni worries about his inadequacies as a writer, especially in comparison with the brother of Jared, and because his writing system, which he elsewhere describes as "Reformed Egyptian," did not allow him to transcribe his vernacular language (cf. Morm. 9:32–33). He is anxious about imperfections, at some points conceding their exist-ence in the work of both himself and his father (Morm. 8:12, 9:31, 33; title page), yet elsewhere denying that he knows of any errors (Morm. 8:17). The result of all this, he fears, will be an almost complete failure to persuade his ultimate audience—the Gentiles of the latter days. He worries that his efforts will spark derision rather than conversion.

Of all the Book of Mormon narrators, Moroni has the clearest sense of his audience. As we saw in Chapter 3, when Nephi directly addresses his readers he seems to have his own people or the Nephite nation in mind, at least until 2 Nephi 25–33, when he begins to suspect that he will eventually have a broader readership consisting of not only the descendants of Lehi in the last days but also Jews and Gentiles. Mormon, coming at the end of Nephite civilization, is more aware that he is writing for people far removed from his time and culture, yet he also assumes that his primary readers will be latter-day Lamanites and only secondarily Jews and Gentiles (4 Ne. 1:49;Morm. 5:12, 7:1–10; cf. 3 Ne. 29:1, Morm. 3:17–18). Twice, fairly late in his history, Mormon addresses brief comments to the Gentiles (3 Ne. 30:1–2 [here he is only repeating Jesus' words] and Morm. 5:22–24), but Moroni knows his core audience intimately; beginning with his first chapter he speaks regularly and explicitly to latter-day Gentiles,[3] though he does not seem overly impressed with us:

> O ye wicked and perverse and stiffnecked people, why have ye built up churches unto yourselves to get gain? Why have ye transfigured the holy word of God, that ye might bring damnation upon your souls? Behold, look ye unto the revelations of God; for behold, the time cometh at that day when all these things must be fulfilled. Behold, the Lord hath shown unto me great and marvelous things concerning that which must shortly come, at that day when these things shall come forth among you. Behold, I speak unto you as if ye were present, and yet ye are not. But behold, Jesus Christ hath shown you unto me, and I know your doing.
>
> And I know that ye do walk in the pride of your hearts; and there are none save a few only who do not lift themselves up in the pride of their hearts, unto the wearing of very fine apparel, unto envying, and strifes and malice, and persecutions, and all manner of iniquities . . . For behold, ye do love money . . . more than ye love the poor and the needy, the sick and the afflicted. O ye pollutions, ye hypocrites, ye teachers, who sell yourselves for that which will canker, why have ye polluted the holy church of God? (Morm. 8:33–38; see also Ether 8:23)

He continues in this manner for a few more verses, and then chastises those who do not believe in Christ (Morm. 9:1–6) as well as those who deny revelations and miracles (Morm. 9:7–29). It is not surprising that, in a contemplative moment, he realizes that his writings are not going to be well received by these same people, that they in fact will "mock at [his] words."[4] (By contrast, Mormon just four chapters earlier was much more sympathetic to the Gentiles, assuming that many of them would "sorrow for the calamity of the House of Israel; yea, they will sorrow for the destruction of this people" [Morm. 5:11].)

Given the hostility that Moroni—perhaps not unreasonably—expects from his readers, we might ask why he writes at all. Once again, Moroni appears quite distinct from Nephi and Mormon in that his motivations are nearly entirely external. He finishes the record because his father instructed him to do so (Morm. 8:1, 3), and later because the Lord gave him even more specific commands (Ether 4:5, 5:1, 8:26, 12:22, 13:13). He seems to write the minimum required to discharge those obligations, with (as we have seen) considerable trepidation. As he attempts to speak to a far-distant, unreceptive audience, he has to keep in mind three separate sets of expectations—those of his father, the Lord, and his Gentile readers. His anxiety about the process means that, in some ways, he has to modify Mormon's historiographical vision in order to achieve his goals.

A Change in Tactics

It is easy to see the differences between Mormon's and Moroni's approaches to history in the book of Ether, Moroni's abridgment of the Jaredite record. Where Mormon tended to provide well-integrated, carefully structured accounts with relatively developed characters and brief, sporadic editorial comments, Moroni does just the opposite. Aside from the first and last major figures, the brother of Jared and Coriantumr, his treatment of the twenty-seven intervening kings reads like a lightly edited chronicle, checking off generations one by one in a much more truncated form than we see even in First and Second Kings (or, less charitably, with the sort of dry synopsis that might characterize a middle-school book report):

> And the country was divided, and there were two kingdoms: the kingdom of Shule, and the kingdom of Cohor, the son of Noah. And Cohor, the son of Noah, caused that his people should give battle unto Shule, in which Shule did beat them and did slay Cohor.
>
> And now Cohor had a son who was called Nimrod; and Nimrod gave up the kingdom of Cohor unto Shule, and he did gain favor in the eyes of Shule; wherefore Shule did bestow great favors upon him and he did do in the kingdom of Shule according to his desires. (Ether 7:20–22)

Shule was fourth in the royal succession, but the style has not changed much by the time we get to the twenty-sixth and twenty-seventh monarchs:

> And it came to pass that Shiblom was slain, and Seth was brought in to captivity, and did dwell in captivity all his days. And it came to pass that

Ahah, his son, did obtain the kingdom, and he did reign over the people all his days. And he did do all manner of iniquity in his days, by which he did cause the shedding of much blood; and few were his days.

And Ethem, being a descendant of Ahah, did obtain the kingdom; and he also did do that which was wicked in his days. (Ether 11:9–11)

The book of Ether has a clear structure—the genealogical list in the first chapter provides the framework for the chronicle of Jaredite kings in chapters 6–11—but Moroni does not appear to be reworking his source material to any appreciable extent; in contrast to his father's abridging, there is not much artistry here.[5] Perhaps he simply did not have much to work with. The twenty-four plates found by the people of Limhi may have consisted of little more than terse annals.

Because his editing is more awkward, with much less literary shaping, Moroni maintains a more pervasive narrator presence. He has to jump in more frequently, and at greater length, to make his points clear. In the first edition of 1830 there were six chapters in the book of Ether (now subdivided into fifteen chapters), and of these, five began with some variation of "And now I, Moroni, proceed to give an account of [the Jaredites] . . ." (Ether 1:1, 5:1, 6:1, 9:1, 13:1).[6] The remaining chapter (originally numbered as V, but now Ether 12) consists almost entirely of Moroni's commentary. In all, the phrase "I, Moroni" appears eleven times in the book of Ether. By comparison, over the course of Mormon's much lengthier abridgment of earlier records, "I, Mormon" occurs only three times (3 Ne. 26:12, 28:24; 4 Ne. 1:23).[7] Moroni employs Mormon's favorite commentarial device, "thus we see," only once (Ether 14:25), preferring to alternate chronicle-like passages of historical synopsis with long editorial interruptions, often aimed directly at his Gentile readers (see Ether 2:9–12, 4:4–19, 8:20–26, 12:6–41).[8]

As we observed in previous chapters, Mormon exhibited a keen interest in evidence and argumentation, especially in demonstrating when prophetic warnings were fulfilled. Moroni, by contrast, appears to have given up on the idea that his readers could be persuaded through historical evidence. Although he certainly believes that God's promises will come to pass (Morm. 8:22, 33), he realizes that many of his readers will "deny the revelations of God, and say that they are done away, that there are no revelations, nor prophecies" (Morm. 9:7). Consequently, he does not bother to note the sort of prophecy/fulfillment connections that characterized Mormon's history. For instance, Jaredite prophets warned that unless the people repented they would be destroyed, their bones would be heaped upon the earth, and God would bring another people to inherit the land (Ether 11:6, 21). Moroni knows that these predictions came true (see Mosiah 8:8; Ether 14:21), but he never explicitly makes the point. Similarly, he never references the startlingly exact prophecies of Alma and Samuel that the Nephites would be destroyed four hundred years after the coming of Jesus (Alma 45:10; Hel. 13:5, 9), even though he saw this take place on schedule (Morm. 8:6). Perhaps most surprisingly, he includes Ether's dramatic prophecy that unless King Coriantumr repented he would be the last survivor of his people (Ether 13:20–22, 14:24)—even pausing to register Coriantumr's growing awareness that such an outcome appeared more and more likely (15:1–3)—yet Moroni ends his account of the Jaredites ambiguously: "And it came to pass that Coriantumr fell to the earth, and became as if he had no life" (Ether 15:32). So is he still alive or not? This is a rather inconclusive conclusion, and it is hard to believe that Mormon would not have made much, much more of this incident (particularly given the additional details of fulfillment provided by Omni 1:20–22, where we learn that Coriantumr had not, in fact, died).[9]

Instead, Moroni seems to believe that only God can convince skeptical latter-day readers of the truth of his account. In a verse beloved by Latter-day Saint missionaries, he urges that "when ye shall receive these things, I would exhort you that ye would ask God, the Eternal Father, in the name of Christ, if these things are not true; and if ye shall ask with a sincere heart, with real intent, having faith in Christ, he will manifest the truth of it unto you, by the power of the Holy Ghost" (Moro. 10:4).[10] Earlier, when we first met Moroni, he assured his readers that God would confirm all his words to "whosoever shall believe in [Jesus'] name, doubting nothing" (Morm. 9:25; cf. v. 21). Similarly, in the book of Ether, Moroni quoted the Lord's promise that "he that believeth these things which I have spoken, him will I visit with the manifestations of my Spirit, and he shall know and bear record. For because of my Spirit he shall know that these things are true" (4:11). Moroni does not think that he can prove the truth of his account; rather, he appeals to his readers to exercise faith, trusting that this will lead the receptive to a personal encounter with God's affirming Spirit.

In his conversation with Jesus in Ether 12 that was quoted above, where Moroni expressed his concern that the Gentiles would mock his weakness in writing, he seems to have hoped that the Lord would respond by making his writing "overpowering," like that of the brother of Jared (Ether 12:23–25). Instead, the Lord counseled patience, assuring him that if people "humble themselves before me, and have faith in me, then will I make weak things become strong unto them." To Moroni he promises, "Because thou hast seen thy weakness thou shalt be made strong, even unto the sitting down in the place which I have prepared in the mansions of my Father." But Jesus' plan for Moroni's audience is just as significant: "Behold, I will show unto the Gentiles their weakness and I will show unto them that faith, hope, and charity bringeth unto me—the fountain of all righteousness." (Ether 12:27–28, 37). In other words, the solution to Moroni's conundrum is not more powerful, Spirit-infused writing, but rather a new type of *reading* characterized by faith and charity. The idea here that knowledge comes through revelation in response to faith is not entirely new to the Book of Mormon—there were earlier examples at 1 Ne. 2:16, 15:6–11, Mosiah 5:2, Alma 5:46, and throughout Jesus' discourses in Third Nephi—but Mormon was never the speaker in those passages, and Moroni shifts the balance between faith and reason substantially away from what Mormon had established in his own narrative. One might imagine Moroni saying to his father, *What you have been doing is not going to work. Why should we bother to try to convince the Gentiles with evidence and arguments when they won't even believe that we existed?*

Since Moroni believes that spiritual knowledge depends more on prayer and revelation than on historical research, we might expect him to take a different approach to the task of writing history than his father, and that is exactly what we find. Moroni apparently did not feel the tension of competing agendas in the same way that Mormon did. As mentioned above, we encounter only one "thus we see" comment in Moroni's record, and there is much less reworking of historical sources, with little attention given to dates and details. The lack of a clear Jaredite chronology may have been the result of sparse sources, but the time line of Moroni's own life is just as obscure. He provides only two dates: AD 400, when he takes over his father's record, and 420, when he makes his last entry (Morm. 8:6; Moro. 10:1); everything else—including the death of his father, his own revelations, his editing of Ether's record, and the dates and circumstances of the letters and sermons he includes—is a chronological blur with virtually no narrative context.[11] Because he edits so differently, Moroni subtly undercuts the significance of his father's literary achievement even as he celebrates it. How important are facts in the end? Does the careful balancing of historical details and literary presentation really matter when all we truly need is the witness of the Spirit? Or perhaps Moroni's attitude reflects not a disagreement over basic principles so much as frustration. In this interpretation, Moroni is not dismissing his father's efforts or sensibilities, but he despairs—rightly, as it turns out—that they will not gain Mormon the respect he deserves. Instead, prideful future readers will mock, and there is really no compelling retort (especially without any culturally specific New World archaeological evidence to support Mormon's scrupulous historiographical details). In either case, a careful analysis of the book of Ether suggests that Moroni was able to adapt his Jaredite sources for the benefit of Gentile readers in ways that might have run counter to the conscientious sensibilities of his historian father.

Minimizing Contrasts

When we first meet Moroni, he tells us twice in three verses that he is writing only "to fulfil the commandment of my father" (Morm. 8:1, 3), yet he never reveals what exactly Mormon had required of him. The omission is curious, somewhat like Nephi's missing blessing from Lehi in 2 Nephi 1–4. Moroni withholds specific information, perhaps because he did not want his readers to weigh what he had produced against what his father had requested. We can imagine it otherwise. Moroni might have dramatized a deathbed scene or reported Mormon's last words with a direct quotation, like the famous Chinese historian Sima Qian (c. 145–86 BC) explaining his own motivation for completing a massive history that his father had begun:

> When his son Qian returned from his mission, he visited his father at the place where he was staying between the Lo and Yellow rivers. The Grand Historian [his father] grasped his hand and said, weeping, "Our ancestors were Grand Historians for the house of Zhou. From the most ancient times they were eminent and renowned . . . Will this tradition end with me? If you in turn become Grand Historian, you must continue the work of our ancestors. . . . I have been Grand Historian, and yet I have failed to set forth a record of all the enlightened rulers and wise lords, the faithful ministers and gentlemen who were ready to die for duty. I am fearful that the historical materials will be neglected and lost. You must remember and think of this!"
>
> Qian bowed his head and wept, saying, "I, your son, am ignorant and unworthy, but I shall endeavor to set forth in full the reports of antiquity which have come down from our ancestors. I shall not dare to be remiss!"[12]

In the next line, Sima Qian's father dies, leaving it to his son to rescue and preserve the historical accounts of men whose fame deserved transmission.

In the absence of any similar scene in the Book of Mormon, we must work backward from Moroni's additions to determine what it was that his father had commanded him to do. It appears that he had been asked to tie up a few loose ends, such as providing an account of the final destruction of the Nephites (Morm. 8) and a history of the Jaredites (the book of Ether; promised by Mormon at Mosiah 28:19), as well as the words by which Jesus had conferred on his disciples the power to give the Holy Ghost (Moro. 2; promised at 3 Ne. 18:37). Another hint was provided by Mormon himself when he expressed his hope that his son would survive "the entire destruction of my people" so that Moroni might "write somewhat concerning them, and somewhat concerning Christ, that perhaps some day it may profit them" (W. of M. 1:2). The bulk of Moroni's writing is taken up by the book of Ether, which begins rather abruptly, though perhaps this is not surprising if readers remember a key passage some three hundred pages earlier:

Now after Mosiah had finished translating these records [the twenty-four gold plates found by the people of Limhi], behold, it gave an account of the people who were destroyed, from the time that they were destroyed back to the building of the great tower, at the time the Lord confounded the language of the people and they were scattered abroad upon the face of all the earth, yea, and even from that time back until the creation of Adam. Now this account did cause the people of Mosiah to mourn exceedingly, yea, they were filled with sorrow; nevertheless, it gave them much knowledge, in the which they did rejoice. *And this account shall be written hereafter*; for behold, it is expedient that all people should know the things which are written in this account. (Mosiah 28:17–19, emphasis added)

With such an explicit declaration of intent, it is evident that Mormon's work is not complete without some explanation of this mysterious, lost civilization, and the fact that the twenty-four plates were discovered in the midst of ruins littered with bones and weapons only heightens our curiosity (Mosiah 8:8–11). Yet judging from the editorial anxiety expressed by Moroni throughout the book of Ether, he found this inherited responsibility anything but easy.

In Ether, we learn that the people referred to by Mormon were descendants of Jared and his brother (a major character who, strangely enough, is never named in the Book of Mormon), who, together with their friends and families, had been led by God from the Tower of Babel to the Americas.[13] There they had created a civilization that lasted over a thousand years before being destroyed by internecine warfare shortly after Lehi and his family arrived in the Promised Land. Although there was never any reported contact between the Lehites and the Jaredites, the last Jaredite survivor, Coriantumr, lived among the Mulekites for nine months, according to a stone inscription that was discovered in the days of King Mosiah$_1$ (Omni 1:20–22; the Mulekites were yet another migrant group from the ancient Near East who had arrived in the New World about 580 BC, lost track of their origins, and then merged with the Nephites under King Mosiah about 200 BC). A record of the Jaredites, written by their last prophet, Ether, on twenty-four gold plates, was discovered by explorers from the colony established by Zeniff as they tried unsuccessfully to reconnect with the main body of Nephites. The reconnaissance party returned to King Limhi with a report of having found ruins and bones (which they assumed were the remains of the Nephites at Zarahemla), along with the plates of Ether, which they could not read. Eventually Mosiah$_2$, king of the Nephites, used "interpreters" or seer stones in his possession to make the translation described above by Mormon. (These events were recounted at Mosiah 8:5–21, 21:25–28, and 28:10–18.)[14]

After reporting the initial discovery of the Jaredite plates, Mormon continues through the rest of his history to give teasers about what was contained in those records—Alma$_2$ charges his son not to make public the details of secret oaths and covenants contained on the twenty-four plates (Alma 37:21–32), and Mormon refers to the role of Satan in the destruction of the Jaredites (Hel. 6:28)—yet he never gets around to actually incorporating a history of the Jaredites into his history. From a naive perspective, he may have just run out of time. Yet a twenty-four-plate account does not seem like a dauntingly lengthy text. Mosiah, after all, had managed a translation to which Mormon presumably had access and could have integrated into his own book or simply appended to his record, much as he did with the Small Plates of Nephi. But he chose not to.

Instead he left the task for his son, who from all indications perceived it as a difficult work indeed. We overhear Moroni complaining that his writing abilities are not up to the assignment (Ether 12:23–25), and he relies heavily on direct instructions from the Lord as to what exactly to do with this text (4:4–5, 5:1, 8:26, 12:22, 26–28, 13:13). It appears that there were elements in the Jaredite record that would have proven awkward or inappropriate to include in their original form. Certainly Moroni feels like he has to intervene regularly as the editor from the very beginning: "Behold, I give not the full account, but a part of the account I give, from the tower down until they were destroyed. And on this wise do I give the account" (Ether 1:6; cf. 3:17). But such an admission is a virtual invitation for readers to ask, "What is missing and why?"

The first omission comes right after Moroni informs us that he is basing his account on the twenty-four plates:

> And as I suppose that the first part of this record, which speaks concerning the creation of the world, and also of Adam and an account from that time even to the great tower, and whatsoever things transpired among the children of men until that time, is had among the Jews—therefore I do not write those things which transpired from the days of Adam until that time. (Ether 1:3–4)

He seems to have in mind the first ten chapters of Genesis, which he would have known from the Brass Plates, but he was probably mistaken in thinking that his readers would have been relieved to be spared a redundant account. Just as modern scholars would be *very* interested in the discovery of a version of the Torah dating back to time of Lehi in 600 BC, so also might we be intrigued by accounts of origins that claimed to predate any Hebrew literature whatsoever (the Jaredites, according to the Book of Mormon, would have left the Old World sometime in the third millennium BC, long before Abraham or Moses).

One wonders what Moroni might have thought of the people whose record he was abridging. Chances are he would have found Jaredite culture almost unimaginably alien. Not only was he separated from them by a considerable language barrier and the passage of more than two thousand years, but—simply on the basis of chronology—they could have known nothing of the Hebrew Bible or the Law of Moses. They were not even of the House of Israel and thus had no part in the covenants and promises that were so central to the Nephites' conception of themselves and their role in God's plan for human history. We learn little of Jaredite customs and lifestyles (though Moroni does mention that they used animals unknown in Nephite times, including elephants, cureloms, and cumoms, whatever those might have been, as well as the very non-Israelite "swine"; Ether 9:18–19), and their government operated on very different principles. Not only was there no reign of judges, but even their form of monarchy was strange: rulers could spend their entire lives in captivity, and kingdoms seem to have been passed down to younger sons, as opposed to the Nephite practice of primogeniture.[15]

Moroni masks how radically different the Jaredite and Nephite civilizations were by giving us a truncated account of the former. More precisely, he seems to reproduce Ether's bare-bones chronicle almost exactly, but then he punctuates that minimal account with relatively lengthy editorial interruptions designed to highlight similarities between the two cultures. The only two periods of Jaredite history for which he provides thicker, more detailed narratives are those that present the most obvious parallels with the Nephites: the beginning and the end. Both peoples were led by God to the same promised land only to embrace wickedness and ultimately self-destruct. Yet even in these sections his narration is designed to help us notice certain elements while ignoring others. For instance, the chapters recounting the Jaredite demise (Ether 13–15) feature a rejection of God's prophets, escalating warfare, a polarized society in which everyone is swept up by one side or the other, a gathering for the final battle, and then a cataclysmic conclusion. It makes for fairly dramatic reading and sounds somewhat like Mormon's account of the end of the Nephites. However, Moroni never points out the rather significant differences: Jaredite troubles arose from rival factions among the leadership rather than from competing ethnic groups, the last prophet had no role in these struggles, the two forces were fairly evenly matched, and one side did not successfully conquer the other (among the Jaredites, the record states that *everyone* died except for Coriantumr and Ether— one a king and the other a prophet).

As John Welch has surmised, "The fact that Moroni felt free to insert his own material into his abridgment of the book of Ether indicates that, in general, he was not attempting to produce a technically rigorous version of Jaredite history."[16] Moroni was not interested in Jaredite culture from an antiquarian or historicist viewpoint; rather, he was intent on using the record of Ether to reinforce lessons that could be drawn from the experience of his own people, the Nephites. He wanted to provide an example of another covenant people that could universalize the Nephite story. But to do so, he had to emphasize parallels while minimizing differences. And he had to work in the history of the Jaredites in such a way that it did not detract or distract from his father's abridgment. The Book of Mormon, to be effective, needed to be a satisfying whole. Welch notices that the book of Ether includes a high proportion of direct narrator comments, at least compared with Mormon's editing, but Moroni has other tools at his disposal as well.

Moroni attempts to shape the book of Ether into a coherent unity with the history of the Nephites in several ways, beginning, at the most didactic, with comments on the Jaredite narrative that make direct comparisons with Nephite events. We see an example of this at Ether 8:20–21, where Moroni explains another omission:

> And now I, Moroni, do not write the manner of their oaths and combi-
> nations, for it hath been made known unto me that they are had among
> all people, and they are had among the Lamanites. And they have caused
> the destruction of this people of whom I am now speaking [the
> Jaredites], and also the destruction of the people of Nephi.

He continues on to generalize the issue—"And whatsoever nation shall uphold such secret combinations, to get power and gain, until they shall spread over the nation, behold they shall be destroyed"—before adding a pointed warning to the Gentiles (vv. 22–24). In similar fashion, after reporting on the brother of Jared's encounter with the preexistent Jesus, Moroni tells us: "[I]t sufficeth me to say that Jesus showed himself unto this man in the spirit, even after the manner and in the likeness of the same body *even as he showed himself unto the Nephites*. And he ministered unto him *even as he ministered unto the Nephites*" (Ether 3:17–18, emphasis added). Elsewhere, he names noteworthy Nephites (among them Alma and Amulek, Ammon, Nephi$_2$, and Lehi$_4$) who, along with the brother of Jared, exercised remarkable faith "even before Christ came" (Ether 12:7–21). And he opens his account of the Jaredites by emphasizing that, aside from all the political details, they were actually "destroyed by the hand of the Lord" (Ether 1:1), just as he began his additions to his father's history with this observation: "[G]reat and marvelous is the destruction of my people, the Nephites. And behold, it is the hand of the Lord which hath done it" (Morm. 8:7–8).

Moroni also explicitly connects the two civilizations through geographic references, informing his readers, for example, that the Jaredite land of Moron was "near the land called Desolation by the Nephites" (Ether 7:6), that the land southward was "called by the Nephites Zarahemla" (Ether 9:31), and—tying each group's final days to the other's—that the hill Ramah "was that same hill where my father Mormon did hide up the records unto the Lord" (Ether 15:11; see also Ether 9:3). These spatial identifications might have helped a Nephite audience picture the story more clearly, but at the time Moroni was writing, he knew that there were no longer any Nephites left. Since his readers in the distant future would be baffled by both sets of geographical references, the point of noting these overlapping locations seems to be connecting the otherwise disparate Jaredites and Nephites.

In a more subtle fashion, Moroni brings the two peoples into conjunction by shaping the Jaredites' story using both parallel narrative elements and distinctive phrasal borrowings from the Nephite account. For example, he reports that Jaredite prophets had warned that unless the people repented, "the Lord God would execute judgment against them to their utter destruction; and that the Lord God would send or bring forth another people [the Nephites] to possess the land, by his power, *after the manner by which he brought their* [Jaredite] *fathers*" (Ether 11:20–21; emphasis added). This replacement of one people by another happened just as foretold, and Moroni highlights the similarities of the Jaredite and Nephite migrations through a series of significant literary parallels:

- The brother of Jared is "large" in stature and "highly favored of the Lord," like Nephi (Ether 1:34; 1 Ne. 2:16; 1:1).
- The people are instructed to "gather together seed of every kind" (Ether 1:41; 1 Ne. 16:11).
- The Lord provides direction for travel (Ether 2:5, 6; 1 Ne. 16:9; 18:5).
- The Lord instructs them to build ships, including design details (Ether 2:16; 1 Ne. 17:8; 18:1, 2).
- They are to be led to "a land of promise . . . choice above all other lands" (Ether 2:7; 1 Ne. 2:20; 2 Ne. 1:5).
- A warning is given concerning those who would possess the land of promise, that the "fulness of the wrath of God" would come upon them when they were "ripened in iniquity" (Ether 2:9; 1 Ne. 17:33, 35).
- The people pitch their tents by the seashore (Ether 2:13; 1 Ne. 17:6).
- They sojourn in the wilderness for many years (Ether 2:13; 1 Ne. 17:4).
- They are anxious about being "swallowed up in the depths of the sea" (Ether 2:25; 1 Ne. 18:10, 15, 20).
- They make implements "molten out of the rock" (Ether 3:1, 3; 1 Ne. 17:16).
- Nephi and the brother of Jared converse with the Lord on a mountain (Ether 3:1–16; 1 Ne. 17:7–14; 18:3)
- Nephi and the brother of Jared are shown a vision of future world events (Ether 3:25; 1 Ne. 11–14).
- The people will "cross the great waters" (Ether 6:3; 1 Ne. 17:17).
- They are "driven forth before the wind . . . towards the promised land" (Ether 6:8; 1 Ne. 18:8).

- They experience "the multitude of [the Lord's] tender mercies" (Ether 6:12; 1 Ne. 8:8).
- Upon arrival in the promised land, they "went forth upon the land" and "began to till the earth" (Ether 6:13; 1 Ne. 18:23–24).
- The people gather before the patriarch dies (Ether 6:19; 2 Ne. 1:1; 4:12).
- The people desire a king; hesitancy is expressed by reluctant leaders (Ether 6:22–25; 2 Ne. 5:18).

Again and again, it seems that Moroni is deliberately employing language from Nephi's writings to tell the story of the first generation of the Jaredites.

There is, of course, another way of interpreting such parallels. Stepping out of the narrative frame, we might view these connections as the result of Joseph Smith's particular imagination and vocabulary—it is only natural that he would tell the same kinds of stories in the same words. This approach was explored by the early twentieth-century Mormon leader and scholar B. H. Roberts, who, after citing a few examples of similar incidents in the wilderness, journeys, and sea voyages of the Jaredites and Nephites, wrote:

> It may be asked, what of this parallelism? What does it amount to? If such a question should be asked, the opponent of the Book of Mormon would answer with emphasis—"This of it. It supplies the evidence that the Book of Mormon is the product of *one mind*, and that, a very limited mind, unconsciously reproducing with only slight variation its visions." And the answer will be accepted as significant at least, if not conclusive.[17]

Yet the parallels are stronger than Roberts realized, especially those that include clear verbal correspondences, and the literary context is more intriguing. Roberts showed little, if any, awareness of what it means to read Ether as the work of Moroni.

Here is yet another list, identifying key words or phrases that connect the founding eras of the Jaredites and the Nephites, along with an indication of how often these terms show up elsewhere in the Book of Mormon:

ETHER	PHRASE	1 NEPHI	NUMBER OF USES ELSEWHERE
1:38	"let us be faithful"	3:16, 4:1, 7:12	0
1:41	seed "of every kind"	16:11	0
1:43	raise up seed unto the Lord	7:1	1
2:3	honey	17:5, 18:6	3 (all 2 Ne. Isaiah)

2:6	"travel(ed) in the wilderness"	2:5	3
2:7, 10, 15	a land "choice above all other lands"	2:20, 13:30	2 (2 Ne. 1:5, Ether 9:20; cf. 2 Ne. 10:19, Ether 12:2)
2:9	God's wrath comes on those who are "ripe(ned) in iniquity"	17:35	1 (Ether 9:20)
2:22; 6:3	cross the "great water(s)"	17:17	0 (cf. Omni 1:16)
2:25	"swallowed up in the depths of the sea"	18:10, 15, 20	0
3:1, 3	"molten out of a/the rock"	17:16	0
3:3	"smit(t)e(n) us because of our iniquity"	18:10	0
6:6	"great and terrible tempest(s)"	18:13	1
6:8	"driven forth before the wind"	18:8, 9	1
6:9	praise God "all the day long"	18:16	0
6:12	"humble(d) themselves/ himself before the Lord"	13:16; 15:20; 16:5, 32; 18:4	2 (incl. Ether 9:35)
6:12	"multitude of his tender mercies"	8:8	0

Some of these phrases might be of particular use when describing a sea voyage to a new land, but many are not. What the list seems to demonstrate is a close, unique literary connection between the first chapters of Ether and First Nephi. This might be explained as inadvertent repetition on Joseph Smith's part, particularly since after the loss of the 116 pages by Martin Harris, Joseph continued his dictation with the books of Mosiah through Moroni before returning to the origins of the Nephites and producing First Nephi through Omni—material from the Small Plates of Nephi. Consequently, Ether and First Nephi were written within a few weeks of each other.[18]

Yet when we reenter the world of the text, other explanations are possible. Mormon describes his discovery of the Small Plates among the records in his possession as a delightful surprise (W. of M. 1:3–5), a small bit of consolation in an era of impending total destruction, sometime before he handed over the records to his son (vv. 1–2). Given the circumstances, we can assume that Moroni would have carefully studied this newfound scriptural treasure. It is therefore not unexpected that his own narrative would be heavily influenced by Nephi's writings or that he might make deliberate allusions to the Small Plates.

When we try to imagine what Moroni might have thought of the twenty-four plates of Ether or how he may have edited them, we are not necessarily assuming the factual historicity of either the narrator or the records. After all, novelists can imagine fictive figures manipulating fictive texts. For instance, in 1726 Jonathan Swift played with his own expected audience by prefacing *Gulliver's Travels* with a note to the reader from the publisher, Richard Sympson (a completely made-up character), who explained:

> The author of these travels, Mr. Lemuel Gulliver, is my ancient and intimate friend; there is likewise some relation between us by the mother's side. . . . Before he quitted Redriff, he left the custody of the following papers in my hands, with the liberty to dispose of them as I should think fit. I have carefully perused them three times. The style is very plain and simple, and the only fault I find is that the author, after the manner of travelers, is a little too circumstantial. . . . This volume would have been at least twice as large if I had not made bold to strike out innumerable passages relating to the winds and tides, as well as to the variations and bearings in the several voyages, together with the minute descriptions of the management of the ship in storms, in the style of sailors. Likewise the account of the longitudes and latitudes, wherein I have reason to apprehend that Mr. Gulliver may be a little dissatisfied. But I was resolved to fit the work as much as possible to the general capacity of readers. However, if my own ignorance in sea-affairs shall have led me to commit some mistakes, I alone am answerable for them. And if any traveler hath a curiosity to see the whole work at large, as it came from the hand of the author, I will be ready to gratify him.[19]

To add to the drollery, in the 1735 edition Swift included a letter from (the fictional) Captain Gulliver to the (fictional) publisher Sympson complaining that he had allowed the (real) printer of the first edition to make (real) changes to the text without permission.

It is important, of course, to ground literary interpretations on evidence in the text, and the case of Moroni is more subtle in that we are working backward from the final form of the book of Ether rather than relying solely on Moroni's explicit declarations, but there are nevertheless patterns in his work that are explainable within the parameters of the narrative. In trying to make sense of the last narrator, I am proposing that when Moroni edited the Jaredite record, he deliberately highlighted connections with the Nephites and Lamanites and minimized differences. There is another striking feature of the book of Ether, and whether it is ultimately ascribed to Joseph Smith or to Moroni, it reflects an aspect of Jaredite culture that the previous narrator, Mormon, would have found truly problematic, a reason he could not simply have appended Mosiah's translation of the twenty-four plates to his own abridgment of history. A close reading of Ether suggests that Jaredite culture was almost entirely non-Christian. Consequently, it is not surprising that Mormon was at a loss as to how to integrate their story into his own account, which was obviously designed to testify of Jesus and his promises. And here Moroni comes to the rescue. With fewer historiographical qualms than his father, Moroni does something that Mormon either could not or would not do. In a startling act of literary appropriation, he Christianizes the Jaredite record.

Disguising a Major Discrepancy

The idea that the Jaredites did not know about Jesus will come as a surprise to most Latter-day Saints. At first glance, the Jaredite story does not seem that different from what we have seen elsewhere in the Book of Mormon; Christ is mentioned regularly and reverently. Yet if one were go through the book of Ether with a red pencil and differentiate Moroni's direct narrator's comments from his paraphrase of the twenty-four plates, it would soon become obvious that, with a single exception, specific references to Jesus Christ appear only in Moroni's editorial remarks.

Jaredite prophets repeatedly preach, it is true, but their message is limited to "repent or be destroyed."[20] And although the Jaredite record refers to "the Lord" more than a hundred times, nothing specifically links this deity to Jesus or his gospel.[21] There are no religious performances, no mention of places of worship, no reported sermons, no discussion of the nature of God or sin or salvation, no warning of a final judgment, and little that would constitute narrative theology. Moroni's paraphrase of the prophecies of Ether, in the very last generation, includes oblique references to New Testament doctrines, but there is still no discussion of redemption through Jesus. The impression we have of how well the book of Ether harmonizes with the Christocentric tone of the rest of the Book of Mormon is due almost entirely to Moroni's editorial skill (or perhaps his adept camouflaging).

The obvious exception to all of this is the brother of Jared's remarkable and very personal encounter with Jesus, as reported in Ether 3. There the Lord appears to his prophet to emphatically declare his identity (more details on this story follow below):

Behold, I am he who was prepared from the foundation of the world to redeem my people. Behold, I am Jesus Christ. I am the Father and the Son. In me shall all mankind have life, and that eternally, even they who shall believe on my name; and they shall become my sons and my daughters. (v. 14)

But as the vision closes, the Lord instructs the brother of Jared to write an account of the experience, seal it up, and not speak of it again (Ether 3:21–22). The remainder of the book of Ether reads as if that is precisely what happened. The language of Christian doctrine vanishes and no specific mention is made of Jesus for the next twenty-eight generations of Jaredite history, until the very end—in marked contrast to the Nephite record, which rarely goes for more than a few verses without "talking of Christ, rejoicing in Christ, preaching of Christ, or prophesying of Christ," to paraphrase 2 Ne. 25:26.[22]

Perhaps no theme was as important to Book of Mormon narrators as demonstrating the universality of the Christian religion, showing that prophets could guide the faithful in every land and era (even before Jesus' birth) to believe in Christ and accept his salvation. The challenge for Moroni, then, was to Christianize Ether's book, making it appear more theologically consistent with his father's history than it actually was. He does this by working an additional eighteen references to Christ's name into his comments on the Jaredite record. His methodology can be easily tracked if we line up the explicit references to Christ with Moroni's six direct comment sections, each of which either begins with some variation of "And now, I, Moroni . . ." or is followed by "And now I proceed with my record . . ."[23]

MORONI'S EDITORIAL INTERRUPTIONS IN ETHER	SPECIFIC REFERENCES TO CHRIST
1:1–6	
2:9–12	2:12
3:17–20	3:17, 19, 20
4:1–5:6	4:1, 2, 3, 7, 8; 5:5
8:20–26	
12:6–41	12:7, 16, 19, 22, 38, 39, 41

The only outlier reference to Christ is at Ether 13:4, which appears in Moroni's paraphrase of Ether's prophecies. Moroni's concerns in these comments are twofold: first, to affirm that Jesus Christ is the God of the new promised land—that is, the Americas—and second, to summarize the characteristics of Jesus' person and mission that had been elaborated in Mormon's writings but were absent from the Jaredite record.

Moroni's first insertion of Jesus into his abridgment sets the pattern for subsequent comments. As the Jaredites were about to sail for the land of promise, the Lord issued a stern decree that "whoso should possess this land of promise, from that time henceforth and forever, should serve him, the true and only God, or they should be swept off when the fulness of his wrath should come upon them" (Ether 2:8). Moroni interrupts here to clarify for Gentile readers the exact identity of the deity referred to: "Behold, this is a choice land, and whatsoever nation shall possess it shall be free . . . if they will but serve the God of the land, *who is Jesus Christ, who hath been manifested by the things which we have written*" (Ether 2:12, emphasis added). The added explanation (with its nicely placed "we") is Moroni's attempt to connect his father's history of the Nephites with his own soon-to-be-related account of the brother of Jared in a demonstration that Jesus Christ had made himself known to both Book of Mormon peoples.

In the Christianizing remarks that follow, Moroni reaffirms his message that Christ is the God of all those who will possess the promised land. In Ether 4:1–3, he reminds us that the Nephites were Christ's people. A few verses later, he reports that Jesus himself told him that he would reveal to the Gentiles the things he had shown the brother of Jared if they had the same sort of faith (Ether 4:7). And so it goes. Moroni fills his editorial interruptions with distinctive phrases about Jesus' characteristics and mission that allude to the Nephites' extensive teachings about him. The ideas are neither organized nor developed as theology. Many are presented in Jesus' own voice. The purpose of their inclusion seems not so much to instruct as to suggest by juxtaposition that the Jaredites shared the Nephite understanding of Christ, despite the fact that the Jaredite narrative was evidently silent on such matters. Below is a list of some of the things that Moroni reminds readers about Christ, with references to a sampling of similar passages elsewhere in the Nephite record. According to Moroni's comments in Ether, Jesus:

- Was prepared from the foundation of the world (Ether 3:14; Mosiah 18:13)
- Is the Father and the Son (Ether 3:14; Mosiah 15:2, Hel. 16:18)
- Is the creator of man after his own image (Ether 3:15; Mosiah 7:27)
- Was lifted up upon the cross (Ether 4:1; 3 Ne. 27:14)
- Is the Son of God (Ether 4:7; 1 Ne. 10:17; Alma 33:14, 17, 18, 22)
- Has power to cause the earth to shake (Ether 4:9; Hel. 12:11)
- Is the source of all that persuades to do good (Ether 4:12; Moro. 7:16–17)
- Is the light, life, and truth of the world (Ether 4:12; Alma 38:9)
- Gave revelations to John (Ether 4:16; 1 Ne. 14:27)

- Bears record of his word with the Father and the Holy Ghost (Ether 5:4; 3 Ne. 11:32)
- Glorified the name of the Father (Ether 12:8; 3 Ne. 9:15)
- Has prepared a place for his followers in the Father's mansions (Ether 12:32–34; Enos 1:27)
- Loves the world and laid down his life for it (Ether 12:33; 2 Ne. 26:24)
- Will be present at the judgment seat (Ether 12:38; Morm. 3:20)

To the casual reader, the Jaredite account appears to support and corroborate theological principles taught in Mormon's history, but everything here comes from the hand of Moroni.

In the one exception to the pattern, at 13:4, we are told that Ether, the last of the Jaredite prophets, "saw the days of Christ." It is here, in the final generation, that Christian language returns to the Jaredite record. Moroni reports that Ether spoke of a "hope for a better world" and "a place at the right hand of God" (Ether 12:4), as well as "a new heaven and a new earth" (13:9), and he offered a lengthy prophecy of the New Jerusalem, whose inhabitants would be those who had been "washed in the blood of the Lamb" (13:11).

It is telling, however, that Ether's message is always conveyed indirectly, and we may wonder how close the paraphrase was, or if there was any embellishment in Moroni's summary. Was, for example, "washed in the blood of the Lamb" a phrase from Ether, or was it Moroni's wording? And what would even the old Jerusalem have meant to Ether, a non-Israelite whose ancestors had left the Old World long before the city was founded? (Did Moroni see a chance to work in more of Jesus' teachings from 3 Ne. 20–21, the only other place in the Book of Mormon that mentions the New Jerusalem?) Then, suddenly, Moroni is cut short by the Lord: "I was about to write more, but I am forbidden" (Ether 13:13; has he gone too far?). In any event, Moroni seems to be wary of giving us Ether's words, and in this he is quite unlike his father, whose inclusion of entire sermons of Alma as embedded documents was a way of saying, *See, I am not just reading my own modern beliefs into these ancient stories—you can look at the original sources yourself.* One might wonder why, if Moroni did not have enough room on the plates for Ether's own words, a few chapters later he is happy to copy a whole sermon and two letters of his father into his record.[24]

Moroni's final and most impressive Christianizing effort occurs in his last comment section (Ether 12:6–41), which is quite separate from his paraphrase of Ether's teachings. The block of text is inserted into the Jaredite history at a position similar to that occupied by Christ's appearance to the Nephites in Mormon's record; that is, it is sandwiched between the people's rejection of the prophets and their road to annihilation. The context here is Ether's preaching about faith and hope even as he prophesies about the people's pending destruction:

For he did cry from the morning, even until the going down of the sun,
exhorting the people to believe in God unto repentance lest they should be
destroyed, saying unto them that by faith all things are fulfilled—

Wherefore, whoso believeth in God,
might with surety hope for a better world,
   yea, even a place at the right hand of God,
which hope cometh of faith,
   maketh an anchor to the souls of men,
which would make them sure and steadfast,
   always abounding in good works,
      being led to glorify God.

And it came to pass that Ether did prophesy great and marvelous
things unto the people, which they did not believe, because they saw
them not. (Ether 12:3–5; the obvious connection here to language from
the book of Hebrews will be taken up in Chapter 9)

At just this moment, Moroni breaks in abruptly with "And now, I, Moroni, would
speak somewhat concerning these things" (Ether 12:6). He then proceeds, by way of
contrast, to describe a series of faithful Nephites, from Alma$_2$ and the sons of Helaman
to the Three Nephites. Not surprisingly, he puts Jesus at the heart of the matter: "It was
by faith that Christ showed himself unto our fathers, after he had risen from the dead"
(Ether 12:7), Moroni tells us.

Then, in keeping with Ether's preaching, he connects faith to hope and extends
an invitation to his readers: "Wherefore, ye may also have hope . . . if ye will but
have faith" (Ether 12:9). In each of the examples of faithful Nephite prophets that
follow, Moroni refocuses Ether's theme of faith in God to faith in Jesus Christ, cul-
minating with the experience of the non-Nephite brother of Jared (Ether 12:20–21).
Moroni then reproduces an exchange that he had with the resurrected Christ,
making Jesus present to his readers by reporting a dialogue in which Jesus adds
charity to Ether's virtues of faith and hope: "I will show unto them [the Gentiles]
that faith, hope, and charity bringeth unto me—the fountain of all righteousness"
(Ether 12:28).

Moroni returns to faith and hope, particularizing and Christianizing the latter
by redefining the hoped-for "better world" mentioned in Ether's preaching as the
place that Jesus has prepared for the righteous in the mansions of the Father (Ether
12:32). In connection with this, Christ's atonement becomes Moroni's prime example of charity. Still addressing the Lord, he says, "thou hast loved the world, even
unto the laying down of thy life for the world . . . and now I know that this love
which thou hast had for the children of men is charity" (Ether 12:33–34). After a
few more verses on the role of charity in the lives of his Gentile readers, Moroni

concludes his comment with a testimony: "I have seen Jesus, and . . . he hath talked with me face to face, and . . . told me in plain humility . . . concerning these things" (Ether 12:39), and then comes a charge to his audience: "And now, I would commend you to seek this Jesus of whom the prophets and apostles have written" (Ether 12:41).[25]

Moroni's Christianizing of the Jaredite experience is subtle and consistent, but his sixteen-year writer's block becomes more understandable when we imagine him reading Mosiah's translation of the record of a non-Israelite, non-Christian society that had missed out on the covenant at Sinai, and then comparing that with the very last words written by his father (directed toward the latter-day descendants of the Lamanites):

> And ye will also know that ye are a remnant of the seed of Jacob;
> therefore ye are numbered among the people of the first covenant; and if
> it so be that ye believe in Christ, and are baptized, first with water, and
> then with fire and with the Holy Ghost, following the example of our
> Savior, according to that which he hath commanded us, it shall be well
> with you in the day of judgment. Amen. (Morm. 7:10)

What could the two records possibly have to do with each other? Mormon had not been able to see his way forward to a solution, yet he was counting on Moroni to fulfill his editorial promise to incorporate the Jaredites into his comprehensive history of the Nephites. In this scenario, Mormon's hope that his son would survive to write "somewhat concerning Christ" (W. of M. 1:2) becomes rather more interesting.

Ultimately, it probably makes little difference to Latter-day Saints whether the Jaredites worshiped Jesus or not—unlike the Lehites, they are completely annihilated with no identifiable posterity, no role to play in the larger story of the House of Israel, and no direct connection to modern readers—yet their non-Christian status seems to have mattered a great deal to Mormon and his conception of the book he was writing. Moroni fulfills his duty by restructuring Ether's account. Through overt, interruptive comments, he is able to transform it into something different from what it seems to have been originally. He reportedly does so with the express permission and guidance of Jesus himself, but it nevertheless appears that his approach would have compromised Mormon's historiographical principles. Mormon cared a great deal about specific facts and dates, because he believed that faith could be derived from a careful analysis of history itself. For Moroni, however, the details of history are less important than the witness of the Spirit, and this flexibility allows him to do something that Mormon could not do himself. His ultimate reliance on spiritual affirmation also helps explain why he devotes a major portion of his abridgment to the story of the brother of Jared.

A Model for the Gentiles

The most complete, rounded narrative in the book of Ether occurs in Ether 2–3 and concerns the brother of Jared. As noted above, it is the only incident in Jaredite history that is unambiguously Christian, yet it is also significant because it illustrates a particular path to religious knowledge. The story begins at the Tower of Babel, when God granted the request of Jared's brother to keep the language of his family and friends intelligible and to lead them to a choice land. God guided them through the wilderness until they came to the seashore, where he gave them instructions on how to build tightly covered, ocean-going barges. When the brother of Jared went to the Lord with concerns about ventilation and interior illumination, the first question was resolved with additional design details, but God asked his prophet to think harder about the second: "What will ye that I should do that ye may have light in your vessels? For behold, ye cannot have windows, for they will be dashed in pieces; neither shall ye take fire with you . . . therefore what will ye that I should prepare for you that ye may have light when ye are swallowed up in the depths of the sea?" (Ether 2:23–25).

In response, the brother of Jared fashioned sixteen molten, glass-like stones, and then returned to the Lord and hesitantly asked him to touch them with his finger so they might shine in the dark. At this point, a remarkable story becomes extraordinary:

> And it came to pass that when the brother of Jared had said these words, behold, the Lord stretched forth his hand and touched the stones one by one with his finger. And the veil was taken from off the eyes of the brother of Jared, and he saw the finger of the Lord; and it was as the finger of a man, like unto flesh and blood; and the brother of Jared fell down before the Lord, for he was struck with fear. (Ether 3:6)

Over the course of the ensuing dialogue, the confidence of the brother of Jared increases until at last he asks the Lord to reveal himself entirely, which the preexistent Christ does, saying, "Because thou knowest these things *ye are redeemed from the fall*; therefore ye are brought back into my presence; therefore I show myself unto you" (Ether 3:13; emphasis added).

It is a stunning culmination, and indeed, several key incidents and phrases seem to indicate that Moroni arranged his abridgment up to this point as a reversal of the fall of man, tracing major events from the Garden of Eden to the Tower of Babel backward (as usual, the connections are to the King James Bible). The following quotations are presented in Book of Mormon form and sequence, though the biblical allusions are quite recognizable:

ALLUSIONS	REFERENCES	ETHER	GENESIS
The tower	The Lord "confounded the language of the people" and they were "scattered upon all the face of the earth."	1:33	11:9
Noah	The Lord commands the brother of Jared to "gather together thy flocks, both male and female, of every kind; and also thy families," along with "fowls of the air" and "swarms of bees," to put into a boat.[26]	1:41 2:2–3	6:18–19 6:20
Antediluvian wickedness	The Lord chastises the brother of Jared, warning him that "my spirit will not always strive with man." Later the prophet confesses that "our natures have become evil continually."	2:15 3:2	6:3 6:5
Expulsion	The Jaredites, like Adam and Eve, are "driven forth" into the wilderness because of their iniquity.	3:3	3:23–24
Catalytic event	God touches the sixteen stones; Adam and Eve touch/eat the forbidden fruit. The eyes of Adam and Eve, as well as Jared, are opened, and all are afraid. God then asks a series of four rhetorical questions.	3:6 3:6 3:7–15	3:3, 6 3:7, 10 3:9–13
Creation	The Lord asks the brother of Jared, "Seest thou that ye are created after mine own image? Yea, even all men were created in the beginning after mine own image."	3:15	1:27

Step by step, Moroni's account takes us back toward creation, reversing the effects of the fall and restoring the close communion between God and man that was present at the beginning.[27]

As the Lord continues his conversation with the brother of Jared—still in his presence and newly "redeemed from the fall"—he refers to a later, more general redemption that was "prepared from the foundation of the world" (Ether 3:14), and he explains that what he has manifested is actually his spirit body, which takes the same shape as the physical form he will someday assume when he comes to the earth as Jesus Christ. The brother of Jared, however, has received a special dispensation, for a particular reason: "And never have I showed myself unto man whom I have created, for never has man believed in me as thou hast" (Ether 3:15).[28]

At this point, Moroni breaks off his narration in order to add a few comments of his own.

Latter-day Saints often use the tale of the brother of Jared and the shining stones as an illustration of the power of prayer or the importance of believers taking some initiative to resolve their difficulties before they turn to God.[29] Moroni, however, highlights a different aspect of the plot when he cuts the story short with a narrative summary:

> And now, as I, Moroni, said I could not make a full account of these
> things which are written, therefore it sufficeth me to say that Jesus
> showed himself unto this man in the spirit . . . And because of the
> *knowledge* of this man he could not be kept from beholding within the
> veil; and he saw the finger of Jesus, which when he saw, he fell with fear;
> for he *knew* that it was the finger of the Lord; and he had faith no longer,
> for he *knew*, nothing doubting. Wherefore, having this perfect *knowledge*
> of God, he could not be kept from within the veil; therefore, he saw Jesus;
> and he did minister unto him. (Ether 3:17, 19–20; emphasis added)

The focus here is on the power of knowledge to open the heavens; as Jesus told the brother of Jared, "Because thou *knowest* these things ye are redeemed from the fall; therefore ye are brought back into my presence" (Ether 3:13). The brother of Jared does not exactly redeem himself—Christ is still at the center of the process—and he acknowledges his sins and weaknesses (3:2–3), but this is not quite the standard gospel story of repentance, baptism, atonement, and forgiveness. It starts with a faith that becomes knowledge, and then God extends his grace by way of self-revelation.

The Lord tells the brother of Jared that the things he has revealed must remain private until after he comes in the flesh and fulfills his mission on the cross. In the meantime, the prophet should record his experience in a secret language ("the language which ye shall write I have confounded," the Lord says, in terms reminiscent of the Tower of Babel), and seal it up, along with two stone "interpreters"—devices that would allow someone someday to recover the hidden account (Ether 3:21–24). Then follows an even more expansive revelation in which God shows the brother of Jared all the people who will ever live upon the earth, again motivated by the same principle: "For he had said unto him in times before, that if he would believe in him that he could show unto him all things—it should be shown unto him; therefore the Lord could not withhold anything from him, for he knew that the Lord could show him all things" (Ether 3:26). This vision as well he is commanded to write, and then seal up with the two stones.

Moroni reports that King Mosiah (whose possession of the interpreters allowed him to translate the twenty-four plates containing Ether's summary version) kept the details of the record concealed until Jesus appeared in the New World, as the

Lord had instructed. After that time, the document apparently circulated freely for several centuries until wickedness again prevailed among the Nephites and Moroni was commanded to hide it up again in the earth (Ether 4:1–3). It is not exactly clear what Moroni's sources are here. He begins his account by informing us that he will be abridging Ether's synopsis of Jaredite history—including the life of the brother of Jared and Ether's own prophecies—but elsewhere he speaks of reading the personal writings of the brother of Jared, and he described them as "mighty . . . unto the overpowering of man to read them" (Ether 12:24). And when he later complains that he cannot write more than "a hundredth part" (of twenty-four plates?), we are left wondering whether he had access to multiple Jaredite records, or whether he simply adopted this phrase from his father as a literary trope (see W. of M. 1:5; Hel. 3:14; 3 Ne. 5:8, 26:6).

What is unmistakable is that Moroni sees his role as record keeper as following the same pattern of writing and sealing established by the brother of Jared:

> Behold, I have written upon these plates the very things which the
> brother of Jared saw; and there never were greater things made manifest
> than those which were made manifest unto the brother of Jared.
> Wherefore the Lord hath commanded me to write them; and I have
> written them. And he commanded me that I should seal them up; and he
> also hath commanded that I should seal up the interpretation thereof;
> wherefore I have sealed up the interpreters, according to the
> commandment of the Lord. (Ether 4:4–5)

This information was obviously pertinent to Joseph Smith—who claimed that he had found the interpreters along with the plates and hence was able to translate the unsealed portion—but there is meaning as well for ordinary readers of the Book of Mormon. They may never possess the sort of knowledge that made possible the epiphany had by the brother of Jared, yet they are nevertheless enjoined to follow his example. Moroni writes: "'In that day that they [the Gentiles] shall exercise faith in me,' saith the Lord, 'even as the brother of Jared did . . . then will I manifest unto them the things which the brother of Jared saw, even to the unfolding unto them all my revelations'" (Ether 4:7).

Similarly, although modern readers do not have the miraculous interpreters employed by Mosiah and Moroni, they are promised another spiritual mechanism by which to ascertain the truth of the Book of Mormon (again in Moroni's quotation of the Lord): "He that believeth these things which I have spoken, him will I visit with the manifestations of my Spirit, and he shall know and bear record. For because of my Spirit he shall know that these things are true . . . Come unto me, O ye Gentiles, and I will show unto you greater things, the knowledge which is hid up because of unbelief" (Ether 4:11–13).

This, of course, is a very different mode of reading from that envisioned by his father. Mormon had assumed that he could persuade his audience through the careful marshaling of historical evidence—that prophecy and its fulfillment, combined with primary documents and a few brief editorial asides, would carry the day. Moroni, knowing more about his audience and facing data that were much less obviously in line with his themes, gives up on strict chronology and the straightforward presentation of historical information, preferring instead to rely on intrusive comment sections and the power of the Spirit to convince his readers. It is an intriguing situation, in which Moroni has to gently subvert the assumptions behind his father's record in order to bring it to a proper conclusion. It is not, however, without parallel.

In the twelfth century Li Qingzhao, often regarded as China's finest female poet, held in her hands a manuscript written by her recently deceased husband. It was his *Records on Metal and Stone*—an annotated collection of inscriptions from ancient bronze artifacts and stone monuments that he had put together over the course of a lifetime of traveling and connoisseurship. Li herself had played a large role in the endeavor, since from the early years of their marriage they had enjoyed buying antiques together, collating old books, and rendering scholarly judgments: "When he got hold of a piece of calligraphy, a painting, a goblet, or a tripod, we would go over it at our leisure, point out faults and flaws, setting for our nightly limit the time it took one candle to burn down. Thus our collection came to surpass all others in fineness of paper and the perfection of the characters." Yet in the Jurchen invasion of 1127, nearly everything—more than ten rooms full of books, scrolls, bronze vessels, and other rare items—was destroyed or lost, a cartload at a time, as the family fled south. Her husband died in the conflict, and in the end she was left alone, with one basket of literary odds and ends and his manuscript of five hundred annotated inscriptions.

Eventually she published his book with an afterword written by herself, in which she celebrated his achievement, describing him in nearly heroic terms, but at the same time hinted at a growing awareness of the ultimate futility of his life's work:

> From the time I was eighteen [the year she married] until now at the age
> of fifty-two—a span of thirty years—how much calamity, how much
> gain and loss I have witnessed! When there is possession, there must be
> lack of possession; when there is a gathering together, there must be a
> dissolution—that is the constant principle of things. Someone loses a
> bow; someone else happens to find a bow—what's worth noticing in
> that? The reason why I have so minutely recorded this story from
> beginning to end is to serve as a warning for scholars and collectors in
> later generations.[30]

So also Moroni, writing what is essentially an appendix to his father's massive history, brings it to a posthumous conclusion and in so doing both honors his father's ambition and calls into question its underlying historiographical principles (with an eye toward later generations). Nevertheless, unlike Li Qingzhao, he never doubts the value of the whole enterprise; both he and Mormon write to persuade future readers to come to Christ and prepare for the judgment day. They simply take different approaches.

Yet there is a certain level of ambivalence in Moroni's writing, at least until Ether 12, where he restates his particular interpretation of the brother of Jared's vision and once more makes a connection between the Jaredite prophet and the latter-day Gentiles:

> And behold, we have seen in this record that one of these was the brother of Jared; for so great was his faith in God, that when God put forth his finger he could not hide it from the sight of the brother of Jared, because of his word which he had spoken unto him, which word he had obtained by faith. And after the brother of Jared had beheld the finger of the Lord, because of the promise which the brother of Jared had obtained by faith, the Lord could not withhold anything from his sight; wherefore, he showed him all things for he could no longer be kept without the veil.
>
> And it is by faith that my fathers have obtained the promise that these things should come unto their brethren [the Lamanites] through the Gentiles; therefore, the Lord hath commanded me, yea even Jesus Christ.
>
> And I said unto him, "Lord the Gentiles will mock at these things, because of our weakness in writing . . ." (vv. 20–23)

This brings us around to the point where we began this chapter, and indeed Moroni's dialogue with Jesus in Ether 12 seems to have been a pivotal event in his development as a writer. Only here is he able to reconcile his feelings of inadequacy at carrying out his father's commandments with his perceptions of what his audience and his God expect of him. For the rest of the Book of Mormon, there are no more complaints about "weakness in writing," and in contrast with both Nephi and Mormon, Moroni concludes his contribution without a direct call for his readers to repent (the word never appears in Moro. 10; contrast 2 Ne. 31:11, 13, 14, 17 and Morm. 7:3, 5, 8). Despite his earlier misgivings about the spiritual receptiveness of the Gentiles, Moroni seems to have taken to heart Jesus' assurance that "if they [the Gentiles] have not charity it mattereth not unto thee, thou hast been faithful" (Ether 12:37), and he trusts that "God shall show unto you [his readers], that that which I have written is true" (Moro. 10:29).

It is tempting, at this point, to see Mormon and Moroni's contributions as a reprise of one of Mormon's favorite forms of parallel narratives: the juxtaposition of stories contrasting the reasonable achievements of skilled professionalism with the sometimes astonishing results that can come when inexperienced, less qualified individuals simply put their trust in the Lord. Recall how Mormon structured the books of Mosiah and Alma to set the faithful competence of Limhi's people, Alma$_2$, and Captain Moroni against the surprising, blessed successes of Alma$_1$'s people, the sons of Mosiah, and Helaman. In each set of parallels, two stories are told in quick succession, with the latter being the more miraculous. The same pattern informs the Book of Mormon as a whole (excluding the Small Plates): Mormon's careful historiographical efforts give way to Moroni's reliance on God to make his writing convincing. In the next chapter, I offer a reading of Moroni's work that suggests that by doing so, he accomplished something extraordinary.

But first a disclaimer. So far, our attention has been directed to features of the text that will, for the most part, be evident to all readers: embedded documents, chronological markers, citations of prophecies, direct narrator comments, and so forth. These narrative elements are clearly the work of a mind attuned to certain organizing principles. It is similarly evident that, at the level of words and phrases, the Book of Mormon can be quite repetitive, yet this characteristic is harder to interpret. Recurring expressions may simply be random, but it is also possible to read some of them as intentional—that is, as allusions deliberately employed by the narrators, or alternatively, as ascribed to the narrators by a clever author. The problem with the latter option is that the degree of intricacy, while not unheard of in fiction, nevertheless seems incongruous with a book that was dictated as an extemporaneous oral composition. Other interpretations are possible, but what follows is a demonstration of one particular way of reading the text, though justifiably skeptical outsiders may regard it (charitably) as a window into how believers might approach the task of narrative analysis. Even when considered as a work of fiction, the inventiveness that seems apparent in Moroni's use of allusion borders on the miraculous. Consequently, it is perhaps an appropriate focus for a chapter that deals with the literary style of a character who professes to look for divine assistance to remedy his writerly inadequacies.

9

Strategies of Conclusion

Allusion

So the question remains, is Moroni a poor writer? Many Latter-day Saints have taken his complaint of "weakness in writing" (Ether 12:23) at face value, paraphrasing it as "Moroni lamented his inability to convey these things powerfully in writing" or "Moroni humbly apologizes to the Lord for the imperfections in the record he was making."[1] Other commentators have read it ironically, noting that some of his prose is "the opposite of what we might consider weak, [featuring] cadences of ascending power" or suggesting that whatever Moroni's earlier literary inadequacies, his last entry in Moroni 10 contains passages that are "elegant and equal to any writing found in the scriptures."[2]

Tone is often difficult to pin down: a humble protestation may reflect genuine emotion, or it may be a rhetorical device for eliciting sympathy, an ironic wink to perceptive readers, a bow to convention (either as an expected authorial pose or an acknowledgment of a traditional distinction between written and oral communication), or an attempt to praise others—the brother of Jared in this case—by deprecating one's own efforts in comparison. But however we take Moroni's confession of weakness, it does appear that he writes differently than other Book of Mormon narrators. We have already noted how in his abridgment of Ether's account, he frequently follows his sparse source material so closely that there are lengthy passages of dry historical data with little literary value. In fact, of the twenty-seven Book of Mormon chapters attributed to Moroni, twenty-one are either copied directly or only lightly edited, and even in the six chapters where he is expressing his own ideas (Morm. 8–9; Ether 5, 12;

Moro. 1, 10), he does so with an unusually high proportion of phrases borrowed from previous Book of Mormon authors.

Although internal repetitions and biblical expressions are pervasive throughout the Book of Mormon, in the sections attributed to Moroni these phenomena are much more insistent, focused, and integrated. The sheer number of identifiable allusions, combined with patterns manifest in their usage, suggest a deliberate strategy at work rather than merely a linguistic patina overlaid on the basic narrative by an author who is well versed in the language of scripture. In this chapter, we will consider evidence for the intentionality of these borrowings in terms of (1) the degree of similarity, (2) their scarcity elsewhere, (3) verbal clusters from proximate verses, (4) related themes, and (5) parallel functions. Then in the last few pages we can return to the question of why Moroni chooses to write in this fashion (or why Joseph Smith chose to present Moroni as writing in this fashion). Moroni's sensibilities are revealed mostly through his style, and whether we see him as a historical figure or a fictional character, it makes him interesting to read.

Mormon apparently handed his lengthy abridgment of Nephite history to his son with a charge to bring it to an appropriate close. Like the commission to add something about the Jaredites, this was not an easy task, and it was sixteen years before Moroni managed to compose a two-chapter conclusion (Morm. 8–9). He excuses himself by noting his struggles to avoid capture and certain death, as well as his lack of writing materials (Morm. 8:1–8), but it may also have been difficult for him to know what kind of ending would transform "the sad tale of the destruction of my people" (8:3) into a book that would promise hope and salvation to future readers. Bringing any sort of long project to a suitable conclusion is a delicate matter, and this is even more the case when the bulk of the work was done by others and the results are expected to become scripture. At some later point, when Moroni found himself with more time and resources, he wrote a second ending (Ether 12, in the midst of his summary of Jaredite history). And then, perhaps after looking over his previous attempts and still not feeling satisfied, he wrote yet another conclusion (Moro. 10), some twenty years after the first. Uniquely among Book of Mormon narrators, Moroni offers us the opportunity to follow the development of his ideas and writing style over the course of decades. We can explore Moroni's distinctive use of allusion by considering each of his three conclusions in turn.

Back to the Beginning

Moroni's first ending occurs right after Mormon 7. He quickly recounts the tragic denouement of Nephite civilization from a personal perspective (Morm. 8:1–12), then writes about the future recovery of the record he is completing:

And I am the same who hideth up this record unto the Lord; the plates thereof are of no worth, because of the commandment of the Lord. For he truly saith that no one shall have them to get gain; but the record thereof is *of great worth*; and whoso shall *bring it to light, him will the Lord bless*. For none can have *power to bring it to light* save it be given him of God; for God wills that it shall be done with an eye single to his glory, or the welfare of the ancient and long dispersed covenant people of the Lord. And blessed be he that shall *bring this thing to light*; for it shall be brought *out of darkness unto light*, according to the word of God; yea, it shall be brought out of the earth, and it shall shine forth *out of darkness*, and come unto the knowledge of the people; and it shall be done by the *power* of God. (Morm. 8:13–16; emphasis added)

One of the notable things about this passage is how much of the language is familiar. Indeed, each of the phrases in italics appeared in a prophecy ascribed to Joseph of Egypt (as quoted by Lehi in 2 Ne. 3), regarding a book that his posterity would someday write:

"which shall be *of great worth* unto them"	2 Ne. 3:7
"unto the *bringing* of them *out of darkness unto light*"	2 Ne. 3:5 (cf. 1 Pet. 2:9)
"that seer *will the Lord bless*"	2 Ne. 3:14
"*power* to bring forth my word"	2 Ne. 3:11

The fact that so much of Mormon 8:13–16 repeats wording from a short passage much earlier in the Book of Mormon may seem like an odd coincidence until we come to Mormon 8:22–25, where the same phenomenon recurs, again connecting Mormon 8 with 2 Nephi 3 (borrowed words are indicated by italics; similar themes are in bold):

The eternal purposes of the Lord shall roll on, until all his *promises shall be fulfilled* . . . Yea, behold I say unto you, that those saints who have gone before me, who have possessed this land, shall *cry*, yea, even *from the dust* will they cry unto the Lord; and as the Lord liveth he will *remember the covenant which he hath made* with them. And he knoweth their prayers, that they were in behalf of their brethren. And *he knoweth their faith*, for in his name could they remove mountains; and in his name could they cause the earth to shake; and by the power of his word did they cause prisons to tumble to the earth; yea, even the fiery furnace could not harm them, neither wild beasts nor poisonous serpents, because of the power of his word. And behold, **their prayers were also in behalf of him that the Lord should suffer to bring these things forth**. And no one need say they shall not come, for they surely shall, for the Lord hath spoken it; **for out of the earth shall they come,** *by the hand of the Lord.*

Once again, phrases and themes (in bold) from 2 Ne. 3 are prominent:

"this *promise . . . shall be fulfilled*"	2 Ne. 3:14
"*cried* unto them *from the dust*"	2 Ne. 3:19–20
"unto the *remembering of the covenant which I made*"	2 Ne. 3:21
"for *I know their faith*"	2 Ne. 3:19
"**because of their faith their words shall proceed forth . . . unto their brethren**"	2 Ne. 3:21
"the *thing* which *the Lord shall bring forth by his hand*"	2 Ne. 3:15

One might argue that this sort of repetition happens all the time, simply as a result of Joseph Smith's limited vocabulary, speech habits, or common Book of Mormon themes, but the possibility of intentionality increases when we recognize that several of these phrases occur *only* in Mormon 8 and 2 Nephi 3, or nearly so:

PHRASE	NUMBER OF OCCURRENCES IN 2 NE. 3/MORM. 8	NUMBER OF OCCURRENCES ELSEWHERE
bring(ing) . . ."out of darkness unto light"	2	1 (Alma 37:25)
[name] "will the Lord bless"	2	0
"promise(s) . . . shall be fulfilled"	2	0
the Lord "know(eth) their faith"	2	0
"cry . . . from the dust"	3	2 (2 Ne. 33:13; Ether 8:24)

It appears that in addition to whatever else he may be doing in Mormon 8:13–26, Moroni is also responding to the prophecy of Joseph of Egypt that was quoted at 2 Nephi 3. The near proximity of a string of closely related allusions means that when we imagine Moroni writing, we are meant to picture him poring over a prior text, reflecting on how its words pertain to him, and pulling out distinctive phrases to reuse in his own writing (much as in the last chapter we saw him borrowing phrases from First Nephi to retell the story of the Jaredites).

This mode of composition, thick with allusions to specific earlier passages, continues. The rest of Mormon 8 describes the skepticism, vices, and destructions that would characterize the period when the Book of Mormon would come forth. The next fifteen verses (Morm. 8:26–41) are so dense with connections to 2 Nephi 26–28, chapters in which Nephi prophetically describes the same era, that they read like a paraphrase. Moroni reports on secret works of darkness; churches built up to get gain; a population lifted up in the pride of their hearts, wearing fine apparel, and occupied with envying, strife, and malice; and the blood of former saints crying to the Lord for vengeance. Oddly enough, even though he claims to have witnessed these conditions for himself in a vision (Morm. 8:34–35), Moroni nevertheless chooses to present his observations in Nephi's words, employing here some two dozen allusions to the earlier writer's account. (In fact, the densely allusive style of writing we see in Moroni's chapters is reminiscent of the way that Nephi synthesized his own prophecies with those of Isaiah and Joseph of Egypt in 2 Nephi 25–33—writings that, according to Book of Mormon chronology, would have recently come into Moroni's hands.)

If Moroni, in Mormon 8, looks to the language of the first narrator in the Book of Mormon, in the next chapter he forges connections with its last author, Mormon, who had also prophesied about the generation when the book would be published. There Moroni borrows the argumentative structure from an earlier exhortation by his father:

> And when ye shall see these sayings coming forth among you, then ye need not any longer spurn at the doings of the Lord, for the sword of justice is in his right hand; and behold, at that day, if ye shall spurn at his doings, he will cause that it shall soon overtake you.
>   [A] Wo unto him that spurneth at the doings of the Lord;
>   yea, *wo unto him that shall deny the Christ* and his works!
>   [B] Yea, *wo unto him that shall deny the revelations of the Lord, and*
>   that shall *say* the Lord *no* longer worketh by *revelation*, or by
>   *prophecy*, or by *gifts*, or by *tongues*, or by *healings*, or by the power of
>   the Holy Ghost! (3 Ne. 29:4–6; emphasis added)

In Mormon 9, Moroni expands Mormon's distinction into separate sections, appealing in turn to each subset of these modern, spurning readers: [A] "those who do not believe in Christ" (Morm. 9:1–6) and [B] those who "deny the revelations of God, and say that they are done away, that there are no revelations, nor prophecies, nor gifts, nor healing, nor speaking with tongues and the interpretations of tongues" (9:7–29). He incorporates several specific phrases from earlier Nephite prophets into this binary framework, such as "souls racked" at 9:3 from the writings of Alma (Mosiah 27:29; Alma 36:12, 14); flames of "unquenchable fire" at 9:5 from King Benjamin's address (Mosiah 2:38; 3:27); "many mighty miracles" at

9:18 from Abinadi's sermon (Mosiah 15:6); "if so, God would cease to be God . . . [but] he ceaseth not to be God" at 9:19, again from Alma's teachings (Alma 42: 22–23); and "days of probation," at 9:28 from Lehi (1 Ne. 10:21; 2 Ne. 2:30). In addition, Moroni also employs a number of apparently anachronistic New Testament phrases including "small and great stand before [God]" at 9:13 and Revelation 20:12; "work out your own salvation with fear and trembling" at 9:27 and Philippians 2:12; and "ask not . . . that ye may consume it upon your lusts" at 9:28 and James 4:3.

Admittedly, these sorts of verbal echoes can be difficult to interpret since it is hard to ascertain the intentionality of such allusions. Yet the case for calculated design becomes stronger when such allusions occur in patterns, as we see when Moroni in these same verses alternates distinctive phrases associated with Nephi and Mormon:

REF.	PHRASE	SOURCE	ELSEWHERE
9:2	"the earth shall be rolled together as a scroll"	**Mormon**: Morm. 5:23	0 (but see 3 Ne. 26:3; Isa. 34:4)
9:2–3	"the Lamb of God"	**Nephi**: 31 times in Nephi's writings	1 (Alma 7:14)
9:7	no revelations, prophecies, gifts, healings, tongues	**Mormon**: 3 Ne. 29:6	0
9:9	God is the same yesterday, today and forever	**Nephi**: 2 Ne. 27:23, 29:9	4 (1 Ne. 10:18; 2 Ne. 2:4; Alma 31:17; Moro. 10:19)[3]
9:10–19	"God of miracles" (5 times)	**Nephi**: 2 Ne. 27:23, 28:6	0
9:19–20	miracles cease	**Mormon**: Moro. 7:27–37 (4 times)	0
9:20–21	"the right way" of one who believes in Christ	**Nephi**: 2 Ne. 25:28–29	0
9:21	whatsoever he shall ask the Father in the name of Christ, it shall be given	**Mormon**: Moro. 7:26	2 (3 Ne. 18:20; 27:28; see also John 14:13)
9:29	"the Son of the Living God"	**Nephi**: 2 Ne. 31:16 **Mormon**: 3 Ne. 30:1; Morm. 5:14	0 (but see Matt. 16:16; John 6:69)
9:29	"and if ye do this . . . ye will in nowise be cast out"	**Nephi**: 2 Ne. 25:29	0 (but see John 6:37)

The borrowings here are not random: all of Nephi's come from the final chapters of his second book, with most (again) deriving from his prophecies of the latter days in 2 Nephi 25–28, while Mormon's are taken from his own late writings (3 Ne. 29–30; Morm. 5) and from his one extant sermon (included later by Moroni in Moro. 7). Again, it appears that Moroni is not so much composing this conclusion as constructing it, extracting phrases from particular texts by Nephi and Mormon in order to weave them together and thereby unify the voices of these two illustrious predecessors.

When we first met Moroni in Mormon 8, he told us that he had "but few things to write" and did not know "how long the Lord will suffer that I might live" (vv. 1, 5). He thought his primary responsibility was to bring his father's monumental history to a quick but adequate conclusion, and Mormon 8–9 is his first attempt to do so. In addition to delivering an urgent message to his skeptical latter-day readers, he alludes to prophecies reported by both Nephi and Mormon concerning the coming forth of their collective writings, linking the first and last generations of Nephite history into an integrated whole.

In his comments at both the opening and closing of this first conclusion, Moroni further suggests that he deliberately adopted the strategy of employing multiple allusions as an effort to unify the record. After summarizing the final destruction of the Nephites, he begins with a poignant self-identification, emphasizing his relation to the book's first and last writers: "Behold, I make an end of speaking concerning this people. I am the son of Mormon, and my father was a descendant of Nephi. And I am the same who hideth up this record unto the Lord" (Morm. 8:13–14). And then, in the last several verses of Mormon 9, he slips from the first-person singular into the plural, speaking not only for himself but also explicitly for his father and all those "who have written before him" (Morm. 9:31–36). It is as if he were saying, *From Nephi to Mormon to me. And it ends here.*

Ether 12, Again

Well actually, it did not end there. With unexpected resources of more ore to fashion plates and more time to write, Moroni at some point appended his abridgment of Jaredite history to his father's book. As we saw in the previous chapter, Ether 12 is a key text in Moroni's self-concept as a writer. It is also his second conclusion, and in an attempt to become, in Henry James' words, "one of the people on whom nothing is lost," we need to return to Ether 12 to review its basic structure and examine how once again Moroni employs extensive allusion as a strategy for completing the entire Book of Mormon.[4]

The chapter can be divided into four sections, as follows:

I (*vv. 1–5*) The final Jaredite prophet, Ether, urges the people to believe in God and repent, warning of impending destruction and noting that faith can lead to hope for a better world. His listeners refuse to believe, because they did not see the "great and marvelous things" of which he had prophesied.

II (vv. 6–21) Moroni expands on this teaching of Ether's, explaining that faith is based on things that are hoped for and not seen. He then gives a dozen examples from the Book of Mormon of miracles or blessings that had resulted from faith. The last of these is that through faith, his fathers obtained a promise from the Lord that a record of the Nephites (in the form of the Book of Mormon) would go to the descendants of the Lamanites, by way of the Gentiles.

III (vv. 22–37) At this moment, recognizing that he is putting the final touches on that same record, Moroni worries that the Gentiles will mock his efforts "because of our weakness in writing." A conversation with the Lord ensues, in which Jesus assures Moroni that he will bless all those who humble themselves because of their weakness, a promise that extends both to Moroni and to the Gentiles (i.e., both the writer and readers of the text). Within this dialogue, Moroni speaks of the virtues of faith, hope, and charity and of the Lord's role in fostering those traits, with Christ's atonement put forward as the preeminent example of charity.

IV (vv. 38–41) Moroni bids farewell to the Gentiles and his brethren (the Lamanites) until he meets them again at the judgment day, and he urges everyone "to seek this Jesus of whom the prophets and apostles have written."

This all seems sufficiently clear and cogent, yet in writing this chapter Moroni will again follow the strategies he employed in Mormon 8–9: incorporating clusters of distinctive phrases as well as argumentative structures from several thematically and verbally linked source texts, and then integrating these varied allusions into a coherent whole. The writings of Nephi and Mormon will again figure prominently, as will a couple of glaringly problematic chapters from the New Testament's Epistle to the Hebrews.

Any quotations in the Book of Mormon from biblical writings composed after 600 BC are anachronistic, potentially challenging both the book's historicity and its credibility. This is all the more so when the borrowed expressions appear in the exact words of the King James Version of 1611.[5] Nonbelievers simply view the English Bible as one of Joseph Smith's sources, while Latter-day Saints look instead for more apologetic explanations. Although a case can be made, for example, for the resurrected Jesus' knowledge of the contents of the gospels, and even perhaps more tenuously for Nephi's citations of Second Isaiah (as we saw in Chapter 2), it is difficult to explain how it is that Moroni and his father before him had access to writings attributed to the apostle Paul. Believers might assume that some of the "things" Jesus himself shared with Moroni when he spoke with him "face to face, in plain humility"(Ether 12:39), included the contents of particular New Testament epistles.[6] But regardless of the explanation, Ether 12 is written as if Moroni is as fully familiar with the text of Hebrews as he is with Nephi's or Mormon's writings.

Moroni's first clear allusion to Hebrews comes in what appears to be a gloss on the Jaredite prophet Ether's message of repentance and faith. He reports that Ether "did cry from the morning, even until the going down of the sun, exhorting the people to believe in God unto repentance lest they should be destroyed, saying unto them that by faith all things are fulfilled" (Ether 12:3). And then Moroni helpfully explains:

Wherefore, whoso believeth in God, might with surety hope for a better world, yea, even a place at the right hand of God *which hope* cometh of faith, maketh an *anchor to the souls* of men, which would make them *sure and steadfast* (Ether 12:4)	Which hope we have as an anchor of the soul, both sure and steadfast (Heb. 6:19)

In continuing his discussion, Moroni incorporates several additional phrases from this particular New Testament chapter, which likewise addresses the relation between faith and hope:

12:8	Christ has "prepared a way that thereby others might be *partakers of the heavenly gift*"	Heb. 6:4	"tasters of the heavenly gift and . . . partakers of the Holy Ghost"
12:17, 22	"by faith . . . *obtained the promise*"	Heb. 6:15	"And so, after he had patiently endured, he obtained the promise"
12:19:	"could not be kept from *within the veil*"	Heb. 6:19	"entereth into that within the veil"

As this cluster of allusions from Hebrews 6 suggests, the common phrases here are not simply the haphazard result of a biblically literate translator putting ideas into an idiom respected by his readers. There appears, rather, to be a direct connection between the contents of the two chapters, with Moroni (or Joseph Smith) deliberately reworking his source, in much the same fashion as we have seen him incorporate prior Book of Mormon texts. This observation is strengthened when we consider the many allusions in Ether 12 to Hebrews 11, another chapter linking faith and hope. The first connection here comes just two verses later in another overt, though unattributed, quotation:

12:6	"And now, I, Moroni . . . would show unto the world that *faith is things which are hoped for and not seen*"	Heb. 11:1	"Now faith is the substance of things hoped for, the evidence of things not seen"

After this famous definition of faith, the author of Hebrews provides a long list of things accomplished by faith, including the creation of the world and specific actions taken by Abel, Enoch, Noah, Abraham, Sarah, Isaac, Jacob, Joseph, Moses' parents, Moses, the children of Israel, Rahab, Gideon, and others. Moroni begins section II of Ether 12 with almost identical language and then proceeds to offer a parallel list of how faith made possible the appearance of Christ among the Nephites, the giving and fulfilling of the law of Moses, the prison escape of Alma$_2$ and Amulek, the receiving of the Holy Ghost by the Lamanite guards of Nephi$_2$ and Lehi$_4$, the missionary successes of Ammon and the other sons of Mosiah, the death-defying transformation of the three Nephites, and the vision the brother of Jared had of the pre-mortal Christ. Both Hebrews 11 and Ether 12 also include numerous repetitions of the expression "by faith" (sixteen times in Hebrews, eleven in Ether). There can be little doubt that Moroni's discourse on faith at Ether 12 is, in some way, based on the Epistle to the Hebrews, but it is more than simply an imitation; it is a creative adaptation.[7] If Moroni seems to have an uncanny knowledge of the New Testament, he also has a firm grasp of his Book of Mormon predecessors, and he relies heavily upon their ideas and phrases as he thoroughly and deftly integrates their voices with that of the author of Hebrews.

As we have just seen, Moroni began this integration by substituting the narratives of several of the Nephite faithful into the argumentative structure of Hebrews 11. He also incorporates several phrases from distinctive occasions of Nephite preaching:

12:8	Christ "*glorified the name of the Father*"	3 Ne. 9:15	"in me hath the Father glorified his name" (the Resurrected Jesus)
12:8	Christ has "*prepared a way*" for those with faith	1 Ne. 3:7 (and 5 other times in Nephi's writings)	"the Lord . . . shall prepare a way for them" (Nephi)
12:14	"*wrought the change* upon the Lamanites"	Mosiah 5:2	"wrought a mighty change in us" (the people's response to King Benjamin's address)
12:16	"all they who *wrought miracles*"/ "wrought them *by faith*"	Moro. 7:37	"it is by faith that miracles are wrought" (Mormon)
12:19	"beheld with an *eye of faith*"	Alma 5:15, 32:40	"eye of faith" (Alma)

Again, it is not always clear whether these kinds of verbal echoes are deliberate or whether Moroni is simply relying on common tropes, but the presence of internal repetition is certainly worth noting.

Moroni presents his final example of Nephite faith in verse 22: "And it is by faith that my fathers have obtained the promise that these things [the Book of Mormon] should come unto their brethren through the Gentiles," and with this he introduces the transition between what we have delimited as sections II and III of Ether 12. He then moves on to his self-conscious conversation with the Lord about his own contribution to the book, a passage we considered at length in the previous chapter. Our renewed discussion of it here will focus on the extent to which Moroni continues to draw extensively from prior texts to present his ideas.

Starting at verse 23, Ether 12 begins to shift its literary dependence from Hebrews 11 to a Nephite source, 2 Nephi 33—yet another text that addresses the relationship between faith and hope. Moroni executes this shift with remarkable dexterity, bidding farewell to the author of Hebrews 11 with an allusion to "mockings," a single distinctive word included there (Heb. 11:36; cf. Eth. 12:23, 25), while simultaneously welcoming Nephi's guidance with an allusion to the notion of being made strong in weakness, a phrase common to both Hebrews and Nephi:

ETHER 12:27	HEBREWS 11:32–34	2 NEPHI 33:4
I give unto men weakness that they may be humble . . . for if they humble themselves before me, and have faith in me, then will I *make weak things become strong* unto them.	The time would fail me to tell of . . . the prophets: who through faith . . . wrought righteousness, obtained promises . . . [and] out of *weakness were made strong.* (cf. 2 Cor. 12:10)	I know that the Lord God will consecrate my prayers for the gain of my people. And the words which I have written in *weakness will be made strong* unto them.

The contexts of these passages are quite different. In Ether 12, the Lord is universalizing a consolation to Moroni; in Hebrews, the author is enumerating the blessings of faith; and Nephi, for his part, is appropriating the prophecy of Joseph of Egypt that played so central a role in Moroni's first conclusion at Mormon 8–9. Their common phrase is indeed distinctive; in addition to these three passages it occurs only in 2 Nephi 3 (twice, in vv. 13 and 21; the latter, which describes the writers of the book who are yet to come—"and the weakness of their words will I make strong in their faith"—is clearly the source of Nephi's own allusion in 2 Ne. 33 above). For all his dependence on 2 Nephi 3 in Mormon 8–9, Moroni here is following Nephi's interpretation of this same text as included in his formal farewell chapter of 2 Nephi 33. (Moroni's double use of "mighty in writing" in vv. 23 and 24 confirms as much, since its only prior usage was by Nephi, responding to 2 Ne. 3 some thirty chapters later; see 2 Ne. 33:1.) I realize that this is a rather thick set of observations, even for those trying to follow along in their copy of the Book of Mormon, but the point is that Moroni in Ether 12 seems to be alluding to Nephi's expansion of Joseph's prophecy (2 Ne. 33) rather than to the original (as found at 2 Ne. 3). The three related chapters are an indication that Moroni—like Nephi before him and Joseph Smith afterward—saw himself as playing a key role in its fulfillment.[8] Indeed, Moroni's admission of "weakness in writing," however sincere and whatever his actual limitations, was also a bid to claim a share in Joseph's prophecy.

Ether 12 and 2 Nephi 33 share similar themes and several common phrases, but they also display a parallel structure. Nephi, picking up the idea in Joseph's prophecies that weak things could be made strong (2 Ne. 3:13, 21), frames his concluding remarks within two corresponding comments: "the words which I have written in weakness will be made strong unto them [his brethren]" (2 Ne. 33:4) and "ye shall know that I have been commanded of him [Christ] to write these things, notwithstanding my weakness" (2 Ne. 33:11). In between he presents a self-reflective meditation that features references to faith, hope, and charity—though the latter two terms appear very infrequently in Nephi's writings.[9]

Moroni appears to have adapted Nephi's model: he sandwiches his own observations on faith, hope, and charity between two admissions of "weakness in writing" (Ether 12:23–25, 40), and he broadens the Lord's promise so that not just weak writing will be made strong but all sorts of weaknesses can be overcome through faith in Christ.[10] This discussion of the three Christian virtues also signals a simultaneous allusion to Mormon, the only other Book of Mormon figure to discuss the three together (again in his sermon at Moro. 7, which itself closely—and anachronistically—reflects Paul's eloquent statement on the same at 1 Cor. 13).[11]

Finally, in section IV, Moroni brings this second conclusion to its end by again interweaving allusions to remarks made earlier by both Nephi and Mormon, the book's first and last writers. In addition to 2 Nephi 33, Moroni draws upon the last lines of a letter from his father recorded in Moroni 9, which will become Mormon's final reported words once Moroni's own book is compiled:

12:38	"And now I, Moroni, bid *farewell* unto the Gentiles ... *until we shall meet before the judgment-seat* of Christ ... all men shall know that my garments are *not spotted* with your blood."	2 Ne. 33:13 2 Ne. 33:7	"Farewell until that great day shall come." "I shall meet many souls spotless at his judgment-seat."

12:39–40	"And then *shall ye know that I have* seen Jesus, and that he hath talked with me *face to face* . . . concerning *these things* . . . and only a few *things have I written,* because of my *weakness in writing.*"	2 Ne. 33:11	"you and I shall stand face to face before his bar; and ye shall know that I have been commanded of him to write these things, notwithstanding my weakness."
12:41	"And now, I would commend you to seek this Jesus of whom the prophets and apostles have written, *that the grace of God the Father, and also the Lord Jesus Christ . . . may be and abide in you forever. Amen.*"	Moro. 9:26	"may the grace of God the the Father . . . and our Lord Jesus Christ . . . be, and abide with you forever. Amen."

In terms of the Book of Mormon's internal chronology, Moroni at Ether 12 is quoting from documents in his possession: the small plates of Nephi and a personal letter from his father. But in light of the fact that Joseph Smith dictated the book of Ether before either Moroni 9 or 2 Nephi 33 (itself dependent on 2 Ne. 3), it may begin to strain credulity when we try to imagine Smith creating a narrator who makes specific allusions to several interrelated texts, none of which had yet been created. From the perspective of believers, it would be rather ironic if Moroni, who eschewed his father's program of evidence-based faith, here inadvertently ended up providing perhaps the strongest textual validation for the historicity of the Book of Mormon. Paradoxically, though, with Ether 12's clear and thorough dependence on Hebrews 6 and 11, Moroni has simultaneously supplied some of the most compelling evidence that the book has its origins in the nineteenth century.[12]

There is certainly a great deal of biblical language in Ether 12, some of it quite specific in its origins, but taken as a whole, the chapter is not a case of easy plagiarism or randomly recalled phrases. Its various elements, both borrowed and original, are interwoven into an integrated, carefully constructed essay. Moroni's remarks make a distinct point about the nature of faith, which applies directly to the narration at hand as well as more broadly to his anticipated readership. In bidding his readers farewell for a second time, he demonstrates a keen awareness of how his predecessors had approached this same task. Again, the allusive character of the chapter allows Moroni to respond to earlier Nephite writers through both incorporation and elaboration. When we note all the textual borrowings, Moroni's prose becomes rather more engaging, despite his complaints of being unable to express himself adequately. In the end, Ether 12 is more than a simple adaptation of Hebrews 11 rounded out with a few Book of Mormon phrases; it offers a merging of the book's first and last authors, combined with a fusing of the biblical and Nephite traditions.

A Curtain Call and the End

The last chapter in the Book of Mormon, Moroni 10, is a complex literary creation in which several of the writing strategies we have come to associate with Moroni are in evidence. The first thing many readers will notice is a discussion of gifts of the spirit that again follows an anachronistic New Testament text, this time based on Paul's similar list in 1 Corinthians 12 (Moro. 10:8–17; 1 Cor. 12:4–11). The presence of this passage, though, is more easily attributable to translator intervention than the adaptations from Hebrews 6 and 11 in Ether 12 because it is much less integrated into the surrounding argument.[13] It still, however, occupies a specific place within a broader structure.

Moroni divides his final farewell into two parts: in the first he addresses "my brethren the Lamanites" (vv. 1–23), and then he directs his attention to "all the ends of the earth" (vv. 24–34), which includes the Gentiles as well as the various descendants of the House of Israel. In doing so, he is reversing a pattern set by his father when Mormon wrote his own separate farewells to "all the ends of the earth" (Morm. 3:17–22) and then later to the Lamanites (Morm. 7:1–10). Mormon and Moroni alike take an urgent, insistent tone, with the father's four instances of "know ye that . . ." in Mormon 7 matching his son's eight repetitions of "I would exhort you that . . ." in Moroni 10 (both of these phrases occur primarily in the segments directed toward the Lamanites and are virtually nonexistent elsewhere in the Book of Mormon).[14]

Moroni's comments to the Lamanites include the 1 Corinthians 12 passage along with additional connections to themes and phrases from his earlier remarks in Mormon 9 and Ether 12 (including "nothing that is good denieth the Christ . . . deny not the gifts of God" [Moro. 10:6, 8], echoing his allusion to Mormon's writings at Morm. 9:1, 7; and God is "the same yesterday, today, and forever" [Moro. 10:19], echoing an allusion to Nephi's writings at Morm. 9:9). Moroni seems to have grown so fond of the strategy of allusion that he now even alludes to himself alluding to others. (The literary critic James Woods has described self-plagiarism as "proof that a style has achieved self-consistency.")[15] At Moroni 10:20, he issues a second appeal for faith, hope, and charity, thereby incorporating his second conclusion at Ether 12.

He ends this section with a quotation, "If ye have faith ye can do all things which are expedient unto me" attributed to Christ (Moro. 10:23), which was cited previously by his father at Moroni 7:33.

The final section, to "all the ends of the earth," begins in Moroni 10:24 and continues its incorporation of allusions to Moroni 7 (his father's sermon, reproduced in that chapter, was apparently still on Moroni's mind). Anticipating the spiritual state of those among whom his book will come forth, he considers the possibility that the power and gifts of God might be done away with, and, like Mormon before him, he indicates that "it shall be because of unbelief" (Moro. 10:24; Moro. 7:37). He later laments a society where "there shall be none that doeth good among you, no, not one" (Moro. 10:25), again clearly echoing Mormon's words from Moroni 7: "for after this manner doth the devil work, for he persuadeth no man to do good, no, not one" (v. 17).[16]

Perhaps not surprisingly, Moroni finishes the Book of Mormon with a series of quick allusions to the farewell comments of the book's preceding editors, especially those who wrote in the Small Plates. (We already know that Moroni cares about last words, since those were the only ones he quoted directly from the Jaredite prophet Ether; see Ether 15:34.) We hear the voices of these characters one more time, in a sort of verbal curtain call:

MORONI 10	PREVIOUS BOOK OF MORMON FAREWELLS
27 And I exhort you to remember these things; for the time speedily cometh that ye shall know that I lie not, for *ye shall see me at the bar of God*; and the Lord God will say unto you, "Did I not declare my words unto you, which were written by this man, like *as one crying from* the dead, yea, even as one speaking out of *the dust*?"	"you and I shall stand . . before his bar" —**Nephi** (2 Ne. 33:11) "as the voice of one crying from the dust" —**Nephi** (2 Ne. 33:13;cf. 2 Ne. 3:19; Isa. 29:4 ‖ 2 Ne. 26:16)
28–29 I declare these things unto the fulfilling of the prophecies. And behold, they shall *proceed forth out of the mouth of* the everlasting God . . . And *God will show unto you, that that* which I have written *is true*	"the words which shall proceed forth out of the mouth of the Lamb of God" —**Nephi** (2 Ne. 33:14; cf. 2 Ne. 3:21) "God will show unto you . . . that they [the things I have spoken] are true" —**Mormon** (Moro. 7:35; cf. 2 Ne. 33:11)

30	And again I would exhort you that ye would *come unto Christ*, and *lay hold upon every good* gift	"I would that ye should come unto Christ" —**Amaleki** (Omni 1:26)[17] "lay hold upon every good thing" —**Mormon** (Moro. 7:19, 20, 25)
31	*Awake, and arise from the dust,* O Jerusalem	"Awake! and arise from the dust" —**Lehi** (2 Ne. 1:14, 23; cf. Isa. 52:1–2)
34	And now *I bid unto all, farewell. I soon go to rest* in the paradise of God, until my spirit and body shall again reunite, and I am brought forth triumphant through the air, to *meet you before the pleasing bar of* the great Jehovah	"I soon go to the place of my rest" —**Enos** (Enos 1:27); "I bid you farewell, until I shall meet you before the pleasing bar of God" —**Jacob** (Jacob 6:13)

In addition, the passage includes an obvious allusion to Isaiah, who was also a major voice from the Small Plates: "strengthen thy stakes and enlarge thy borders forever, that thou mayest no more be confounded" (Moro. 10:31 ‖ Isa. 54:2–4).

Moroni 10 is Moroni's final attempt to bring the Book of Mormon to a close. His first conclusion, at Mormon 8–9, alluded to connections between himself, his father, Nephi, and the prophecies of the biblical Joseph included on the Brass Plates. His second ending, at Ether 12, highlighted examples of faith from Nephite history, connected his perceived "weakness in writing" with the earlier efforts of Nephi, and brought together the last testimonies of both Nephi and Mormon. Finally, in his third effort, written some twenty years after the first, Moroni puts on a striking display of allusive virtuosity as he borrows from the farewell speeches of his predecessors in order to construct an urgent appeal to readers that is, at the same time, an homage to all the editors—not only Nephi and Mormon but several of the minor narrators from the Small Plates as well. In this way Moroni forges a still stronger connection between the beginning and the end of Nephite history while also emphasizing the general unity of purpose among all its contributors. The gradual development of his ideas on how to compose a formal farewell can be set against his evolving conception of how best to complete his father's history.

Each opportunity for yet another installment seems to have come as something of a surprise to Moroni. When he appended a brief ending to Mormon's autobiographical book, he did not think he would survive long, noting that he would have written more "if I had room upon the plates, but I have not . . . and how long the Lord will suffer that I may live I know not" (Morm. 8:5). Contrary to his expectations, he found an opportunity to fulfill Mormon's promise at Mosiah 28:19 by adding a synopsis of Jaredite history, but he thought that those chapters would be his terminal contribution as well. Consequently, he wrote a second farewell at Ether 12, in which he alluded to perhaps his most personal document from his father—a private letter that he apparently had not intended at that point to provide to his readers (compare Ether 12:41 and Moro. 9:26). Later, he begins his own book of Moroni by observing that "after having made an end of abridging the account of the people of Jared, I had supposed not to have written more, but I have not as yet perished . . . wherefore, I write a few more things, contrary to that which I had supposed" (Moro. 1:1, 4).

The task of finishing Mormon's abridgment seems to have been a daunting one, and over the course of many years Moroni rethinks his strategy of conclusion at least twice. Even though his writings are relatively concise and densely allusive, we can trace the development of his thought as follows:

(1) In Mormon 8–9, expecting to hide up the records in short order (Morm. 8:4), Moroni quickly narrates the tragic end of the Nephites and then adds his own prophecies concerning social and religious conditions at the time when the record would again be brought to light, along with specific warnings to his skeptical Gentile readers. In this way, he suggests that a new beginning will someday come from the final destruction of his civilization, one that fulfills ancient prophecies such as those pronounced by Joseph of Egypt.

(2) With the book of Ether, Moroni extends and universalizes the Nephite story by reaching back further into the past and narrating the tale of yet another civilization that is destroyed because of wickedness. This places Mormon's history in a context even larger than the destiny of the House of Israel with its various offshoots and scattered remnants (since the Jaredites had no connection to the twelve tribes of Israel). There are particular messages that Moroni draws out—as well as points he deliberately obscures—for his latter-day Gentile readers, and the emotional climax of his work occurs when he confesses his fears that his audience, whom he has seen in vision, will mock his writing (see Morm. 8:34–35). The Lord reassures him, and though Moroni admits that he has added "only a few [things] . . . because of my weakness in writing," he nevertheless seems reconciled to his role and his capabilities, and he ends on a fairly positive note, commending his readers to Jesus and invoking the grace of God upon them (Ether 12:40–41). It is striking that he places his farewell in Ether 12, before he actually recounts the final and brutal annihilation of the Jaredites (Ether 13–15), but this arrangement allows him to avoid the sudden shift in tone or the softening of tragedy that would have resulted from following unmitigated disaster with his personal experience of divine affirmation.

(3) If the book of Ether was an extended glance backward, the book of Moroni looks forward, being almost entirely concerned with the future needs of his audience of Gentiles and Lamanites. The whole book, consisting mainly of quoted

material, offers guidance on how to remain faithful in times of turmoil and how to retain a vision of Christian community in a world that is falling apart. Perhaps in the intervening twenty years Moroni's heart had softened toward his Gentile readers (similarly, he has come around to referring to the Lamanites as his "beloved brethren"; Moro. 10:18–19); certainly they would be skeptical and prideful, but they too would find themselves in the midst of political and spiritual chaos. The first six chapters of Moroni's book provide brief but specific information on performing ordinances and regulating the church (these instructions, derived from Jesus' teachings among the Nephites, may reflect a profound nostalgia for the kind of sustaining faith community in which Moroni himself had once participated, and which he would never be part of again).[18] The next three chapters, all taken from Mormon's writings, contain advice on discerning good from evil and developing faith, hope, and charity (ch. 7), eradicating the unacceptable practice of infant baptism (ch. 8), and responding to unequivocal evil and the suffering of its victims (ch. 9). The last of these three chapters, fortunately not lengthy, is probably the most unpleasant in the Book of Mormon. It is a personal letter from Mormon to Moroni, and unlike the previous depictions of warfare that we have seen in Mormon's history, it is raw and direct. This is what Mormon's voice sounds like when he is not editing or sanitizing for a latter-day audience, and in it we confront graphic, explicit references to massacre, rape, torture, and even cannibalism. Moroni immediately follows this with his final conclusion (ch. 10), which emphasizes the gifts of the spirit and coming to Christ. The jarring juxtaposition serves his purposes here, since the contrast between living with or without God could not be made more strongly.[19]

At this point—with the conclusion of chapter 10—Moroni's voice goes silent, but not for Joseph Smith, who asserted that he again saw and heard Moroni, now an angel, on the night of September 23, 1823, still avidly quoting (and adapting) scripture.[20] For other readers, the situation is more nuanced. When we first met Moroni, he confessed with some frustration that "were it possible, I would make all things known unto you" (Morm. 8:12); by the last chapter, however (and in contrast to his father's dominant mode of persuasion), he has relinquished that role to a higher power, one that can keep speaking long after his own demise: "by the power of the Holy Ghost ye may know the truth of all things" (Moro. 10:5). Actually, this theme of spiritual confirmation has been building through each of his three conclusions, from a brief mention at Mormon 9:25, quoting Jesus ("whosoever shall believe in my name, doubting nothing, unto him will I confirm all my words"), to a longer discussion at Ether 12 of how a "witness" comes only after "a trial of your faith" (v. 6), to specific instructions in Moroni 10 for how to "ask God . . . in the name of Christ . . . with a sincere heart, with real intent" so that he might "manifest the truth of it unto you, by the power of the Holy Ghost" (v. 4). Whether one regards that promise as real or fanciful, it is nevertheless a fitting conclusion to a book that wishes to be much more than a book, a text that wants to envelop readers in a world of its own making. In this respect, the Book of Mormon is very much like the Bible, of which Erich Auerbach famously wrote: "Far from seeking, like Homer, merely to make us forget our own reality for a few hours, [the Bible] seeks to overcome our reality: we are to fit our own life into its world, feel ourselves to be elements in its structure of universal history."[21]

It is natural to try to understand the character of Moroni by searching his writings for themes or concerns that would afford him a degree of consistency and coherence. Indeed, this sort of approach has been a central tendency of the present study, weighing parts against wholes to imaginatively reconstruct what I hope are plausible portrayals of the Book of Mormon's narrators, even though their constant presence is at times hidden in the background rather than being placed front and center. These figures each possess a distinct literary identity, which is manifest not just by what they say but by how they say it.

In Moroni's case, it appears that he has nearly succeeded in achieving an ambition of the literary critic and essayist Walter Benjamin, who, according to Hannah Arendt, wanted "to produce a work consisting entirely of quotations."[22] Moroni's exact method for composing formal farewells varies over time, but his first inclination is always to use the words of his predecessors, and his strategy for doing so remains remarkably consistent. He carefully constructs his parting comments by interweaving distinctive phrases and structural schemes from multiple, thematically related sources. And although this type of intricate, densely allusive composition may not automatically meet the standards of great literature, it does bespeak a text more cerebral than many readers might have expected. This much seems clear enough, but the question for inquisitive readers is, what do these observations reveal about Moroni himself?

For my purposes here, it makes no difference whether readers regard Moroni as an actual historical figure or a strongly imagined fictional character; either way, we know him only through what is revealed in the last fifty pages of the Book of Mormon. As we try to construct a persona that fits the literary evidence, it is perhaps easiest to assume that Moroni was a hesitant, reluctant writer. He took a long time and produced little because he was awed, even overwhelmed, by the power of what the brother of Jared had written (Ether 12:24), and undoubtedly by Nephi's and Mormon's writings as well. Or perhaps, like many a college freshman, he found it easier to borrow the words of others rather than write original sentences. Either hypothesis could explain Moroni's penchant for relying so heavily upon the language of his predecessors. Yet while such interpretations are certainly reasonable, there is another possibility. Perhaps Moroni was simply taking time to do things well. Not every culture values originality in writers, and rather than seeing Moroni's work as mind-numbingly derivative, we might instead view it as a deliberate aesthetic choice, particularly since his method involved a high level of integration rather than simple cutting and pasting. There could be a particular artistic sensibility in operation here, one that may be foreign to contemporary tastes, but which nevertheless constitutes a distinct poetics where repetition is a virtue (and novelty is not).

From this perspective, extensive allusion makes a great deal of sense. By employing the words of others, Moroni shifts the notion of authorship and makes himself the self-effacing inheritor, or spokesman, for an entire literary tradition. He is able to appeal to the authority of past prophets and record keepers (while at the same time reinforcing the respect due them), and he can reward close readers who are able to recognize phrases and make connections. His allusions and quotations are a call to remembrance and a recognition of how dependent he is on the faithfulness of those who preceded him. Above all, his particular mode of writing serves to consolidate the text, joining together beginning and end, and unifying the entire book in a theologically and aesthetically pleasing manner. Moroni's contributions to his father's record provide both a sense of closure and also an intimation of an overall design for the Book of Mormon—a literary enactment of the all-encompassing plan that God has for human history and for individuals. With an appropriate conclusion in place, the structure of the book replicates and emphasizes its message.

Moroni's style represents the pinnacle of the use of allusion in the Book of Mormon, but similar observations might apply to the book as a whole. Joseph Smith, whether as author or translator, presents his message through the words of others. The text seeks credibility by claiming a connection to a long literary tradition, and it exhibits an unexpected level of complexity and coherence. Its language, dense with biblical phrases, offers comfort to modern readers seeking a new revelation consistent with the scripture they already know, as well as an invitation to recognize and interpret particular references and variations.[23] At the same time, there is a hint of what Robert Alter, with regard to the Bible, has described as "the most serious playfulness, endlessly discovering how the permutations of narrative conventions, linguistic properties, and imaginatively constructed personages and circumstances can crystallize subtle and abiding truths of experience in amusing or arresting or gratifying ways."[24] When read verse by verse, the Book of Mormon can sink under the weight of its repetitive, awkward sentences, but when viewed from the perspective of the narrators—who are envisioned as deliberately shaping the texts they create—it exhibits a literary exuberance that frustrates quick judgments and reductive analyses.

Afterword

Curiously enough, one cannot *read* a book: one can only reread it.
—Vladimir Nabokov

It is difficult to know how to bring this study to a conclusion as well. I have tried to offer what Robert Alter once described as "a continuous *reading* of the text instead of a nervous hovering over its various small components," but I am very aware that this volume constitutes only a first run-through of the Book of Mormon.[1] There is much more to discover in terms of narrative techniques, connections between various people and events, thematic development, and the specific language employed by different speakers. The key to reading the Book of Mormon well is to start with the organizing principle of the text—the fact that it presents itself as the work of narrators with distinct voices and perspectives. Understanding the book on its own terms, recognizing its structure and form, and identifying the means by which it conveys its message are the first steps to any further inquiries, whether they be historical, literary, or religious.

Terryl Givens has observed that for early adherents and critics alike, the Book of Mormon functioned primarily as a sign of Joseph Smith's prophetic claims: "the 'message' of the Book of Mormon *was* its manner of origin."[2] Consequently, its actual contents could often seem of secondary importance when compared to the sheer fact of its existence. Yet Joseph's story of an angel, gold plates, and a miraculous translation all could have been corroborated by First Nephi alone. Instead, we have a lengthy, rather convoluted text, and because it is a narrative mediated by narrators—unlike the Qur'an or even the LDS Doctrine and Covenants—it is open to literary analysis and rich interpretive possibilities of the sort that are evident only upon attentive, multiple rereadings. For those who believe the book to be a revelation from God, there is more than enough to work with as they uncover new meanings and applications to their lives. There is also enough substance to Mormon scripture to reward the attention of outside scholars.

The place of the Book of Mormon in American history is secure. Because it was one of the most significant religious publications in the nineteenth century, historians of the Jacksonian era will always be interested in how this book absorbed and influenced political, religious, and cultural currents of the time. Historians specializing in subsequent periods will want to account for the growth and increasing visibility of the Mormon Church by examining its founding scripture, among other things. Latter-day Saints, for their part, will continue to identify points of connection with the ancient world in an attempt to better understand the text and lend support to its claims of historicity. Each group, however, will have more success if they read the Book of Mormon as a narrative, interpreting its message in an accurate but nuanced way, and giving greater weight to the themes that are actually more important to the story.

In the field of American literature, the Book of Mormon has generally been overlooked, perhaps because scholars assumed it was shallow and uninteresting, or perhaps because, even when viewed as fiction, it could only be bad fiction. Today novels are most often read and acclaimed to the extent that they exhibit a sparkling style and an ironic detachment—qualities sorely lacking in the Book of Mormon. Its narrators are didactic and painfully sincere. Worse still, they want to save their readers' souls in very specific ways, at a time when moralistic narration and religious exclusivism have fallen out of favor. Yet if the Book of Mormon does not qualify as a literary masterpiece, it is nevertheless a complex and coherent work of literature, and its narratological strategies are of more than just passing interest. Professors in English departments are probably not used to thinking of the Book of Mormon as a puzzle along the lines of Vladimir Nabokov's *Pale Fire*, but both works display a similar intricacy; indeed, to confuse Mormon and Joseph Smith would be a category mistake of the same order as failing to distinguish Charles Kinbote, the editor of *Pale Fire*, from Nabokov himself.[3] When analyzed closely, the book produced by Smith exhibits a literary verve and subtlety that make it more than simply a period piece. And, quite unusually among writings from the early nineteenth century, it still has numerous devoted readers to this day.

Yet the most promising academic approaches to the Book of Mormon may come from the field of religious studies. The category of "scripture" both incorporates and transcends the genres of history and fiction, and thus offers new ways of thinking about sacred texts. What role do they play within the community of believers? How are such writings authenticated and canonized? How do they convey their ideas? How do they depend upon and also challenge earlier scriptures? These types of questions are significant, but they can be adequately addressed only after a searching examination of a book's contents and structure—one that takes into account the internal, organizing logic of the text.

The Book of Mormon has outgrown its American roots and can now be comfortably regarded as world scripture, that is, a sacred writing that through numerous translations has crossed cultural divides and can claim several million believers around the globe (in fact, most of the more than thirteen million Latter-day Saints in the world today live outside the United States). This is remarkable, because the emergence of a new world scripture is a rather rare phenomenon. In the last thousand years, it has happened perhaps only a dozen times. Many of the possible candidates, such as the Zen classics *Biyan Lu* and *Wumenguan* (Blue Cliff Record and Gateless Gate, twelfth and thirteenth centuries), the Jewish Zohar (thirteenth century), and the Tibetan *Bar-do Thos-grol* (Book of the Dead, fourteenth century) are revered and employed in religious practice but have not been accepted as part of the canon of their respective faiths. The only new religions whose scale and reliance upon distinctive scriptures are comparable to the Mormons are the six million Baha'is who consider the writings of Baha'u'llah (1817–1892) and other founders to be sacred, and the twenty-three million Sikhs whose veneration of the Adi Granth (a collection of religious poetry compiled in the seventeenth century) is extraordinary.[4]

Comparative studies reveal differences as well as similarities, and uniquely among new scriptures of the last millennium, the Book of Mormon consists of an extended, integrated, history-like narrative. Other recent holy books are generally collections of doctrinal expositions, moral exhortations, devotional poetry, manuals of ritual, or commentaries on scripture, and each must be read in ways appropriate to its genre. For instance, the following song attributed to the fifteenth-century Hindu saint Ravi Dass appears in the aforementioned Adi Granth:

> Like a well filled with frogs
> that know nothing of other lands,
> so my heart,
> rapt with worldly delight, knows nothing of this world
> or the next.

> O Lord of all creation,
> show Yourself for an instant. (Rest)

> My mind is sullied, O Madho [Krishna];
> I cannot grasp the substance

of Your reality.
Have mercy and lift my confusion.
Grant me wisdom
that I may come to understand.

Even great yogis
cannot begin to describe
all Your virtues.
I want to love You
and worship You,
so says Ravi Dass the cobbler.[5]

(Adi Granth, "Raga Gauri-Purbi")

The spiritual yearning exhibited here, along with the startling juxtaposition of the Lord of all creation and a man from the lowest caste, makes this hymn immediately accessible and moving.[6] Yet to understand it more fully as lyric poetry, one would have to know more about the language it was composed in, the metrical form, and the literary precedents of its imagery (there is a famous Indian story of frogs in a well). Not much is known of Ravi Dass' life, but it would be helpful to compare this poem with the forty other hymns of his that were included in the Adi Granth. In addition, we would want to consider the role played by songs of Hindu and Muslim saints within the holy book of the Sikhs (who are neither Hindus nor Muslims), and our perceptions of the piece are bound to be influenced by its position within the Adi Granth, which is organized by ragas—a musical mode—rather than by author. This poem might be read by believers, yet it is just as likely to be heard as a song in a Sikh temple, perhaps in the forty-eight-hour nonstop musical recitations of the entire Adi Granth that mark festivals and commemorate significant occasions such as births, weddings, and funerals. Outsiders might well ponder what it would be like to have one's life measured out by the rhythms of medieval, mystic verse.

Next consider an excerpt from the Book of Mormon:

O, remember, my son, and learn wisdom in thy youth;
    yea, learn in thy youth to keep the commandments of God.
Yea, and cry unto God for all thy support;
    yea, let all thy doings be unto the Lord,
    and whithersoever thou goest let it be in the Lord;
yea, let all thy thoughts be directed unto the Lord;
    yea, let the affections of thy heart be placed upon the Lord forever.
Counsel with the Lord in all thy doings,
    and he will direct thee for good.
Yea, when thou liest down at night lie down unto the Lord,

that he may watch over you in your sleep;
　　and when thou risest in the morning
　　　　let thy heart be full of thanks unto God
　　And if ye always do these things,[7]
　　　　ye shall be lifted up at the last day. (Alma 37:35–37)

The poetic power of these very direct, didactic lines may not equal that of Ravi Dass, yet the passage is not without aesthetic qualities—the repetitions give it a memorable cadence (as in some forms of political oratory or the preaching tradition of the black church), and the concluding parallel between getting up in the morning and being raised by God at the judgment day is appealing.[8] Nevertheless, the resonance and poignancy of this passage come less from its poetic form than from its place within the narrative.

The words are Alma₂'s as he is giving advice to his oldest son, Helaman₂, on the momentous occasion of his handing over the sacred records to the next generation. This transfer takes place at a time of national crisis, and there are indications elsewhere in the text that Alma has had concerns about this particular son, who is probably no longer a youth. The speech is also the first of three that Alma addresses to each of his sons the year before his death. At a higher narratological level, this quotation comes from a primary source document that was inserted by Mormon into a crucial juncture of his abridgment of Nephite history, between the preaching to the Zoramites that leads to a devastating war, and his account of the war itself. And finally, we will see Helaman putting his father's advice into practice just a few years later, when he is placed in command of an army of two thousand young Ammonite soldiers, despite the fact that his prior experience has been as a church leader rather than as a military man. He reports to his superior, Captain Moroni, that "we did pour out our souls in prayer to God, that he would strengthen us and deliver us" (Alma 58:10), and in the end Helaman and his troops enjoy astonishing success, surpassing even that of Moroni, a man who brought to the task an entire lifetime of military training and experience. The Book of Mormon is a complex, sometimes perplexing text, but it is worth considering how such a narrative can infuse the lives of believers with meaning.

Donald Akenson, at the end of his marvelous history of the origins of the Bible and the Talmuds, writes:

> None of this should make most readers uncomfortable. For most, the
> arguments that I have presented throughout this book should be
> belief-neutral. They can be entertained and subsequently evaluated on
> their merits and on the degree of their consonance with the primary
> evidence. My hope is that agnostics, atheists, and the amiably indifferent,

all will appreciate the beauty and integrity of the process of invention
and the character of the final texts, even if they are unable to grant to
these processes and documents any degree of spiritual authority. And I
hope that believers (using the term in the most inclusive sense) will see
in the complex filigree of invention of the Bible and of the Rabbinic
texts, the hand of their god.[9]

Such sentiments are in line with my own hopes for this introduction to the Book
of Mormon, though I am cognizant of the vast changes in the study of religions
over the last century that have made these sorts of nonpolemical approaches
possible.

A hundred years ago, in 1909, the world-renowned historian Eduard Meyer
took a year's leave of absence from the University of Berlin to live in the United
States, where, among other projects, he gathered information about the Mormons,
hoping thereby to gain insights into the early development of Islam and Christianity. When he published his results, however, he had little to say about Mormon
scripture. In fact, he admitted that he had "not been able to read the complete Book
of Mormon," excusing himself with the observation that "no human except a
believer could find the strength to read the whole thing," and describing it as
"clumsy, monotonous in the extreme, repetitious, . . . [and as] incoherent as one
would expect it from a totally uneducated man who dictated it in a state of half-
sleep."[10] Today this sort of breezy dismissal would not be just an embarrassment; it
would be wrong.

Mark Twain, who once memorably referred to the Book of Mormon as "chloroform in print," is also our source for the quip that Wagner's music is "better than
it sounds."[11] Somewhat surprisingly, it may actually be the latter description that
more accurately describes the Book of Mormon. There is no denying that the words
can sound awkward, repetitious, and derivative, but if we direct our attention deeper,
to the level of form and structure, there is much more going on than first meets the
eye (or ear). The music of Wagner can take some getting used to, but there is a defi-
nite aesthetic manifest there, even if it is not immediately discernible. And given
enough attention and study, something that might at first seem unattractive or dis-
cordant can become appreciated and even loved. John W. Welch, of Brigham Young
University, relates an experience he had with the distinguished general editor of the
Anchor Bible series: "After Professor David Noel Freedman and I had read through
Alma 36 together with chiasmus in mind, he remarked to me, 'Mormons are very
lucky. Their book is very beautiful.'"[12] It was a kind and generous comment by a
scholar who was willing to take a fresh look at someone else's scripture. Whether
Joseph Smith worked by craftiness, by genius, or by revelation, the Book of Mormon
is a remarkable text, one that is worthy of serious study. It is better than it sounds.

Notes

INTRODUCTION

1. Richard Lyman Bushman, *Believing History: Latter-day Saint Essays*, ed. Reid L. Neilson and Jed Woodworth (New York: Columbia University Press, 2004), viii.

2. Nathan O. Hatch, *The Democratization of American Christianity* (New Haven, CT: Yale University Press, 1989), 115; Gordon S. Wood, "Evangelical America and Early Mormonism," *New York History* 61 (1980): 381.

3. Daniel Walker Howe, *What Hath God Wrought: The Transformation of America, 1815–1848*, Oxford History of the United States (New York: Oxford University Press, 2007), 314.

4. Thomas F. O'Dea, *The Mormons* (Chicago: University of Chicago Press, 1957), 28, 33.

5. Douglas J. Davies, *An Introduction to Mormonism* (Cambridge: Cambridge University Press, 2003), 48.

6. Klaus J. Hansen, *Mormonism and the American Experience* (Chicago: University of Chicago Press, 1981), 64–74.

7. Richard L. Bushman, *Joseph Smith and the Beginnings of Mormonism* (Urbana: University of Illinois Press, 1984), 139.

8. Hatch, 116–17. See also Kenneth Winn's unusually extensive treatment in "The Book of Mormon as a Republican Document," which is the second chapter of his *Exiles in a Land of Liberty: Mormons in America, 1830–1846* (Chapel Hill: University of North Carolina Press, 1989). Winn reads the Book of Mormon as a "stirring, if veiled, critique of Jacksonian America" (20).

9. Robert N. Hullinger, *Joseph Smith's Response to Skepticism* (Salt Lake City: Signature, 1992), 32. An earlier version of this book was published as

Mormon Answer to Skepticism: Why Joseph Smith Wrote the Book of Mormon (St. Louis: Clayton Publishing House, 1980).

10. Dan Vogel, *Indian Origins and the Book of Mormon* (Salt Lake City: Signature, 1986).

11. Dan Vogel and Brent Lee Metcalfe, eds., *American Apocrypha: Essays on the Book of Mormon* (Salt Lake City: Signature, 2002). The essay that most clearly articulates the idea in the title is Robert M. Price, "Joseph Smith: Inspired Author of the Book of Mormon," 321–66.

12. Clyde R. Forsberg, *Equal Rites: The Book of Mormon, Masonry, Gender, and American Culture* (New York: Columbia University Press, 2004).

13. Robert D. Anderson, *Inside the Mind of Joseph Smith: Psychobiography and the Book of Mormon* (Salt Lake City: Signature, 1999), 65, xxi.

14. This subtitle was added by the Church of Jesus Christ of Latter-day Saints in 1982.

15. Jan Shipps, *Mormonism: The Story of a New Religious Tradition* (Urbana: University of Illinois Press, 1985).

16. Dan Vogel, *Joseph Smith: The Making of a Prophet* (Salt Lake City: Signature, 2004).

17. Richard Dilworth Rust, *Feasting on the Word: The Literary Testimony of the Book of Mormon* (Salt Lake City: Deseret Book and FARMS, 1997).

18. The most ambitious attempt to read the Book of Mormon as an ancient text is John L. Sorenson, *An Ancient American Setting for the Book of Mormon* (Salt Lake City: Deseret Book and FARMS, 1985). The Foundation for Ancient Research and Mormon Studies (FARMS), a Book of Mormon research institute housed at Brigham Young University (and now part of the Neal A. Maxwell Institute for Religious Scholarship), has generated an impressive array of short studies aimed at demonstrating the text's historicity. Many of the evidences they have identified have been conveniently summarized in Donald W. Parry, Daniel C. Peterson, and John W. Welch, eds., *Echoes and Evidences of the Book of Mormon* (Provo, UT: FARMS, 2002). For other examples of LDS scholarly approaches, see Noel B. Reynolds, ed., *Book of Mormon Authorship Revisited: The Evidence for Ancient Origins* (Provo, UT: FARMS, 1997) or back issues of the *Journal of Book of Mormon Studies* (available online at http://farms.byu.edu). Full commentaries focusing on doctrinal issues have been produced by members of BYU's Religion Department. Representative examples include Joseph Fielding McConkie and Robert L. Millet, *Doctrinal Commentary on the Book of Mormon* (Salt Lake City: Bookcraft, 1987–92) and Monte S. Nyman's six-volume commentary (different volumes have different titles), published by Granite Publishing of Orem, UT, 2003–6. The most interesting of recent commentaries is Brant A. Gardner's *Second Witness: Analytical and Contextual Commentary on the Book of Mormon* (Draper, UT: Greg Kofford Books, 2007), also in six volumes. Gardner's analysis can veer into the speculative and the devotional, but his systematic attention to narrative, culture, rhetoric, and redaction is a welcome development in LDS approaches.

19. The history of the reception of the Book of Mormon is admirably laid out, with a great deal of provocative cultural context, by Terryl L. Givens in *By the Hand of Mormon: The American Scripture That Launched a New World Religion* (New York: Oxford University

Press, 2002). In the last chapter he identifies "dialogic revelation" as one major theme of the Book of Mormon.

20. Dominick LaCapra, *Rethinking Intellectual History: Texts, Context, Language* (Ithaca: Cornell University Press, 1983), 14.

21. O'Dea, 26.

22. David A. Bell, "The Bookless Future: What the Internet Is Doing to Scholarship," *The New Republic*, May 2 and 9, 2005, 30–31.

23. John W. Barber and Henry Howe, *Historical Collections of the State of New York* (New York: S. Tuttle, 1841), 581.

24. The situation for non-Mormons is similar to what Adam Thirlwell described in his recent study of literary form when he complained about the first English translation of Tolstoy's *War and Peace*, which excerpted passages thematically, in the manner of an anthology: "Once again, a novel with a complicated form was gutted for its ideas. An anthology is the paradigm of bad fictional reading, because it believes in reading as a way of gathering information. And this is not true in a novel. The facts in a novel are not like other facts: they have a place in a larger form. But an anthology destroys this form." Adam Thirlwell, *The Delighted States* (New York: Farrar, Straus and Giroux, 2007), 234.

25. This scheme does leave out a handful of minor narrators in the books of Jacob, Enos, Jarom, and Omni, but these writers account for only about twenty-five pages of the Book of Mormon (out of over five hundred).

26. Quotations from the Book of Mormon in the pages that follow will usually be given with the formatting from my *Reader's Edition*.

27. See, for example, Edwin Dolan, "Odysseus in Phaeacia," reprinted in *The Odyssey: A New Verse Translation*, trans. and ed. Albert Cook, Norton Critical Edition (New York: Norton, 1974), 495–505.

28. Bushman, *Joseph Smith and the Beginnings*, 119.

29. Meir Sternberg explores this issue persuasively in his *Poetics of Biblical Narrative: Ideological Literature and the Drama of Reading* (Bloomington: Indiana University Press, 1985), 23–35. For instance, he notes that judging solely from stylistic or compositional elements, "one simply cannot tell fictional from historical narrative" (29). Indeed, the distinction does not even lie in the accuracy of historical information since fiction often includes true assertions about the past while history has to be written with surmised details, motivations, and connections (some of which may later be disproved); the difference is rather "the commitment to truth value" (25). See also Peter Lamarque, *Fictional Points of View* (Ithaca: Cornell University Press, 1996), 24–26. *The Poetics of Biblical Narrative* may be one of the best books ever written about the Book of Mormon—an assessment that would undoubtedly surprise Professor Sternberg given the fact that he never mentions Mormon scripture and perhaps has never even looked at it. Nevertheless, he demonstrates a method of close reading that is extraordinarily useful in trying to make sense of the Book of Mormon, even as it highlights both similarities and differences with patterns of biblical narrative.

30. Hans W. Frei, *The Eclipse of Biblical Narrative: A Study in Eighteenth and Nineteenth Century Hermeneutics* (New Haven, CT: Yale University Press, 1974), 135. Sternberg makes a similar distinction between "source-oriented inquiry" and "discourse-oriented analysis" (*Poetics*, 15).

31. For a basic introduction to narrative theory as it might be applied to scripture, see Mark Allan Powell, *What is Narrative Criticism?* (Minneapolis: Fortress Press, 1990).

32. Michael Sells, *Approaching the Qur'an: The Early Revelations* (Ashland, OR: White Cloud Press, 1999).

33. Again, Sternberg: "Personal opinion about fact or faith is one thing, and interpretive strategy another. Interpreters must either invent their own biblical text or grant the storyteller all the storytelling authority (divine and otherwise) he enjoys in cultural context. . . . To make sense of the Bible in terms of its own conventions, one need not believe in either, but one must postulate both" (81; cf. 33–34).

34. Bernard Duyfhuizen, *Narratives of Transmission* (Rutherford, NJ: Fairleigh Dickinson University Press, 1992), 179, 135.

35. Ezra Taft Benson, "The Book of Mormon Is the Word of God," *Ensign*, May 1975, 64–65; he repeated his admonition after he became president of the church in "The Book of Mormon—Keystone of Our Religion," *Ensign*, Nov. 1986, 4. In August 2005, President Gordon B. Hinckley called for renewed attention to the Book of Mormon and challenged members of the church throughout the world to read it again by the end of the year; Gordon B. Hinckley, "A Testimony Vibrant and True," *Ensign*, August 2005, 3–6.

CHAPTER 1

1. The last of these books may be less familiar to readers, but information can found at Isabelle Robinet, *Taoism: Growth of a Religion*, trans. Phyllis Brooks (Stanford, CA: Stanford University Press, 1997), 114–48, and Stephen R. Bokenkamp, *Early Daoist Scriptures* (Berkeley: University of California Press, 1997), 275–372.

2. The story has been told many times, but two of the most careful and thorough analyses are Richard L. Bushman's sympathetic account in *Joseph Smith and the Beginnings of Mormonism* (Urbana: University of Illinois Press, 1984), and Dan Vogel's more skeptical version in *Joseph Smith: The Making of a Prophet* (Salt Lake City: Signature, 2004). Also well worth reading is Terryl L. Givens's overview in *By the Hand of Mormon: The American Scripture That Launched a New World Religion* (New York: Oxford University Press, 2002), 8–42. Givens's book is the finest study of the origins and reception of the Book of Mormon written to date.

3. For more on the Book of Mormon as a sacred sign, see Givens, 62–88, 235–39.

4. Andrew Jenson, *Latter-day Saint Biographical Encyclopedia: A Compilation of Biographical Sketches of Prominent Men and Women in the Church of Jesus Christ of Latter-day Saints* (Salt Lake City: Andrew Jenson History Co., 1901), 1:74.

5. The earliest assertion was Sidney B. Sperry's 1935 article "The Book of Mormon as Translation English," reprinted in the *Journal of Book of Mormon Studies* 4, 1 (1995): 209–17. John A. Tvedtnes makes a case for "Hebraisms" in the Book of Mormon in "The Hebrew Background of the Book of Mormon," in *Rediscovering the Book of Mormon*, ed. John L. Sorenson and Melvin J. Thorne (Salt Lake City: Deseret Book and FARMS, 1991), 77–91. There he notes the regular presence of the construct state ("plates of brass" instead of "brass plates"), adverbials ("with patience" instead of "patiently"), and cognates ("I have dreamed a dream"), among others. The problem is that most of these forms also appear in

the Bible, where Joseph Smith could have learned them. More striking is Royal Skousen's discovery of "if-and" conditional clauses in the original manuscript of the Book of Mormon, which match Hebrew usage but do not appear in the English translations of the Bible. See Royal Skousen, "Translating the Book of Mormon: Evidence from the Original Manuscript," in *Book of Mormon Authorship Revisited: The Evidence for Ancient Origins*, ed. Noel B. Reynolds (Provo, UT: FARMS, 1997), 88–90. Nevertheless, Latter-day Saints generally ignore the presence of pseudo-Hebraicisms like "cavity of a rock" (1 Ne. 3:27) for "cave." Hebrew has an ordinary word for cave, *mĕ'ārâ*, and does not use a construct state to convey the idea (nor does the KJV). For a comprehensive catalog of literary forms, see Hugh W. Pinnock, *Finding Biblical Hebrew and Other Ancient Literary Forms in the Book of Mormon* (Provo, UT: FARMS, 1999).

6. The definitive work on the original grammar of the Book of Mormon will be Volume 3 of Royal Skousen's Critical Text of the Book of Mormon project. Volumes 1 and 2 have already been published by the Foundation for Ancient Research and Mormon Studies (FARMS), as well as Volume 4, in six book-length parts.

7. Paul C. Gutjahr, *An American Bible: A History of the Good Book in the United States, 1777–1880* (Stanford: Stanford University Press, 1999), 152–53. According to Gutjahr, the original edition of the Book of Mormon bore a striking resemblance to the 390,000 Bibles printed by the American Bible Society in 1829 with the goal of getting one into each household in the United States.

8. Miriam A. Smith and John W. Welch, "Joseph Smith: 'Author and Proprietor,'" in *Reexploring the Book of Mormon*, ed. John W. Welch (Salt Lake City: Deseret Book and FARMS, 1992), 154–57. See also Nathaniel Hinckley Wadsworth, "Copyright Laws and the 1830 Book of Mormon," *BYU Studies* 45, 3 (2006): 77–99.

9. See Givens, 165–84, and Paul Y. Hoskisson, ed., *Historicity and the Latter-day Saint Scriptures* (Provo, UT: BYU Religious Studies Center, 2001).

10. In 1920, the LDS Church added a three-page excerpt from Joseph Smith's 1838 history in which he tells the story of how he came into possession of the plates; that same excerpt still appears in the official edition.

11. Theoretically, there may be other potential explanations, but they have few supporters today. These include the idea that the Book of Mormon was written by someone else and then stolen or plagiarized by Joseph Smith (as many nineteenth-century critics asserted in the now-discredited Spaulding Theory), or that it might be the product of demons, or that it might be a work of fiction written by God and revealed verbatim to Joseph.

12. Royal Skousen, *Analysis of Textual Variants of the Book of Mormon, Part Four* (Provo, UT: FARMS, 2007), 2647–49, 2676–78.

13. Interview of Emma Smith with Joseph Smith III in Nauvoo, Illinois, 1879, in Joseph Smith III, "Last Testimony of Sister Emma," *Saints' Herald* 26 (October 1, 1879): 289–90. See Grant Hardy, ed., *The Book of Mormon: A Reader's Edition* (Urbana: University of Illinois Press, 2003), 641–42; or Dan Vogel, ed., *Early Mormon Documents* (Salt Lake City: Signature, 1996–2003), 1:541–42.

14. The warning that "inasmuch as ye shall keep my commandments ye shall prosper in the land; but inasmuch as ye will not keep my commandments ye shall be cut off from my presence" (2 Ne. 1:20) is a constant refrain in the book, being repeated some twenty

times (with variations). See 1 Ne. 2:20–21, 4:14, 17:13; 2 Ne. 1:9, 4:4, 5:20; Jarom 1:9; Omni 1:6; Mosiah 1:7, 2:22, 2:31; Alma 9:13–14, 36:1, 36:30, 37:13, 38:1, 48:15, 48:25, 50:20.

15.   "It is written: 'And it came to pass in the days of Ahasuerus.' R. Levi, according to others R. Jonathan, said: This is a tradition among us from our ancestors—the men of the Great Assembly—that wherever it is written וַיְהִי [*wayĕhî*, it came to pass], was some disaster." Babylonian Talmud, Tractate Megillah, ch. 1. I am indebted to Lauren F. Winner's *Girl Meets God: On the Path to a Spiritual Life* (Chapel Hill. NC: Algonquin Books of Chapel Hill, 2002),241, for the Talmud reference.

16.   It would be fitting if the LDS Church, in a future edition of the Book of Mormon, emphasized Nephi's thematic introduction by making his comment on mercy, faith, and deliverance a separate verse (it is currently the second half of 1 Ne. 1:20). The versification was not original to the text, having been added in 1879, and because the sentence comes at the very end of the first chapter, giving that chapter twenty-one verses would not confuse already existing commentaries or references.

17.   Meir Sternberg, *The Poetics of Biblical Narrative: Ideological Literature and the Drama of Reading* (Bloomington: Indiana University Press, 1985), 50.

18.   See also Jacob 6:13; Moro. 10:27, 34.

19.   John W. Welch began to explore some of the implications of this in his "Preliminary Comments on the Sources Behind the Book of Ether," FARMS Preliminary Report (Provo, UT, 1986), 16–17.

20.   See, for example, Richard Dilworth Rust, *Feasting on the Word: The Literary Testimony of the Book of Mormon* (Salt Lake City: Deseret Book and FARMS, 1997), 9, 11. Despite this assertion, Rust has written a perceptive book about the literary techniques used by various Book of Mormon narrators, whom he treats as fully historical individuals.

21.   Fawn M. Brodie, *No Man Knows My History: The Life of Joseph Smith the Mormon Prophet*, 2nd ed. (New York: Knopf, 1971; orig. pub. 1945), 55–56. Compare Jan Shipps, *Mormonism: The Story of a New Religious Tradition* (Urbana: University of Illinois Press, 1985), 16–20.

22.   The page counts are from the 1830 edition.

23.   Royal Skousen, personal communication. Skousen will analyze the evidence for this hypothesis in Volume 3 of his Critical Text of the Book of Mormon Project.

24.   Daniel Walker Howe, *What Hath God Wrought: The Transformation of America, 1815–1848*, Oxford History of the United States (New York: Oxford University Press, 2007), 314.

25.   Details about Joseph Smith, the angel Moroni, gold plates, and a miraculous translation could constitute yet another framing story, but this tale never intrudes directly into the text; it is information that readers must bring to the book. Since 1920, official editions of the Book of Mormon have included a brief excerpt from Joseph Smith's 1838 history telling the story of how he found and translated the Gold Plates. In 1830, however, the preface and testimonies of the witnesses only vaguely referred to a translation "by the gift and power of God," with a general indication of where the plates had been found and no mention at all of the angel Moroni, repeated visits to the hill, or the seer stone. As Richard Bushman has noted: "The first edition said virtually nothing about Joseph himself. The preface contained one sentence about his part in the work: 'I would also inform you

that the plates of which hath been spoken, were found in the township of Manchester, Ontario county, New York.' His own name appeared only on the title page and in the testimony of the eight witnesses at the back. It was an unusually spare production, wholly lacking in signs of self-promotion." Bushman, 112–13.

26. This episode was mentioned, somewhat obliquely, in the one and a half page preface to the first edition, which is in the voice of Joseph Smith. For the text of the Preface, see Hardy, 654–55.

27. Seymour Chatman, *Story and Discourse: Narrative Structure in Fiction and Film* (Ithaca: Cornell University Press, 1978), 62–63.

28. The most careful investigation of the relationship between Nephi's and Lehi's accounts is S. Kent Brown, "Recovering the Missing Record of Lehi," in his *From Jerusalem to Zarahemla: Literary and Historical Studies of the Book of Mormon* (Provo, UT: BYU Religious Studies Center, 1998), 28–54. For more on First and Second Nephi as a second, revised version of Nephi's memoirs, see the brief essays by John Welch in *Pressing Forward With the Book of Mormon: The FARMS Updates of the 1990s*, ed. John W. Welch and Melvin J. Thorne (Provo, UT: FARMS, 1999), 75–83.

29. There is more. As an autodiegetic narrative, First Nephi exhibits fixed internal focalization (we see everything through Nephi's eyes). Nephi also proves to be an intrusive narrator, and the fact that he comments on his own writing makes him self-reflexive as well. Nephi's voice is privileged above all others—as editor and sole narrator he always has the final say—and his standing as a prophet reinforces his unique authority to interpret the events he recounts. This results in a monologic narrative, defined by Gerald Prince as one in which "the narrator's views, judgments, and knowledge constitute the ultimate authority with respect to the world represented." Gerald Prince, *A Dictionary of Narratology* (Lincoln: University of Nebraska Press, 1987), 54.

30. On paratexts, see Gérard Genette, *Paratexts: Thresholds of Interpretation*, trans. Jane E. Lewin (New York: Cambridge University Press, 1997). H. Porter Abbott, *The Cambridge Introduction to Narrative* (Cambridge: Cambridge University Press, 2002), 77–78. Seymour Chatman had earlier noted that "we might better speak of the 'inferred' than of the 'implied' author." Seymour Chatman, *Coming to Terms: The Rhetoric of Narrative in Fiction and Film* (Ithaca: Cornell University Press, 1990), 77. The concept of the implied author is controversial, with some theorists such as Gérard Genette arguing that it is an unnecessary construct, but even he would allow it for "apocryphal" works (*apocryphe*), which claim to have been written by someone other than the apparent author (see his *Narrative Discourse Revisited*, trans. Jane E. Lewin [Ithaca: Cornell University Press, 1988], 146–47). For the Book of Mormon, the distinction is absolutely crucial.

31. The first quotation is from an 1831 letter to the editor of the *Painesville (OH) Telegraph*; it is reproduced in Vogel, *Early Mormon Documents*, 3:9. The second quote is from Eber D. Howe, *Mormonism Unvailed* (Painesville, OH: Eber D. Howe, 1834), 23. Books tracing the Book of Mormon to popular culture include Dan Vogel, *Indian Origins and the Book of Mormon: Religious Solutions from Columbus to Joseph Smith* (Salt Lake City: Signature, 1986), David Persuitte, *Joseph Smith and the Origins of the Book of Mormon*, 2nd ed. (Jefferson, NC: McFarland, 2000), and Grant H. Palmer, *An Insider's View of Mormon Origins* (Salt Lake City: Signature, 2002). On "free association," see Robert D. Anderson,

Inside the Mind of Joseph Smith: Psychobiography and the Book of Mormon (Salt Lake City: Signature, 1999), xxvii.

32. See Sorenson and Thorne, *Rediscovering*; Pinnock, *Finding Ancient Hebrew*; and Donald W. Parry, *The Book of Mormon Reformatted According to Parallelistic Patterns* (Provo, UT: FARMS, 1992). Richard Rust's *Feasting on the Word* is among the more sophisticated LDS studies; James Duke's book is the most comprehensive. See James T. Duke, *The Literary Masterpiece Called the Book of Mormon* (Springville, UT: Cedar Fort, 2004).

33. Sternberg, 2.

34. Shimon Bar-Efrat, *Narrative Art in the Bible* (Sheffield, England: Sheffield Academic Press, 2000), 23–30.

35. Robert Alter, *The Art of Biblical Narrative* (New York: Basic Books, 1981), 22–23; see also Robert Alter, "Introduction to the Old Testament," in *The Literary Guide to the Bible*, ed. Robert Alter and Frank Kermode (Cambridge, MA: Harvard University Press, 1987), 22–23.

36. I have in mind here not just the formal introductions and farewells by which we keep track of narrators, but also the way they organize their accounts into various discourses, sermons, father's blessings, visions, extended scriptural quotations, missionary journeys, military campaigns, and so forth. The original chapter divisions seem also to be presented as the work of the narrators. In any case, all these units are much clearer in my *Reader's Edition*. See also Thomas W. Mackay, "Mormon as Editor: A Study of Colophons, Headers, and Source Indicators," *Journal of Book of Mormon Studies* 2, 2 (1993): 90–109; and on chapter divisions, see Royal Skousen, "Translating the Book of Mormon: Evidence From the Original Manuscript," in *Book of Mormon Authorship Revisited: The Evidence for Ancient Origins*, ed. Noel B. Reynolds (Provo, UT: FARMS, 1997), 85–87.

37. The narrative is actually somewhat vague about timing. The estimation of two weeks for the journey, based on probable geography, is from S. Kent Brown, *Voices from the Dust: Book of Mormon Insights* (American Fork, UT: Covenant Communications, 2004), 3–6.

38. The Hebrew word *'ebed* usually denotes a slave, but because it can also refer to persons in subordinate positions (especially in relation to God, a king, or high officials) it was generally translated as "servant" in the King James Bible. The Book of Mormon adopts this ambiguous usage, though 1 Ne. 4:33 clearly indicates Zoram's unfree status. In addition, an alternative, Lamanite version of Zoram's fleeing with Nephi and his brothers, suggesting an element of coercion in his decision, is implicit at Alma 54:23.

39. Nephi's full statement, one of the most oft-cited verses from the Book of Mormon, reads: "And it came to pass that I, Nephi, said unto my father, 'I will go and do the things which the Lord hath commanded, for I know that the Lord giveth no command-ments unto the children of men, save he shall prepare a way for them that they may accomplish the thing which he commandeth them.'" Note that in this case Nephi is not shy about revealing his father's reaction; the narrative continues: "And it came to pass that when my father had heard these words he was exceedingly glad, for he knew that I had been blessed of the Lord" (1 Ne. 3:7–8).

40. Sternberg, 236.

41. One of the most engaging things about the *Book of Mormon Movie* is observing where the film-makers felt compelled to add details to round out the narrative. Equally entertaining is observing how thoroughly modern in sensibility—and foreign to the Book

of Mormon—most of that filler is. (The script tends to respond to gaps; the very nature of cinema requires everyone involved to continuously fill in blanks.)

42. S. Kent Brown, "What Were Those Sacrifices Offered by Lehi?" in *From Jerusalem to Zarahemla*, 1–8.

43. The phrase "after this manner of language" is not a regular way for the Book of Mormon to end quotations; it is unique to Nephi. It appears six times in 1 Nephi and it never occurs in the Bible (reducing the phrase to "manner of language" yields exactly the same results).

44. This structure may be a bit difficult to perceive in the version interspersed with commentary that I provided above, but in the *Reader's Edition* it is much clearer: the passage is formatted as a separate unit (with the heading "Lehi's Family Reunited") and there are three paragraphs, one for each of the quotations.

45. Thomas F. O'Dea, *The Mormons* (Chicago: University of Chicago Press, 1957), 29; cf. 33.

46. L. C. Knights, *How Many Children Had Lady Macbeth? An Essay in the Theory and Practice of Shakespeare Criticism* (Cambridge, UK: Minority Press, 1933). Knights never addresses the question in his title, which actually is of some interest since Shakespeare's play is ambiguous on the subject: at I.vii.54–55 Lady Macbeth speaks of nursing a baby, while Macbeth meditates on his childlessness at III.i.60–73 and Macduff bluntly states "he has no children" at IV.iii.216. See John Britton, "A. C. Bradley and those Children of Lady Macbeth," *Shakespeare Quarterly* 12, 3 (Summer 1961): 349–51. While Knights rejects character studies, his own interpretations, which see *Macbeth* as a "dramatic poem" or "a statement of evil" are far from satisfactory.

47. Chatman, 117.

48. Peter Lamarque, *Fictional Points of View* (Ithaca, NY: Cornell University Press, 1996), 57, 61. Lamarque's book offers a particularly detailed and lucid account of the interpretive process (especially 55–70), but see also Wolfgang Iser's classic description of the phenomenology of reading in his *Implied Reader* (Baltimore: Johns Hopkins University Press, 1974), 274–94.

49. Lamarque, 64–66.

50. Baruch Hochman, *Character in Literature* (Ithaca: Cornell University Press, 1985), 28–58.

51. Chatman, 117–18.

52. The phrase "history-like narrative" is borrowed from Hans W. Frei, *The Eclipse of Biblical Narrative: A Study in Eighteenth and Nineteenth Century Hermeneutics* (New Haven: Yale University Press, 1974).

53. Stanley Fish, *Is There a Text in This Class? The Authority of Interpretive Communities* (Cambridge, MA: Harvard University Press, 1980).

54. Noble Ross Reat, "Insiders and Outsiders in the Study of Religious Traditions," *Journal of the American Academy of Religion* 51, 3 (1983): 459–76.

CHAPTER 2

1. Richard Lyman Bushman, *Joseph Smith: Rough Stone Rolling* (New York: Knopf, 2005), 87–88.

2. Dan Vogel, *Joseph Smith: The Making of a Prophet* (Salt Lake City: Signature, 2004), 119. Vogel structures much of his monograph around major figures in the Book of Mormon, with chapter titles that tag such characters with brief descriptions (e.g., "Abinadi, Prophet Martyr," "Alma, Church Founder," "Moroni, Military Hero"), but his readings are consistently and relentlessly reductive. He sees everything in the Book of Mormon as a reflection of Joseph Smith's psyche or immediate environment. As a result, his analysis of the book's characters never takes them seriously, even as literary creations.

3. For other explicit declarations of his intentions, see 1 Ne. 19:18 and 2 Ne. 25:23.

4. Noel B. Reynolds, "The Political Dimension in Nephi's Small Plates," *BYU Studies* 27, 4 (1987): 15.

5. At 1 Ne. 18:19 Nephi's wife (unnamed) pleads for his life; we might assume that this is the same daughter of Ishmael. For a careful accounting of the probable members of Lehi's extended family, see John L. Sorenson, "The Composition of Lehi's Family" in *By Study and Also By Faith: Essays in Honor of Hugh W. Nibley on the Occasion of His Eightieth Birthday, 27 March 1990*, ed. John M. Lundquist and Stephen D. Ricks (Salt Lake City: Deseret Book and FARMS, 1990), 2:174–96.

6. Latter-day Saints are partial to reading "[the Lord] did visit me" as the descent of a divine being, much like the experience that Joseph Smith recounted in his First Vision. The verb *visit* in the Hebrew Bible (*pāqad*) does not generally mean to "pay a personal call"; rather it means "to aid," "to care for," "to appoint," or "to punish."

7. Again, similarities and contrasts with the Hebrew Bible are both significant. As Robert Alter has noted, "By and large, the biblical writers prefer to avoid indirect speech." The Book of Mormon has no such compunction, and indeed, indirect speech is pervasive and extensive. On the other hand, Alter also observes that in any story "the point at which dialogue first emerges will be worthy of attention, and in most instances, the initial words spoken by a personage will be revelatory, perhaps more in manner than in matter, constituting an important moment in the exposition of character"—a description that fits Book of Mormon narrative exactly. See Robert Alter, *The Art of Biblical Narrative* (New York: Basic Books, 1981), 67, 74.

8. John Bright, *Jeremiah*, Anchor Bible, vol. 21 (Garden City, New York: Doubleday, 1965), 153. Nephi, for example, never reports any divine dreams of his own, and in fact the only other individual in the Book of Mormon who receives a revelation through a dream is the Jaredite king Omer (Ether 9:3).

9. Jack R. Lundbom, *Jeremiah 1–20*, Anchor Bible, vol. 21A (New York: Doubleday, 1999), 143, 462–63; see also Elaine R. Follis, "Zion Traditions," in the *Anchor Bible Dictionary*, ed. David Noel Freedman et al. (New York: Doubleday, 1992), 6:1098–102. It is perhaps significant that Nephi never mentions David aside from his quotations of Isaiah (which do *not* include Isa. 31 or 37), and even his brother Jacob mentions David only negatively (Jacob 1:15, 2:23–24).

10. By contrast, Lehi (and by extension Nephi) were clearly not orthodox Jews in several significant ways. For instance, as early as 1831, Alexander Campbell pointed out the implausibility of the non-Levite Lehi performing sacrifices (1 Ne. 2:7, 5:9, 7:22). Mormons regarded this as a serious enough criticism that they responded in the official church newspaper. Today Latter-day Saints justify Lehi's sacrifices by making a distinction between

the Aaronic (or Levitical) Priesthood and the Melchizedek Priesthood, although this distinction is foreign to the Book of Mormon itself (Melchizedek is mentioned only at Alma 13:14–18 and the term "Melchizedek Priesthood" never appears anywhere.) See Alexander Campbell, "Delusions," *The Millennial Harbinger* 2, 2 (February 1831); Oliver Cowdery, "Delusion," *Messenger and Advocate* 1, 6 (March 1835): 90–91; Joseph Fielding McConkie and Robert L. Millet, *Doctrinal Commentary on the Book of Mormon* (Salt Lake City: Bookcraft, 1987), 1:31; David R. Seely, "Lehi's Altar and Sacrifice in the Wilderness," *Journal of Book of Mormon Studies* 10, 1 (2001): 62–69.

11.   Lehi is the patriarch of the clan until his death. In the power struggle that follows, Laman and Lemuel again threaten Nephi and he takes into the wilderness those members of the family who are willing to accept his leadership. Adding to the general level of resentment, he mentions that his followers included his sisters (2 Ne. 5:6), who by this time had probably married the sons of Ishmael—staunch allies of Laman and Lemuel—and who would have thereby left their husbands.

12.   This is S. Kent Brown's estimate of the mileage. See S. Kent Brown, *Voices From the Dust: Book of Mormon Insights* (American Fork, UT: Covenant Communications, 2004), 3–6.

13.   This reading of 1 Ne. 3:16 is supported by Royal Skousen's magisterial work of textual criticism of the Book of Mormon. The current text reads: "for behold, he [Lehi] left gold and silver, and all manner of riches. And all this he hath done because of the commandments of the Lord." Skousen points out that the original manuscript had the singular "commandment," and observes that this "implies a specific commandment for Lehi to leave his wealth behind." See Royal Skousen, *Analysis of Textual Variants of the Book of Mormon, Part One* (Provo, UT: FARMS, 2004), 89.

14.   Latter-day Saints have noted the correspondences between the travels of Lehi's family and the Exodus. See Terrence L. Szink, "Nephi and the Exodus" and Alan Goff, "Mourning, Consolation, and Repentance at Nahom," both in *Rediscovering the Book of Mormon*, ed. John L. Sorenson and Melvin J. Thorne (Salt Lake City: Deseret Book and FARMS, 1991), 38–51, 92–99; and S. Kent Brown, "The Exodus Pattern in the Book of Mormon," in his *From Jerusalem to Zarahemla: Literary and Historical Studies of the Book of Mormon* (Provo, UT: BYU Religious Studies Center, 1998), 75–98. Nate Oman's blog posts on 1 Nephi 17 seem to independently parallel my own impressions. He notes that "where Nephi experiences the story of Moses in the story of his family's exodus, Laman and Lemuel experience the story of Moses in the correct application of the law." Nate Oman, "Commentary on 1 Ne. 17," four parts, January 15–February 3, 2009, starting with http://timesandseasons.org/index.php/2009/01/commentary-on-1-nephi-17-pt-1.

15.   1 Nephi, chaps. 4, 5, 17, 19; 2 Ne. 3, 5, 11, 25. For many readers, Nephi's slaying of Laban seems to require some justification beyond the revenge and expediency offered by the angel at 1 Ne. 4:11–13: "It is better that one man should perish than that a nation should dwindle and perish in unbelief." Was it really necessary for Laban to die? Couldn't his drunken stupor have been so profound that Nephi could have stolen his clothes and identity without killing him? Might not God have dispatched him at the right moment, say, with a heart attack? Or why didn't an angel simply take the plates from Laban's treasury and deliver them to Lehi's family? The connections with Moses provide one possible

answer: as with Moses' killing of the Egyptian at Ex. 2:11–15, Nephi's decisive action marks a sharp transition, a point of no return that forces the family to flee into the wilderness as fugitives. Compare John W. Welch, "Legal Perspectives on the Slaying of Laban," *Journal of Book of Mormon Studies* 1, 1 (1992): 119–41.

16.   Such parallels have been noted before; see Reynolds, 33.

17.   See Richard Lyman Bushman, "The Lamanite View of Book of Mormon History" in *Believing History: Latter-day Saint Essays*, ed. Reid L. Neilson and Jed Woodworth (New York: Columbia University Press, 2004), 79–92.

18.   The mention of Nephi's "children" at 2 Ne. 4:15 and 11:2 may be generic references to his descendants.

19.   Nephi's wife was also among those reproved for their faithlessness by the words written by God on the Liahona (1 Ne. 16:27).

20.   Perhaps this "raw meat" was cured or dried. At 1 Ne. 17:12, Nephi connects their unusual diet with a general prohibition against the use of fire.

21.   Eldin Ricks noted this long ago in his *Book of Mormon Commentary*, 2nd ed. (Salt Lake City: Deseret News Press, 1953), 1:204.

22.   In Jacob's words, Nephi handed over the record with a charge "that I should preserve these plates and hand them down unto my seed, from generation to generation" (Jacob 1:3).

23.   In 1 Ne. 19:4, Nephi makes a mid-sentence correction that seems to indicate an acknowledgement of the unexpected succession: "This have I done [i.e., kept a record on the Large Plates], and commanded my people that they should do after I was gone; and that these plates [the Small Plates] should be handed down from one generation to another, *or from one prophet to another*, until further commandments of the Lord" (the reading "that they should do" rather than the current "what they should do" is from the original manuscript; see Skousen, 402). Nephi eventually hands the Small Plates not to the next generation, but rather to the next prophet, Jacob, who as a brother belongs to the same generation as Nephi. Another possibility, first suggested by John Sorenson, is that Jacob married one of Nephi's daughters. In this case, Jacob's descendants would also be in Nephi's direct line. See Sorenson, "The Composition of Lehi's Family," in Lundquist and Ricks, 2:184.

24.   In the original manuscript of the Book of Mormon, 1 Ne. 9:4 read "an account of the reigns of the kings." See Skousen, 191–92. Noel B. Reynolds finds Nephi's connection to monarchy so problematic that he suggests the line of Nephite kings may have started with the next generation; see his "Nephite Kingship Reconsidered," in *Mormons, Scripture, and the Ancient World: Studies in Honor of John L. Sorenson*, ed. Davis Bitton (Provo, UT: FARMS 1998), 151–89.

25.   See also the title and headnote to the book of Third Nephi, where descent from Nephi is attributed to six of the primary record keepers.

26.   Leo G. Purdue, Joseph Blenkinsopp, John J. Collins, and Carol Meyers, *Families in Ancient Israel* (Louisville, Kentucky: Westminster John Knox, 1997), 182, 191.

27.   Robert Alter, *The Five Books of Moses* (New York: W. W. Norton, 2004), 65.

28.   These verses are also quoted by Jacob in 2 Ne. 8:24–25. In Lehi's allusion, Isaiah's "beautiful garments" have been transformed into the New Testament "armor of righteousness" (2 Cor. 6:7; see also Eph. 6:13–17).

29. This point is made by S. Kent Brown in *Voices From the Dust*, 54–55.

30. Nephi's placement of this incident may be another example of editorial manipulation of chronology. In the narrative, Lehi's dream immediately follows the arrival of Ishmael and his family, but the fact that Ishmael, with his wife, sons, and daughters, are not mentioned at all is puzzling. Perhaps Lehi had this dream at an earlier date, when his concerns were limited to his immediate family.

31. It is not clear whether Lehi saw the rest of the vision as well. Nephi states that "I saw the things which my father saw" (1 Ne. 14:29), but this might mean that his own vision incorporated Lehi's dream. If Lehi saw the full-sweep of the future of his descendants, Nephi does not report that he ever mentioned it. A difference in visions would go a long way in explaining their difference in attitudes toward Laman and Lemuel; Nephi had seen unequivocally that the Lamanites would continue along the rebellious path set by their fathers.

32. Again, Royal Skousen's recent work on the text of the Book of Mormon makes the connection even more explicit. In all printed editions of the Book of Mormon, the angel's explanation at 1 Ne. 12:18 has read "a great and a terrible gulf divideth them, yea, even the word of the justice of the Eternal God." The original manuscript, however, clearly has "the sword of the justice of the Eternal God." Skousen, 257–58.

33. However, in Royal Skousen's reconstruction of the original text, the verse should read "the wicked are *separated* from the righteous and also from that tree of life." Skousen, 334.

34. Dan Vogel notices differences between Nephi's and Lehi's accounts of the tree, which he explains as due to a combination of Joseph Smith's confusion and a literary projection of his own desire to counter his father's universalist tendencies. But Vogel fails to recognize that the details adhere to the internal logic of the larger narrative and that Smith's family dynamics were in fact quite different from Lehi's. See Vogel, 395. Any discussion of Lehi's dream, however, should note that Joseph's father had a very similar dream several years before the dictation of the Book of Mormon manuscript; our source for this is Lucy Mack Smith, Joseph's mother. See Lavina Fielding Anderson, ed., *Lucy's Book: A Critical Edition of Lucy Mack Smith's Family Memoir* (Salt Lake City: Signature, 2001), 294–98.

35. Michael D. Coogan, ed., *The New Oxford Annotated Bible*, 3rd ed. (Oxford: Oxford University Press, 2001), 1074.

36. For fuller analyses of this passage, see Steven P. Sondrup, "The Psalm of Nephi: A Lyric Reading," *BYU Studies* 21, 3 (1981): 357–72, and Matthew Nickerson, "Nephi's Psalm: 2 Nephi 4:16–35 in the Light of Form-Critical Analysis," *Journal of Book of Mormon Studies* 6, 2 (1997): 26–42. Either Nephi or Joseph Smith was an astute reader of the Psalms since, as Nickerson explains, Nephi's example closely follows the generally accepted pattern (first identified in the 1920s by Hermann Gunkel) of an "individual lament" psalm: invocation, complaint, petition, confession of trust, and vow of praise. (In the Psalm of Nephi, the third and fourth elements are switched; compare Claus Westermann, *The Psalms: Structure, Content, and Message*, trans. Ralph D. Gehrke [Minneapolis: Augsburg Publishing House, 1980], 53–70.)

37. Royal Skousen argues that the current text reflects a misunderstanding on the part of the typesetter and should actually read "hath visited *me* in so much mercy."

Skousen, 546. We might wonder whether Nephi's displeasure here, at his own weakness despite having seen such "great things," is an echo of his earlier condemnation of Laman and Lemuel.

CHAPTER 3

1. The only exception is his comment that he consecrated his younger brothers Jacob and Joseph as priests and teachers over his people (2 Ne. 5:26).

2. This cannot be entirely due to the Lord's injunction to focus his writing on spiritual rather than political matters, or it would seem to imply that Nephi had had no particular spiritually edifying experiences in the last several decades that were worth recording.

3. Later narrators followed Nephi's lead, and perhaps the most significant failure of the Book of Mormon as either history or fiction is the almost complete lack of individual women (in over five hundred pages, there are only three named female characters, three direct quotations ascribed to women, and a couple references to mother/child relationships; there are *no* accounts of Nephite marriages other than the brief exchange in 1 Ne. 5 between Lehi and Sariah). Even compared with texts as patriarchal as the Bible, the invisibility of women in the Book of Mormon is striking—a fact that was noted before the rise of modern feminism. In the words of nineteenth-century Mormon leader George Reynolds, "It is somewhat noticeable how little prominence is given to womankind in the historical narrative of the Book of Mormon, and unfortunately when mention is made of them it too frequently grows out of man's sins and their misfortunes" (George Reynolds, *The Story of the Book of Mormon*, 3rd ed. [Chicago: Henry C. Etten and Co. 1888], 237). Since Joseph Smith's own life at the time of the translation included influential women such as his mother and his wife of less than a year, those seeking the origins of the book in his personal history have to somehow explain the absence of any accounts of courtship, romance, or maternal interaction. For Latter-day Saints, answers can be found in Nephite "biography, culture, and genre" (in the words of Kevin and Shauna Christensen), though ultimately, given what we might assume about Nephite society from the text, it may be an advantage to the LDS Church that the particulars of women's lives are so rare; the Book of Mormon's status as scripture might have made extremely restrictive Nephite attitudes toward women normative for the Mormon faith. On the general topic, see Carol Lynn Pearson, "Could Feminism Have Saved the Nephites?" *Sunstone* 19, 1 (March 1996): 32–40; Kevin and Shauna Christensen, "Nephite Feminism Revisited: Thoughts on Carol Lynn Pearson's View of Women in the Book of Mormon," *FARMS Review* 10, 2 (1998): 9–61; and Camille Williams, "Women in the Book of Mormon," *Journal of Book of Mormon Studies* 11, 1 (2002): 66–79. One of the more successful attempts to discover family values in the Book of Mormon is E. Douglas Clark and Robert S. Clark, *Fathers and Sons in the Book of Mormon* (Salt Lake City: Deseret Book, 1991).

4. Jan Shipps has pointed out how significant this same phenomenon has been in later Latter-day Saint religiosity—as when Mormon pioneers spoke of Brigham Young as a new Moses, again leading God's people through the wilderness to a promised land—noting that "this replication was not conscious ritual re-creation of events, but

rather experiential 'living through' of sacred events in a new age." Jan Shipps, *Mormonism: The Story of a New Religious Tradition* (Urbana: University of Illinois Press, 1985), 41–65; quote from52.

5. Jacob's book of seven chapters consists primarily of one sermon and a lengthy quotation from the prophet Zenos in the Brass Plates. His appearance in Nephi's record (a sermon in 2 Ne. 6–10) does include some biblical commentary, but he was obviously under the strong influence of his older brother at that point. In fact, Jacob admits that he is citing Isaiah because "they are the words which my brother has desired that I should speak unto you" (2 Ne. 6:4).

6. Richard Lyman Bushman, *Joseph Smith: Rough Stone Rolling* (New York: Knopf, 2005), 102.

7. In addition, Nephi had just quoted another early, extrabiblical prophet—Zenos—and he also works in phrases from that text. As with Mahayana Buddhism, where later scriptures appear that claim both earlier provenance and a clearer understanding of dharma, the words of Zenos preach a pre-Christian gospel more clearly than anything in the Hebrew Bible. See 1 Ne. 19:10–17.

8. For a thorough overview of Latter-day Saint scholarship on the connection between Isaiah and the Book of Mormon, see Donald W. Parry and John W. Welch, eds., *Isaiah in the Book of Mormon* (Provo, UT: FARMS, 1998).

9. This can most easily be seen in Grant Hardy, ed., *The Book of Mormon: A Reader's Edition* (Urbana: University of Illinois Press, 2003), 122–27.

10. 1 Ne. 15:27–29 demonstrates that prophets can fail to perceive the full import of their revelations: "the water which my father saw [in his dream] was filthiness; and so much was his mind swallowed up in other things that he beheld not the filthiness of the water . . . [which represented] that awful hell, which the angel said unto me was prepared for the wicked." Nevertheless, there is at least one verse (1 Ne. 19:21) in which Nephi suggests that ancient prophets specifically foresaw Lehi's family.

11. For convenient examples, see Michael Warner, ed., *American Sermons: The Pilgrims to Martin Luther King, Jr.* (New York: Library of America, 1999). The volume includes a very useful "Note on the Sermon Form" (889–91) which mentions the importance attached to "simple and plain speech" —a value also espoused by Nephi (2 Ne. 25:4, 7, 28, 31:2–3. 33:6)—as well as a late sermon by Joseph Smith in a very different style from what we read in the Book of Mormon.

12. Ethan Smith, *View of the Hebrews*, 2nd ed. (Provo, UT: BYU Religious Studies Center, 1996; orig. publication 1825). Ethan Smith was writing in nearly the same time and place as Joseph Smith (no relation) and their ideas exhibit many similarities, though LDS authors have been quick to point out significant differences as well. For instance, although both *View of the Hebrews* and the Book of Mormon quote the Bible extensively, they focus on different chapters, and Ethan did not frame his ideas as a historical narrative. See John W. Welch, "View of the Hebrews: An Unparallel," in *Reexploring the Book of Mormon* (Salt Lake City: Deseret Book and FARMS, 1992), 83–87. A key text in the debate is the list of parallels put together by the nineteenth-century Mormon leader Brigham H. Roberts, which can be found in B. H. Roberts, *Studies of the Book of Mormon*, ed. Brigham D. Madsen (Urbana: University of Illinois Press, 1985).

13. Krister Stendahl, former dean of the Harvard Divinity School, argued that the Book of Mormon's version of the Sermon on the Mount could be understood as a nineteenth-century targum. See his "Sermon on the Mount and Third Nephi," in *Reflections on Mormonism: Judaeo-Christian Parallels*, ed. Truman G. Madsen (Provo, UT: BYU Religious Studies Center, 1978), 139–54; reprinted in Krister Stendahl, *Meanings: The Bible as Document and as Guide* (Philadelphia: Fortress Press, 1984), 99–113.

14. Good introductions can be found in the articles on pesharim in the *Anchor Bible Dictionary* or the *Encyclopedia of the Dead Sea Scrolls*, ed. Lawrence H. Schiffman and James C. VanderKam, 2 vols. (New York: Oxford University Press, 2000).

15. See, for example, Fawn M. Brodie, *No Man Knows My History*, 2nd ed. (New York: Knopf, 1971), 58, and Dan Vogel, *Joseph Smith: The Making of a Prophet* (Salt Lake City: Signature, 2004), 426. Vogel also suggests that Smith may have had Oliver Cowdery copy from Isaiah in his absence, but the evidence from the manuscripts do not support this hypothesis. The Isaiah chapters appear to have been written from dictation rather than copied from the Bible; we observe, for instance, that names are frequently spelled differently, and the 1830 chapter divisions in the Book of Mormon do not correspond to those of the biblical Isaiah. See Royal Skousen, *Analysis of Textual Variants of the Book of Mormon, Part Two* (Provo, UT: FARMS, 2005), 655–803.

16. For example, see Monte S. Nyman, *Great are the Words of Isaiah* (Salt Lake City: Bookcraft, 1980), 9.

17. For side by side comparisons of Isaiah in the King James Bible and the Book of Mormon, with variants marked, see Hoyt W. Brewster Jr., *Isaiah Plain and Simple: The Message of Isaiah in the Book of Mormon* (Salt Lake City: Deseret Book, 1995). All detailed analyses, however, must be redone in light of Royal Skousen's work on the original text of the Book of Mormon.

18. Skousen, *Variants, Part Two*, 781–84.

19. Royal Skousen, "Textual Variants in the Isaiah Quotations in the Book of Mormon," in Parry and Welch, *Isaiah in the Book of Mormon*, 381–82.

20. Skousen, *Variants, Part Two*, 670–71 (omitted *be* verb), 751–52 (increased parallelism); David P. Wright, "Isaiah in the Book of Mormon: or Joseph Smith in Isaiah," in *American Apocrypha: Essays on the Book of Mormon*, ed. Dan Vogel and Brent Lee Metcalfe (Salt Lake City: Signature, 2002), 178–82 (disrupted parallelism).

21. Skousen, *Variants, Part Two*, 689–90, 692, 757.

22. Hardy, 641.

23. There are many examples of this distinction made in Adam Clarke, *The Holy Bible . . . with a Commentary and Critical Notes . . .* (New York: Ezra Sargent, 1811). Clarke's commentary can be searched in an on-line version at http://www.godrules.net/library/clarke/clarke.htm.

24. B. H. Roberts, *Defense of the Faith and the Saints* (Salt Lake City: Deseret News, 1907), 1:272–73; Sidney B. Sperry, *Our Book of Mormon* (Salt Lake City: Bookcraft, 1950), 172; Daniel H. Ludlow, *A Companion to Your Study of the Book of Mormon* (Salt Lake City: Deseret Book, 1976), 141.

25. Royal Skousen, working from a believer's perspective and a close analysis of the manuscripts, suggests that Joseph received the text in a fairly exact form; that is to say,

he seems to have been a conduit rather than an active translator. See Royal Skousen, "Translating the Book of Mormon: Evidence from the Original Manuscript," *Book of Mormon Authorship Revisited: The Evidence for Ancient Origins*, ed. Noel B. Reynolds (Provo, UT: FARMS, 1997), 61–93.

26. David P. Wright, "Joseph Smith's Interpretation of Isaiah in the Book of Mormon," *Dialogue* 31, 4 (Winter 1998): 185. David J. Shepherd argues that the presence of the King James Version of Isaiah in the Book of Mormon is the most telling evidence of its status as a "pseudotranslation," albeit "the most complex, ambitious, and influential pseudotranslation that the world has ever seen"; see his "Rendering Fiction: Translation, Pseudotranslation, and the Book of Mormon," in *The New Mormon Challenge*, ed. Francis J. Beckwith, Carl Mosser, and Paul Owen (Grand Rapids: Zondervan, 2002), 367–95.

27. The most ambitious attempt to date to identify parallels between Book of Mormon readings and variants in other ancient sources is John Tvedtnes, "The Isaiah Variants in the Book of Mormon," FARMS Preliminary Report (Provo, UT, 1981). A shorter version was published as "Isaiah Variants in the Book of Mormon," in *Isaiah and the Prophets*, ed. Monte S. Nyman (Provo, UT: BYU Religious Studies Center, 1984), 165–76. Wright offers a critical response in "Isaiah in the Book of Mormon," 187–208.

28. For Mormon perspectives, see Nyman, 253–57; Victor L. Ludlow, *Isaiah: Prophet, Seer, and Poet* (Salt Lake City: Deseret Book, 1982), 541–48; and John W. Welch, "Authorship of the Book of Isaiah in Light of the Book of Mormon," in Parry and Welch, *Isaiah in the Book of Mormon*, 423–37. Latter-day Saints, however, have never undertaken the sort of phrase by phrase analysis in Hebrew that characterizes works like Joseph Blenkinsopp's three-volume Anchor Bible commentary (2000–3), which reveals just how much of what we see in Isaiah is best explained by the Second Isaiah hypothesis. The level of consensus on this issue, especially in a field as contentious as biblical studies, is remarkable (and certainly includes scholars who believe in inspiration and prophecy).

29. William Hamblin, "'Isaiah Update' Challenged" [letter to the editor], *Dialogue* 17, 1 (Spring 1984): 4–8.

30. R. Coggins, "First Isaiah," in the *Anchor Bible Dictionary*, ed. David Noel Freedman et al. (New York: Doubleday, 1992), 3:474–88. As an example, see H. G. M. Williamson, *The Book Called Isaiah: Deutero-Isaiah's Role in Composition and Redaction* (Oxford: Oxford University Press, 1994), which argues that Second Isaiah edited and augmented Isaiah 1–39.

31. Mormon teachings could allow for Joseph to have dictated a translation that had been produced in the spirit world by God, angels, or even Nephi himself, all of whom could have known the King James Version intimately by 1829. Nephi might have updated and revised his book posthumously. Joseph Smith might have—with divine approbation—expanded the core text of Nephi's writings, or he could have been inspired to open his Bible and make corrections as he read it aloud. Or the Isaiah chapters in the Book of Mormon may be an example of a translation of "dynamic equivalence" rather than "formal correspondence"; that is to say, the Brass Plates may have included a version of Isaiah that was recognizable but non-standard, which is precisely what the Book of Mormon provided to nineteenth-century Americans. We might even hypothesize that God could even have directly placed in the Brass Plates writings still to be created in the future. As Meir

Sternberg once described rabbinical approaches to Biblical authorship, "Given divine inspiration, Moses could compose the rest of the Bible as well as the Pentateuch to the last letter. So could any of his successors—Joshua, Samuel, David, Jeremiah, Ezra—regardless of their position in history. . . . Where the Holy Spirit operates, in short, all earthbound notions like access and competence lose their force as criteria of authorship." To be a Latter-day Saint is to accept the miraculous, divine origin of the Book of Mormon (most often defined as including the existence of angels, ancient plates, and historical Nephites), but within those basic parameters, there are still many faithful possibilities. Few Mormon scholars have investigated these options; I don't expect that non-Mormons will find any of them remotely plausible.

The idea of an inspired expansion is explored in Blake T. Ostler, "The Book of Mormon as a Modern Expansion of an Ancient Source," *Dialogue* 20, 1 (Spring 1987): 66–123. B. H. Roberts hypothesized that Joseph may have used the Bible while translating the Book of Mormon; see his *New Witnesses for God* (Salt Lake City: Deseret News, 1909), 3:425–40. The concept of "dynamic equivalence" is from Eugene A. Nida and Charles R. Taber's classic study, *The Theory and Practice of Translation* (Leiden: E. J. Brill, 1969), 12–32. Another example is the rendition of John 1:1 in the Bible used by Chinese Protestants (and Chinese Latter-day Saints). The Greek word *logos* meant "word," but it was also a philosophically rich term in New Testament times. Rather than using the regular Chinese character for "word," the translators adopted a philosophical term that was equivalently evocative, so the opening of John literally reads, "In the beginning was the Dao, and the Dao was with God, and the Dao was God." The Sternberg quotation is from his *Poetics of Biblical Narrative: Ideological Literature and the Drama of Reading* (Bloomington: Indiana University Press, 1985), 61.

32. R. J. Zwi Werblowsky and Geoffrey Wigoder, eds., *Oxford Dictionary of the Jewish Religion* (New York: Oxford University Press, 1997), 463.

33. Vogel, 426.

34. When Nephi₂, living more than five centuries later, exclaims, "Oh, that I could have had my days in the days when my father Nephi first came out of the land of Jerusalem, that I could have joyed with him in the Promised Land; then were his people easy to be entreated, firm to keep the commandments of God, and slow to be led to do iniquity; and they were quick to hearken unto the words of the Lord—Yea, if my days could have been in those days, then would my soul have had joy in the righteousness of my brethren" (Hel. 7:7), it is hard not to smile at his misplaced nostalgia. Either he has been reading a very different version of early Nephite history or he hasn't been paying attention.

35. Another careful attempt to answer these questions, with somewhat different results, can be found in S. Kent Brown, *From Jerusalem to Zarahemla: Literary and Historical Studies of the Book of Mormon* (Provo, UT: BYU Religious Studies Center, 1998), 9–27. Brown highlights the situation in Jerusalem and the hardships of the desert years rather than Nephi's conflicts with his brothers over their resistance to prophecy.

36. Nephi's gloss here (if that is what it is) is a way to reshape the text of Isaiah so that it makes more sense in light of his current situation; some scholars see a similar process at work in the received text. Joseph Blenkinsopp raises the possibility that the phrase *but not*

in truth and sincerity in the previous verse was "inserted by a disillusioned scribe reflecting a later and less-promising situation." Joseph Blenkinsopp, trans., *Isaiah 40–55*, Anchor Bible, vol. 19A (New York: Doubleday, 2000), 288.

37. The changes made in Joseph's revision of the Bible, usually referred to in Mormon circles as the Joseph Smith Translation (JST), seem more programmatic and generally easier to account for in terms of obvious theological issues. See Royal Skousen, "The Earliest Textual Sources for Joseph Smith's 'New Translation' of the King James Bible," *FARMS Review* 17, 2 (2005): 451–70; Scott H. Faulring, Kent P. Jackson, and Robert J. Matthews, eds., *Joseph Smith's New Translation of the Bible: Original Manuscripts* (Provo, UT: BYU Religious Studies Center, 2004), 3–13; Philip L. Barlow, *Mormons and the Bible: The Place of the Latter-day Saints in American Religion* (New York: Oxford University Press, 1991), 46–61; and Robert J. Matthews, *"A Plainer Translation:" Joseph Smith's Translation of the Bible* (Provo, UT: Brigham Young University Press, 1975). For a provocative analysis of the JST from a religious studies perspective, see Kathleen Flake, "Translating Time: The Nature and Function of Joseph Smith's Narrative Canon," *Journal of Religion* 87 (October 2007): 497–527. Flake is certainly right about Smith's privileging narrative forms over propositional theologizing, but despite Smith's broad definition of the term "translation," I am not sure that the mode of production for the JST matched that of the Book of Mormon, even for the extended Isaiah passages in 1 and 2 Nephi.

38. John Barton, "Prophecy (Postexilic Hebrew)," in the *Anchor Bible Dictionary*, 5:489–95. Whatever the status of the Hebrew canon in 597 BC, Lehi and his family had a de facto canon—scripture was defined as what was included on the Brass Plates.

39. Ludlow, 407–10; Andrew C. Skinner, "Nephi's Lessons to his People: The Messiah, the Land, and Isaiah 48–49 in 1 Nephi 19–22," in Parry and Welch, *Isaiah in the Book of Mormon*, 106–9.

40. For those looking for parallels with Joseph Smith's life, it would be useful to compare Nephi's seeing himself in Isaiah 49 with Joseph's excitement at realizing that he himself was the unlearned reader of Isaiah 29:11–12, as evidenced by Martin Harris's visit with Prof. Charles Anthon in New York City. See Bushman, *Rough Stone*, 63–66.

41. The major features of Lehi's dream are given an allegorical interpretation by the angel and then a historical counterpart in the apocalyptic survey of future events that follows. I would line them up in this way:

DREAM	ALLEGORY	FUTURE HISTORY
Tree	Love of God	Life of Jesus
River	Hell	Wars and wickedness
Rod of Iron	Word of God	Bible and Book of Mormon
Mists of Darkness	Temptations	Missing scripture
Great Building	Vanity and pride	Great and abominable church

This list is similar to, though not identical with, the discussion in John W. Welch, "Connections between the Visions of Lehi and Nephi," in *Pressing Forward with the Book of Mormon*, ed. John W. Welch and Melvin J. Thorne (Provo, UT: FARMS, 1999), 49–53.

42. John J. Collins, ed., "Apocalypse: The Morphology of a Genre," *Semeia* 14 (1979): 9. The part of this definition that does not fit is the absence in 1 Nephi 11–14 of a cosmic journey through the heavens. That would have to wait, in Mormonism, until Joseph Smith's vision in 1832 of the three degrees of glory in the Doctrine and Covenants, section 76.

43. Mark Thomas has written cogently about how 1 Nephi 11–14 can be read as an example of apocalyptic literature. Mark D. Thomas, *Digging in Cumorah: Reclaiming the Book of Mormon Narratives* (Salt Lake City: Signature, 1999), 99–109.

44. In 2 Ne. 29:5, Nephi quotes God as directly addressing the Gentiles, but he himself has not done so yet.

45. Interestingly, the tone changes here, as Nephi adopts the intimate form of address "my beloved brethren" from his younger brother. The phrase appears sixteen times in 2 Ne. 25–33 and nowhere else in Nephi's writings, with the exception of 2 Ne. 6–10 (Jacob's discourse), where it was used thirteen times. Jacob's fondness for the phrase is evident in the additional seven times that "beloved brethren" appears in his own brief book (though one of the instances, at Jacob 4:11, seems to have been added by the 1830 compositor; see Skousen, *Variants, Part Two*, 990–91).

46. Frederick Axelgard has noted some of the specific connections between Nephi's vision in 1 Ne. 11–14 and his comments inspired by Isaiah in 2 Ne. 25–30. See Frederick W. Axelgard, "1 and 2 Nephi: An Inspiring Whole," *BYU Studies* 26, 4 (Fall 1986): 53–65. This article is one of the few attempts to make sense of the larger literary organization of Nephi's writings, and it raises many of the issues that I have tried to deal with in this chapter.

47. See Richard Bushman's remarks on the Book of Mormon's fascination with records and the ways in which they come together, in his essay "The Book of Mormon in Early Mormon History," a chapter in his *Believing History: Latter-day Saint Essays*, ed. Reid L. Neilson and Jed Woodworth (New York: Columbia University Press, 2004), 65–78.

48. James J. O'Donnell, *Augustine: A New Biography* (New York: HarperCollins, 2005), 6. Another of O'Donnell's comments could also be applied to Nephi's writings: "Though friends and family get carefully scripted parts to play in the *Confessions*, the book as a whole is a one-man show, and a virtuoso performance at that. And for all that it is a testimony of faith and confidence, it is permeated with anxiety" (36).

49. For example, the break between First and Second Nephi—which apparently takes place within a single family discussion—is unexpected, and requires some sort of explanation. Noel Reynolds has proposed that First Nephi was carefully constructed with multiple parallels and chiastic features, and that Second Nephi was a "collection of odds and ends" that he could not fit into his tight literary structure. Noel B. Reynolds, "Nephi's Outline," *BYU Studies* 20, 2 (Winter 1980): 131–49; reprinted in *Book of Mormon Authorship: New Light on Ancient Origins*, ed. Noel B. Reynolds and Charles D. Tate (Provo, UT: BYU Religious Studies Center, 1982). I have an alternative suggestion, based on the original chapter divisions, as to how Nephi may have tried to bring order and balance to his account (modern chapter numbers appear in parentheses):

FIRST NEPHI		SECOND NEPHI	
I–II (1–9)	Lehi's teachings	I–II (1–3)	Lehi's Teachings
III (10–14)	Lehi concludes, Nephi responds (his vision)	III (4)	Lehi concludes, Nephi responds (his psalm)
IV (15)	His brothers rebel	IV (5)	His brothers rebel
V (16–19)	Nephi rescues the family, preaches	V–VII (6–10)	Jacob preaches
VI (19–20)	Isaiah chapters	VIII–X (11–24)	Isaiah chapters
VIII (22)	Nephi's prophetic expansion	XI–XV (25–33)	Nephi's prophetic expansion

50.   There is much more going on in just First and Second Nephi than Philip L. Barlow acknowledges in his otherwise fine *Mormons and the Bible: The Place of the Latter-day Saints in American Religion*. His discussion of biblical interpretation in the entire Book of Mormon occupies just twelve pages (26–38).

CHAPTER 4

1.   The reading "wild wilderness" is in both the original and printer's manuscripts, though the first word has been omitted in all printed editions of the Book of Mormon. See Royal Skousen, *Analysis of Textual Variants of the Book of Mormon, Part Two* (Provo, UT: FARMS, 2005), 1069–70.

2.   For a preliminary literary assessment of Jacob, see John S. Tanner, "Jacob and his Descendants as Authors," in *Rediscovering the Book of Mormon*, ed. John L. Sorenson and Melvin J. Thorne (Salt Lake City: Deseret Book and FARMS, 1991), 52–66. There is also a volume devoted to Jacob 5: Stephen D. Ricks and John W. Welch, eds., *The Allegory of the Olive Tree: The Olive, the Bible, and Jacob 5* (Salt Lake City: Deseret Book and FARMS, 1994).

3.   The two places where Mormon addresses God's plan for Israel are at 3 Ne. 5:21–26 (in which he uses the relatively rare term "House of Jacob" exclusively) and perhaps Morm. 5:10–24. One of Nephi's uses of the word "messiah" (at 1 Ne. 12:18) is due to a later revision; the original manuscript has "Jesus Christ"; see Royal Skousen, *Analysis of Textual Variants of the Book of Mormon, Part One* (Provo, UT: FARMS, 2004), 258–59.

4.   Meir Sternberg, *The Poetics of Biblical Narrative: Ideological Literature and the Drama of Reading* (Bloomington: Indiana University Press, 1985), 41–48; quote from 42. Sternberg is not the only one to read the Bible in this three-fold mode, and indeed, it may be a natural way to approach scripture. For instance, N. T. Wright, as he begins his massive, multi-volume study of the origins of Christianity, devotes a chapter each to the New Testament as literature, history, and theology. See N. T. Wright, *Christian Origins and the Question of God* (Minneapolis: Fortress, 1992), 1:chs. 3–5.

5.   The subscripts help distinguish characters who share the same name. The Book of Mormon reports that the Nephites often named their children after ancestors or famous figures

from the past, and thus there are two Almas (father and son), two Moronis (separated by five hundred years), three Helamans, and so forth. The convention of subscripts is becoming more common in Mormon scholarship, being used, for example, in the *Encyclopedia of Mormonism*, ed. Daniel H. Ludlow, 4 vols. (New York: Macmillan, 1992), and Grant Hardy, ed., *The Book of Mormon: A Reader's Edition* (Urbana: University of Illinois Press, 2003). Nephite naming practices stand in contrast with those of the Bible; see Sternberg, 329–30.

6. By contrast, Nephi is not quite sure whom he is addressing until the last chapter of Second Nephi, which may be surprising if one considers Joseph Smith the author of the Book of Mormon. Since Smith dictated the (little *b*) book of Mormon before 1 and 2 Nephi, the lost awareness of an audience would indicate strongly imagined narrators.

7. I am assuming that Mormon is the narrator here, even though he does not explicitly identify himself until 3 Ne. 5:12 (aside from Words of Mormon). One might be tempted to ascribe these remarks to the prophets whose names appear in the book titles, but many of the direct comments make more sense as the work of Mormon; for instance, when the unnamed narrator tells us that "thus ended the record of Alma" (Alma 44:24), or promises more details in later books (Mosiah 28:9, 19), or explains Nephite customs (Alma 8:7, which presumes a non-Nephite audience).

8. For more on this chapter, see Thomas W. Mackay, "Mormon's Philosophy of History: Helaman 12 in the Perspective of Mormon's Editing Procedures," in *The Book of Mormon: Helaman Through 3 Nephi 8, According To Thy Word*, ed. Monte S. Nyman and Charles D. Tate Jr. (Provo, UT: BYU Religious Studies Center, 1992), 129–46. The poetic format here is intended to reflect and highlight the rough parallelism of the phrases.

9. Perhaps a better comparison would be with Mormon's autobiographical writings. "I, Mormon" appears three times in the single chapter of Words of Mormon, and an additional eight times in the seven chapters of the book of Mormon that were written by Mormon himself, but this is still quite sparse compared to Nephi. The loss of the 116 pages complicates the discussion since Mormon could have introduced himself at the beginning of his record (in the now lost "book of Lehi") in much the way that Nephi did. From Mosiah to 3 Nephi, whenever the narrator uses the pronoun "I," he seems to assume that readers already know who he is.

10. Susan Taber, "Mormon's Literary Technique" in the *Mormon Letters Annual 1983* (Salt Lake City: The Association for Mormon Letters, 1984), 123–24. Taber's article was one of the first attempts to deal with Mormon's contributions in a comprehensive fashion.

11. John L. Sorenson, *The Geography of Book of Mormon Events: A Source Book*, rev. ed. (Provo, UT: FARMS, 1992), 221–306.

12. Royal Skousen argues for emending Alma 51:26 by replacing *Nephihah* with *Moroni*, and changing "in the land of Nephi" at Alma 53:6 to "in the land of the Nephites." See his *Analysis of Textual Variants of the Book of Mormon, Part Four* (Provo, UT: FARMS, 2007), 2647–9, 2676–8.

13. I have done this myself at Hardy, 675–85. For additional charts and tables, see John W. Welch and J. Gregory Welch, *Charting the Book of Mormon: Visual Aids for personal Study and Teaching* (Provo, UT: FARMS, 1991). For more on Book of Mormon geography, see John L. Sorenson, *Mormon's Map* (Provo, UT: FARMS, 2000).

14.   The phrase "people of Anti-Nephi-Lehi" appears eight times between Alma 23:17 and 27:25 (with the first occurrence being the variant "Anti-Nephi-Lehies"); "people of Ammon" can be found eighteen times between Alma 27:26—when the change was made—and Hel. 3:12. One verse, Alma 43:11, has both forms as a gloss. Apparently this sudden shift in nomenclature escaped the notice of Oliver Cowdery, who seems to have used the term "Anti-Nephi-Lehites" in a heading that he added to the top of page 338 of the original manuscript (above the text of Alma 53:10–22). See Royal Skousen, ed., *The Original Manuscript of the Book of Mormon: A Typographical Facsimile of the Extant Text* (Provo, UT: FARMS, 2001), 429.

15.   There is, however, a discrepancy when we try to correlate the standard Western calendar with that of the Nephites. They counted six hundred years from the time Lehi left Jerusalem to the birth of Jesus (1 Ne. 10:4, 19:8; 2 Ne. 25:19; 3 Ne. 1:1), yet Lehi fled in the first year of the reign of Zedekiah (1 Ne. 1:4), or 597 BC, while Jesus was born no later than 4 BC. Latter-day Saints have dealt with this problem in several ways, including speculations that the Nephites used a shorter, lunar calendar. See John L. Sorenson, "Comments on Nephite Chronology," *Journal of Book of Mormon Studies* 2, 2 (1993): 207–11; and Randall P. Spackman, "The Jewish/Nephite Lunar Calendar," *Journal of Book of Mormon Studies* 7, 1 (1998): 48–59. In the present study, I treat dates in a straightforward manner as if Lehi had left in 600 BC and Jesus was born six hundred years later, in the same way as the running chronology at the bottom of pages in the official edition of the Book of Mormon.

16.   Thucydides, *History of the Peloponnesian War*, I, 22.

17.   See Richard Dilworth Rust, *Feasting on the Word: The Literary Testimony of the Book of Mormon* (Salt Lake City: Deseret Book and FARMS, 1997), 101–68.

18.   Mormon's strangest omission is at 3 Ne. 7:17: "And he [Nephi₃] did minister many things unto them, and all of them cannot be written, and a part of them would not suffice, therefore they are not written in this book." Many readers would have been grateful for even an imperfect summary.

19.   H. D. F. Kitto, *Poesis: Structure and Thought* (Berkeley: University of California Press, 1966), 261.

20.   The phrase "Captain Moroni" never appears in the Book of Mormon, but it is a standard LDS usage. On the Book of Mormon as a lineage history, see John L. Sorenson, *An Ancient American Setting for the Book of Mormon* (Salt Lake City: Deseret Book and FARMS, 1985), 50–56. The Book of Mormon is, of course, named after its primary narrator, but given the relatively narrow focus of his history on the church established by Alma₁ at the Waters of Mormon, it might be useful to think of his work not just as "The Book of [the person named] Mormon," but also "The Book of [what began at the place called] Mormon."

21.   Alma 1:1 is a possible exception, but see, for example, John Bytheway, *Righteous Warriors: Lessons from the War Chapters in the Book of Mormon* (Salt Lake City: Deseret Book, 2004).

22.   On Mormon's use of typology, I disagree with the interpretation that Richard Rust presents in his *Feasting on the Word*, 196–218. There are three important articles on the subject—Bruce W. Jorgensen, "The Dark Way to the Tree: Typological Unity in the Book of Mormon"; Richard Dilworth Rust, "'All Things Which Have Been Given of God . . . Are the Typifying of Him': Typology in the Book of Mormon"; and George S. Tate, "The Typology of the Exodus Pattern in the Book of Mormon"—all of which appear in *Literature of Belief: Sacred Scripture and Religious Experience*, ed. Neal A. Lambert (Provo, UT: BYU Religious

Studies Center, 1981). To my mind, this mode of scriptural exegesis is too general to adequately account for the details of Mormon's narration. As a matter of hermeneutics, readers can always find similarities between objects or events that might suggest one is a "type" of the other, but these are less important than the connections which Nephites themselves perceived and acknowledged. (Book of Mormon authors never make one person a "type" for another.)

23. We will see the phrase "fair sons and daughters" one more time—at Ether 13:17, when Moroni describes how the prophet Ether withdrew from society at the beginning of the final conflict that would annihilate the Jaredites. All three occurrences connect the destruction of a civilization with the failure to repent.

24. "Verily, verily I say unto you" appears twenty times in the NT (always in John) and twenty-three times in the BofM (always in 3 Nephi). If we shorten the phrase to "verily I say unto you," the exceptional nature of Alma 48:17 is still evident: it occurs sixty-eight times in the NT (but only in the gospels), and forty-six times in the BofM (only in 3 Nephi and only spoken by Christ, with one exception—Mosiah 26:31, another instance of God speaking directly).

25. Taber's article is actually more nuanced than this. She also finds parallels among all four figures, noting, for example, numerous similarities between Benjamin and Abinadi. See her "Mormon's Literary Techniques," *passim.*

26. See Rust, 19–46, and in general, Mark D. Thomas's *Digging in Cumorah: Reclaiming Book of Mormon Narratives* (Salt Lake City: Signature Books, 2000).

27. In fact, aside from Old Testament quotations generally associated with the end of times (Isa. 11:4–9 || 2 Ne. 30:8–16; Mal. 3–4 || 3 Ne. 24–25), there are only four places in the entire Book of Mormon that directly reference the Second Coming or the Millennium: 1 Ne. 22:24–26; 3 Ne. 26:3, 28:7–8, and 29:2. Book of Mormon prophecies are concerned with general conditions in the last days rather than the culminating event that will bring them to a conclusion, and in particular, Third Nephi speaks much, much more about the gathering of Israel than about the second coming of Christ.

28. The complete list, again, is 1 Ne. 2:20–21, 4:14, 17:13; 2 Ne. 1:9, 1:20, 4:4, 5:20; Jarom 1:9; Omni 1:6; Mosiah 1:7, 2:22, 2:31; Alma 9:13–14, 36:1, 36:30, 37:13, 38:1, 48:15, 48:25, 50:20.

29. Miguel de Cervantes, *Don Quixote*, trans. Edith Grossman (New York: HarperCollins, 2003), 513.

30. The complexities, and humor, are compounded when Cervantes also reports complaints made about the (fictional) author by a (fictional) translator. Howard Mancing makes the striking argument that Benengeli "emerges as the most consistently comic character in part II of the novel," whose main role is to "replace—or at least rival—Don Quixote as an object of laughter." He explains, "What is generally not realized is that the butt of this laughter is now less the comic antics of the mad knight-errant and more the absurdities of the historian/author and the narrative structure of the work." But the effect is achieved through the interplay of Cervantes and Benengeli rather than through the interaction of Benengeli and the narrative itself. See Howard Mancing, *The Chivalric World of* Don Quijote: *Style, Structure, and Narrative Technique* (Columbia: University of Missouri Press, 1982), 192–209; quotes from 209.

31. An earlier version of this reading appeared in Grant R. Hardy, "Mormon as Editor," in *Rediscovering the Book of Mormon*, ed. John L. Sorenson and Melvin J. Thorne (Salt Lake City: Deseret Book and FARMS, 1991), 15–28.

CHAPTER 5

1. See Grant R. Hardy and Robert E. Parsons, "Book of Mormon Plates and Records," in the *Encyclopedia of Mormonism*, ed. Daniel H. Ludlow (New York: Macmillan, 1992), 1:195–201. The chart accompanying that article, which was developed by John W. Welch, is reproduced at Grant Hardy, ed., *The Book of Mormon: A Reader's Edition* (Urbana: University of Illinois Press, 2003), 674.

2. Gordon K. Thomas has written about how the famous literary frauds of the late eighteenth century, namely those of Thomas Chatterton and James Macpherson, would have influenced early British perceptions of the Book of Mormon. See his "The Book of Mormon in the English Literary Context of 1837," *BYU Studies* 27, 1 (1987): 37–45.

3. On the paucity of documents in classical histories, see Michael Grant, *Greek and Roman Historians: Information and Misinformation* (London and New York: Routledge, 1995), 34–36. The letters can be found at Josephus, *Life*, 65, and Thucydides, *History of the Peloponnesian War*, VII, 10–15. Chinese historians since Sima Qian (ca. 100 BC) have always quoted extensively from edicts, memorials, letters, essays, reports, and other documents found in the imperial archives.

4. Bernard Duyfhuizen, *Narratives of Transmission* (Rutherford, New Jersey: Fairleigh Dickinson University Press, 1992), 106. With regard to the Book of Mormon, the term *extradiegetic* is complicated because different narrators are personally involved in various portions of their narratives to different degrees.

5. Although Mormon, as the narrator, never inserts scriptural passages, he does recount how Abinadi recited the Ten Commandments and Isaiah 53 (Mosiah 13–14), how Alma$_2$ quoted Zenos and Zenock (two extrabiblical Hebrew prophets) in his sermon to the Zoramites at Antionum (Alma 33), and how Jesus quoted Isaiah, Micah, and Malachi (3 Ne. 20–22, 24–25).

6. Zeniff's memoir (Mosiah 9:1–10:22). Revelation to Alma$_1$ (Mosiah 26:15–32; note v. 33). King Mosiah's edict (Mosiah 29:5–32, though v. 33 identifies this as an excerpt). Letters: Moroni$_1$ to Ammaron (Alma 54:5–14); Ammaron to Moroni$_1$ (Alma 54:16–24); Helaman$_2$ to Moroni$_1$ (Alma 56:2–58:41); Moroni$_1$ to Pahoran (Alma 60:1–36); Pahoran to Moroni$_1$ (Alma 61:2–21); and Giddianhi to Lachoneus (3 Ne. 3:2–10). For a literary appreciation of Book of Mormon epistles, see Richard Dilworth Rust, *Feasting on the Word: The Literary Testimony of the Book of Mormon* (Salt Lake City: Deseret Book and FARMS, 1997), 149–66.

7. Directly quoted sermons: King Benjamin (Mosiah 2:9–4:30); Alma$_2$ at Zarahemla (Alma 5:3–62); Alma$_2$ at Gideon (Alma 7:1–27); Alma$_2$ at Ammonihah (Alma 9:8–30); Alma$_2$ to Helaman$_2$ (Alma 36:1–37:47); Alma$_2$ to Shiblon (Alma 38:1–15); and Alma$_2$ to Corianton (Alma 39:1–42:31). The indications of the original sources are at Mosiah 2:8–9 (though it is not clear whether the circulated transcript would have included Benjamin's apparently extemporaneous remarks in chap. 4), Alma 5:2, 35:16, and the headnotes to Alma 7 and 9.

The headnote to Alma 9, which promises a narrative "according to the record of Alma," mentions speeches of both Alma and Amulek as well as their prison experience, so chapters 9–15 seem to be intended, but the actual first-person narration ends at Alma 9:33, shortly after Alma's sermon.

In addition to the embedded-source sermons listed above, other significant speeches—which may have been reworked by Mormon and usually include interruptions from listeners—include orations by King Limhi (Mosiah 7:18–33), Abinadi (Mosiah 12:1–16:15), Amulek at Ammonihah (Alma 10:2–11, with a note at 9:34 that what follows is an excerpt), Alma₂ at Antionum (Alma 32:8–33:23), Amulek at Antionum (Alma 34:2–41), Nephi₂ (Hel. 7:13–29), Samuel the Lamanite (Hel. 13:5–15:17), Jesus' First Discourse to the Nephites (3 Ne. 12:1–16:20), Jesus' Second Discourse (3 Ne. 20:10–23:5), and Jesus' Instructions to the Twelve Disciples (3 Ne. 27:2–28:12). Other sermons in the sections of the Book of Mormon attributed to Nephi or Jacob or Moroni include speeches by Nephi (1 Ne. 17:23–47), Jacob (2 Ne. 6:2–9:54, 10:1–25; Jacob 2:2–3:11), Lehi (2 Ne. 1:1–4:12), and Mormon (Moro. 7:2–48). For comments on several of these sermons, see Rust, 101–43. S. Kent Brown provides a detailed analysis of part of Samuel's sermon in his "The Prophetic Laments of Samuel the Lamanite," in *From Jerusalem to Zarahemla: Literary and Historical Studies of the Book of Mormon* (Provo, UT: BYU Religious Studies Center, 1998), 128–45. Other possible speeches that are shorter or less formal include the words of King Anti-Nephi-Lehi (Alma 24:7–16), Ammon's rejoicing over missionary success (Alma 26:1–37), and Alma's comments on missionary work (Alma 29:1–17).

8. Duyfhuizen, 123.

9. Daniel Defoe, *Robinson Crusoe*, ed. Michael Shinagel, Norton Critical Edition, 2nd ed. (New York: W. W. Norton, 1994), 52. Some early readers found the verisimilitude of Defoe's novels disturbing and accused him of deliberate deception—a charge that today sounds odd since modern boundaries of fiction and nonfiction are generally acknowledged and accepted. See Leonard J. Davis, *Factual Fictions: The Origins of the English Novel* (New York: Columbia University Press, 1983), 154–73.

10. Michael Seidel, *Robinson Crusoe: Island Myths and the Novel* (Boston: Twayne, 1991), 80–81.

11. The subscripts that I use with names are adopted from my *Reader's Edition*, and sometimes they do not match up exactly with those in the index of the official 1981 edition. This is because I took into account all the biblical names that occur in the Book of Mormon. At 2 Ne. 21:14, in a quotation of Isaiah, we read the phrase "children of Ammon." Because of this, Ammon the rescuer of the Zeniffites is Ammon₂ (rather than Ammon₁) and Ammon the missionary to the Lamanites is Ammon₃.

12. Note that Enos loved the Lamanites in the abstract, but found it very difficult to work up much fellow-feeling for any individual Lamanites that he knew (compare Enos 1:13 and 1:20).

13. It appears that when Limhi reports that his grandfather was "over-zealous to inherit the land of his fathers" and hence was deceived by the "cunning and craftiness of King Laman," who wanted to "bring this people . . . into bondage" (Mosiah 7:21–22), he is quoting Zeniff's record even before we read the record itself (compare Mosiah 9:3, 10).

14. The next verse continues, "And it came to pass that I went again with four of my men into the city, in unto the king, that I might know of the disposition of the king . . ."

(Mosiah 9:5). The word "again" suggests that Zeniff had already entered into negotiations with the Lamanite king before fighting broke out among the members of the first expedition.

15. See Bernard Dupriez, *A Dictionary of Literary Devices*, trans. and adapted by Albert W. Halsall (Toronto: University of Toronto Press, 1991), s. v. "suspension"; and Shlomith Rimmon-Kenan, *Narrative Fiction: Contemporary Poetics*, 2nd ed. (London: Routledge, 2002), 126–28.

16. Several Book of Mormon authors refer to the "traditions of the Lamanites" (see Mosiah 1:5; Alma 3:8, 9:16–17, 60:32; Hel. 5:51, 15:4), and belief in the correct traditions of the Nephites seems to have been the most important criteria in deciding who was or was not a Nephite (apparently this acceptance of tradition was of more significance than actual lineage; see Alma 3:11), but only Zeniff goes to the trouble of specifying exactly what the "traditions of the Lamanites" were.

17. Actually, Noah is not the embodiment of aggressive evil; rather he is lazy, gluttonous, easy-going, eager to please, and he tries to avoid confrontation at all cost. He is hypersensitive to criticism (Mosiah 11:27, 17:8, 11–12), he worries that Abinadi's preaching will "stir up my people to anger one with another, and to raise contentions among my people" (11:28), and his only battle strategy against the Lamanites was to retreat as quickly as possible, even if it meant abandoning wives and children (19:9–11). In short, Noah's vices were exactly those that would have arisen from growing up with a nonjudgmental, tender-hearted, overly optimistic father.

18. John Paul Riquelme, "Pretexts for Reading and for Writing: Title, Epigraph, and Journal in *A Portrait of the Artist as a Young Man*," *James Joyce Quarterly* 18 (1981): 301.

19. The repetitions include spying (Mosiah 9:1, 10:7), possessing the land in peace (9:5, 10:1), tilling the ground (9:9, 10:4, 10:21), battling in the strength of the Lord (9:17, 10:10), and the cunning and craftiness of King Laman (9:10, 10:18).

20. John Tvedtnes has proposed that the "king-men" who attempted to restore the monarchy later in Alma 51 may have been disgruntled Mulekite scions. See John A. Tvedtnes, "Book of Mormon Tribal Affiliation and Military Castes," in *Warfare in the Book of Mormon*, ed. Stephen D. Ricks and William J. Hamblin (Salt Lake City: Deseret Book and FARMS, 1990), 298–99.

21. For additional examples, see John W. Welch, "Benjamin, The Man: His Place in Nephite History," in *King Benjamin's Speech: "That Ye May Learn Wisdom,"* ed. John W. Welch and Stephen D. Ricks (Provo, UT: FARMS, 1998), 42–48. Welch, however, misses a few other connections between Alma 5 and Mosiah 5, including having names "blotted out" (Mosiah 5:11; Alma 5:57) and knowing "the name by which ye are called" (Mosiah 5:14; Alma 5:38).

22. Mosiah 5:2, 7; Alma 5:7, 12, 13, 14, 26, 19:33; Hel. 15:7.

23. To take only connections between Alma 5 and Mosiah 11–16, both Alma and Abinadi have much to say of bondage and deliverance (both refer to the same events, but Alma alludes to them retrospectively while Abinadi was speaking prophetically). The phrase "bands of death" appears twelve times in the Book of Mormon; it is first introduced by Abinadi, who employs it five times, and then it occurs three times in Alma 5. We could also compare these two passages:

(1) Even this mortal shall put on immortality, and this corruption shall put on incorruption, and shall be brought to stand before the bar of God, to be judged of him according to their works . . . (Abinadi at Mosiah 16:10)

(2) Do you . . . view this mortal body raised in immortality, and this corruption raised in incorruption, to stand before God to be judged according to the deeds which have been done in the mortal body. (Alma at Alma 5:15).

This means that Alma's citation is much closer to Abinadi's formulation than to anything in the New Testament. We may still wonder how these phrases showed up in Mosiah 16, but Alma, at least, is clearly quoting Abinadi rather than Paul (see 1 Cor. 15:53–54). The "corruption/incorruption" distinction appears six times in the Book of Mormon, but only Alma and Abinadi add the "mortal/immortality" corollary, and the two verses quoted above are the only ones in the Book of Mormon that add the specific wording of standing before God to be judged.

24. In Gideon, Alma is mild and straightforward, with some of the clearest prophecies in the Book of Mormon of Jesus' life; in Ammonihah, he offers a stinging condemnation (the comparison between the Lamanites and Nephites is not to the advantage of the latter); and in Zarahemla he asks a long series of about fifty rhetorical questions intended to provoke, intrigue, and tease his listeners into rethinking their lives. For these questions in a list format, see John W. Welch and J. Gregory Welch, *Charting the Book of Mormon: Visual Aids for Personal Study and Teaching* (Provo, UT: FARMS, 1999), charts 62–65. By contrast, Alma 7 contains just one query: "Do you believe these things?" (v. 17).

25. The only other instances are from Amulek (Alma's missionary companion) at Alma 34:36, Mormon at Hel. 3:30, and Jesus at 3 Ne. 28:10.

26. The one stray occurrence of "bands of death" is at Alma 22:14.

27. This particular repetition is required by the chiastic structure of Alma 36.

28. Though Captain Moroni draws on this language once, in Alma 60:20.

29. "born again" (4,0,3): Mosiah 27:25, Alma 5:49, 7:14 (2x); John 3:3,7, 1 Pet. 1:23. "born of God" (9,0,6): Mosiah 27:25, 28, Alma 5:14, 22:15 (Lamanite king), 36:5, 23, 24, 26, 38:6; all NT references from 1 John. (In this notation, the first number in parentheses is the number of times the phrase appears in the BofM, the second is the OT, and the third is the NT.)

30. Mosiah 27:26; Alma 5:51, 7:14, 9:12, 11:37 (2x, Amulek), 39:9, 40:26; 3 Ne. 11:38 (Jesus); 1 Cor. 6:9, 10, 15:50; Gal. 5:21.

31. Kent Brown points out, in a personal communication, that the concepts are related: birth into a family assures one of an inheritance.

32. This idea is explored in S. Kent Brown's essay "Alma's Conversion: Reminiscences in His Sermons," in Brown, 113–27. When Alma makes his famous exclamation at Alma 29:1—"O that I were an angel, and could have the wish of mine heart, that I might go forth and speak with the trump of God, with a voice to shake the earth, and cry repentance unto every people!"—he probably has in mind the particular angel who spoke to him "with a voice to shake the earth" (Mosiah 27:11, 15; this same angel was the one who commanded him to return to Ammonihah at Alma 8:15). See John A. Tvedtnes, "The Voice of an Angel," in *Book of Mormon Authorship Revisited: The Evidence for Ancient Origins*, ed. Noel B. Reynolds (Provo, UT: FARMS, 1997), 311–21. Alma dedicates his life to spreading the

message he first received from the angel, though he has to use human means to do so, such as rhetorical devices in sermons.

33. There is also a passage at which Mormon could have included yet another account of Alma's conversion but chose not to: "And Alma also related unto them his conversion, with Ammon and Aaron, and his brethren [the sons of Mosiah]. And it came to pass that it did cause great joy among them [the Lamanite converts of the sons of Mosiah]" (Alma 27:25–26).

34. The references here to "fruit" and "tasting" may be an allusion to the imagery of Lehi's dream in 1 Ne. 8, particularly since verse 22 features an explicit connection to "father Lehi."

35. Dan Vogel, *Joseph Smith: The Making of Prophet* (Salt Lake City: Signature, 2004), 196.

36. Vogel, 241–42.

37. Grant H. Palmer, *An Insider's View of Mormon Origins* (Salt Lake City: Signature, 2002), 99–104.

38. "born of God" appears five times in 1 John; "pains of hell"—Ps. 116:3; "gall of bitterness"—Acts 8:23; "Jesus, thou son of God/David, have mercy on me"—Mk. 10:47 ‖ Luke 18:38; "marvelous light"—1 Pet. 2:9; "see(n) eye to eye"—Isa. 52:8. Clearly the Book of Mormon draws upon the Authorized Version and thus postdates it, though Latter-day Saints might reframe the observation as "clearly the Book of Mormon, as a modern English translation, draws upon the Authorized Version and thus postdates it."

39. John W. Welch, "Chiasmus in the Book of Mormon," in *Book of Mormon Authorship: New Light on Ancient Origins*, ed. Noel B. Reynolds (Provo, UT: BYU Religious Studies Center, 1982), 33–52; and John W. Welch, "A Masterpiece: Alma 36," in *Rediscovering the Book of Mormon*, ed. John. L. Sorenson and Melvin J. Thorne (Salt Lake City: Deseret Book and FARMS, 1991), 114–31. There are several additional chiastic elements that appear before and after the excerpt from Alma 36 that I quoted: vv. 1–4 and 27–30 each contain references to keeping the commandments, prospering in the land, remembering the captivity of previous generations, bondage and deliverance, and being supported by God in trials, troubles and afflictions—all in the proper sequence for an extended chiasmus. Welch has also argued that minor discrepancies between various versions of the story do not compromise the reliability of Alma's testimony. See his "Three Accounts of Alma's Conversion" in *Reexploring the Book of Mormon*, ed. John W. Welch (Salt Lake City: Deseret Book and FARMS, 1996), 150–53. In this particular essay he does not discuss the brief narrative in Alma 26:17–20 that tells the story from the perspective of one of the sons of Mosiah.

40. John Welch has responded to these sorts of criticisms in several essays, including "Criteria for Identifying and Evaluating the Presence of Chiasmus," *Journal of Book of Mormon Studies* 4, 2 (1995): 1–14; "What Does Chiasmus in the Book of Mormon Prove?" in *Book of Mormon Authorship Revisited*, ed. Noel Reynolds (Provo, UT: FARMS, 1997), 199–224; and "How Much Was Known about Chiasmus in 1829 When the Book of Mormon Was Translated?" *FARMS Review* 15, 1 (2003): 47–80. A critical rejoinder can be found in Earl M. Wunderli, "Critique of Alma 36 as an Extended Chiasm," *Dialogue* 38, 4 (Winter 2005): 97–112; with additional debate with Boyd F. Edwards and W. Farrell Edwards at *Dialogue* 39, 3 (Fall 2006): 164–73. In my opinion, Welch opens himself up for criticism when he tries too hard to incorporate as many elements as possible in his chiastic schema,

while on the other hand Wunderli's criteria for what constitutes matching components are too stringent. Nevertheless, the general chiastic structure of the chapter is obvious once one starts to look for it.

41.   John Welch makes this point in "Chiasmus in the Book of Mormon," 51.

42.   Similarly emotional language can be found at Mosiah 27:29, where Mormon reports Alma's words as he came out of his inert state:

> My soul hath been redeemed
>   from the gall of bitterness
>   and the bonds of iniquity.
> I was in the darkest abyss;
>   but now I behold the marvelous light of God.
> My soul was racked with eternal torment;
>   but I am snatched,
>   and my soul is pained no more.

Here we see consecutive contrasts rather than chiasmus, but in any event this speech is entirely omitted from Alma's retelling of the story at Alma 36 (though he alludes to it at 36:23: "I . . . did manifest unto the people that I had been born of God").

43.   See footnote #6 above for a list. Moroni later includes two additional letters from his father Mormon at Moro. 8 and 9.

44.   It is also telling that when Alma is giving advice to his rebellious third son, Corianton, he says "I have somewhat more to say unto thee than what I said unto thy brother; for behold, have ye not observed the steadiness of thy brother, his faithfulness, and his diligence in keeping the commandments of God? Behold, has he not set a good example for thee? For thou didst not give so much heed unto my words as did thy brother, among the people of the Zoramites" (Alma 39:1–2). Despite the fact that these words immediately follow Alma's admonitions to his sons Helaman and Shiblon, only one brother—Shiblon—is held up as an example. Helaman's character and behavior apparently did not merit the same unqualified approbation. This is so surprising in the context that when Oliver Cowdery took the dictation for the original manuscript, he twice mistakenly wrote the plural "brothers" in the passage above before going back to cross out the superfluous "s." See Royal Skousen, *Analysis of Textual Variants in the Book of Mormon, Part Four* (Provo, UT: FARMS, 2007), 2387–8. (But note that at 39:10, Alma urges Corianton to counsel with both his elder brothers; he seems to expect that Helaman will do fine from this point on.)

A final observation is that Alma or Mormon (or Joseph Smith) has structured the first two-thirds of the book of Alma according to a series of parallels. Although Alma preached in at least five cities during the Nephite Reformation (Alma 4–16), we have extended reports—actually, embedded primary documents—for only three sermons: Zarahemla (whose situation was morally ambiguous), Gideon (clearly righteous, with the shortest discourse), and Ammonihah (obviously wicked, with the longest speech). The same number, sequence, and relative length appear again at Alma 36–42 in another series of primary sources—Alma's words of counsel to his three sons. Helaman, with some evidences of moral ambiguity, comes first; then Shiblon, who is clearly righteous, gets the shortest discourse; and finally Corianton, who is reproved for his transgressions, receives the longest sermon. There is even considerable overlap in content between the messages that Alma delivered to the city of Ammonihah and to his third son: both focus on the themes of resurrection and redemption. Happily, however, Corianton, unlike Ammonihah, repents.

45.   Usually, a clear transition of record-keepers merits independent status as a separate book. We can see a deliberately demarcated transition at Alma 44:24, but Helaman$_2$'s actual contributions were probably minimal or fragmentary, like those of the record-keepers in the book of Omni. The book of Helaman, as another counterexample, was considered from first to last as jointly authored by Helaman$_3$ and his sons; see the headnote to the book as well as Hel. 16:25, with a transition implied, rather than specified, at Hel. 3:37.

46.   Jarom 1:1, 15; Omni 1:1, 3, 8, 25; Mosiah 1:16, 28:20; Alma 45:2–9.

47.   The phrase "death by fire" occurs six times in the Book of Mormon, but always in relation to the martyrdom of Abinadi; Mosiah 17:15, 18, 20, 19:20; Alma 25:9, 11.

48.   This last example is obviously related in some way to 1 Cor. 15:54–57, but it does seem to be a favorite of Mormon's, appearing not only in another paraphrase at Alma 22:14, but also in his direct appeal to readers at Morm. 7:5. Paul himself was quoting Isa. 25:8 and Hos. 13:14.

49.   There may also be a connection to the discussion of offerings for unintentional sins at Numbers 15:22–31.

50.   It may also be worth observing that Mormon at one point inserts an editorial comment into Helaman's long letter of Alma 56–58, indicated by a shift from 1st person to 3rd (see 56:52–53).

51.   One possible connection is that when Alma addresses his youngest son, Corianton, he speaks at length of death, judgment, and resurrection—issues that the rebellious Corianton had been worried about. This discourse is particularly poignant given that Mormon has placed it at the beginning of the Zoramite War; before the year is out, a large number of young men are going to be dead (Alma 44:21–24).

CHAPTER 6

1.   Hans Frei, *The Eclipse of Biblical Narrative: A Study in Eighteenth and Nineteenth Century Hermeneutics* (New Haven: Yale University Press, 1974), 14.

2.   Frei, 135. This is very much the way that Dan Vogel reads the Book of Mormon in *Joseph Smith: The Making of a Prophet* (Salt Lake City: Signature, 2004). As a result, his interpretations of Mormon scripture tend to be simplistic and reductionist.

3.   Mormon tells us that he is abridging earlier records and, from an internal perspective, it is possible that some of the parallels I identify in this chapter came from his sources rather than his editing; that is to say, the original authors of the books of Mosiah and Alma might have been responsible for organizing their accounts in allusive, aesthetically pleasing ways. Yet because the Book of Mormon text generally does not provide enough information to unpack these sorts of literary puzzles (we're not even sure who wrote Mosiah; could it have been Alma$_2$?), I give Mormon credit for the finished narrative. Nonbelievers, of course, can credit Joseph Smith with creating the character of Mormon, who in turn creates an edited narrative from hypothetical sources. Gary Sturgess, in one of the best essays ever written on the book of Mosiah, has attempted a comprehensive reading

that speculates on Mormon's source text. He offers a great deal of conjecture, but in his astute identification of structure and themes—including kingship and deliverance—he provides a workable interpretation of Mosiah as a whole. I tend to focus on other features of the text, but Sturgess's reading is a reminder that my approach is not the only way of making sense of the Book of Mormon. See Gary L. Sturgess's "The Book of Mosiah: Thought about its Structure, Purposes, Themes, and Authorship," *Journal of Book of Mormon Studies* 4, 2 (1995): 107–35.

4. Richard Dilworth Rust, *Feasting on the Word: The Literary Testimony of the Book of Mormon* (Salt Lake City: Deseret Book, 1997), 22.

5. Rust, 21, 23–24. Mark D. Thomas uses type-scenes as the principle mode of analysis in his *Digging in Cumorah: Reclaiming Book of Mormon Narratives* (Salt Lake City: Signature, 1999).

6. Robert Alter, *The Art of Biblical Narrative* (New York: Basic Books, 1981), 51; see 47–62.

7. Alter, 181.

8. Thucydides, *History of the Peloponnesian War*, trans. Rex Warner (Harmondsworth, England: Penguin, 1954), I:22.

9. From a Latter-day Saint perspective, the first type of reading (attending to what Mormon says explicitly) is aimed at conversion, the second type (focused on implications) can lead to sanctification. For a fuller explication of these ideas, see Heather Hardy, "Another Testament of Jesus Christ: Mormon's Poetics," *Journal of Book of Mormon Studies* 16, 2 (2007): 16–27.

10. It appears that Abinadi was killed about 150 BC; Ammon arrives sometime around 120 BC. There is one piece of evidence that Abinadi's murder was regarded as a national tragedy for centuries afterward: when Mormon introduces himself, he says, "Behold, I am called Mormon, being called after the land of Mormon, the land in which Alma did establish the church among the people, yea, the first church which was established among them after their transgression" (3 Ne. 5:12). The historical context here suggests that the unspecified "transgression" was the execution of Abinadi.

11. So the first quotation, at Mosiah 11:20, in full reads: "And it came to pass that there was a man among them whose name was Abinadi; and he went forth among them, and began to prophesy, saying, 'Behold, thus saith the Lord, and thus hath he commanded me, saying, "Go forth, and say unto this people: 'Thus saith the Lord—Wo be unto this people, for I have seen their abominations, and their wickedness, and their whoredoms; and except they repent I will visit them in mine anger.'"'"

12. Of course, I am not the first person to make this observation. See Joseph Fielding McConkie and Robert L. Millet, *Doctrinal Commentary on the Book of Mormon* (Salt Lake City: Bookcraft, 1987–92), 2:204, and Alan Goff, "Apologetic and Critical Assumptions about Book of Mormon Historicity," *FARMS Review* 7, 1 (1995): 193. There is another echo of this key phrase at Alma 9:6, when another soon-to-be-destroyed interlocutor in Ammonihah demands, "Who is God, that . . ."

13. There are also three instances of hardened hearts in the New Testament, and the wording in this verse may be influenced by John 12:40: "He hath blinded their eyes and hardened their heart."

14. See S. Kent Brown, *From Jerusalem to Zarahemla: Literary and Historical Studies of the Book of Mormon* (Provo, UT: BYU Religious Studies Center, 1998), 79–80. Alan Goff offers a detailed and provocative reading of Exodus allusions in the book of Mosiah in his "Historical Narrative, Literary Narrative—Expelling Poetics from the Republic of History," *Journal of Book of Mormon Studies* 5, 1 (1996): 84–100. He notes that "Abinadi is a new Moses come down to reassert the law of Moses in a crucial time in Nephite history" (90).

15. "Redeem his people" occurs nine times in the Book of Mormon; of those, five references belong to these two narratives (Mosiah 13:33, 15:1, 11; Alma 11:40; Hel. 5:10; the last is a quotation of Amulek at Ammonihah).

16. The shorter construction "very Eternal Father" is similarly restricted in its use to these two parallel accounts, appearing only at Mosiah 15:4, 16:15 and Alma 11:38, 39.

17. There are two possible connections between the Exodus and tragedy of Ammonihah—the citizens there ask the dangerous question, "Who is God, that . . ." (Alma 9:6), and there is some mention of a prophet stretching forth his hand (though at Alma 14:10–11, they pointedly refrain from doing so)—yet the story overall is not reminiscent of Moses. Both of these elements also occur in the Abinadi story (see Mosiah 11:27, 12:2).

18. Nephi$_2$ will later be drawn into a legal confrontation (Hel. 9) that will share many elements with Alma and Amulek's experience, but not so much with Abinadi's.

19. There are actually three distinctive connections between Hel. 5 and 1 Ne. 17; I am not sure why.

> "durst not lay their hands upon them" / "neither durst they lay their hands upon me"—Hel. 5:25; 1 Ne. 17:52
> "still voice" / "still small voice"—Hel. 5:30; 1 Ne. 17:45 (cf. 1 Kings 19:12)
> "the earth shook as if it were about to divide asunder" / "cause the earth to shake as if it were to divide asunder"—Hel. 5:33; 1 Ne. 17:45

20. Vogel notices parallels between the prison story at Hel. 5 and Christ's visit to the Nephites in 3 Nephi, but he does not make much of it. He simply guesses that "the reason for this similarity may have something to do with Smith's sense of the imminent destruction of the wicked preceding Jesus' second advent and Smith's desire to save his father" (276). In the interest of comprehensiveness, I should note that a single Amalekite (one of the ex-Nephite dissenters) was converted at Alma 23:14.

21. Up to this point, there was only a single passage in Nephite scripture that used the phrase (2 Ne. 31:13–17), and this was in a chapter that is anomalous in many ways.

22. Meir Sternberg, *The Poetics of Biblical Narrative: Ideological Literature and the Drama of Reading* (Bloomington: Indiana University Press, 1985), 141.

23. Sternberg, 141.

24. Hunter R. Rawlings III, *The Structure of Thucydides' History* (Princeton: Princeton University Press, 1981), 50–51. Not all classicists were persuaded by Rawlings's analysis, but a sampling of reviews reveals that his book was generally well-received as a substantial contribution to Thucydidean studies.

25. Rawlings, 3–4.

26.   There is a dramatic increase in church membership at Hel. 3:24–26 which rapidly dissipates in the next chapter (4:1, 23), but it is only at Hel. 11:21 that the church encompasses a majority of the people—both Nephites and Lamanites—a situation that lasts for less than fifty years (3 Ne. 6:14). Of course, the two hundred years following Jesus' postresurrection visit are a different story, but we know almost nothing about that time period.

27.   The notation that this account is "according to the record of Alma" seems to be an identification of Mormon's major source rather than an indication of an embedded document. Alma is still referred to in the third-person (as at Alma 17:2 and 27:16). Nevertheless, there are expressions such as "at this day" (Alma 25:9) and "down to the present time" (Alma 18:38, 23:5), that might best be explained as Mormon following his source very closely. Certainly the first-person summary at Alma 28:8–14 and the reflections of Alma 29 are in Alma's voice.

28.   Despite his impressive sermons—so many of which Mormon included as embedded documents—Alma's career as a whole seems to have been only moderately successful. Alma's first challenge as the founding chief judge in 91 BC was a heretic named Nehor who argued that the clergy should be professionalized and that because God would save all men at the last day there was no need for repentance (Alma 1:3–4). He was executed for murder, but his followers—the Amlicites—joined with the Lamanites, started a war, and were soundly defeated in 87 BC, though at the cost of many thousand lives. Alma, in fact, killed their leader Amlici with his own sword on the battlefield. Unfortunately, the ideas of Nehor and the Amlicites continued to plague Alma throughout his life. They were prominent in the city of Ammonihah, the site of a major confrontation with Alma in 82 BC. That city was destroyed the next year—"it was called the 'Desolation of Nehors'" (Alma 16:11; cf. 14:16–18, 15:15)—but the Amlicite movement continued among both the Nephites and Lamanites. (I am following Royal Skousen here in reading the current "Amalekites" as a variant spelling of "Amlicites"). The apostate views of the Zoramites were similar to the Amlicites—though the former group taught an ethnic rather than a universal salvation—and after Alma's preaching at Antionum, the Amlicites are always mentioned in conjunction with the Zoramites (Alma 43:6, 13, 20, 44) until their destruction in battle in 74 BC.

As J. Christopher Conkling has observed, this means that Alma's public career begins with a war with the Amlicites—"and now, as many of the Lamanites and the Amlicites who had been slain upon the bank of the river Sidon were cast into the waters of Sidon; and behold, their bones are in the depths of the sea, and they are many" (Alma 3:3)—and it ends with a war with the Amlicites: "the number of their dead was exceedingly great, both on the Nephites and on the Lamanites [under Amlicite commanders]. And it came to pass that they did cast their dead into the waters of Sidon, and they have gone forth and are buried in the depths of the sea" (Alma 44:21–22). In this context, Alma's carefully recorded admonitions to his sons in his old age represent the distillation of a life-long struggle against a particular set of false ideas; it is no wonder that key passages highlight the need for repentance and the individualized nature of Christ's atonement (to Helaman at Alma 36–37), as well as the certainty that all mankind will someday be raised from the dead to stand before God to be judged of their sins (to Corianton at Alma 39–42).

There are hints that Alma himself may have been a proto-Amlicite before his conversion, though Mormon doesn't make much of this connection. The tenets ascribed to unbelievers in Mosiah 26:1–2 (among whom were counted Alma and the sons of Mosiah; Mosiah 27:8) included rejecting doctrines of the resurrection—with its corollary of a last judgment—and the coming of Christ. In this reading, Alma's long flirtation with these heretical viewpoints (he was probably converted in his thirties) would have been something like Augustine's years as a Manichaean, and Alma's son Corianton apparently struggled with the same sorts of false doctrines that had once entangled Alma himself.

See Royal Skousen, *Analysis of Textual Variants of the Book of Mormon, Part Three* (Provo, UT: FARMS, 2006), 1605–1609, and J. Christopher Conkling, "Alma's Enemies: The Case of the Lamanites, Amlicites, and Mysterious Amalekites," *Journal of Book of Mormon Studies* 14, 1 (2005): 108–17. If we were to flout my methodological advice and bring Joseph Smith back into the discussion, we might note how similar Nehor's ideas were to the Universalism of nineteenth-century America; on the other hand, the identification of Amlicites and Amalekites is a crucial aspect of the narrative to which Joseph seemed entirely oblivious—in his editing of both the 1837 and 1840 versions of the Book of Mormon, he never caught the error.

29. Does it make a difference in their relationship that Alma is probably at least ten years older than the sons of Mosiah? This can be surmised from the fact that Alma's father was born about 173 BC and Mosiah was born around 154 BC (see Mosiah 29:45–46). Alma seems to have been the oldest son, or perhaps the only son.

30. In a moment of crisis that predated the Nephite Reformation (when he fought face-to-face with Amlici), Alma prayed that he might be "an instrument in [God's] hands to save and preserve this people," a request that was apparently granted (Alma 2:30–31). And then several years later, after he had preached to the Zoramites at Antionum alongside the sons of Mosiah, the entire party was described as having been "instruments in the hands of God of bringing many of the Zoramites to repentance" (Alma 35:14).

31. Note that when Moroni retires, he is able to pass the position of chief captain to his son, Moronihah (Alma 62:43). He probably had received his own command in much the same way.

32. In the seventeen years in which we follow the career of Moroni closely, we only observe him praying once (Alma 46:16), citing scriptures twice (Alma 46:24–26, 60:23–24), and claiming one revelation (Alma 60:33), which turns out to be mistaken, as we shall see.

33. At Alma 53:2, the narrator tells us that the general Lehi₃ was "a man like unto Moroni," and this seems a much more apt comparison.

34. Latter-day Saints most often use the non–Book of Mormon phrase "stripling warriors" when writing and speaking about these youthful combatants, perhaps in an attempt to heighten the drama or emphasize the manliness of these role models.

CHAPTER 7

1. Latter-day Saints, trying to make sense of this in scientific terms, have speculated that the darkness may have been the result of volcanoes spewing large amounts of ash into

the atmosphere. The most detailed analysis is Bart J. Kowallis, "In the Thirty and Fourth Year: A Geologist's View of the Great Destruction in 3 Nephi," *BYU Studies* 37, 3 (1998): 137–90; but earlier studies include John L. Sorenson, *An Ancient American Setting for the Book of Mormon* (Salt Lake City: Deseret Book and FARMS, 1985), 318–23; James L. Baer, "The Third Nephi Disaster: A Geological View," *Dialogue* 19, 1 (Spring 1986): 129–32; Russell H. Ball, "An Hypothesis Concerning the Three Days of Darkness among the Nephites," *Journal of Book of Mormon Studies* 2, 1 (1993): 107–23; and John A. Tvedtnes, "Historical Parallels to the Destruction at the Time of the Crucifixion," *Journal of Book of Mormon Studies* 3, 1 (1994): 170–86. The darkness, variously described as a "vapor" or "mists" that could be felt, was associated with suffocating smoke, which made it impossible to light fires (3 Ne. 8:20–22, 10:13).

2. The Transfiguration accounts add the imperative "hear him," as does 3 Ne. 11:7; the language is closest to Matt. 17:5.

3. Technically, Mormon's version would be a fourth-century abridgment of a record written at the time of Jesus.

4. Wing-tsit Chan has described the Lotus Sutra as "a drama on the greatest scale ever conceived by man. Its stage is many Buddha-worlds. Its time is eternity. And its actors are the Lord Buddha Sakyamuni and innumerable beings." See Wing-tsit Chan, "The Lotus Sutra," in *Eastern Canons: Approaches to the Asian Classics*, ed. Wm. Theodore de Bary and Irene Bloom (New York: Columbia University Press, 1990), 220–31, quote from221; and Tamura Yoshiro, "The Ideas of the *Lotus Sutra*," in *The Lotus Sutra in Japanese Culture*, ed. George J. Tanabe Jr. and Willa Jane Tanabe (Honolulu: University of Hawaii Press, 1989), 37–51. The Lotus Sutra exhibits a very different sort of religious sensibility from that found in Third Nephi, even though both describe the teachings of divine beings with power that extends throughout the cosmos.

5. There are also two ambiguous passages in which Alma speaks of a day not far off when "the Son of God cometh in his glory" (Alma 5:50–51, 9:26). This obviously refers to a postresurrection appearance, but it is not clear whether it would be in the Old or New World.

6. See Brent Lee Metcalfe, "The Priority of Mosiah: A Prelude to Book of Mormon Exegesis," in *New Approaches to the Book of Mormon: Explorations in Critical Methodology*, ed. Brent Lee Metcalfe (Salt Lake City: Signature, 1993), 417–18.

7. Hel. 13:7 suggests a possible reason—Samuel says that he had originally intended to declare "glad tidings" concerning Christ that had been revealed to him by an angel, but when he was rejected by the Nephites he had to change his message.

8. Hel. 16:19–20 continues, "Why will he not show himself in this land as well as in the land of Jerusalem? But behold, we know that this is a wicked tradition, which has been handed down unto us by our fathers," and it might seem as if this "wicked tradition" included the notion of a postresurrection appearance of Jesus in the New World. Nevertheless, the rejected tradition here is akin to those labeled "foolish traditions of your fathers" elsewhere (Alma 8:11, 21:8, 30:14, 16, 23, 27, 31; 31:16–17), and refers to Christ's life in general, along with a suspicion that religious authorities manipulate the people with predictions that will be impossible to verify. Again, Hel. 16:20: ". . . we know that this is a wicked tradition, which has been handed down unto us by our fathers, to cause us that we should believe in some great and marvelous thing

which should come to pass, *but not among us*, but in a land which is far distant, a land which we know not; therefore they can keep us in ignorance, *for we cannot witness with our own eyes that they are true.*"

9. Jesus does mention his crucifixion once in a conversation with the twelve, but not in his sermons to the multitude (3 Ne. 27:14; with an oblique reference to being "lifted up by the Jews" at 28:6). Similarly, his voice from heaven preceding his bodily appearance had stated, "Behold, for such [those who repent and become as little children] I have laid down my life, and have taken it up again" (3 Ne. 9:22).

10. In his instructions to Nephi₃ about record keeping, Jesus mentions a particular prophecy of Samuel's, but it does not figure in his teachings to the people (3 Ne. 23:6–14).

11. Alexander Campbell, "Delusions," *The Millennial Harbinger* 2, 2 (February 1831); reprinted as a separate pamphlet in 1832; available online at http://www.mun.ca/rels/restmov/texts/acampbell/delusions.html.

12. The four lengthy comments are at 3 Ne. 5:7–26, 10:11–19, 26:6–12, and 28:24–30:2. These are discrete, readily identifiable sections, each of which contains the phrase "I make an end of my sayings/speaking" (3 Ne. 5:19, 10:19, 26:12, 28:24).

13. The fact that, during this time period, the Lamanites are described as being more righteous than the Nephites may come as a surprise to readers of the Book of Mormon, which is sometimes regarded as racist in its treatment of the Lamanites (with implications for Joseph Smith and the LDS Church). Obviously Nephite ideas about race are not those of twenty-first century Americans, but their attitudes toward the Lamanites are complex. Nephite racism or ethnocentrism is not really a matter of skin color, which is very rarely mentioned; instead their prejudice is most clearly manifest in their assumption of Lamanite passivity. It seems that the Lamanites cannot do anything without the incitement and leadership of Nephite dissenters, or without adopting innovations of the Nephites. Yet the narrative of Samuel the Lamanite, along with the large-scale reversal of Nephite/Lamanite spiritual conditions in his day, demonstrates how the Book of Mormon sometimes sets up categories only to subvert them later. For LDS perspectives on such matters, see John A. Tvedtnes, "The Charge of 'Racism' in the Book of Mormon," *FARMS Review* 15, 2 (2003): 183–98; and Richard Lyman Bushman, *Joseph Smith: Rough Stone Rolling* (New York: Knopf, 2005), 97–99.

14. Mormon uses similar terms to describe the prophecies of Samuel's contemporary, Nephi₂: "telling them of things which must shortly come, that they might know and remember at the time of their coming that they had been made known unto them beforehand, to the intent that they might believe" (Hel. 16:5). All this is reminiscent of Isa. 48:3–5, cited by Nephi at 1 Ne. 20:3–5.

15. The words of the crowd echo, perhaps, Matt. 23:30: "And [you] say, If we had been in the days of our fathers, we would not have been partakers with them in the blood of the prophets."

16. Perhaps the gathering together of all the faithful Nephites and Lamanites in one land (3 Ne. 3:13–16, 22–26) was an indication that they saw this as a last stand. Certainly this same strategy was adopted by Mormon himself several centuries later when he attempted, unsuccessfully as it turned out, to prevent the extermination of his own people (see Morm. 5:1–7, 6:1–5). He may downplay the military aspects of the events in 3 Nephi 3–4 (which

apparently included one of the most destructive battles in all of Nephite history; see 3 Ne. 4:11) in order to keep the focus on the prophesied signs.

17. Readers of the modern Book of Mormon will have encountered Mormon earlier in the Words of Mormon, but according to both the book's internal chronology and its dictation order, that brief editorial note was written after Third Nephi.

18. Isaiah quotations: 1 Ne. 20:1, 2 Ne. 12:5, 6, 18:17, 20:20, 24:1, 27:33; Jesus: 3 Ne. 20:16, 21:2; Mormon: 3 Ne. 5:21, 25 (3 times), 4 Ne. 1:49, Morm. 5:12. In my *Reader's Edition*, I labeled this section "Mormon₂'s Prophecies," but on further reflection, I think this was a mistake. His use of the intensifiers "surely" (3 Ne. 5:21, 23) and "as the Lord liveth" (vv. 24, 26) seems to indicate that these comments represent his own judgment and belief rather than the self-evident, authoritative voice of prophecy. He is here deferring to the prophets, not acting as one himself.

19. In the Book of Mormon, the words "seams" and "cracks" each appear only in these two verses.

20. Zenos and Zenock were Old World prophets whose writings had been preserved in the Brass Plates; compare 3 Ne. 10:15–17 with 1 Ne. 19:10–12 and Alma 33:15–16. One wonders if there was additional information about these men included in the lost 116 pages. Apparently the two prophets were ancestors of Lehi (3 Ne. 10:16), which may explain how their words got into the Brass Plates. That collection was a lineage record of some sort, complete with genealogies (1 Ne. 5:14–16).

21. See, for example, S. Kent Brown, "When Did Jesus Visit the Americas?" in his *From Jerusalem to Zarahemla: Literary and Historical Studies of the Book of Mormon* (Provo, UT: BYU Religious Studies Center, 1998), 146–56. I think that John Tvedtnes adequately answers most of the difficulties Brown points out concerning the traditional view, and assuming that the damage from natural disasters was not equal everywhere, it makes sense to think of Jesus' advent as following fairly quickly after the widespread destruction. See John A. Tvedtnes, *The Most Correct Book* (Salt Lake City: Cornerstone, 1999), 251–69. This would be a reason for Mormon not to include a separate date for Christ's arrival in Bountiful. The reference to the "ending of the thirty and fourth year" (3 Ne. 10:18) is certainly cryptic, but as Tvedtnes observes, there is much that has to happen before Mormon finally notes that "the thirty and fourth year passed away" (4 Ne. 1:1). Mormon's insistence that the visit occurred "soon after the ascension of Christ into heaven" (3 Ne. 10:18) is also puzzling. (Does it mean after his resurrection? At the conclusion of his forty-day ministry described at Acts 1:1–12?)

22. This is exactly the scenario imagined in film *The Testaments of One Fold and One Shepherd* (2000). This cinematic dramatization of the events of Third Nephi was an official production of the LDS Church and was shown daily at the Joseph Smith Building in Salt Lake City as well as in temple visitors' centers across the United States.

23. In fact, Nephi₃ himself had been very actively engaged in baptizing in the years that preceded Jesus' coming (3 Ne. 1:23, 7:23–26) and he is the first to initiate the new baptisms (3 Ne. 19:11–12). We might reasonably ask what authority Nephi now has that he was formerly lacking, or how the ordinance has been transformed. Clearly something has changed, but Mormon does not provide an explanation. Believers and critics alike have rushed to fill the gap, suggesting that the rebaptisms were "Christocentric" rather than "penitent"—a distinction that does not exactly hold up in the text—or that they were

necessary in light of a newly reorganized church, or that they represented a renewal of covenants in a new age. Brent Metcalfe, in an article seeking to demonstrate Joseph Smith's authorship, argued that Christocentric baptisms occurred only in portions of the Book of Mormon that were dictated later (including 2 Nephi), however Matthew Roper has identified a number of counterexamples. See Metcalfe, 418–22; and Matthew Roper, "A More Perfect Priority?" *FARMS Review* 6, 1 (1994): 367–69. The other hypotheses come from mainstream Latter-day Saint sources; see James E. Talmage, *Jesus the Christ: A Study of the Messiah and His Mission According to Holy Scriptures Both Ancient and Modern* (1915; repr., Salt Lake City: Deseret Book, 1983), 690, and Joseph Fielding Smith, *Doctrines of Salvation: Sermons and Writings of Joseph Fielding Smith*, ed. Bruce R. McConkie (Salt Lake City: Bookcraft, 1954–56), 2:336.

24. Stan Larson, "The Historicity of the Matthean Sermon on the Mount in 3 Nephi," in *New Approaches to the Book of Mormon: Explorations in Critical Methodology*, ed. Brent Lee Metcalfe (Salt Lake City: Signature, 1993), 115–63; Ronald V. Huggins, "Did the Author of 3 Nephi Know the Gospel of Matthew?" *Dialogue* 30, 3 (Fall 1997): 137–48. John W. Welch has responded at length to these criticisms in "Approaching New Approaches," *FARMS Review* 6, 1 (1994): 145–86 and *Illuminating the Sermon at the Temple and the Sermon on the Mount* (Provo, UT: FARMS, 1999), 179–237. Welch does not dispute the dependence of 3 Nephi on Matthew, but he downplays the importance of passages where the Book of Mormon adopts King James readings based on mistranslations or problems in the Greek text, and he draws attention to some of the places where 3 Nephi differs from the Authorized Version, such as 3 Ne. 12:22 which, along several early Greek manuscripts, drops the phrase "without a cause" from Matt. 5:22.

25. More specifically, an omniscient Christ could have delivered essentially the same discourse that Matthew would someday compose; our familiar Sermon on the Mount might have been a reasonable sampling of Jesus' characteristic Aramaic teachings (in fact, as Jesus concludes he informs the Nephites that "ye have heard the things which I taught before I ascended to my Father," 3 Ne. 15:1); the translator could have borrowed heavily from the Authorized Version; or the entire section might be like the "dramatic reenactments" that sometimes appear in documentary films, that is, staged re-creations for new audiences—in this case modern readers—that stand in for authentic historical events. Critical scholar Ronald Huggins brought up the first possibility only to dismiss it quickly with the comment that "such an explanation makes a sham of all textual and source-critical studies"; but we are speaking here of a book that bills itself as delivered by an angel and translated through a seer stone—the ordinary rules may not apply, at least not from a Latter-day Saint perspective. See Huggins, 145–46.

26. Welch, *Illuminating the Sermon*, 23–122. Welch puts forward the idea that the Sermon on the Mount, and even more so the Sermon at the Temple, can be read coherently as a ritual text that bears a striking resemblance to LDS temple ordinances. This type of analysis may be of interest to Mormons, but his argument relies heavily on inference, suggestion, and the liberal use of specific phrases from the LDS endowment ceremony. It seems unlikely that an outsider trying to ritualize the Sermon on the Mount or imaginatively reconstruct a ceremonial context would come up with anything like the Mormon temple experience. Rather than being a central concept, the word "temple"

appears only twice in Third Nephi: once in a quotation of Mal. 3:1 (3 Ne. 24:1), and once in a description of the setting (3 Ne. 11:1) which sounds conventional rather than integral to the meaning of the sermon. Jacob, Benjamin, and Limhi all addressed their people at temples (Jacob 1:17, 2:2, 11; Mosiah 1:18, 2:1, 5–7, 7:17).

27.   Jorge Luis Borges, "Pierre Menard, Author of the *Quixote*," in *Collected Fictions*, trans. Andrew Hurley (New York: Viking Penguin, 1998), 88–95, quotation from 94.

28.   Interestingly, in the Sermon at the Temple the first part of this formula has been consistently modified to "it is written . . ." Perhaps there is an indication here that religion in Nephite culture (or in Joseph Smith's conception of it) was based on concepts of a written canon rather than oral tradition. See Welch, *Illuminating the Sermon*, 131–32.

29.   Differences between the two versions can be easily seen at Welch, *Illuminating the Sermon*, 255–76. It is intriguing that in Third Nephi, the seemingly impractical injunction in the Sermon on the Mount to "take no thought for the morrow" was directed specifically to the disciples rather than to Christians in general (3 Ne. 13:25–14:1).

30.   Krister Stendahl, "The Sermon on the Mount and Third Nephi," in *Reflections on Mormonism*, ed. Truman G. Madsen (Provo, UT: BYU Religious Studies Center, 1978), 143.

31.   It is surprising that in an entire book devoted to tracing the possible sources and implications of the Sermon at the Temple, Welch never mentions the obvious connection between the inserted phrase at 3 Ne. 12:47—"old things are done away, and all things have become new"—and 2 Cor. 5:17: "old things are passed away; behold, all things are become new." When Jesus refers to this saying in his discussion after the Sermon, he quotes the Pauline version: "Marvel not that I said unto you that 'old things had *passed* away, and that all things had become new'" (3 Ne. 15:3; emphasis added, cf. 15:2). Victor Paul Furnish has observed that Paul borrowed this idea from apocalyptic Judaism (with a precedent at Isa. 43:18–19), and it refers not just to a transformation in individual believers, but to "a new age which stands over against this present evil age." See his *Second Corinthians*, Anchor Bible, vol. 32A (New York: Doubleday, 1984), 315, 332.

32.   The most comprehensive study of the differences between the Sermon on the Mount in the Bible and the Book of Mormon is Welch, *Illuminating the Sermon*, esp. 125–50 and 255–76. He points out that Sermon on the Mount appears to have been revised in a few places to better fit Nephite society: references to scribes, Pharisees, officers, and publicans are omitted, as is swearing by the city of Jerusalem (3 Ne. 12 || Matt. 5, vv. 20, 25, 35, 46–47). So also the British coin "farthing" has been replaced by the Nephite measure "senine," and the repeated refrain "it hath been said" has been transformed to "it is written" (3 Ne. 12 || Matt. 5, vv. 21, 26, 27, 31, 33, 38, 43). We should note, however, that this cultural adaptation is not complete. 3 Nephi still includes the Aramaic words "Mammon" and "Raca," as well as references to cubits (not mentioned elsewhere in the Book of Mormon), jots and tittles, figs, grapes, lilies, swine, the Sanhedrin ("council"), and the Roman practice of compelling civilians to carry their baggage for a mile (3 Ne. 12 || Matt. 5, vv. 18, 22, 41; 3 Ne. 13 || Matt. 6, vv. 24, 27, 28; 3 Ne. 14 || Matt. 7, vv. 6, 16).

33.   There is also an echo of Jesus and his disciples at Gethsemane, where he stepped away from them three time to pray, in each instance returning to find that they had fallen asleep. In Bountiful, the same sequence of events is reenacted, but rather than dozing off, his Nephite disciples "pray steadfastly, without ceasing." Jesus commends them saying, "So

great faith have I never seen among all the Jews." Compare 3 Ne. 19:15–36 with Matt. 26:36–46 and Mark 14:32–42.

34.   The incident with the children physically enacts or literalizes Jesus' teaching at 3 Ne. 11:37–38: "And again I say unto you, ye must repent, and become as a little child, and be baptized in my name, or ye can in nowise receive these things [salvation and the kingdom of God]. And again, I say unto you, ye must repent, and be baptized in my name, and become as a little child, or ye can in nowise inherit the kingdom of God" (cf. Matt. 18:2–5; Mark 10:15; Luke 18:17).

35.   This opportunity is mentioned at least four times in Third Nephi (3 Ne. 16:13, 21:6, 22, 30:2) and Latter-day Saints take it quite literally. After baptism and a confirmation by which they receive the gift of the Holy Ghost, they are encouraged to get a blessing from a church patriarch that will, among other personal promises and warnings, declare which tribe of Israel they belong to (or perhaps are assigned to). Most discover that they are affiliated with Ephraim.

36.   In his study of the relationship between Mormons and Jews, Steven Epperson downplayed this last point, observing that "The Book of Mormon repeatedly asserts that Israel's restoration depends on realizing the *territorial* terms of the covenant not in its conversion to, or identity with, the church." It may be that "Jewish missions were explicitly rejected by most leaders of the LDS Church and were never part of the church's program in the nineteenth century," but the Book of Mormon is nevertheless clear that eventually Jews will become Christians: "I will remember the covenant . . . that I would give unto them again the land of their fathers for their inheritance, which is the land of Jerusalem . . . And it shall come to pass that the time cometh, when the fulness of my gospel shall be preached unto them; and they shall believe in me, that I am Jesus Christ, the Son of God, and shall pray unto the Father in my name" (3 Ne. 20:29–31; cf. 2 Ne. 25:14–19; 3 Ne. 16:4, 11–12, 20:13; Morm. 5:14). Steven Epperson, *Mormon and Jews: Early Mormon Theologies of Israel* (Salt Lake City: Signature, 1992), 30, 36. See also Bushman, *Rough Stone Rolling*, 98–99, 102–5.

37.   There is something of a precedent for this in the Hebrew Bible at Deut. 5:3, where Moses proclaims to the children of Israel, shortly before they enter the Promised Land, "the Lord made not this covenant with our fathers, but with us, even us, who are all of us here alive this day." *The New Oxford Annotated Bible* (3rd ed.) notes that this is "inconsistent with the earlier emphasis that the generation who experienced these events has now died off (2.14–15). The aim is to overcome the limits of historical time and place through participation in the covenant, which makes revelation 'present.'"

38.   In LDS literature from 1830 to 1846, 3 Nephi 21 was the single most quoted chapter (with vv. 1–7 being the most frequently referenced block of text within that chapter). See Grant Underwood, "Book of Mormon Usage in Early LDS Theology," *Dialogue: A Journal of Mormon Thought* 17, 3 (August 1984): 39–40; and Grant Underwood, *The Millenarian World of Early Mormonism* (Urbana: University of Illinois Press, 1993), 78–79. Underwood has observed that for the first generation of Latter-day Saints, "the coming forth of the Book of Mormon served as an invaluable prophetic landmark, a millenarian milestone which helped the Saints to locate themselves in the eschatological timetable" (*Millenarian World*, 91).

39.   The wording here is more similar to the New Testament than the Old. The entire passage (3 Ne. 20:23–26), very closely follows Peter's speech at Acts 3:22–26, as can be seen

from 20:25, where Jesus says "ye are the children of the prophets" and refers to God's promise at Gen. 22:18 that all the nations would be blessed through Abraham's descendants. In his 1838 autobiography, Joseph Smith wrote that the first time the angel Moroni appeared to him, he quoted "the third chapter of Acts, twenty-second and twenty-third verses precisely as they stand in our New Testament. He said that that prophet was Christ; but the day had not yet come when 'they who would not hear his voice should be cut off from among the people,' but soon would come." See Joseph Smith—History 1:40 (this section of Joseph's autobiography has been canonized as part of the Pearl of Great Price).

40.   Although Jesus states that Mal. 3–4 are new to the Nephites, phrases from Mal. 4:1–2 were quoted at 1 Ne. 22:15, 23–24 and 2 Ne. 26:4, 6, 9. The first of these citations is ascribed to an otherwise unidentified "prophet," probably Zenos (cf. 1 Ne. 19:8–20). This means that for Latter-day Saints, Malachi could be a composite book that incorporated earlier prophecies, some of which were on the Brass Plates (much as Mic. 4:1–5 seems to quote Isa. 2:2–5). See Bruce R. McConkie, "The Doctrinal Restoration," in *Joseph Smith Translation: The Restoration of Plain and Precious Things*, ed. Monte S. Nyman and Charles D. Tate Jr. (Provo, UT: BYU Religious Studies Center, 1985), 17–18. For non-Mormons, the easiest explanation is that Joseph Smith made a mistake.

41.   It is remarkable how often Jesus specifies that covenants with Israel were made by *the Father*. See 3 Ne. 16:5, 11–12; 20:12, 29, 46; 21:4, 7; 29:1. He also credits the Father with the covenant with Abraham (3 Ne. 20:25, 27).

42.   Of course, Christians and Jews who would someday read the Book of Mormon already had access to Malachi in the Bible, so the idea here must be that Malachi's message needed to be reaffirmed, or put in the context of prophecies concerning the last days.

43.   The phrase "Lord of the whole earth" is quite similar, but its usage is also limited. It appears in the Bible only at Ps. 97:5, Micah 4:13, and Zech. 4:14. Jesus picks up the second of these references when he quotes Micah 4:13 at 3 Ne. 20:19.

44.   Royal Skousen prefers the reading in brackets, which matches Mal. 4:2. The original dictation of the Book of Mormon would not have distinguished between *son* and *sun*. See his *Analysis of Textual Variants of the Book of Mormon, Part Two* (Provo, UT: FARMS, 2005), 830–33.

45.   The relationship of Mormon's readers to his own book is similar—they also, through divine intervention, have been presented with a text that reveals that previously unknown prophets had foreseen and written about their lives.

46.   Omitted from the Book of Mormon here is any recognition that early Christians believed that Malachi's prophecy of a messenger who would prepare the way before the Lord had been fulfilled in John the Baptist (see Matt. 11:10–11 and Luke 7:27–28). According to Joseph Smith, in 1823 the angel Moroni quoted to him the third and fourth chapters of Malachi "with a little variation from the way it reads in our Bibles" along with a few other scriptures that were "about to be fulfilled." See Joseph Smith—History 1:36–41. Latter-day Saints believe that Malachi's prophecy at Mal. 4:5 of Elijah's return was fulfilled at the Kirtland Temple on April 3, 1836. See Doctrine and Covenants 110:13–16.

47.   Even in Abinadi's original reading, he suggested that some prophecies might be continuously operable, identifying the welcoming heralds of Isa. 52:7 as prophets "who have

published peace," as well as "those that are still publishing peace" and "those who shall hereafter publish peace, yea, from this time henceforth and forever" (Mosiah 15:14–17).

48. Mormon's clearest identification of his presumed audience is at Morm. 3:17–22, where he lists four distinct groups: the Gentiles, the Jews, other scattered descendants of Israel, and the remnants of the Lehites.

49. We are told at least eight times that participants "did bear record" of events during Christ's visit. For example, after we read of fire encircling the children and angels coming down to minister to them, Mormon adds: "And the multitude did see and hear and bear record; and they know that their record is true for the all of them did see and hear, every man for himself" (3 Ne. 17:25). See also 3 Ne. 11:15, 17:15–17, 21, 18:37, 39, 19:14, 33; cf. 10:1, 3. The only other portion of the Book of Mormon with this degree of attention to "bearing record" is Nephi's Vision at 1 Ne. chaps. 11–14. There may be a connection here with the recurring observation in Exodus that "all the people" witnessed various miraculous events; see Ex. 19:11, 16, 20:18, and 33:10.

50. The argument he is setting up seems to equate the signs among the Nephites of Christ's birth with the sign of the coming forth of the Book of Mormon. These are preliminary warnings, which will be followed by a brief probationary period and then the destructions accompanying Jesus' death will have their counterpart in the devastation that will take place at the Second Coming. On both latter occasions, doubt will be impossible and it will be too late for repentance.

51. Arnaldo Momigliano, *Essays in Ancient and Modern Historiography* (Middletown, CT: Wesleyan University Press, 1977), 195.

52. Royal Skousen has argued that the original reading of the verse was probably "*changed* from mortality to immortality" rather than "cleansed." See Royal Skousen, *Analysis of Textual Variants of the Book of Mormon: Part Six* (Provo, UT: FARMS, 2009), 3542.

53. Compare Terryl Givens' comments on the Book of Mormon and dialogic revelation in his *By the Hand of Mormon*, 218–28.

CHAPTER 8

1. Jacob, the most important of the minor narrators, offers a alternative ending with his "Brethren, adieu" (Jacob 7:27), though his conclusion in the previous chapter followed the standard pattern (6:13). (Perhaps Jacob 7 was an afterthought or an epilogue.)

2. The second *I* in this sentence was inadvertently deleted in 1837 and has never appeared in any subsequent editions. It was, however, undoubtedly in the original manuscript. See Royal Skousen, *Analysis of Textual Variants of the Book of Mormon: Part Six* (Provo, UT: FARMS, 2009), 3653.

3. Note that three of Moroni's six distinct comment-sections in the book of Ether include the evocation "O ye Gentiles": Ether 2:11, 4:13, 8:23.

4. Moroni does state that his compilation of the book of Moroni was for the benefit of his brethren the Lamanites (Moro. 1:4), but he seems to be entrusting these materials to the Gentiles, expecting that they will eventually make them accessible to the descendants of Lehi. Only at Moroni 10:1–23 does he address these "brethren" directly, and then he

concludes by speaking "to all the ends of the earth," that is, his wider, primary audience (Moro. 10:24–34). One other passage where the House of Israel is addressed directly is Ether 4:14–15, but this is Jesus speaking rather than Moroni.

5. As I noted in my introduction to the *Reader's Edition*: "The book of Ether offers one more striking example of narrative complexity: the genealogy in the first chapter provides the framework for the chronicle of Jaredite kings in chapters 6–11. That is, Joseph dictated a long string of twenty-seven unusual names and then several pages later repeated the list, but this time with stories attached to each name. If he were composing as he went along, this would be quite a feat of memory, especially since the names in the narrative portion are in reverse order from the way they appear in the genealogical list." Grant Hardy, *The Book of Mormon: A Reader's Edition* (Urbana: University of Illinois Press, 2003), xiii.

6. Richard Rust noted this pattern in his *Feasting on the Word* (Salt Lake City: Deseret Book and FARMS, 1997), 239.

7. I am excluding from this count the times "I, Mormon" appears in his autobiographical book or in the Words of Mormon. My point here has to do with the number of times the editors explicitly identify themselves within their redactions of earlier sources, rather than when they are recounting their personal life-stories. For the record, the phrase "I, Mormon" occurs eight times in the book of Mormon, and "I, Moroni" appears four times in the book of Moroni, but in those cases the usage is more like "I, Nephi" in 1 and 2 Nephi.

8. Of course, Mormon used other phrases as well to quickly point up morals from his stories; see George A. Horton Jr., "And Thus We See," in the *Book of Mormon Reference Companion*, ed. Dennis L. Largey (Salt Lake City: Deseret Book, 2003), 57–59. Nevertheless, the only other similar construction I have found in Ether occurs at 2:9: "And now, we can behold the decrees of God concerning this land, that it is a land of promise."

9. Moroni does report that Ether later "went forth [from his hiding place] and beheld that the words of the Lord had all been fulfilled" (Ether 15:33), but this concerns the destruction of the Jaredite people rather than the individual fate of Coriantumr. One counter-example to the pattern I am highlighting here occurs at Ether 7:5 where Moroni notes that a coup "brought to pass the saying of the brother of Jared that they would be brought into captivity," yet the original prediction was never labeled a prophecy and does not read as anything more than an astute political judgment: "the people desired of [Jared and his brother] that they should anoint one of their sons to be a king over them. And now, behold, this was grievous unto them. And the brother of Jared said unto them, 'Surely this thing leadeth into captivity'" (Ether 6:22–23).

10. Using Moroni 10:4 as a missionary tool is primarily a twentieth-century phenomenon. Early church members did not cite the verse, as can be seen in Grant Underwood's "Book of Mormon Usage in Early LDS Theology," *Dialogue: A Journal of Mormon Thought* 17, 3 (Autumn 1984): 35–74. The one exception occurred in 1832 when the editor of a church magazine reprinted the tenth chapter of Moroni in its entirety, noting that it provided "a guide by which the world may inquire of the Lord and know of a truth, that these things are so," but this idea was not followed up until 1884, when George Q. Cannon cited Moroni 10:4 as an afterthought to a conference talk and asked if this was not the way that his

listeners in the congregation had gained a testimony of the Book of Mormon (*Evening and Mormon Star* 1, 5 [October 1832]: 38; *Journal of Discourses* 25 [year TK]: 128–29). Such a strategy of proselytizing was brought to the forefront by B. H. Roberts in a series of articles and pamphlets that culminated in his *New Witnesses for God* (Salt Lake City: Deseret News, 1909), 2:7, 378–80; 3:234.

11.   John Sorenson once put together a preliminary chronology of Jaredite history. It is a very rough estimate, but it is still much more than Moroni ever provided. See John L. Sorenson, "The Years of the Jaredites," a 1968 article from *BYU Today* republished as a FARMS Preliminary Paper at http://farms.byu.edu/publications/transcripts/?id=28.

12.   Burton Watson, *Ssu-ma Ch'ien: Grand Historian of China* (New York: Columbia University Press, 1958), 48–50. The romanization has been changed from Wade-Giles to Pinyin.

13.   This is a puzzle, because no other major Book of Mormon character is identified only by a relationship. Oliver Cowdery gave the name of the brother of Jared as "Moriancumer" in a letter to W. W. Phelps published in the *Messenger and Advocate* in 1835, and George Reynolds in 1892 reported that William F. Cahoon in 1834 had heard Joseph Smith bless a baby and give it the name "Mahonri Moriancumer," then turn to the father and inform him that this was the name of the brother of Jared. Despite its late, second-hand nature, this tradition has been accepted by Latter-day Saints. Oliver Cowdery, "Letter VI," *Latter Day Saints' Messenger and Advocate* 1, 7 (April 1835): 112; George Reynolds, "The Jaredites," *Juvenile Instructor* 27 (May 1, 1892): 282n. The full name also appeared in an unattributed set of questions and answers in the *Contributor* 3, 2 (November 1881): 64, and was mentioned again in 7, 1 (October 1885): 12.

14.   The linking of these passages is intriguing. Mosiah 8:5–21 reports a lengthy conversation between King Limhi and Ammon, the leader of the rescue party, about the significance of seers and their ability to read lost languages. Mormon immediately follows this with a multi-chapter flashback (including an embedded primary source) that recapitulates the history of Zeniff's colony, ending with a second recounting of the discovery of the twenty-four plates and then returning to the same exact point in the original conversation: "And now Limhi was again filled with joy in learning from the mouth of Ammon that King Mosiah had a gift from God, whereby he could interpret such engravings" (Mosiah 21:28). (Early versions of the Book of Mormon read "King *Benjamin* had a gift from God . . ." The names were switched in 1837, presumably to correct for a chronological difficulty [a related verse, Ether 4:1, was changed for the same reason in 1849], but there are other ways to explain the chronology and so the earlier readings are probably correct. See Royal Skousen, *Analysis of Textual Variants of the Book of Mormon, Part Three* [Provo, UT: FARMS, 2006], 1418–21.)

Susan Staker has written an interesting essay on centrality of the concepts of seers, seer stones, and discovered texts in Joseph Smith's own sense of mission. She takes a naturalistic view of how the structure of the Book of Mormon developed over the course of Joseph's dictation, but she is mistaken when she asserts that "the Book of Mormon is characterized by [a Bible-like] authoritative third-person discourse" until Hel. 2:13–14, when "quite unexpectedly, the voice of a first-person 'I'-narrator appears." Actually, we have heard this voice all along, starting in Mosiah 1:8 (and with explicit "I" references beginning at Mosiah

8:1). See Susan Staker, "Secret Things, Hidden Things: The Seer Story in the Imaginative Economy of Joseph Smith," in *American Apocrypha*, ed. Dan Vogel and Brent Lee Metcalfe (Salt Lake City: Signature, 2002), 235–74; the quotations are from 254.

15.   There are enough examples of royal heirs being born in their fathers' old age, after many other children, that it seems to be a pattern; see Ether 7:3, 7, 9:14; 10:4, 10:13–14. Some Latter-day Saint readers have suggested that there is evidence from place names, personal names, and a few particular crops of a lingering Jaredite influence on the Nephites, probably through the intermediary of the Mulekite people, but the evidence is sparse (as is always the case with the Jaredites). See John L. Sorenson, "When Lehi's Party Arrived in the Land, Did They Find Others There?" *Journal of Book of Mormon Studies* 1, 1 (1992): 19–24.

16.   John W. Welch, "Preliminary Comments on the Sources behind the Book of Ether" (FARMS Preliminary Report, 1986), 7.

17.   B. H. Roberts, *Studies of the Book of Mormon*, ed. Brigham D. Madsen (Urbana: University of Illinois Press, 1986), 251–63, 280–83; emphasis in the original. The quotation is from 259. There has been considerable debate about just how serious Roberts was in advancing these sorts of objections to the historicity of the Book of Mormon. George D. Smith takes Roberts's skepticism at face value in "'Is There Any Way to Escape These Difficulties?' The Book of Mormon Studies of B. H. Roberts," *Dialogue: A Journal of Mormon Thought* 17, 2 (Summer 1984), 94–111; as does Brigham D. Madsen, "B. H. Roberts' 'Studies of the Book of Mormon,'" *Dialogue: A Journal of Mormon Thought* 26 3 (Fall 1993), 77–86. Latter-day Saints have been anxious to defend Roberts as a faithful thinker who at times played devil's advocate. See, for example, Truman G. Madsen, "B. H. Roberts and the Book of Mormon," in *Book of Mormon Authorship*, ed. Noel B. Reynolds (Provo, UT: BYU Religious Studies Center, 1982), 7–31; Truman G. Madsen and John W. Welch, "Did B. H. Roberts Lose Faith in the Book of Mormon?" (FARMS Preliminary Report, 1985); and Davis Bitton, "B. H. Roberts and Book of Mormon Scholarship," *Journal of Book of Mormon Studies* 8, 2 (1999): 60–69.

18.   Critics who believe that Joseph Smith was making it up as he went along have pointed out discrepancies between material attributed to the Small and the Large Plates (such as Alma's apparent ignorance of Nephi's very specific prophecies about Jesus' visit to the Nephites and the timing of his birth; e.g., Alma 13:25), and they have highlighted connections between the last and first portions of the Book of Mormon (seeing, for example, development in theological concepts like baptism and church that begin in the latter half of the book and continue through the dictation of First and Second Nephi). See Brent Lee Metcalfe, "The Priority of Mosiah: A Prelude to Book of Mormon Exegesis," in *New Approaches to the Book of Mormon*, ed. Brent Lee Metcalfe (Salt Lake City: Signature, 1993), 395–444; and Edwin Firmage Jr., "Historical Criticism and the Book of Mormon: A Personal Encounter," in *American Apocrypha*, ed. Dan Vogel and Brent Lee Metcalfe (Salt Lake City: Signature, 2002), 1–16. Dan Vogel has taken this approach in the comprehensive, critical reading of the Book of Mormon that undergirds his *Joseph Smith: The Making of a Prophet* (Salt Lake City: Signature, 2004). An attempt to reconstruct the production of the Book of Mormon from a naturalistic perspective can be found at Quinn Brewster, "The Structure of the Book of Mormon: A Theory of Evolutionary Development," *Dialogue: A Journal of Mormon Thought* 29, 2 (1996): 109–40.

Latter-day Saints, naturally, have been eager to demonstrate just the opposite. See Matthew Roper, "A More Perfect Priority," *FARMS Review* 6, 1 (1994): 362–78; and Alan Goff, "Positivism and the Priority of Ideology in Mosiah-First Theories of Book of Mormon Production," *FARMS Review* 16, 1 (2004): 11–36. Of particular interest is John Welch's observation that Alma 36:22—"Yea, methought I saw, even as our father Lehi saw, God sitting upon his throne, surrounded with numberless concourses of angels, in the attitude of singing and praising their God"—is an attributed quotation that replicated twenty-one words from 1 Ne. 1:8 exactly, which means that Smith dictated the later citation before the original source of the quotation. See John W. Welch, "Textual Consistency," in *Reexploring the Book of Mormon*, ed. John W. Welch (Salt Lake City: Deseret Book and FARMS, 1992), 21–23.

19.   Jonathan Swift, *Gulliver's Travels* (New York: Oxford University Press, 1977); spelling and punctuation modernized.

20.   Ether 7:23; 9:28, 29; 11:1, 2, 12, 13, 20–22; 12:2; 15:3. There is a notion in Mormon scripture that "all the prophets who have prophesied ever since the world began—have they not spoken more or less concerning these things [the coming of the Messiah and the redemption of his people]?" (Mosiah 13:33). But perhaps the Jaredites preached somewhat less about Christ, and in any case the speaker of these words, Abinadi, knew nothing of Ether's record (this is also true of Nephi's brother Jacob, who makes a similar statement at Jacob 4:4). Other statements about the universal Christian message of prophets are limited to those who taught since the time of Moses or Samuel (Hel. 8:16, 3 Ne. 20:24; compare Acts 3:24).

21.   The English term *Lord*, of course, is a translation of the Hebrew *Yahweh*, which itself is attested no earlier than the 14th century BC. Since the Jaredites predate that by at least another thousand years (according to the rough chronology in the Book of Mormon), it is not clear what original divine title might have been behind Moroni's use of *Lord*. Henry O. Thompson, "Yahweh," in the *Anchor Bible Dictionary*, ed. David Noel Freedman et al. (New York: Doubleday, 1992), 6:1011–2.

22.   There is one other less obvious exception. In Ether 9:22, we are told that good King Emer, in the sixth generation of the Jaredites, "saw peace in the land; yea, and he even saw the Son of Righteousness, and did rejoice and glory in his day" (Royal Skousen believes that the original reading should be "Sun of righteousness," thus matching Mal. 4:2; see his comments in *Analysis of Textual Variants of the Book of Mormon, Part Two* [Provo, UT: FARMS, 2005], 830–33.) Moroni offers no elaboration, refraining to equate the "sun of righteousness" with deity, let alone with Christ (as Nephi does at 2 Ne. 26:9, the only other time this phrase is used by Nephite prophets). The usage in Mal. 4:2 is vague; a literal translation from Hebrew would be, "But a sun of righteousness will arise for you, those revering my name; and healing [is] in her wings." This is not obviously a reference to either Yahweh or Christ, and scholars have read it as "a figurative description of the eschatological day; the dawning of a new day ushering in an era of righteousness," or as an allusion to Babylonian or Canaanite solar deities, or as an image based on "the winged sun disk pervasive in [Ancient Near Eastern] iconography" (Andrew E. Hill, *Malachi*, Anchor Bible, vol. 25D [New York: Doubleday, 1998], 349–52; the translation of Mal. 4:2 is from page 326).

23. My demarcations of comment sections are similar to those identified by John W. Welch in his "Preliminary Comments on the Sources Behind the Book of Ether," 7, but he missed Moroni's comments in Ether 2.

24. The single instance of Moroni offering a direct quotation of Ether's actual words is in his final sentence: "Now the last words which are written by Ether are these, 'Whether the Lord will that I be translated, or that I suffer the will of the Lord in the flesh, it mattereth not, if is so be that I am saved in the kingdom of God. Amen.'" (Ether 15:34). I concede the Christian provenance of the phrase "kingdom of God," but it nevertheless is a simple phrase rather than a developed idea. Moroni is keeping tight control of his material.

25. The apostles mentioned here are those Jesus chose in Palestine. The Book of Mormon scrupulously avoids calling the twelve Nephite disciples "apostles" and indicates that the Nephite twelve will in some way be subordinate to Jesus' original twelve. See 1 Ne. 12:9–10; Morm. 3:18–19.

26. Bees are not mentioned in the Noah story, but there are several references to "creeping things of the earth" (Gen. 6:7, 20, 7:8, 14, 21, 23), which are categorically related to insects and flying insects. See David P. Wright, "Crawling and Creeping Things," in the *Anchor Bible Dictionary*, 1:1203. Noah's ark is specifically referred to as a model for the Jaredite barges at Ether 6:7, and Hugh Nibley has suggested that the luminous stones lighting the Jaredite vessels had their counterpart in the Zohar associated with the ark. See Hugh Nibley, *An Approach to the Book of Mormon*, ed. John W. Welch, 3rd ed. (Salt Lake City: Deseret Book and FARMS, 1988), 336–39, 348–58. Nibley is often considered by Latter-day Saints to have been the foremost authority on the Book of Mormon in the second half of the twentieth century, but because his work is so relentlessly focused on ancient Near Eastern parallels rather than the narrative structure of the book itself, his voluminous writings have not been particularly useful to the present study.

27. Mark Thomas views this section as organized around two sets of three prayers. The first set, each marked by the formula "and it came to pass that the brother of Jared did cry unto the Lord . . . and the Lord had compassion," is clearly indicated by intentional repetitions. The second set is less obviously composed as a coherent unit, and Thomas's identification of Matt. 20:30 as the key underlying text does not seem compelling to me. See Mark D. Thomas, *Digging in Cumorah* (Salt Lake City: Signature, 1999), 73–77.

28. Mormons have been anxious to reconcile this statement with other accounts in LDS scripture of God manifesting himself to early figures from Genesis such as Enoch. See, for example, Joseph Fielding McConkie and Robert L. Millet, *Doctrinal Commentary on the Book of Mormon* (Salt Lake City: Bookcraft, 1987–92), 4:277–78. Moroni himself notes that other prophets had the same experience; see Ether 12:19–20.

29. These topics have been the basis for countless sermons and lessons; see, for example, Daniel H. Ludlow, *A Companion to Your Study of the Book of Mormon* (Salt Lake City: Deseret Book, 1976), 315–17. In more scholarly sources, see Thomas, 74–76, and Terryl L. Givens, *By the Hand of Mormon* (New York: Oxford University Press, 2002), 220.

30. Stephen Owen, ed. and trans., *An Anthology of Chinese Literature: Beginnings to 1911* (New York: Norton, 1996), 591–96. The quotations are from pages 592 and 596; the translator's bracketed comments were omitted. See also Stephen Owen's comments in his

Remembrances: The Experience of the Past in Classical Chinese Literature (Cambridge, MA: Harvard University Press, 1986), 80–98.

CHAPTER 9

1. Jeffrey R. Holland, *Christ and the New Covenant: The Messianic Message of the Book of Mormon* (Salt Lake City: Deseret Book, 1997), 330; George Reynolds and Janne M. Sjodahl, *Commentary on the Book of Mormon*, ed. Philip C. Reynolds (Salt Lake City: Deseret Book, 1955–61), 6:168.

2. Richard Dilworth Rust, *Feasting on the Word: The Literary Testimony of the Book of Mormon* (Salt Lake City: Deseret Book and FARMS, 1997), 12; Gary Layne Hatch, "Mormon and Moroni: Father and Son," in *Fourth Nephi through Moroni: From Zion to Destruction*, ed. Monte S. Nyman and Charles D. Tate Jr. (Provo, UT: BYU Religious Studies Center, 1995), 114.

3. The first two references are in Nephi's writings, but they are quotations from Lehi. The phrase is obviously related to Heb. 13:8: "Jesus Christ the same yesterday, and today, and for ever."

4. The phrase is from Henry James's 1884 essay, "The Art of Fiction," reprinted in *The Art of Criticism: Henry James on the Theory and the Practice of Fiction*, ed. William Veeder and Susan M. Griffin (Chicago: University of Chicago Press, 1986), 173.

5. Latter-day Saints have long been wary of acknowledging just how much of the language of the Book of Mormon is derived from the Bible for this reason. It is telling that the most comprehensive list in print of biblical phrases in the Book of Mormon appears in a rather amateurish, avowedly anti-Mormon, self-published volume: Jerald and Sandra Tanner, *Covering Up the Black Hole in the Book of Mormon* (Salt Lake City: Utah Lighthouse Ministry, 1990).

6. When Moroni urges readers to "seek this Jesus of whom the prophets and apostles have written" (Ether 12:41), it may be important to note that the word *apostles* in the Book of Mormon never refers to the Nephite twelve; it is exclusively reserved for Jesus' chief followers in the Old World. So there may be an intimation here that Moroni knows something of New Testament writings. But such speculations will always be matters of faith rather than evidence.

7. A similar point is made, with much more detail, by David P. Wright in his "'In Plain Terms that We May Understand': Joseph Smith's Transformation of Hebrews in Alma 12–13," in *New Approaches to the Book of Mormon: Explorations in Critical Methodology*, ed. Brent Lee Metcalfe (Salt Lake City: Signature, 1993), 165–29. (Wright also mentions the connection between Ether 12 and Heb. 11 on 204, 221–23.) For responses to Wright's article, see John W. Welch, "Approaching New Approaches," *FARMS Review* 6, 1 (1994): 168–81, and John A. Tvedtnes, "New Approaches to the Book of Mormon: Explorations in Critical Methodology," in the same issue, 19–23. Royal Skousen's exhaustive examination of the early manuscripts of the Book of Mormon has shown that in their original form, many quotations of the Bible were even closer to the King James Version than they now appear. See Royal Skousen, "Textual Variants in the Isaiah Quotations in the Book of Mormon," in *Isaiah in the Book of Mormon*, ed. Donald W. Parry and John W. Welch (Provo, UT: FARMS, 1998), 379–81.

8. Early Latter-day Saints read Joseph of Egypt's prediction of a future prophet whose "name shall be called after me; and it shall be after the name of his father" (2 Ne. 3:15) as an obvious reference to Joseph Smith Jr. See Grant Underwood, "Book of Mormon Usage in Early LDS Theology," *Dialogue: A Journal of Mormon Thought* 17, 3 (Autumn 1984): 47.

9. Apart from 2 Ne. 33, Nephi uses the word "charity" in just one verse, 2 Ne. 26:30; "hope" appears in his writings only at 1 Ne. 19:24; 2 Ne. 31:20, and 33:9.

10. Oddly enough, Nephi's emphasis is on the charity he has for his future readers, whereas Moroni's main concern is the lack of charity his future readers will have for him (2 Ne. 33:8–9; Ether 12:34–36). Both men contrast the power of the spoken word with the weakness they perceive in their own writings (2 Ne. 33:1–2; Ether 12:23).

11. There is one exception: in a passing reference, Alma$_2$ urges the inhabitants of Gideon to "see that ye have faith, hope, and charity" (Alma 7:24).

12. Let me try to clarify what I am claiming here and elsewhere in this chapter. (1) There are distinctive shared phrases that occur in Moroni's writings and other key passages in the Book of Mormon. (2) These often focus on the themes of writerly farewells and Joseph's prophecy at 2 Ne. 3 of a future book. (3) The connections fall into patterns and fit the narrative so well that it makes sense to read them as deliberate allusions rather than as coincidences (say, the result of Joseph Smith drawing upon favorite phrases to describe similar motifs). (4) Discerning patterns is always something of a subjective judgment—there is, after all, a difference between poetics and hermeneutics—but the same types of intricate links that I see between Ether 12 and Hebrews 11 (which should be relatively unproblematic for outsiders) are also evident among Book of Mormon texts.

The situation is complicated by the fact that Moroni appears to be drawing upon passages that had not yet been dictated by Smith, but I am not thereby arguing that Smith could not have produced the book without divine assistance. Some may see it as evidence of revelation, but it is also possible that Smith had worked out in his mind or even prewritten the key passages in question before he started dictating the parts of the text ascribed to Moroni. In any case, Moroni's extensive allusions suggest that, as either history or fiction, the Book of Mormon is a carefully written, well-integrated piece of literature.

13. This explanation is advanced by Sydney B. Sperry in *Our Book of Mormon* (Salt Lake City: Bookcraft, 1947), 194–96. Sperry further suggests that Paul himself may have gotten his ideas from Jesus, who also had taught them to the Nephites when he visited the New World. Again, these are defenses of faith rather than the results of textual analysis.

14. Morm. 7:2, 3, 4, 5; cf. 7:9–10; Moro. 10:3, 4, 7, 8, 18, 19, 27, 30, with a couple of minor variations. The only occurrence of either of these phrases elsewhere is a "know you that" at 3 Ne. 27:27.

15. James Woods, *How Fiction Works* (New York: Farrar, Straus and Giroux, 2008), 65.

16. There is a New Testament connection here with Rom. 3:10, which itself echoes Psalms 14:3 and 53:3.

17. The phrase "come unto Christ," now a favorite of Latter-day Saints, occurs only four times in the Book of Mormon: twice in Moro. 10 (vv. 30 and 32), and then at Jacob 1:7 and Omni 1:26. Nevertheless Christ's invitation to "come unto me" occurs nearly thirty times, particularly in Third Nephi. We might note that "come unto Christ" does not appear in the Bible either.

18. Or alternatively, the situation may be similar to the Rabbis of the second century who tried to record in the Mishnah everything they could remember about the recently destroyed Second Temple. Donald Akenson observes, "Remembering and, later, recording the Second Temple's physical characteristics of course was not an exercise in nostalgia: controlled recall, however, is one of the chief analgesics for extreme grief. But more: as we saw when we encountered a similar situation earlier, after the destruction of Solomon's Temple—parts of the Book of Kings read like the transcription of an architectural seminar—recording the physical details of the structure was one of the prerequisites for its rebuilding. Memorizing, passing on, writing down these details was in itself a holy piece of work, a first step toward reconstruction." Moroni's transcriptions of liturgy became the basis for LDS practices, in what modern Mormons refer to as "The Restoration." Donald Harman Akenson, *Surpassing Wonder: The Invention of the Bible and the Talmuds* (Chicago: University of Chicago Press, 2001), 308. Scott H. Faulring, "The Book of Mormon: A Blueprint for Organizing the Church," *Journal of Book of Mormon Studies* 7, 1 (1998): 60–69.

19. Mark D. Thomas has also compared Moroni's three endings in his "Moroni: The Final Voice," *Journal of Book of Mormon Studies* 12, 1 (2003): 88–99.

20. See Joseph Smith—History 1:27–54, in the LDS Pearl of Great Price. In vv. 36–41, Joseph reports that the angel Moroni quoted Mal. 3–4 (with some significant differences from the KJV), Isa. 11, Acts 3:22–23, and Joel 2:28–32, along with "many other passages of scripture." According to the Book of Mormon's internal chronology, Moroni may have written the Title Page after he had completed Moroni 10, but most readers will have encountered this at the beginning of the book.

21. Erich Auerbach, *Mimesis: The Representation of Reality in Western Literature*, trans. Willard R. Trask (Princeton: Princeton University Press, 1953), 15.

22. Hannah Arendt, *Men in Dark Times* (New York: Harcourt, Brace and World, 1968), 202.

23. See Timothy L. Smith, "The Book of Mormon in a Biblical Culture," *Journal of Mormon History* 7 (1980): 3–21, which is one of the most astute analyses of the major themes in the Book of Mormon ever written by an outsider.

24. Robert Alter, *The Art of Biblical Narrative* (New York: Basic Books, 1981), 46.

AFTERWORD

1. Robert Alter, "Introduction to the Old Testament," in *The Literary Guide to the Bible*, ed. Robert Alter and Frank Kermode (Cambridge: Harvard University Press, 1987), 26. Emphasis in the original.

2. Terryl L. Givens, *By the Hand of Mormon: The American Scripture That Launched a New World Religion* (New York: Oxford, 2002), 82–88, 235–39. The quotation is from 84, with emphasis in the original.

3. See Vladimir Nabokov, *Pale Fire* (New York: G. P. Putnam's Sons, 1962), as well as Brian Boyd's fascinating *Nabokov's Pale Fire: The Magic of Artistic Discovery* (Princeton: Princeton University Press, 1999)—a book with a number of similarities to this present study. The long poem in Nabokov's novel, ostensibly written by John Shade, includes the

line "Not flimsy nonsense, but a web of sense" (63), which might also be charitably applied to the Book of Mormon.

4. For more thoughts along these lines, see my introduction to Royal Skousen, ed., *The Book of Mormon: The Earliest Text* (New Haven: Yale University Press, 2009), vii–xxviii.

5. Nirmal Dass, trans., *Songs of the Saints from the Adi Granth* (Albany: State University of New York Press, 2000), 90.

6. Unfortunately, perhaps, the poem is "accessible" only in translation. The original was written in a syncretic dialect so archaic that even native Punjabi speakers understand very little of it without recourse to dictionaries and commentaries. It is instructive to compare the observations of the Adi Granth's first English translator, Ernest Trumpp, with Eduard Meyer's and Mark Twain's assessments of the Book of Mormon (below). According to Trumpp, the Sikh scripture is "incoherent and shallow in the extreme, and couched at the same time in dark and perplexing language, in order to cover these defects. It is for us Occidentals a most painful and almost stupefying task, to read only a single Rāg, and I doubt if any ordinary reader will have the patience to proceed to the second Rāg, after he shall have perused the first. It would therefore be a mere waste of paper to add also the minor Rāgs which only repeat, in endless variations, what has already been said in the great Rāgs over and over again, without adding the least to our knowledge." And this from a man who spent seven years producing a translation of over 700 pages! It is always a challenge to try to understand other people's scriptures. Ernest Trumpp, trans., *The Adi Granth* (London: W. H. Allen, 1877), preface, vii.

7. The addition of the word *always* in the last sentence brings the current text into line with the original manuscript. See Royal Skousen, *Analysis of Textual Variants in the Book of Mormon, Part Four* (Provo, UT: FARMS, 2007), 2369–70.

8. Alma began his speech to Helaman with the observation that "whosoever shall put their trust in God shall be supported in their trials, and their troubles, and afflictions, and shall be lifted up at the last day" (Alma 36:3). Then he retold the story of his own conversion by an angel, in chiastic form, to illustrate the point. The second appearance of the phrase "lifted up at the last day," near the end of his remarks, gives the speech a coherent focus. The phrase "lifted up at the last day" occurs seven more times in the Book of Mormon.

9. Donald Harman Akenson, *Surpassing Wonder: The Invention of the Bible and the Talmuds* (Chicago: University of Chicago Press, 2001), 411. By coincidence, Akenson has recently completed a study of the Latter-day Saints' global genealogical project; see his *Some Family: The Mormons and How Humanity Keeps Track of Itself* (Montreal: McGill-Queen's University Press, 2007).

10. Eduard Meyer, *The Origin and History of the Mormons, with Reflections on the Beginnings of Islam and Christianity*, trans. Heinz F. Rahde and Eugene Seaich (German ed., 1912; Salt Lake City: Univ. of Utah Press, 1961), iii, 24; the translations here are from James K. Lyon, "Mormon and Islam through the Eyes of a 'Universal Historian' [Eduard Meyer]," *BYU Studies* 40, 4 (2001): 221–36.

11. The line about Wagner is from the humorist Bill Nye (1850–1896), though our only record of the remark is *Mark Twain's Autobiography* (New York: Harper and Brothers, 1924), 1:338. Twain's description is probably the most influential brush-off of the Book of

Mormon in American letters. The broader passage reads: "The book is a curiosity to me, it is such a pretentious affair, and yet so 'slow,' so sleepy; such an insipid mess of inspiration. It is chloroform in print. If Joseph Smith composed this book, the act was a miracle—keeping awake while he did it was, at any rate" (*Roughing It* [New York: Library of America, 1984; original ed., 1872], 617). Mark Twain was reaching for laughs here, but his analysis had enough sense in it to make Mormons uncomfortable. In fact, I suspect that the "chloroform in print" line was the reason the official "Pronouncing Vocabulary," from its inception in 1920 until 1981, stipulated that Ether begin with a short *e*; only after other anesthetics had replaced ether on the operating table did that particular jibe lose its sting. (This observation applies only to the suggested pronunciation in the inexpensive editions of the Book of Mormon that were intended for investigators. For information on the origin of the pronouncing vocabulary, see Mary Jane Woodger, "How the Guide to English Pronunciation of Book of Mormon Names Came About," *Journal of Book of Mormon Studies* 9, 1 [2000]: 52–57. Compared to other suggested pronunciations on the list for names beginning with E, *Ether* with a short *e* was clearly an anomaly.) See also Richard H. Cracroft, "The Gentle Blasphemer: Mark Twain, Holy Scripture, and the Book of Mormon," *BYU Studies* 11, 2 (1971): 119–40.

12.   John W. Welch, "What Does Chiasmus in the Book of Mormon Prove?" in *Book of Mormon Authorship Revisited: The Evidence for Ancient Origins*, ed. Noel B. Reynolds (Provo, UT: FARMS, 1997), 206.

Index

Scripture Index

Note: **Boldface type** indicates that there are several verses within the chapters that are discussed on the corresponding pages